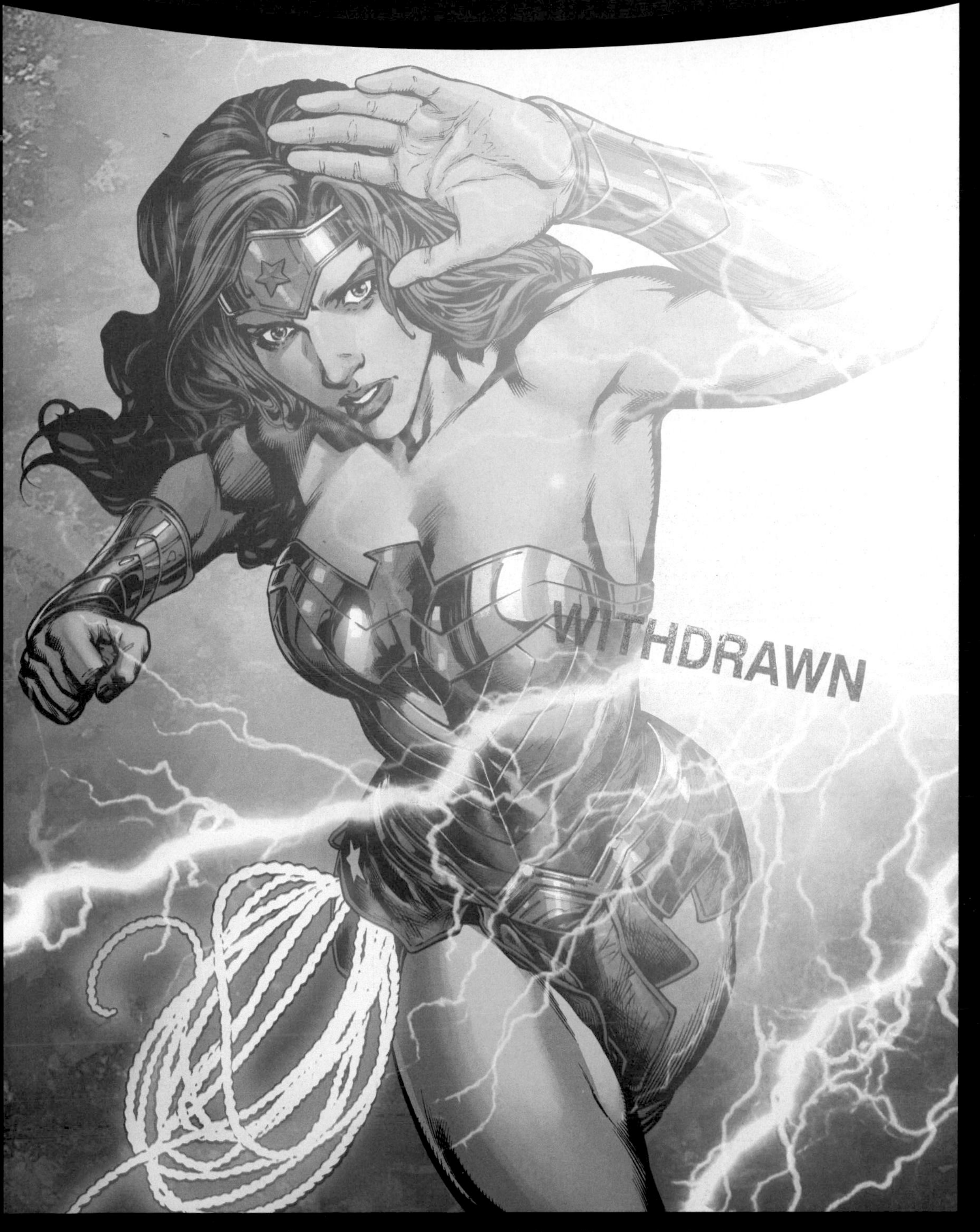
WITHDRAWN

WONDER WOMAN

VOL.6 CHILDREN OF THE GODS

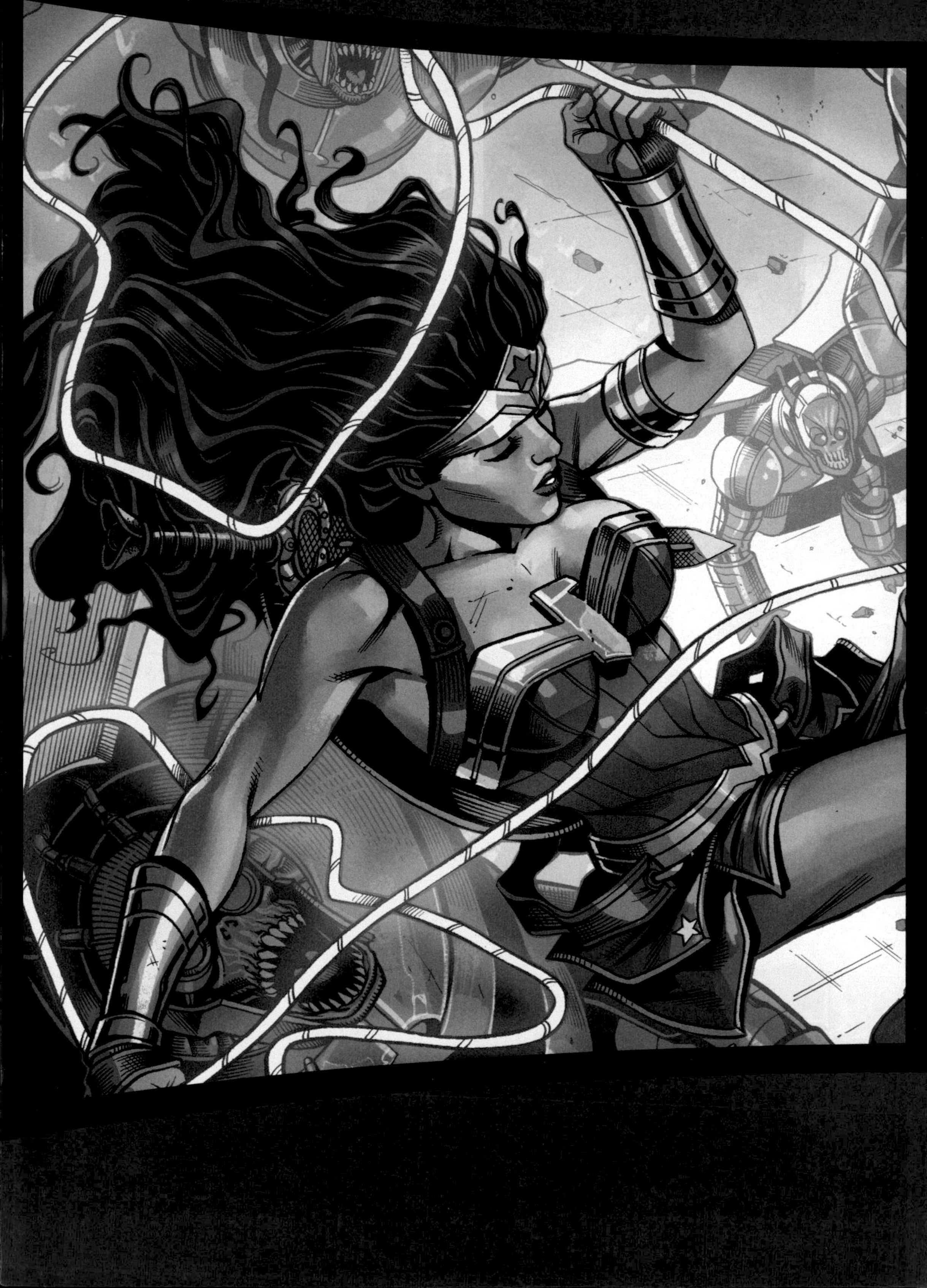

WONDER WOMAN
VOL.6 CHILDREN OF THE GODS

JAMES ROBINSON
writer

CARLO PAGULAYAN * **SERGIO DAVILA**
EMANUELA LUPACCHINO * **STEPHEN SEGOVIA**
pencillers

RAUL FERNANDEZ * **EBER FERREIRA** * **MICK GRAY**
SCOTT HANNA * **RAY McCARTHY** * **MARK MORALES**
SEAN PARSONS * **JASON PAZ** * **ART THIBERT**
inkers

ROMULO FAJARDO JR.
colorist

SAIDA TEMOFONTE
letterer

JENNY FRISON
collection cover artist

WONDER WOMAN created by WILLIAM MOULTON MARSTON
SUPERMAN created by JERRY SIEGEL and JOE SHUSTER
By special arrangement with the Jerry Siegel family
FOURTH WORLD created by JACK KIRBY

CHRIS CONROY Editor - Original Series * **ANDREW MARINO** Assistant Editor - Original Series
JEB WOODARD Group Editor - Collected Editions * **ROBIN WILDMAN** Editor - Collected Edition
STEVE COOK Design Director - Books * **SHANNON STEWART** Publication Design

BOB HARRAS Senior VP - Editor-in-Chief, DC Comics
PAT McCALLUM Executive Editor, DC Comics

DAN DiDIO Publisher * **JIM LEE** Publisher & Chief Creative Officer
AMIT DESAI Executive VP - Business & Marketing Strategy, Direct to Consumer & Global Franchise Management
BOBBIE CHASE VP & Executive Editor, Young Reader & Talent Development * **MARK CHIARELLO** Senior VP - Art, Design & Collected Editions
JOHN CUNNINGHAM Senior VP - Sales & Trade Marketing * **BRIAR DARDEN** VP - Business Affairs
ANNE DePIES Senior VP - Business Strategy, Finance & Administration * **DON FALLETTI** VP - Manufacturing Operations
LAWRENCE GANEM VP - Editorial Administration & Talent Relations * **ALISON GILL** Senior VP - Manufacturing & Operations
HANK KANALZ Senior VP - Editorial Strategy & Administration * **JAY KOGAN** Senior VP - Legal Affairs * **JACK MAHAN** VP - Business Affairs
NICK J. NAPOLITANO VP - Manufacturing Administration * **LISETTE OSTERLOH** VP - Digital Marketing & Events
EDDIE SCANNELL VP - Consumer Marketing * **COURTNEY SIMMONS** Senior VP - Publicity & Communications
JIM (SKI) SOKOLOWSKI VP - Comic Book Specialty Sales & Trade Marketing
NANCY SPEARS VP - Mass, Book, Digital Sales & Trade Marketing * **MICHELE R. WELLS** VP - Content Strategy

WONDER WOMAN VOL. 6: CHILDREN OF THE GODS

Published by DC Comics. Compilation and all new material Copyright © 2018 DC Comics. All Rights Reserved.
Originally published in single magazine form in WONDER WOMAN 31-37. Copyright © 2017, 2018 DC Comics. All Rights Reserved.
All characters, their distinctive likenesses and related elements featured in this publication are trademarks of DC Comics.
The stories, characters and incidents featured in this publication are entirely fictional.
DC Comics does not read or accept unsolicited submissions of ideas, stories or artwork.

DC Comics, 2900 West Alameda Ave., Burbank, CA 91505
Printed by LSC Communications, Owensville, MO, USA. 8/10/18. First Printing.
ISBN: 978-1-4012-8424-4

Library of Congress Cataloging-in-Publication Data is available.

PEFC Certified

Printed on paper from
sustainably managed
forests, controlled
sources

PEFC/29-31-337   www.pefc.org

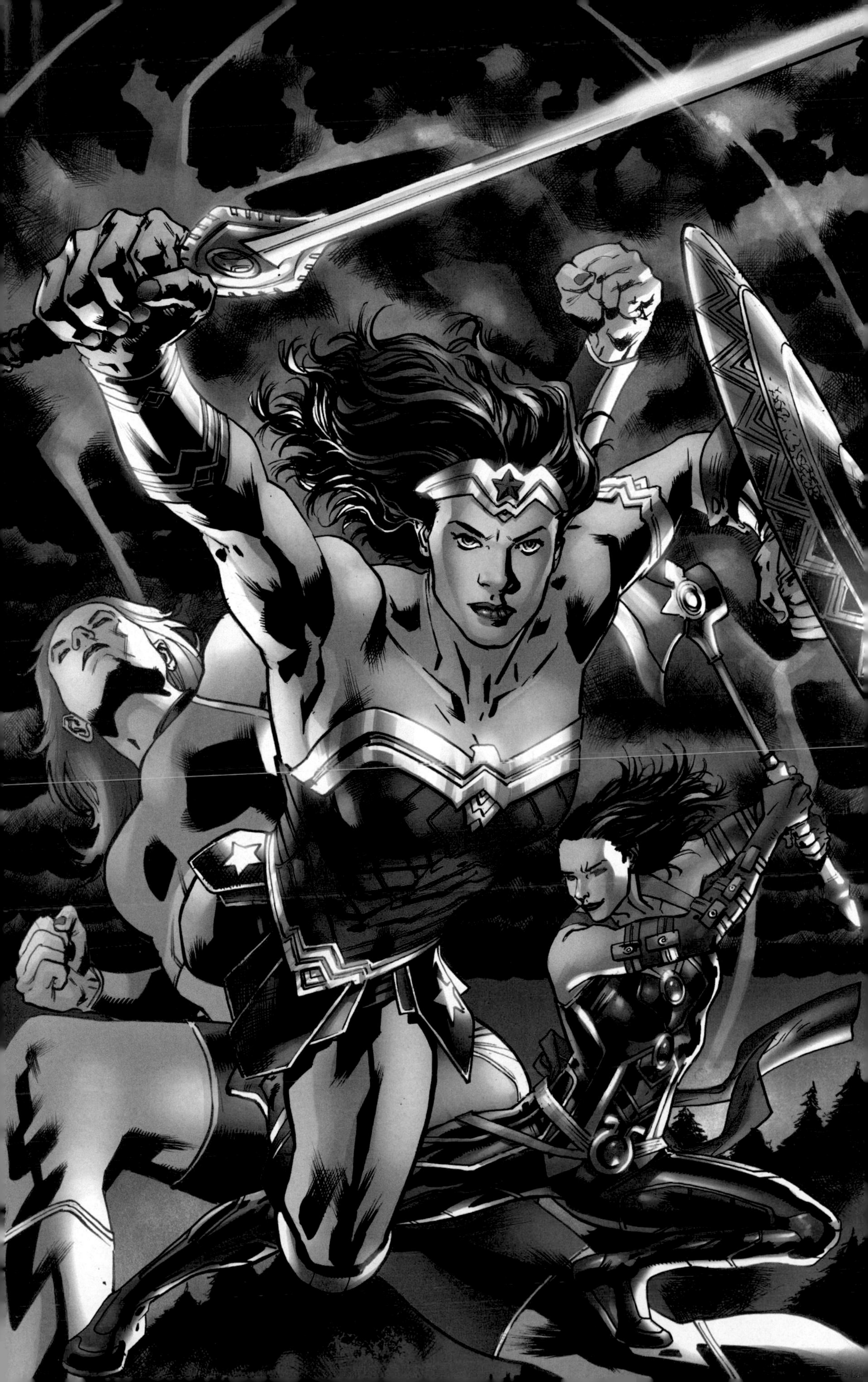

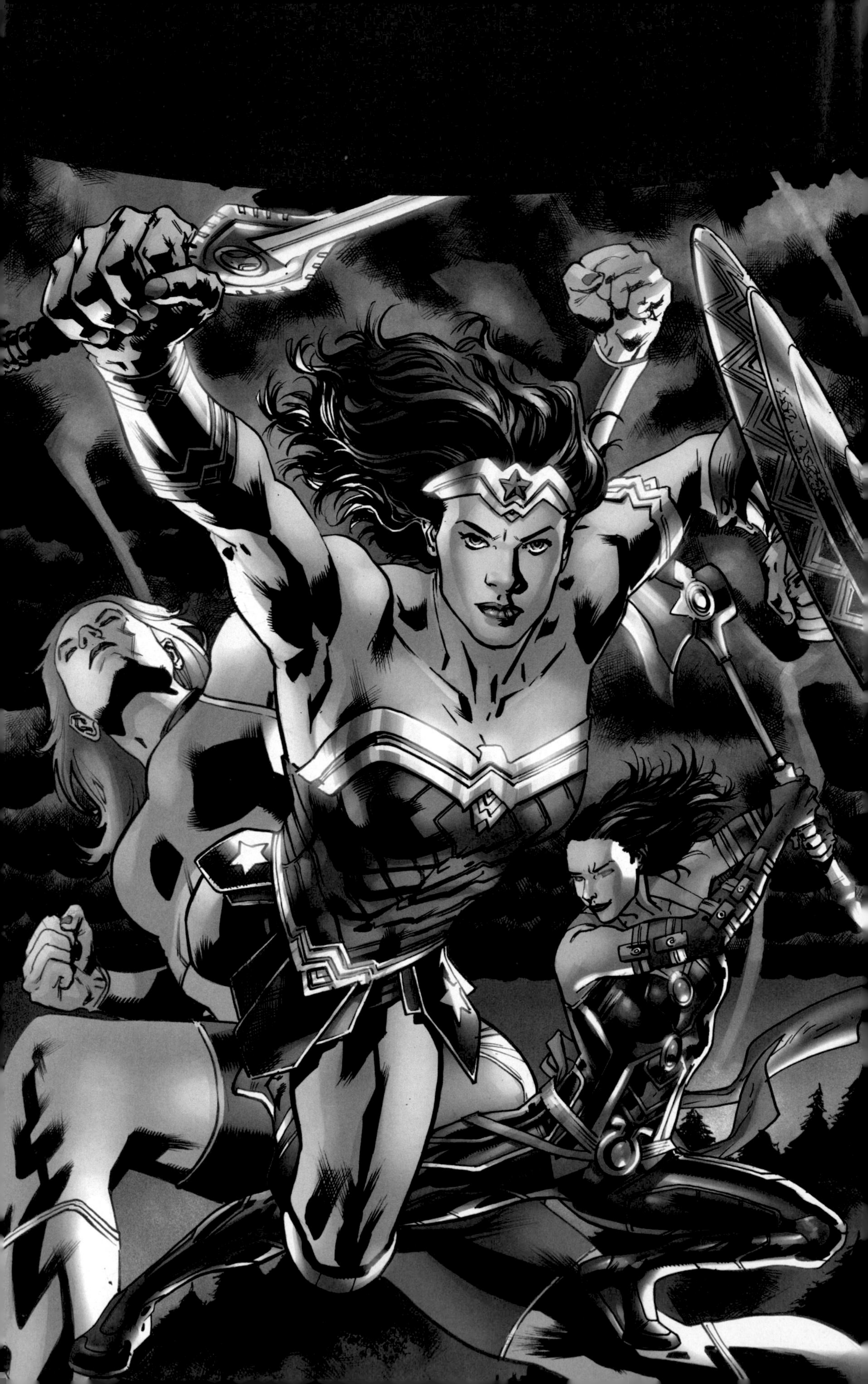

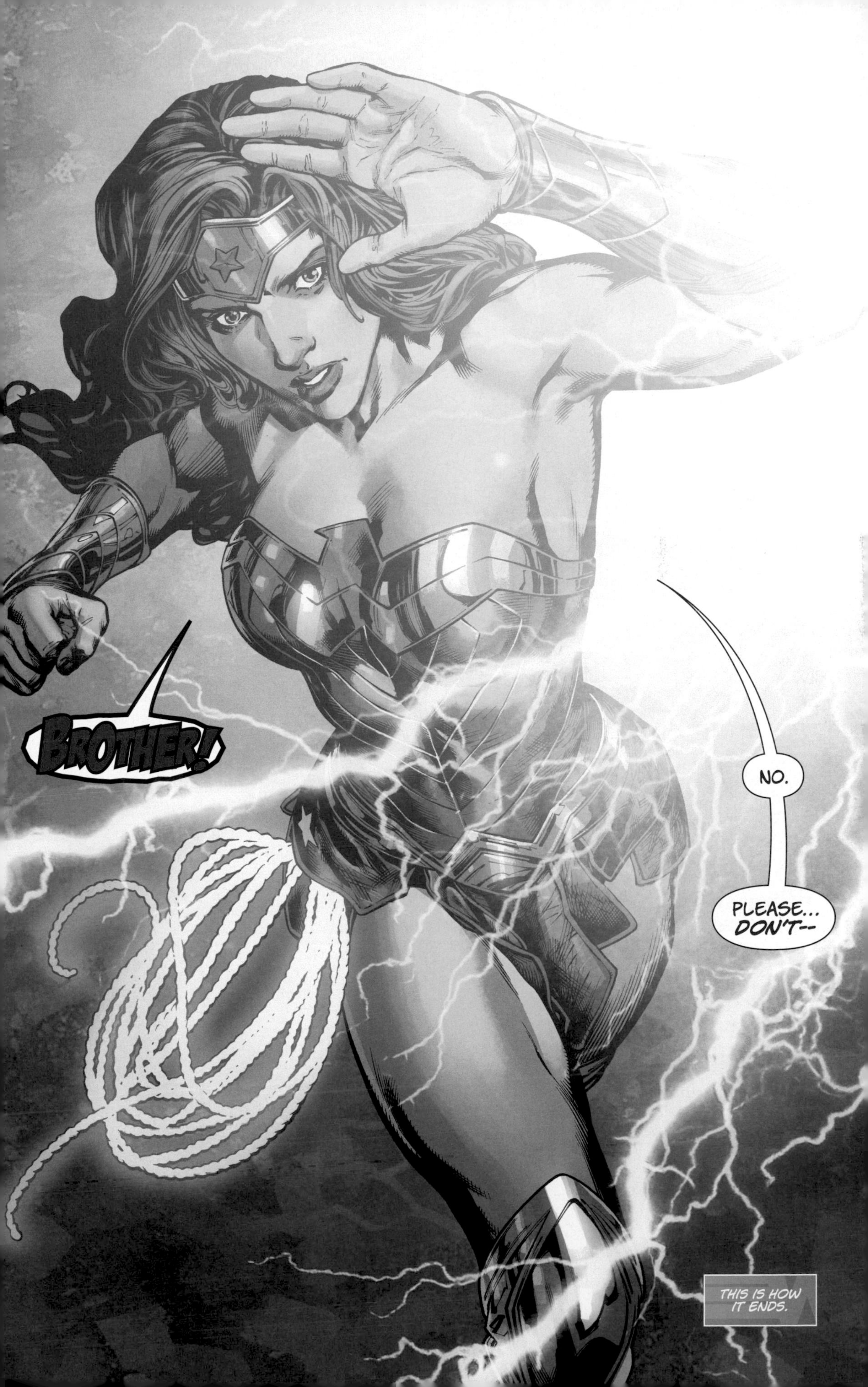
BROTHER!
NO.
PLEASE... DON'T--
THIS IS HOW IT ENDS.

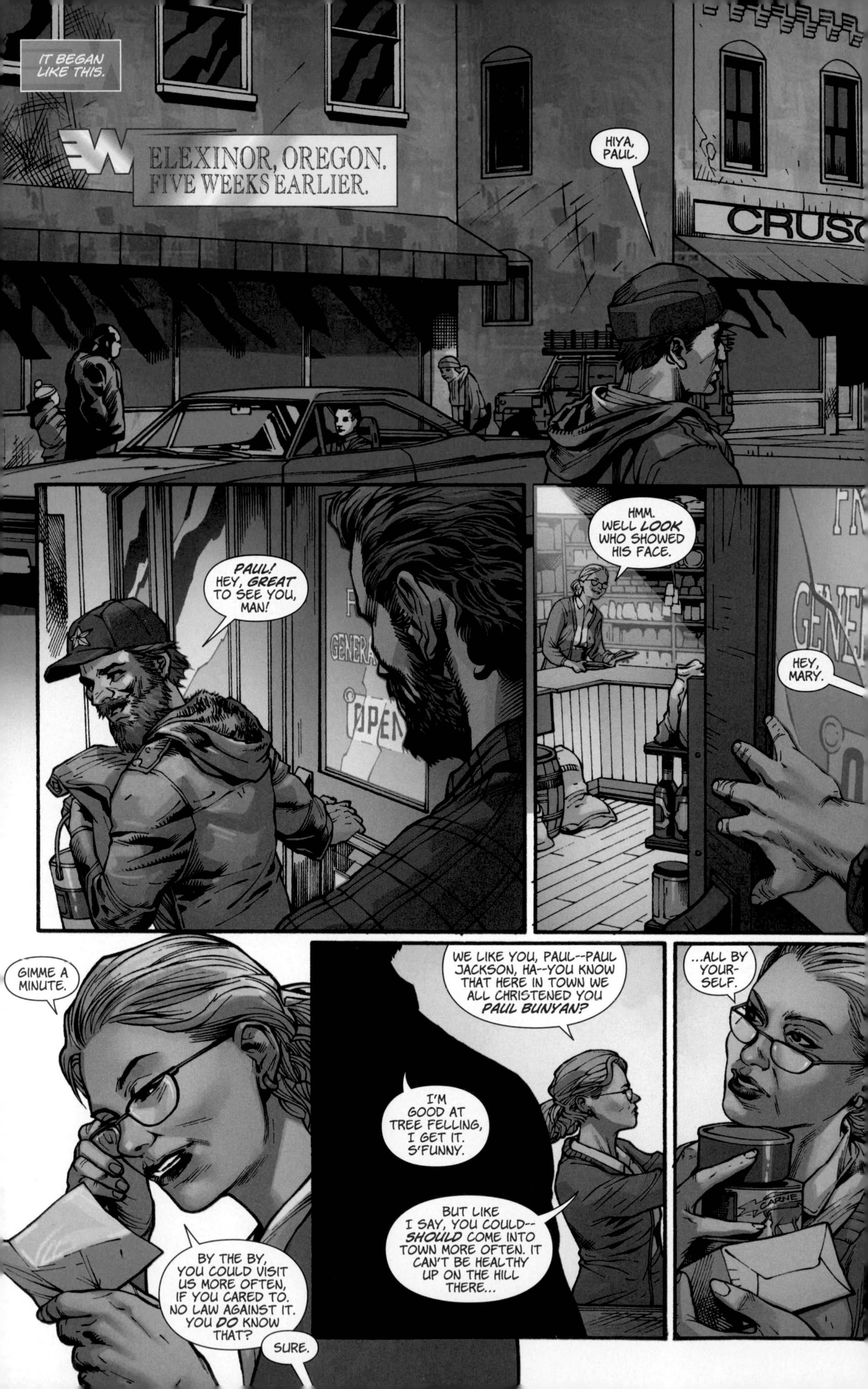
IT BEGAN LIKE THIS.
ELEXINOR, OREGON. FIVE WEEKS EARLIER.
CRUSO
HIYA, PAUL.
PAUL! HEY, GREAT TO SEE YOU, MAN!
OPEN
HMM. WELL LOOK WHO SHOWED HIS FACE.
HEY, MARY.
GIMME A MINUTE.
BY THE BY, YOU COULD VISIT US MORE OFTEN, IF YOU CARED TO. NO LAW AGAINST IT. YOU DO KNOW THAT?
SURE.
WE LIKE YOU, PAUL--PAUL JACKSON, HA--YOU KNOW THAT HERE IN TOWN WE ALL CHRISTENED YOU PAUL BUNYAN?
I'M GOOD AT TREE FELLING, I GET IT. S'FUNNY.
BUT LIKE I SAY, YOU COULD--SHOULD COME INTO TOWN MORE OFTEN. IT CAN'T BE HEALTHY UP ON THE HILL THERE...
...ALL BY YOUR-SELF.
CARNE

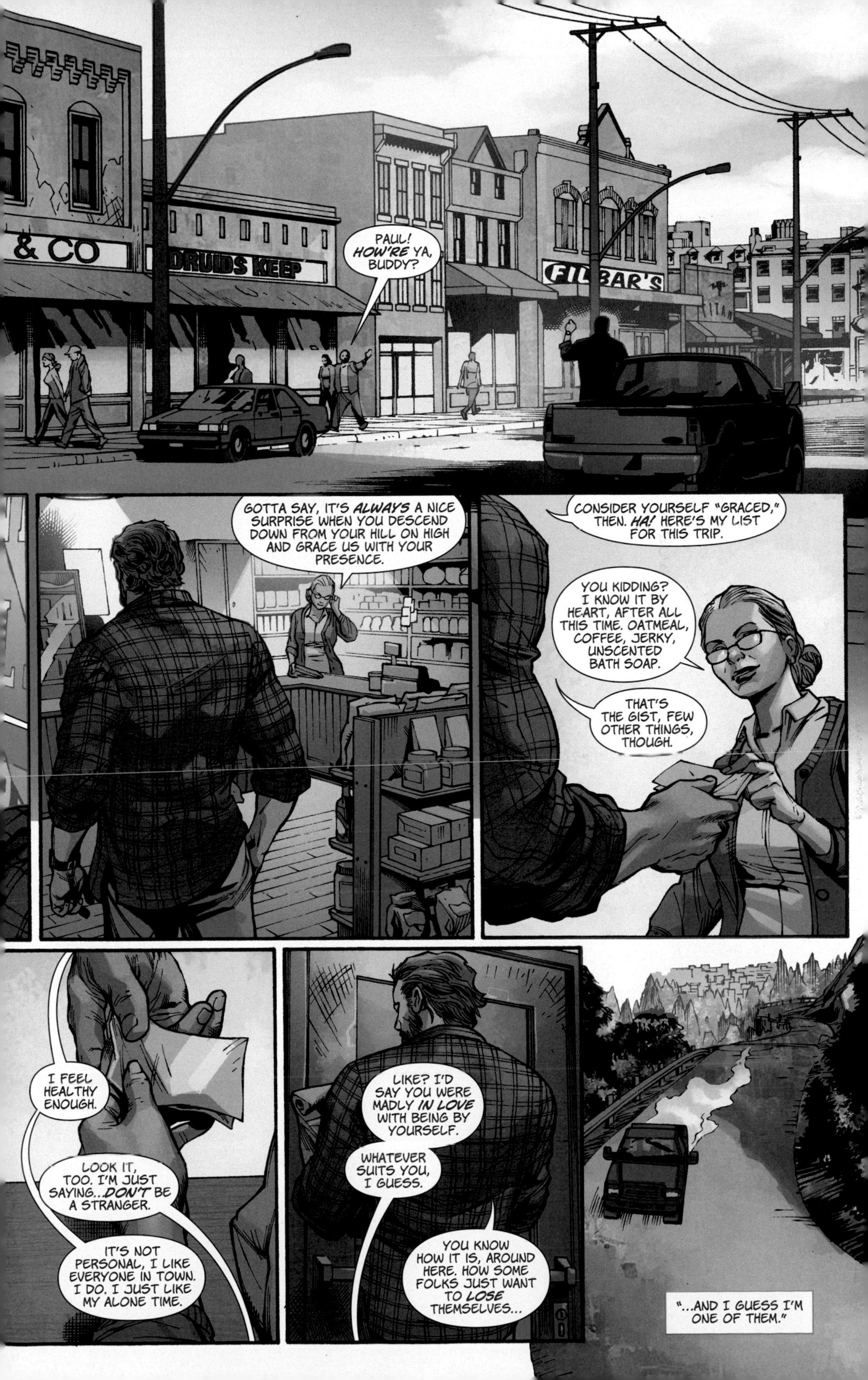
& CO
DRUIDS KEEP
PAUL! HOW'RE YA, BUDDY?
FILBAR'S
GOTTA SAY, IT'S ALWAYS A NICE SURPRISE WHEN YOU DESCEND DOWN FROM YOUR HILL ON HIGH AND GRACE US WITH YOUR PRESENCE.
CONSIDER YOURSELF "GRACED," THEN. HA! HERE'S MY LIST FOR THIS TRIP.
YOU KIDDING? I KNOW IT BY HEART, AFTER ALL THIS TIME. OATMEAL, COFFEE, JERKY, UNSCENTED BATH SOAP.
THAT'S THE GIST, FEW OTHER THINGS, THOUGH.
I FEEL HEALTHY ENOUGH.
LOOK IT, TOO. I'M JUST SAYING...DON'T BE A STRANGER.
IT'S NOT PERSONAL, I LIKE EVERYONE IN TOWN. I DO. I JUST LIKE MY ALONE TIME.
LIKE? I'D SAY YOU WERE MADLY IN LOVE WITH BEING BY YOURSELF.
WHATEVER SUITS YOU, I GUESS.
YOU KNOW HOW IT IS, AROUND HERE. HOW SOME FOLKS JUST WANT TO LOSE THEMSELVES...
"...AND I GUESS I'M ONE OF THEM."

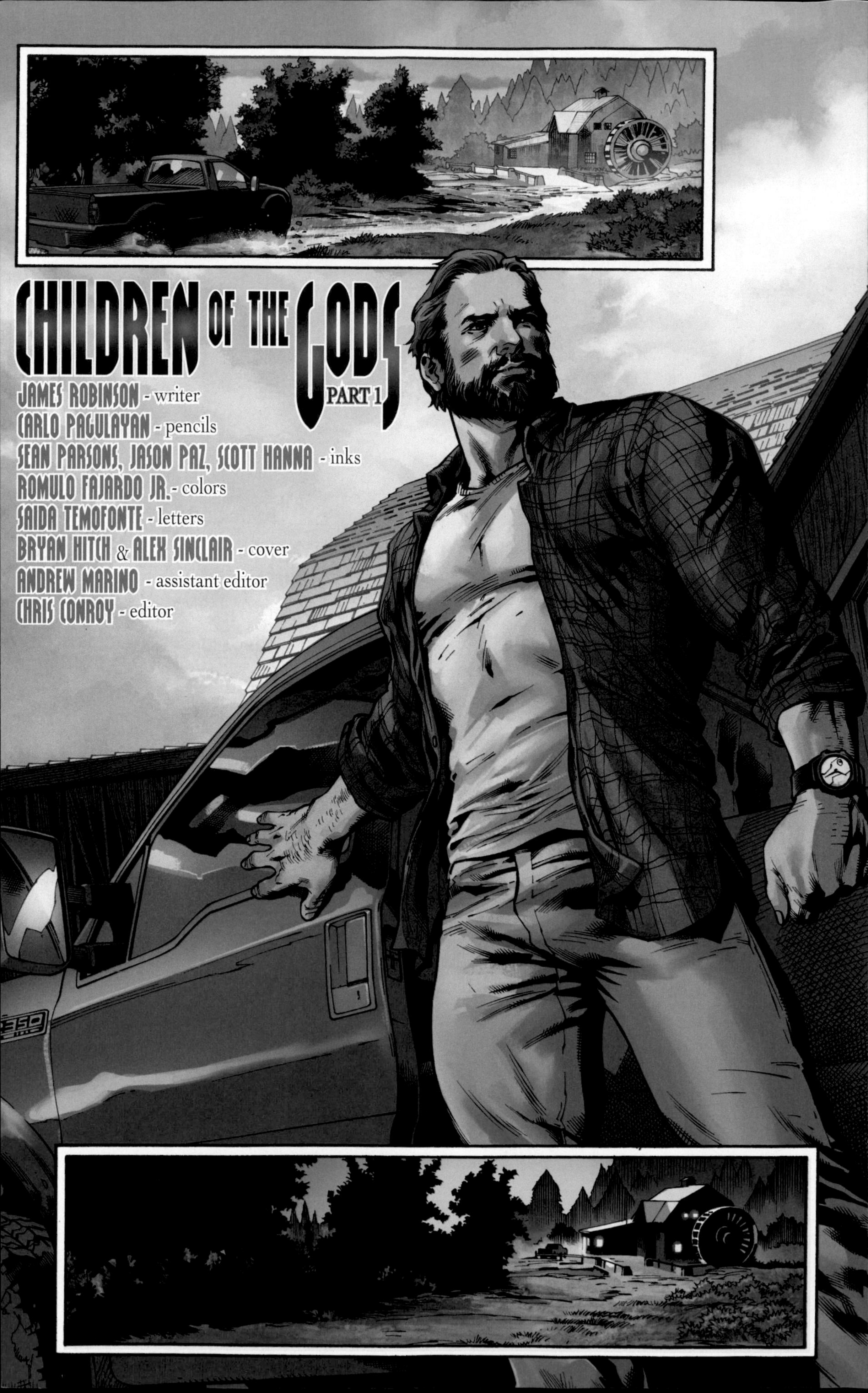
CHILDREN OF THE GODS
PART 1
JAMES ROBINSON - writer
CARLO PAGULAYAN - pencils
SEAN PARSONS, JASON PAZ, SCOTT HANNA - inks
ROMULO FAJARDO JR. - colors
SAIDA TEMOFONTE - letters
BRYAN HITCH & ALEX SINCLAIR - cover
ANDREW MARINO - assistant editor
CHRIS CONROY - editor

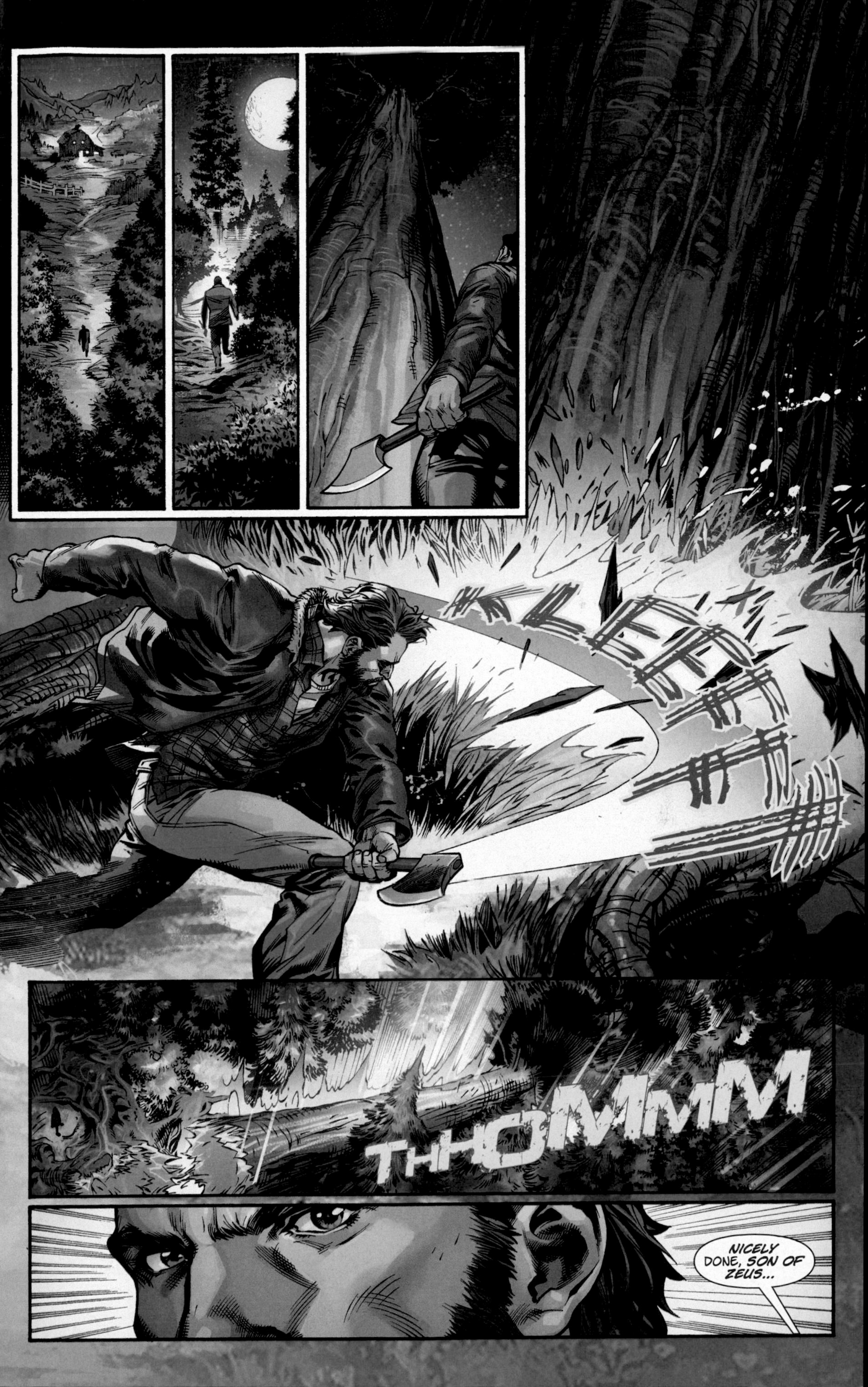
THHOMMMM
NICELY DONE, SON OF ZEUS...

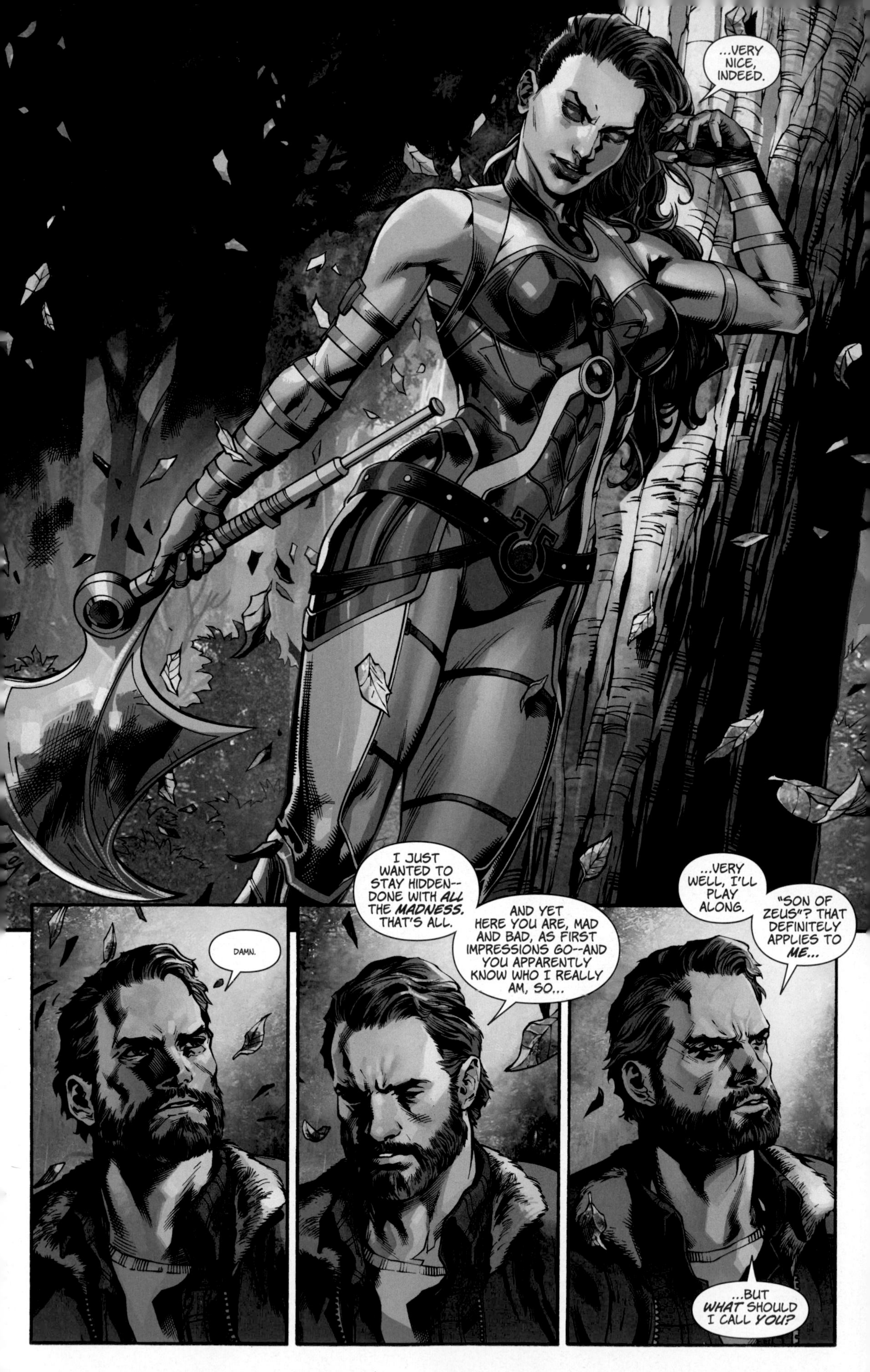
...VERY NICE, INDEED.
DAMN.
I JUST WANTED TO STAY HIDDEN-- DONE WITH ALL THE MADNESS. THAT'S ALL.
AND YET HERE YOU ARE, MAD AND BAD, AS FIRST IMPRESSIONS GO--AND YOU APPARENTLY KNOW WHO I REALLY AM, SO...
...VERY WELL, I'LL PLAY ALONG.
"SON OF ZEUS"? THAT DEFINITELY APPLIES TO ME...
...BUT WHAT SHOULD I CALL YOU?

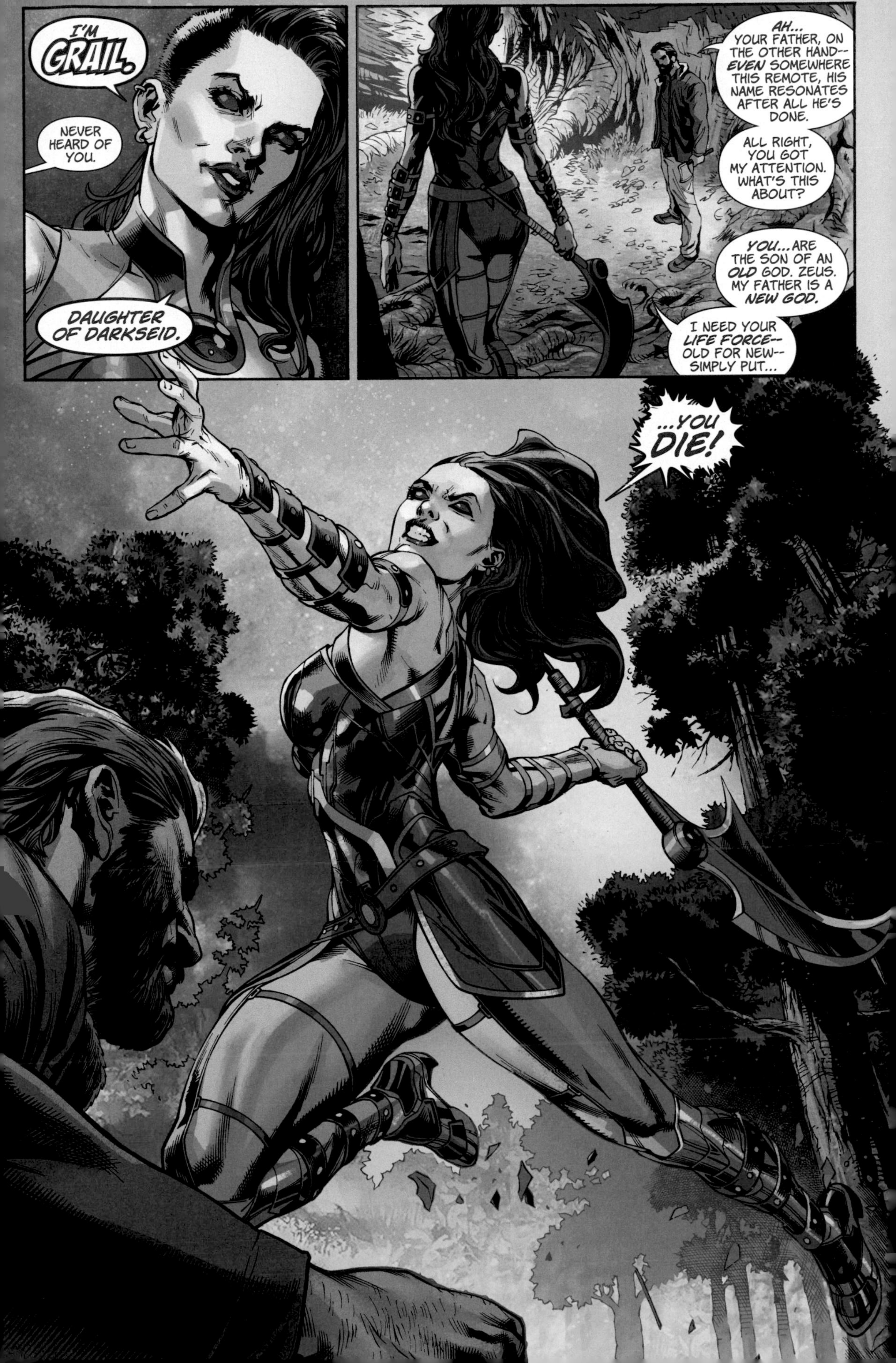
I'M GRAIL.
NEVER HEARD OF YOU.
DAUGHTER OF DARKSEID.
AH... YOUR FATHER, ON THE OTHER HAND-- EVEN SOMEWHERE THIS REMOTE, HIS NAME RESONATES AFTER ALL HE'S DONE.
ALL RIGHT, YOU GOT MY ATTENTION. WHAT'S THIS ABOUT?
YOU... ARE THE SON OF AN OLD GOD. ZEUS. MY FATHER IS A NEW GOD.
I NEED YOUR LIFE FORCE-- OLD FOR NEW-- SIMPLY PUT...
...YOU DIE!

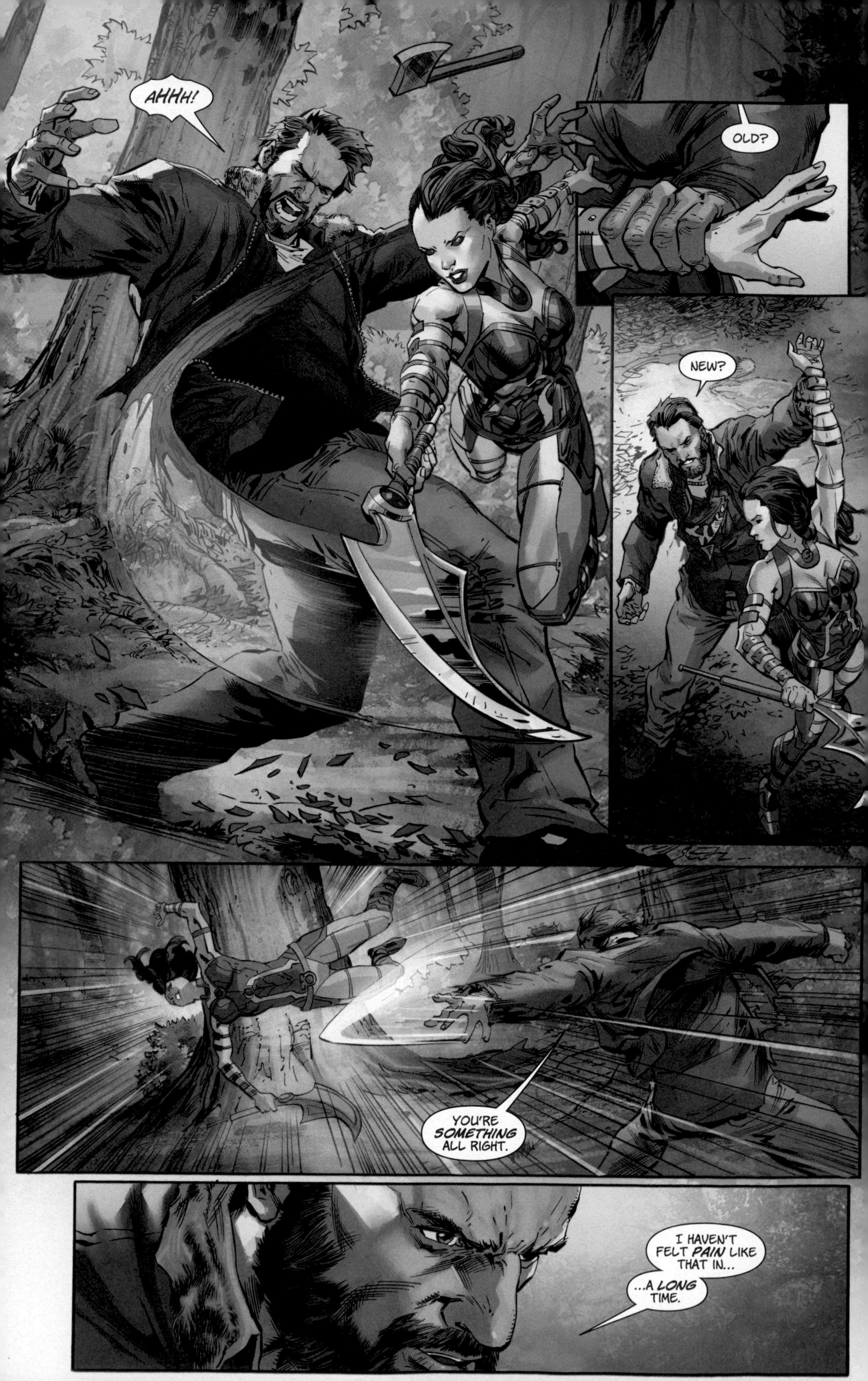
AHHH!
OLD?
NEW?
YOU'RE SOMETHING ALL RIGHT.
I HAVEN'T FELT PAIN LIKE THAT IN...
...A LONG TIME.

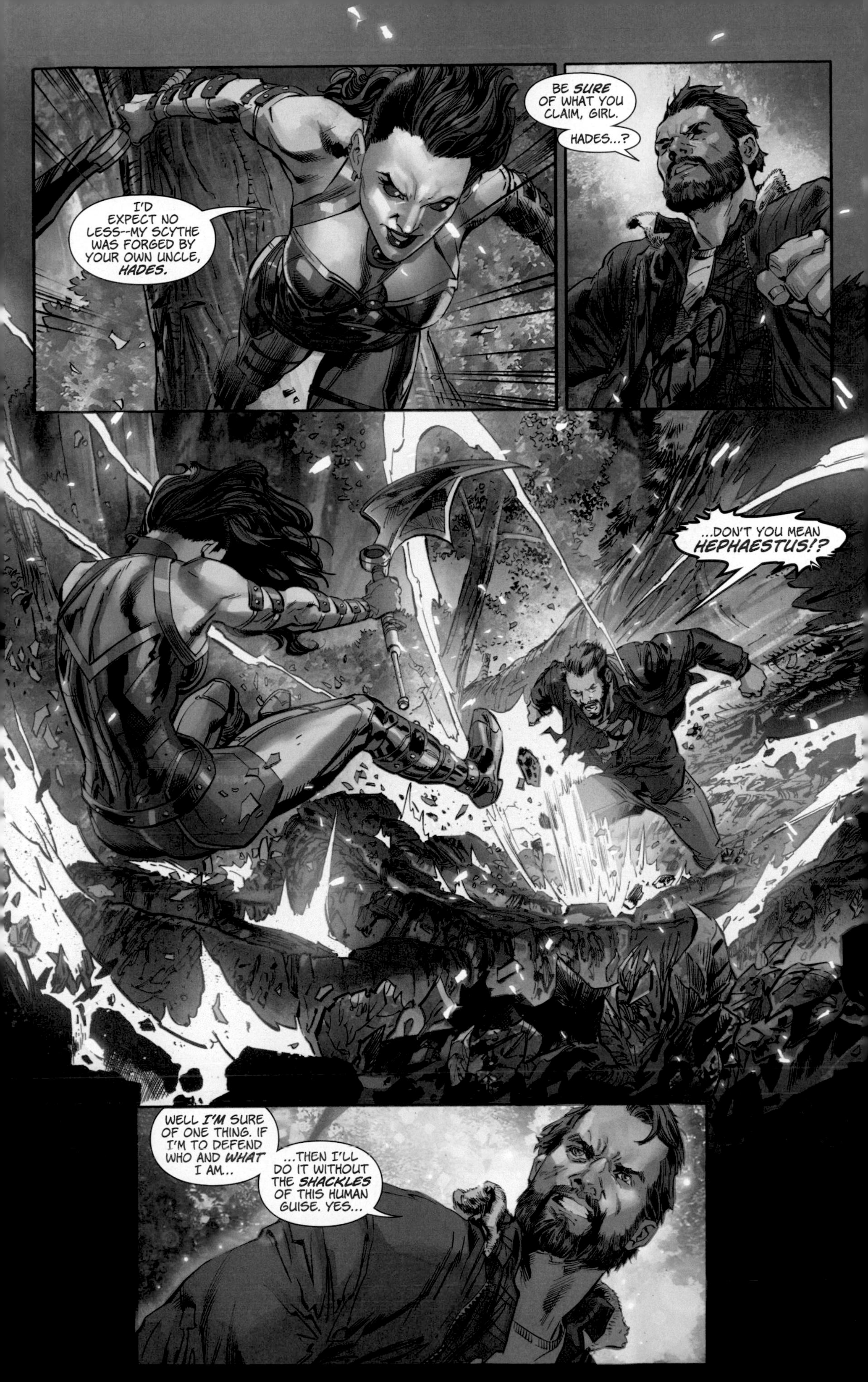
I'D EXPECT NO LESS--MY SCYTHE WAS FORGED BY YOUR OWN UNCLE, HADES.
BE SURE OF WHAT YOU CLAIM, GIRL.
HADES...?
...DON'T YOU MEAN HEPHAESTUS!?
WELL I'M SURE OF ONE THING. IF I'M TO DEFEND WHO AND WHAT I AM...
...THEN I'LL DO IT WITHOUT THE SHACKLES OF THIS HUMAN GUISE. YES...

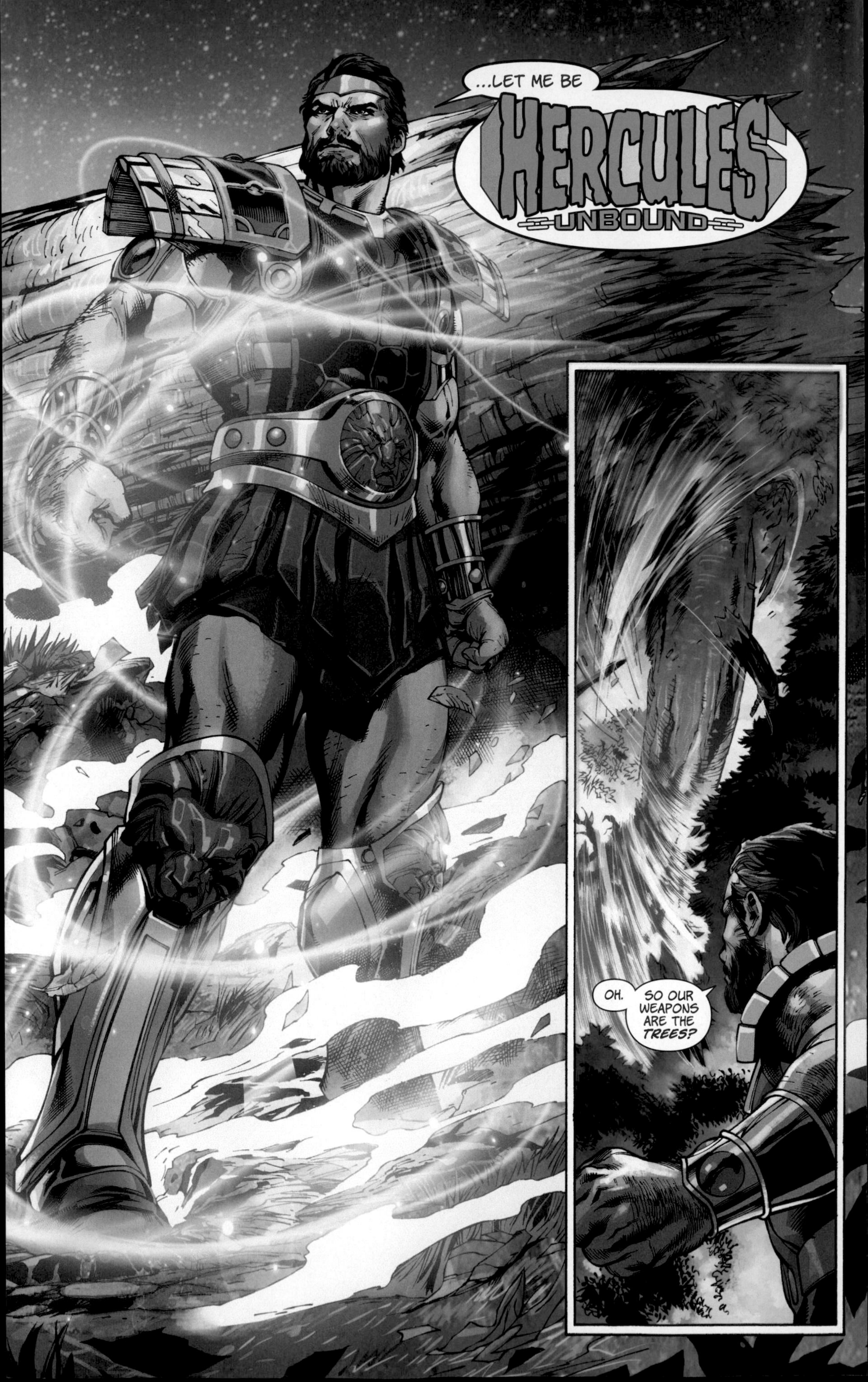

...LET ME BE
HERCULES UNBOUND
OH.
SO OUR WEAPONS ARE THE TREES?

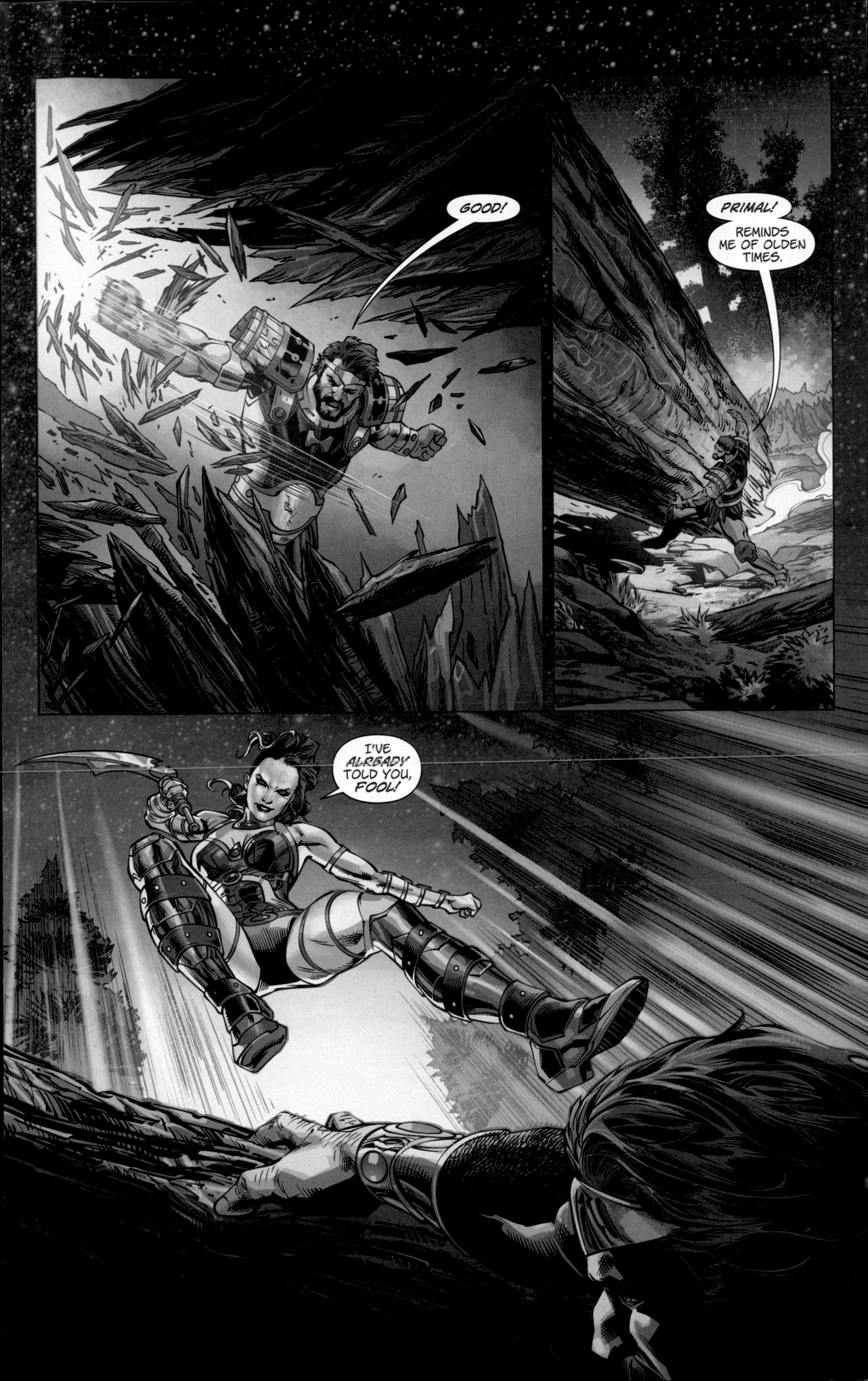
GOOD!
PRIMAL!
REMINDS ME OF OLDEN TIMES.
I'VE ALREADY TOLD YOU, FOOL!

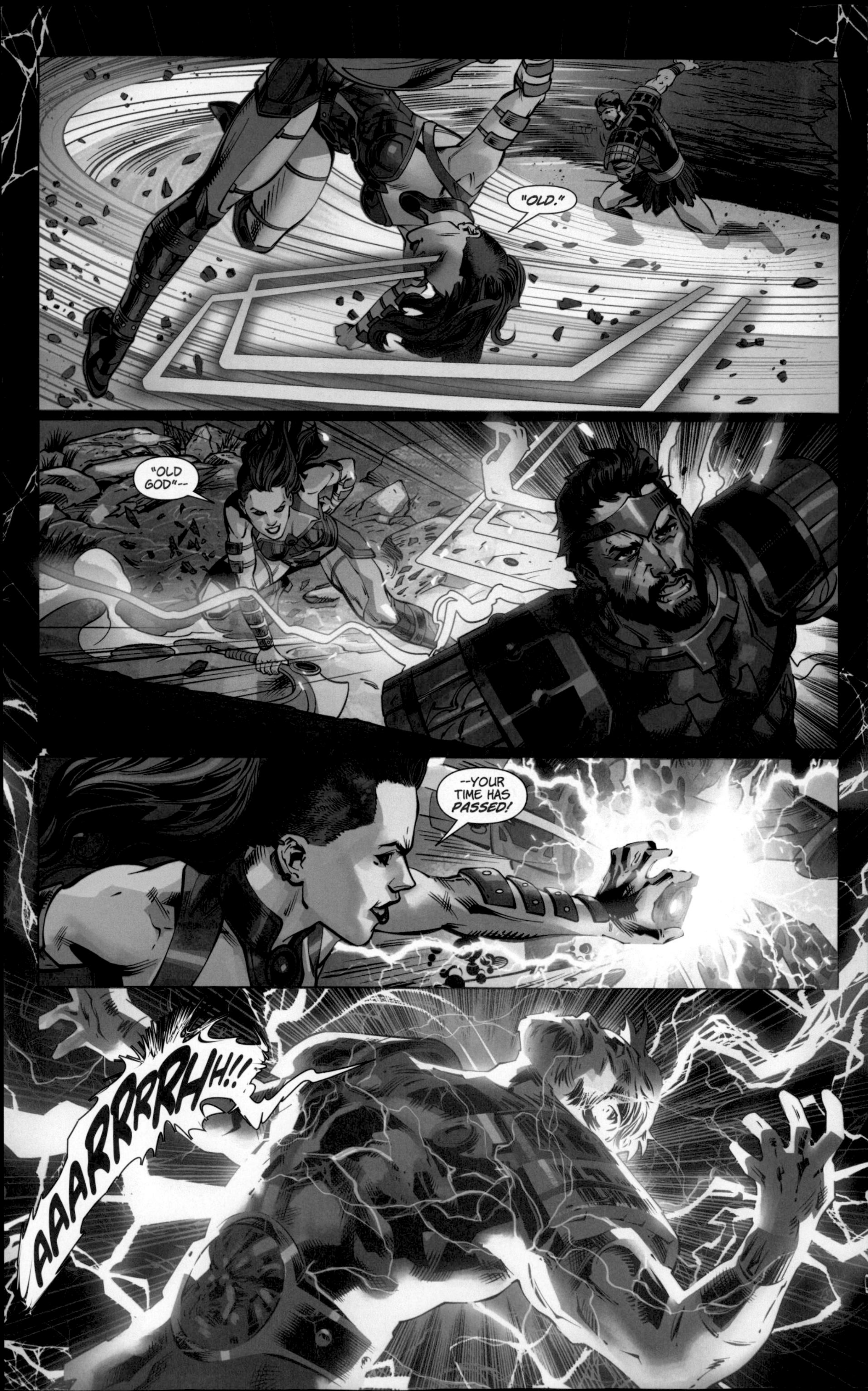
"OLD."
"OLD GOD"--
--YOUR TIME HAS PASSED!
AAARRRRHH!!

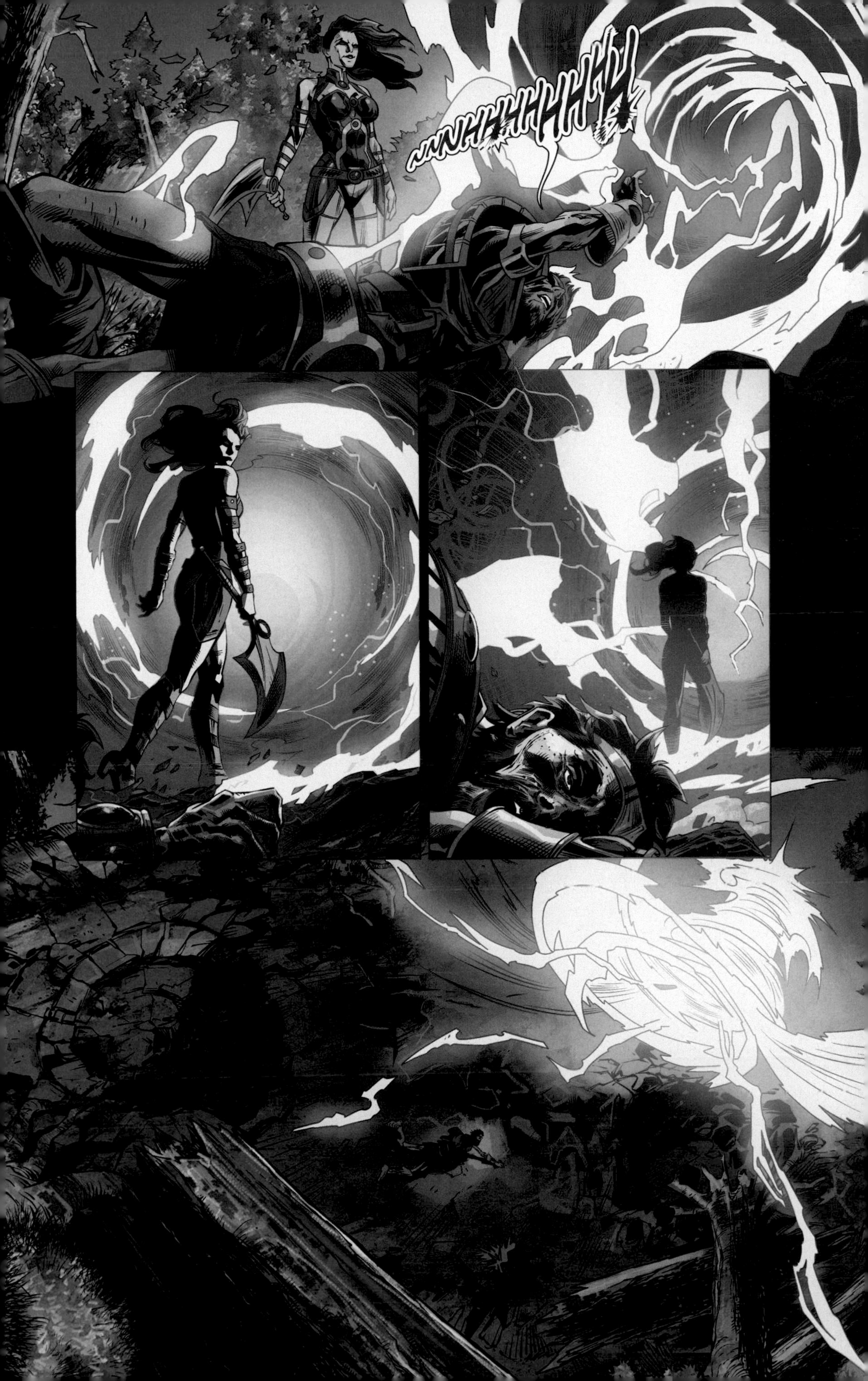
NNNHHHHHHH!

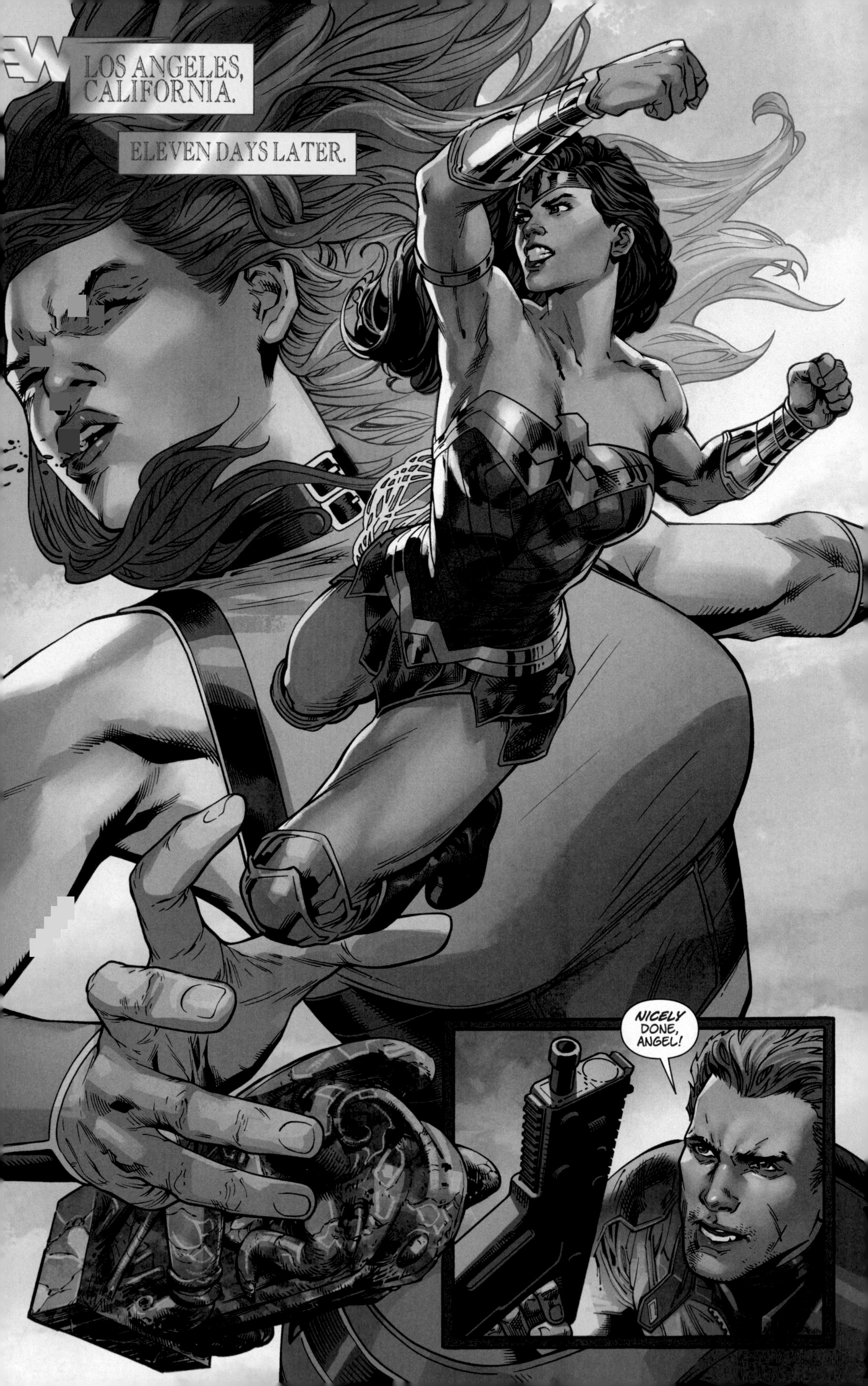
LOS ANGELES, CALIFORNIA.
ELEVEN DAYS LATER.
NICELY DONE, ANGEL!

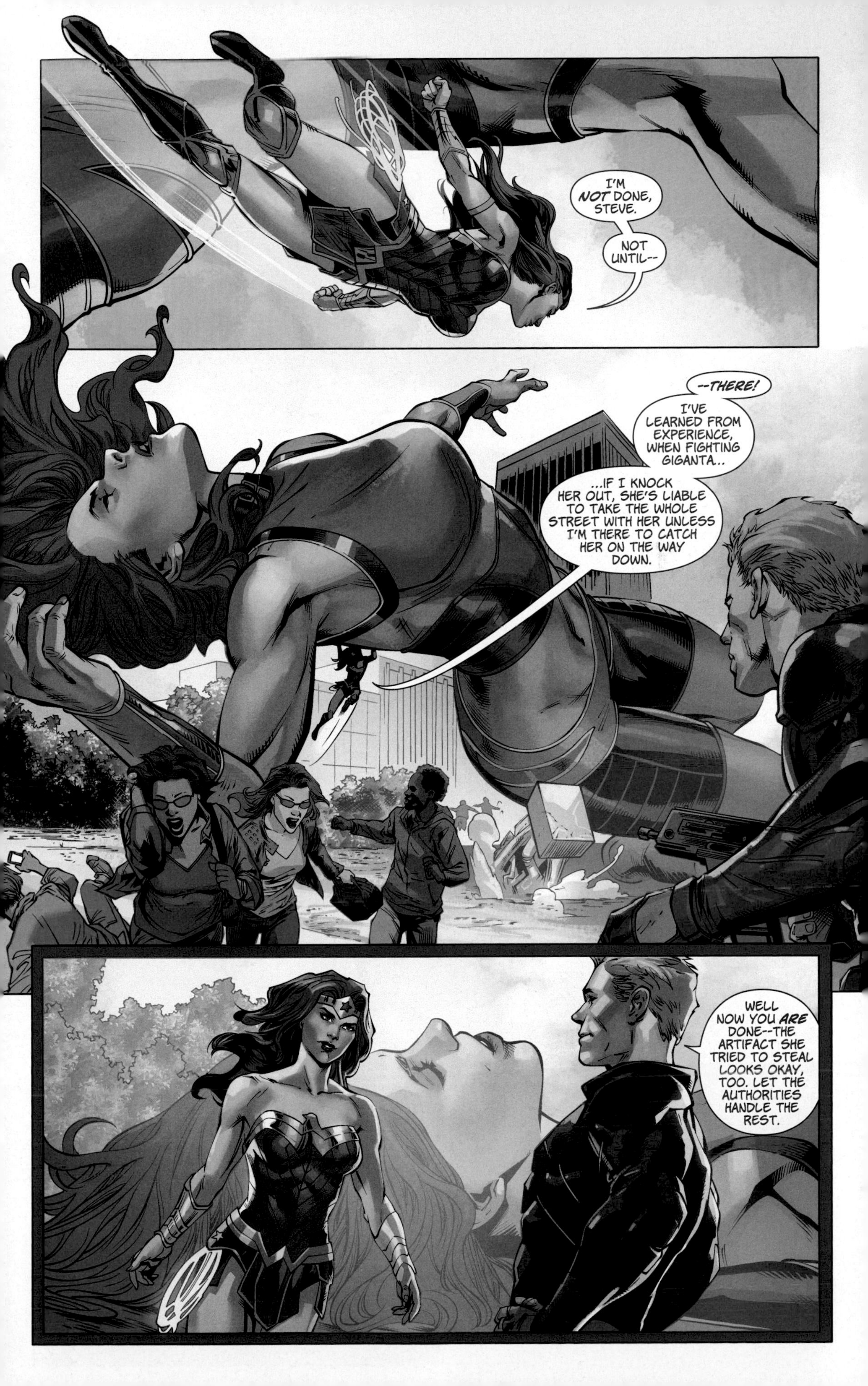
I'M NOT DONE, STEVE.
NOT UNTIL--
--THERE!
I'VE LEARNED FROM EXPERIENCE, WHEN FIGHTING GIGANTA...
...IF I KNOCK HER OUT, SHE'S LIABLE TO TAKE THE WHOLE STREET WITH HER UNLESS I'M THERE TO CATCH HER ON THE WAY DOWN.
WELL NOW YOU ARE DONE--THE ARTIFACT SHE TRIED TO STEAL LOOKS OKAY, TOO. LET THE AUTHORITIES HANDLE THE REST.

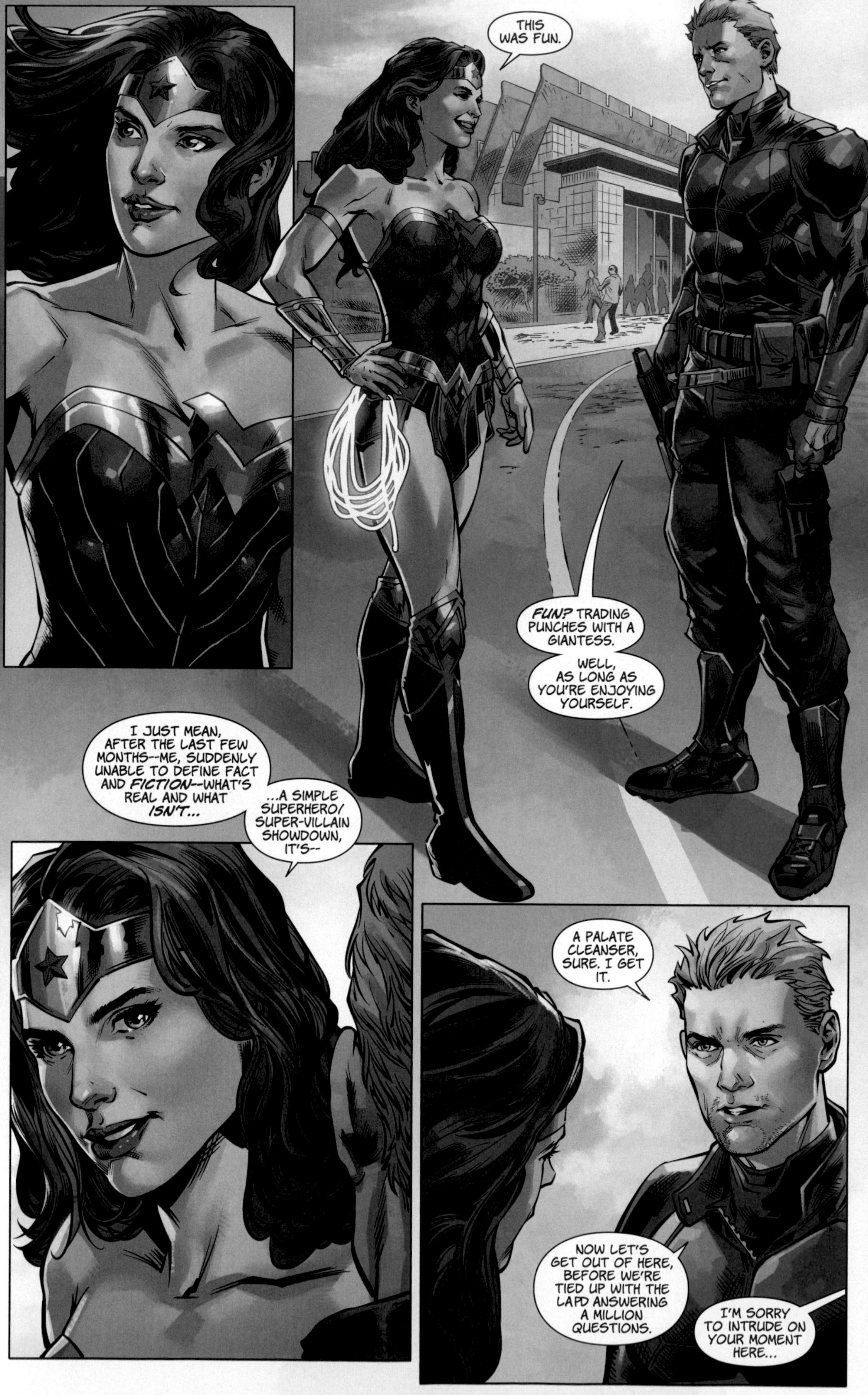
THIS WAS FUN.
FUN? TRADING PUNCHES WITH A GIANTESS.
WELL, AS LONG AS YOU'RE ENJOYING YOURSELF.
I JUST MEAN, AFTER THE LAST FEW MONTHS--ME, SUDDENLY UNABLE TO DEFINE FACT AND FICTION--WHAT'S REAL AND WHAT ISN'T...
...A SIMPLE SUPERHERO/ SUPER-VILLAIN SHOWDOWN, IT'S--
A PALATE CLEANSER, SURE. I GET IT.
NOW LET'S GET OUT OF HERE, BEFORE WE'RE TIED UP WITH THE LAPD ANSWERING A MILLION QUESTIONS.
I'M SORRY TO INTRUDE ON YOUR MOMENT HERE...

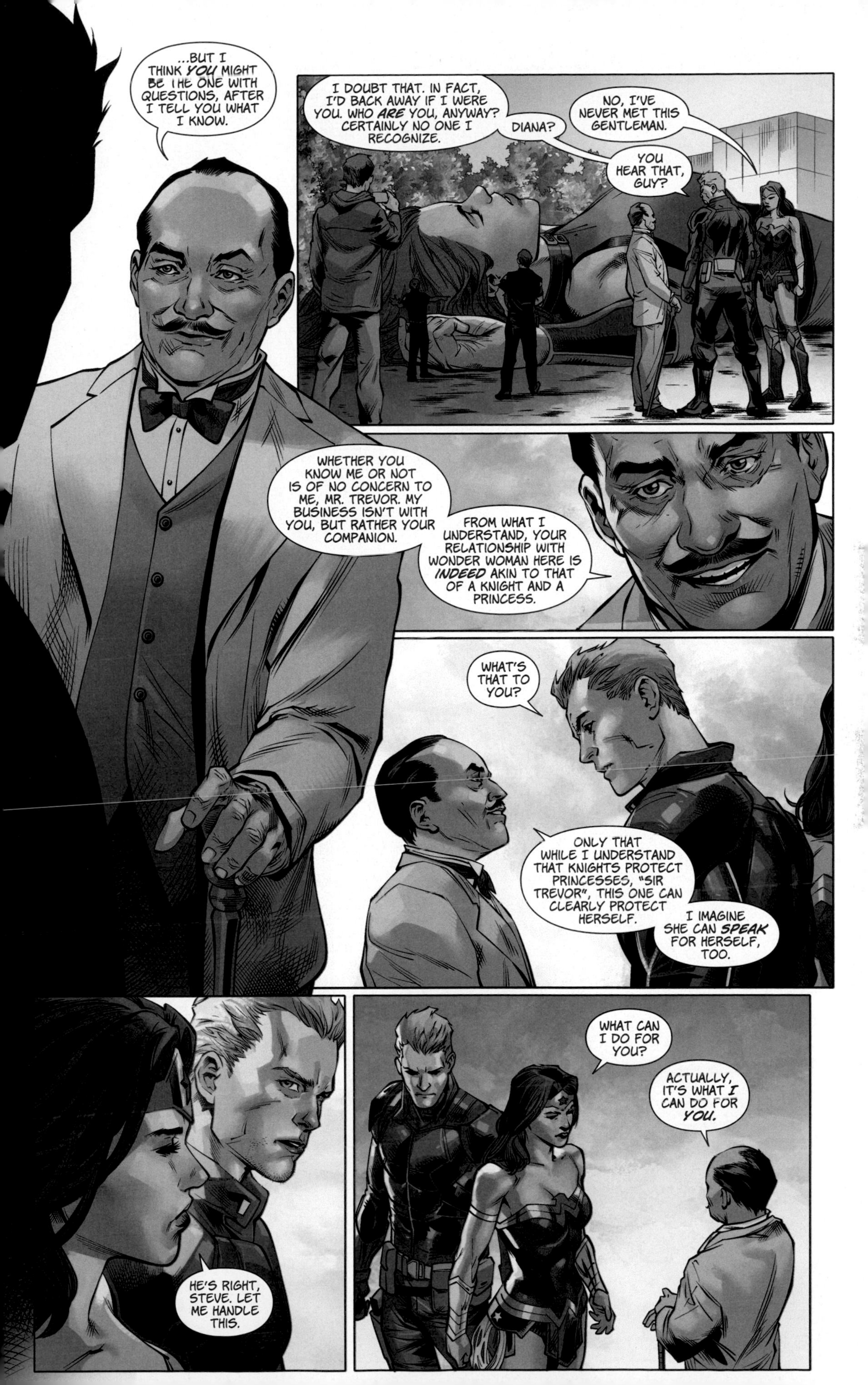
...BUT I THINK YOU MIGHT BE THE ONE WITH QUESTIONS, AFTER I TELL YOU WHAT I KNOW.
I DOUBT THAT. IN FACT, I'D BACK AWAY IF I WERE YOU. WHO ARE YOU, ANYWAY? CERTAINLY NO ONE I RECOGNIZE.
DIANA?
NO, I'VE NEVER MET THIS GENTLEMAN.
YOU HEAR THAT, GUY?
WHETHER YOU KNOW ME OR NOT IS OF NO CONCERN TO ME, MR. TREVOR. MY BUSINESS ISN'T WITH YOU, BUT RATHER YOUR COMPANION.
FROM WHAT I UNDERSTAND, YOUR RELATIONSHIP WITH WONDER WOMAN HERE IS INDEED AKIN TO THAT OF A KNIGHT AND A PRINCESS.
WHAT'S THAT TO YOU?
ONLY THAT WHILE I UNDERSTAND THAT KNIGHTS PROTECT PRINCESSES, "SIR TREVOR", THIS ONE CAN CLEARLY PROTECT HERSELF.
I IMAGINE SHE CAN SPEAK FOR HERSELF, TOO.
HE'S RIGHT, STEVE. LET ME HANDLE THIS.
WHAT CAN I DO FOR YOU?
ACTUALLY, IT'S WHAT I CAN DO FOR YOU.

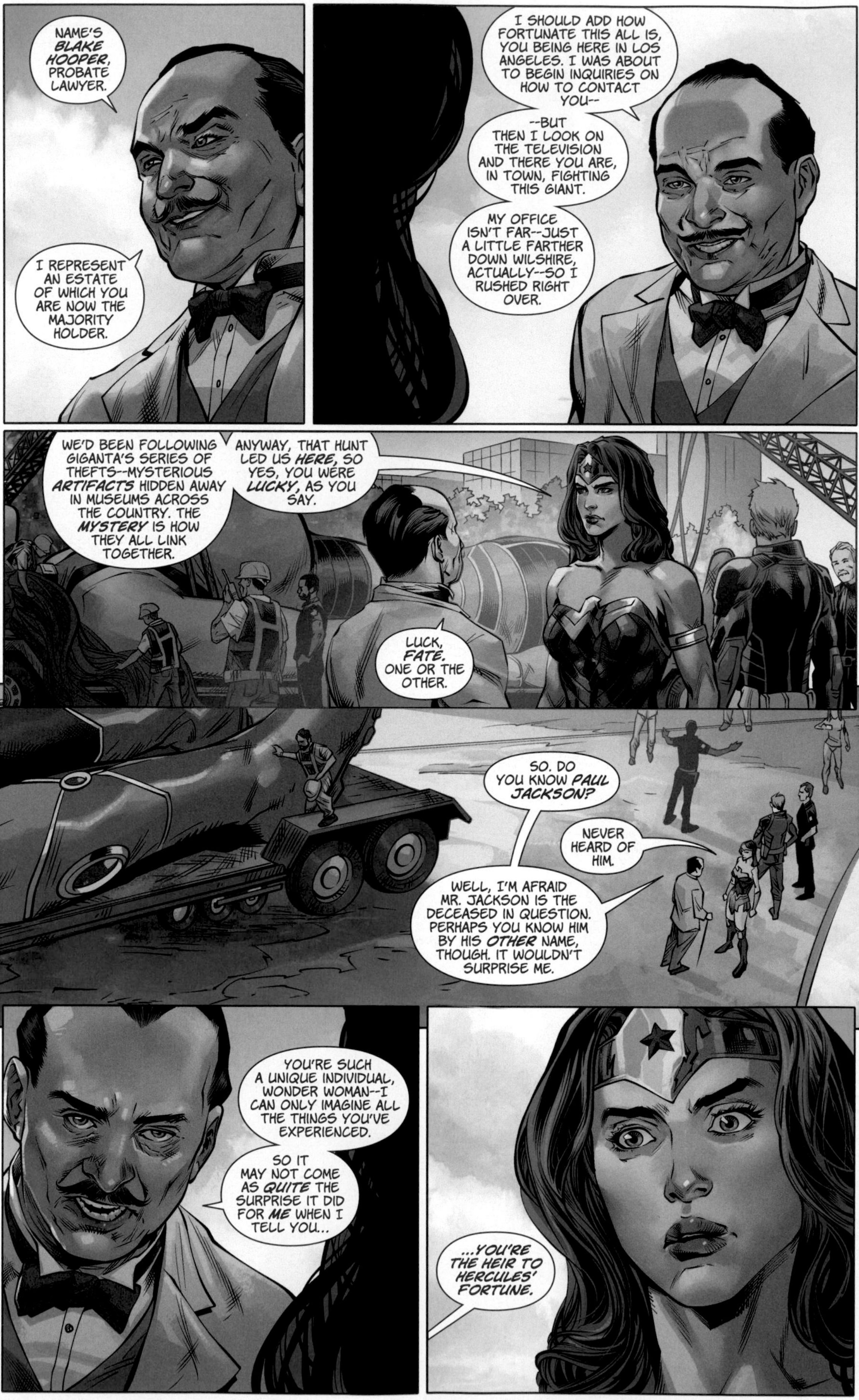
NAME'S BLAKE HOOPER, PROBATE LAWYER.
I REPRESENT AN ESTATE OF WHICH YOU ARE NOW THE MAJORITY HOLDER.
I SHOULD ADD HOW FORTUNATE THIS ALL IS, YOU BEING HERE IN LOS ANGELES. I WAS ABOUT TO BEGIN INQUIRIES ON HOW TO CONTACT YOU--
--BUT THEN I LOOK ON THE TELEVISION AND THERE YOU ARE, IN TOWN, FIGHTING THIS GIANT.
MY OFFICE ISN'T FAR--JUST A LITTLE FARTHER DOWN WILSHIRE, ACTUALLY--SO I RUSHED RIGHT OVER.
WE'D BEEN FOLLOWING GIGANTA'S SERIES OF THEFTS--MYSTERIOUS ARTIFACTS HIDDEN AWAY IN MUSEUMS ACROSS THE COUNTRY. THE MYSTERY IS HOW THEY ALL LINK TOGETHER.
ANYWAY, THAT HUNT LED US HERE, SO YES, YOU WERE LUCKY, AS YOU SAY.
LUCK, FATE. ONE OR THE OTHER.
SO. DO YOU KNOW PAUL JACKSON?
NEVER HEARD OF HIM.
WELL, I'M AFRAID MR. JACKSON IS THE DECEASED IN QUESTION. PERHAPS YOU KNOW HIM BY HIS OTHER NAME, THOUGH. IT WOULDN'T SURPRISE ME.
YOU'RE SUCH A UNIQUE INDIVIDUAL, WONDER WOMAN--I CAN ONLY IMAGINE ALL THE THINGS YOU'VE EXPERIENCED.
SO IT MAY NOT COME AS QUITE THE SURPRISE IT DID FOR ME WHEN I TELL YOU...
...YOU'RE THE HEIR TO HERCULES' FORTUNE.

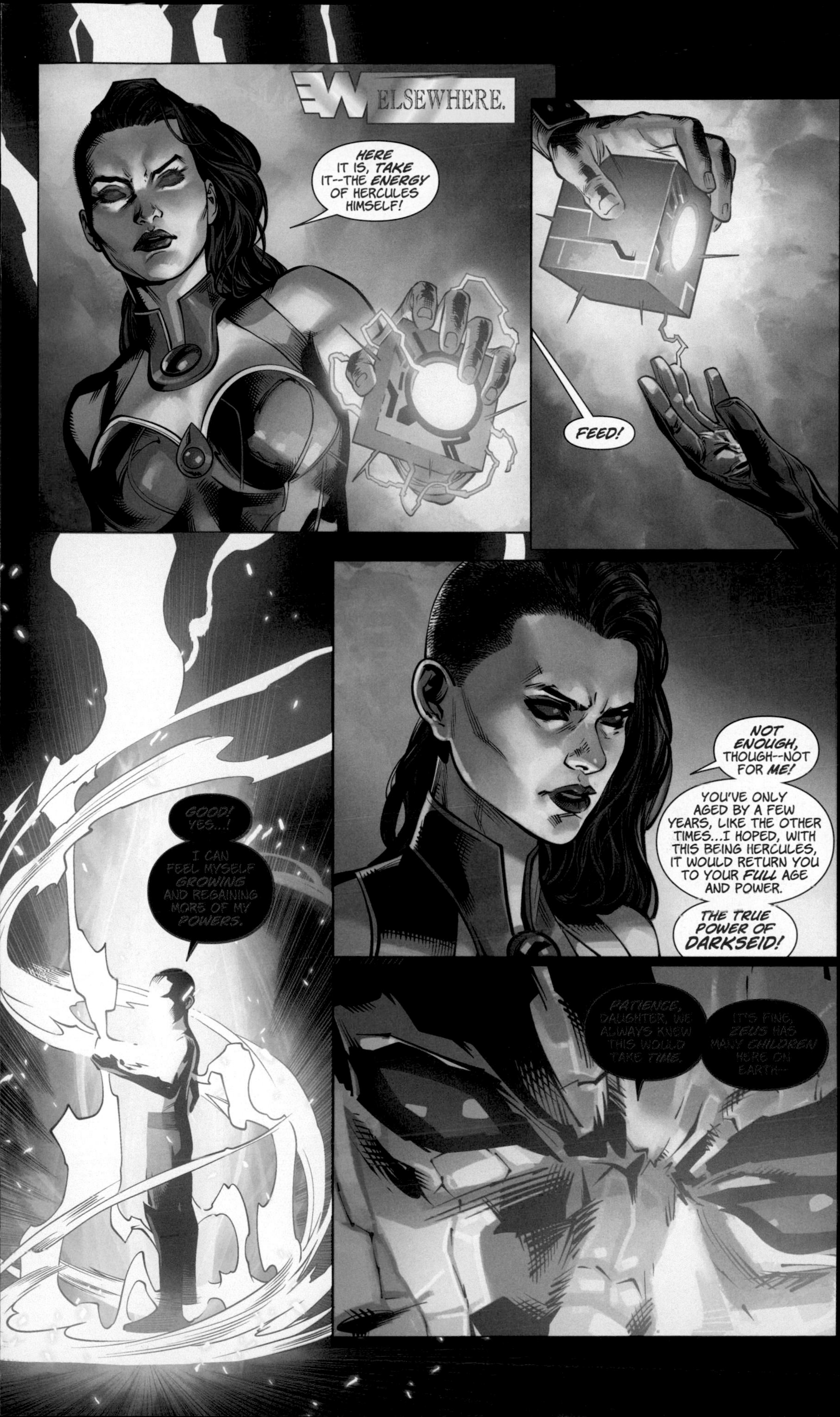
ELSEWHERE.
HERE IT IS, TAKE IT--THE ENERGY OF HERCULES HIMSELF!
FEED!
GOOD! YES...!
I CAN FEEL MYSELF GROWING AND REGAINING MORE OF MY POWERS.
NOT ENOUGH, THOUGH--NOT FOR ME!
YOU'VE ONLY AGED BY A FEW YEARS, LIKE THE OTHER TIMES...I HOPED, WITH THIS BEING HERCULES, IT WOULD RETURN YOU TO YOUR FULL AGE AND POWER.
THE TRUE POWER OF DARKSEID!
PATIENCE, DAUGHTER, WE ALWAYS KNEW THIS WOULD TAKE TIME.
IT'S FINE, ZEUS HAS MANY CHILDREN HERE ON EARTH--

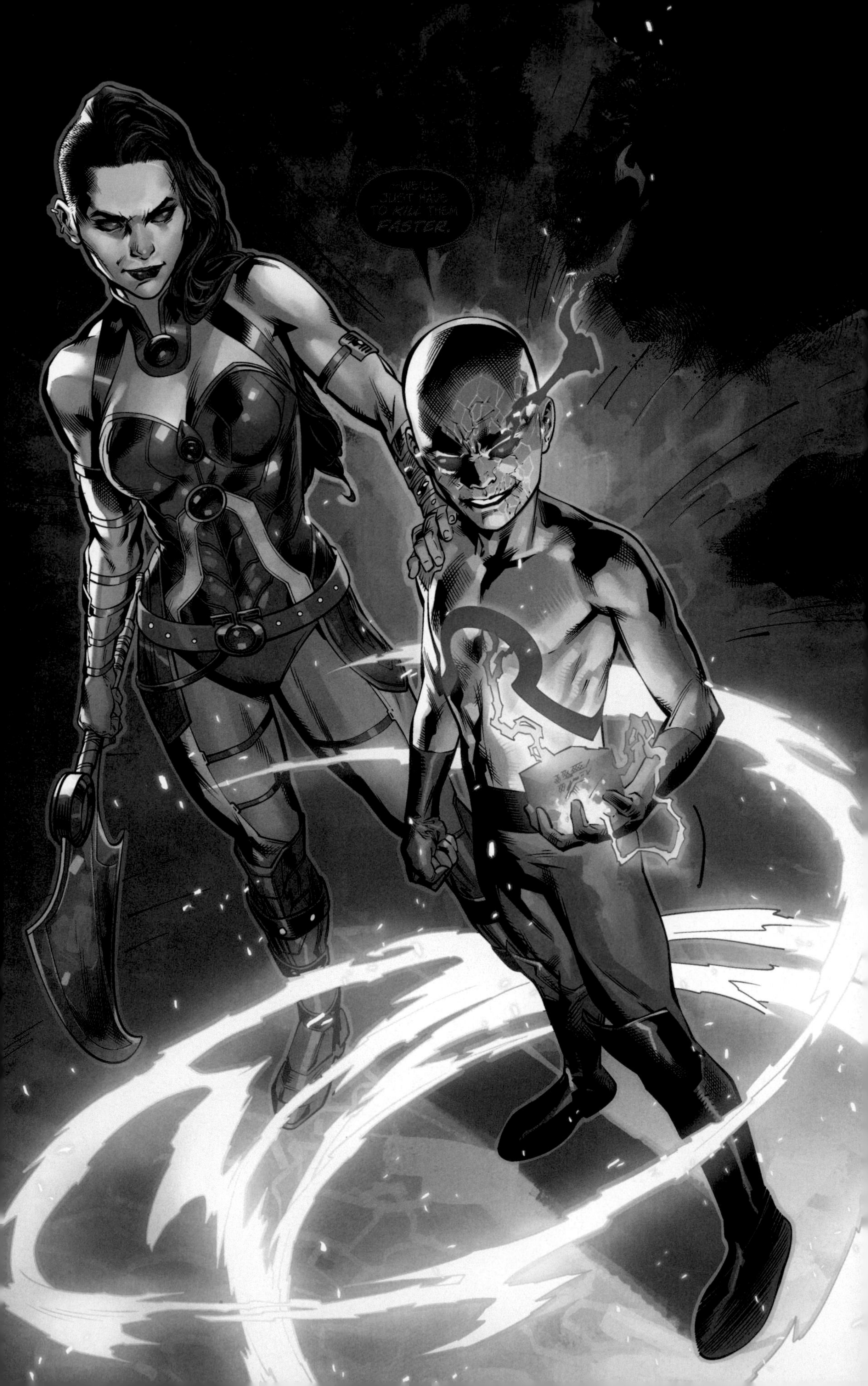
–WE'LL JUST HAVE TO KILL THEM FASTER.

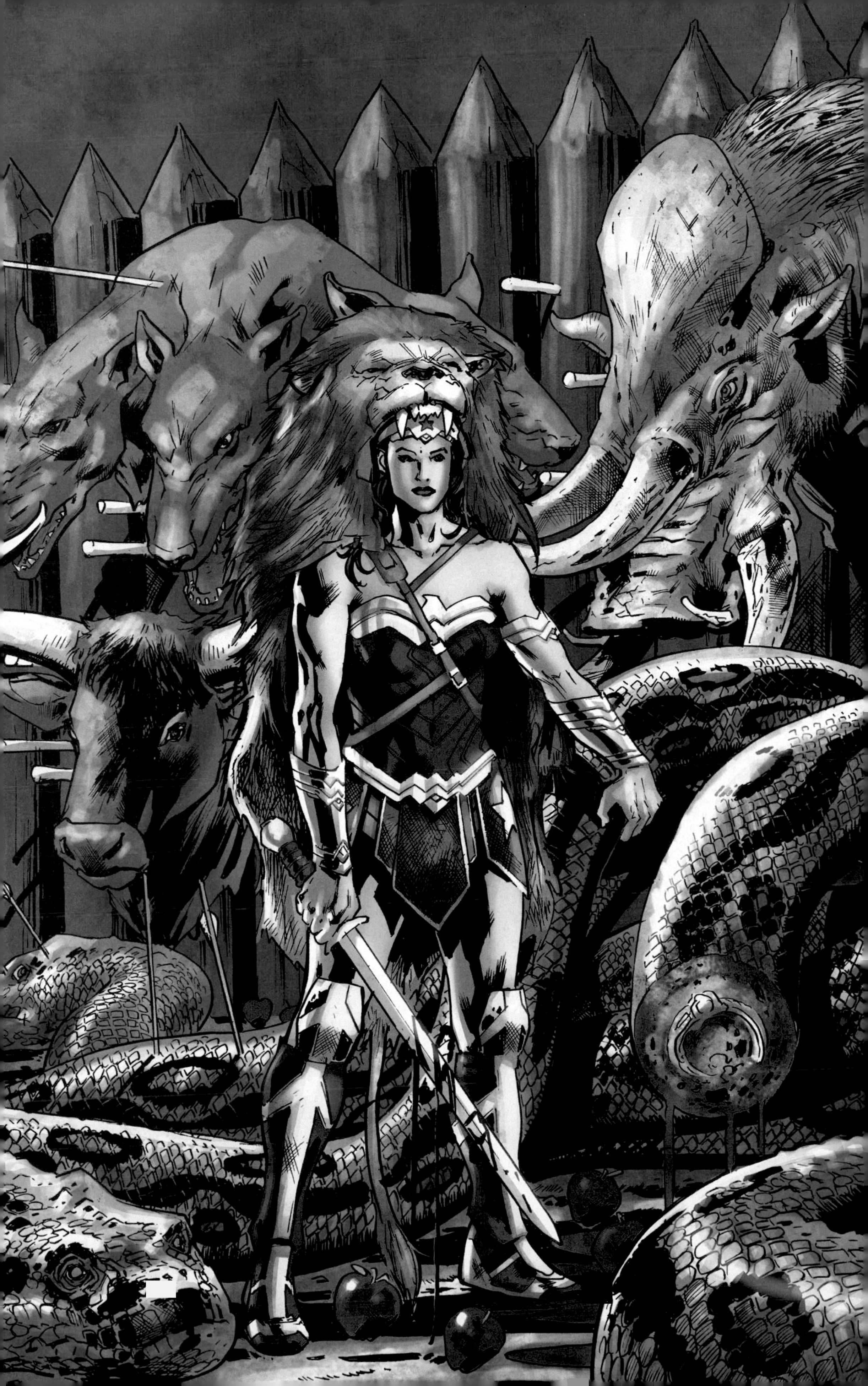

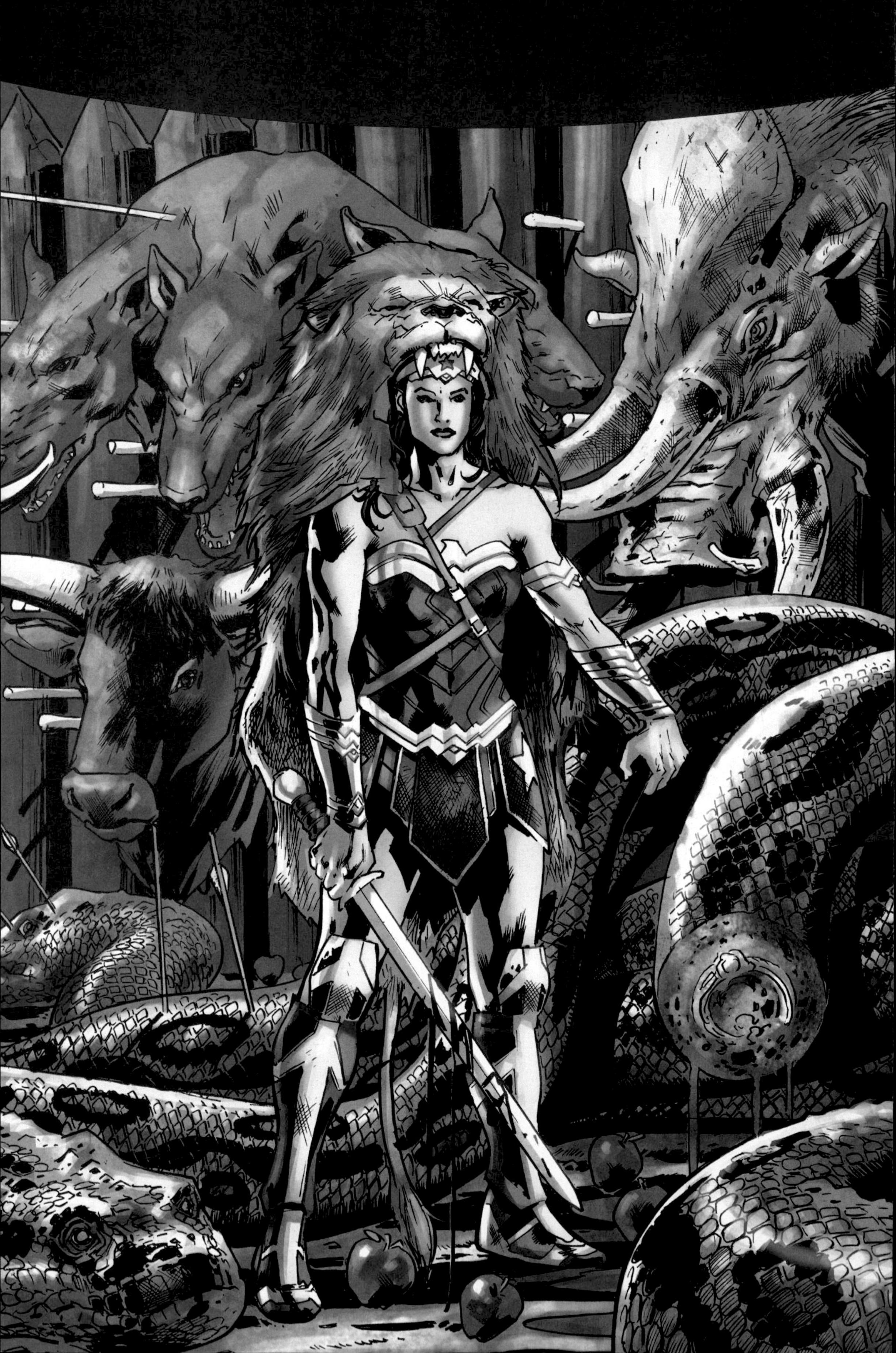

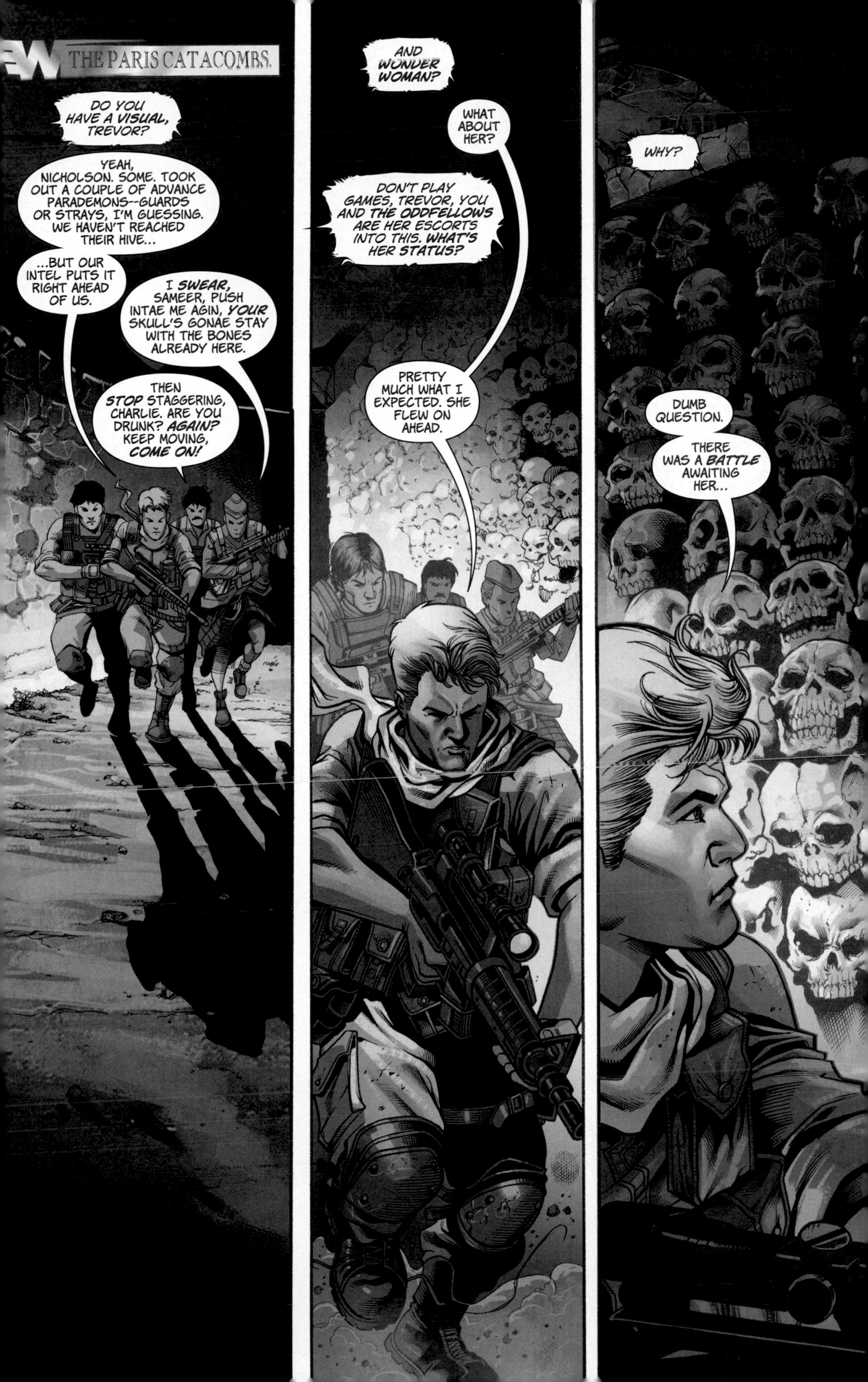
THE PARIS CATACOMBS.
DO YOU HAVE A VISUAL, TREVOR?
YEAH, NICHOLSON. SOME. TOOK OUT A COUPLE OF ADVANCE PARADEMONS--GUARDS OR STRAYS, I'M GUESSING. WE HAVEN'T REACHED THEIR HIVE...
...BUT OUR INTEL PUTS IT RIGHT AHEAD OF US.
I SWEAR, SAMEER, PUSH INTAE ME AGIN, YOUR SKULL'S GONAE STAY WITH THE BONES ALREADY HERE.
THEN STOP STAGGERING, CHARLIE. ARE YOU DRUNK? AGAIN? KEEP MOVING, COME ON!
AND WONDER WOMAN?
WHAT ABOUT HER?
DON'T PLAY GAMES, TREVOR, YOU AND THE ODDFELLOWS ARE HER ESCORTS INTO THIS. WHAT'S HER STATUS?
PRETTY MUCH WHAT I EXPECTED. SHE FLEW ON AHEAD.
WHY?
DUMB QUESTION.
THERE WAS A BATTLE AWAITING HER...

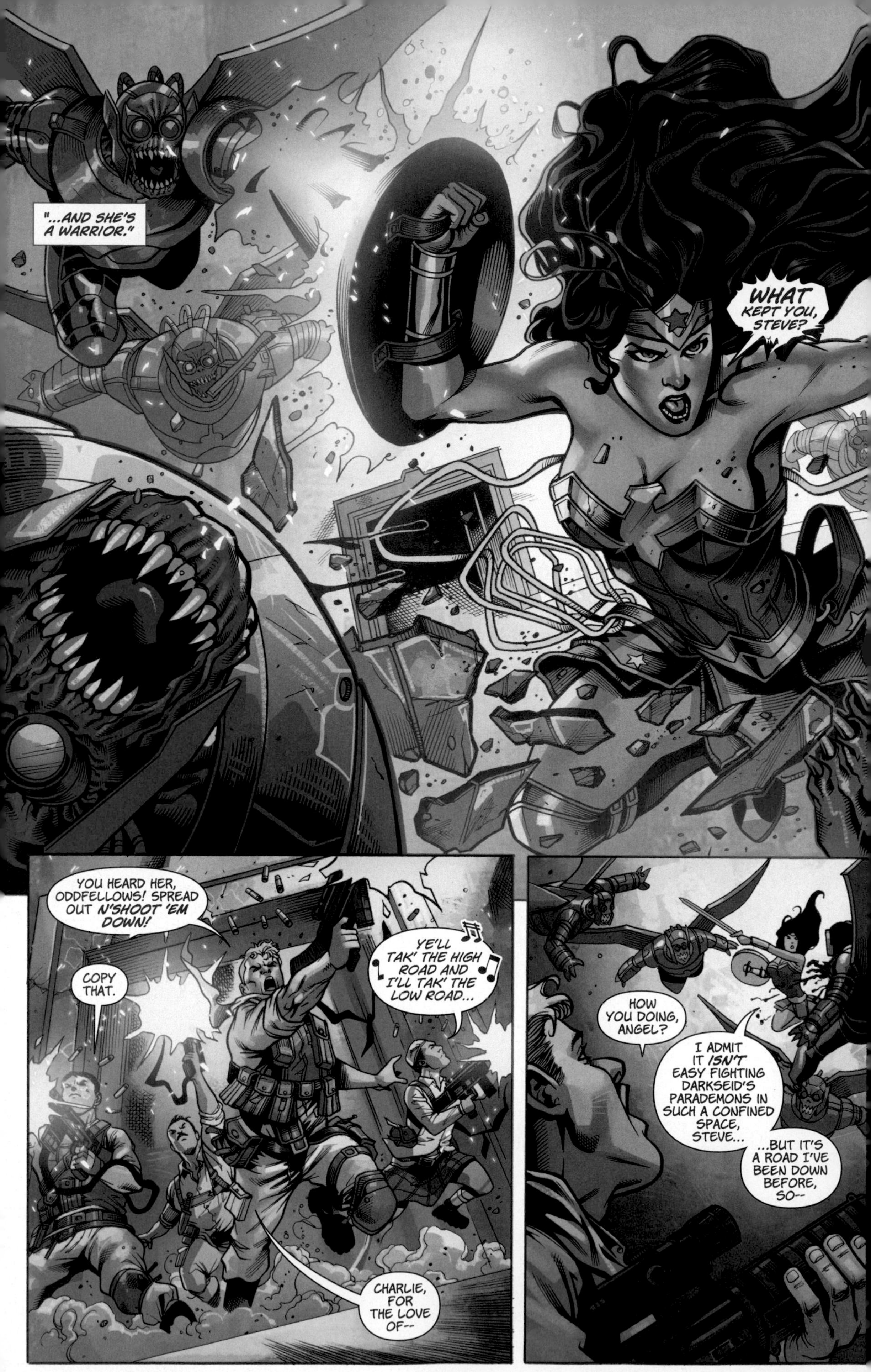
"...AND SHE'S A WARRIOR."
WHAT KEPT YOU, STEVE?
YOU HEARD HER, ODDFELLOWS! SPREAD OUT N'SHOOT 'EM DOWN!
COPY THAT.
YE'LL TAK' THE HIGH ROAD AND I'LL TAK' THE LOW ROAD...
CHARLIE, FOR THE LOVE OF--
HOW YOU DOING, ANGEL?
I ADMIT IT ISN'T EASY FIGHTING DARKSEID'S PARADEMONS IN SUCH A CONFINED SPACE, STEVE...
...BUT IT'S A ROAD I'VE BEEN DOWN BEFORE, SO--

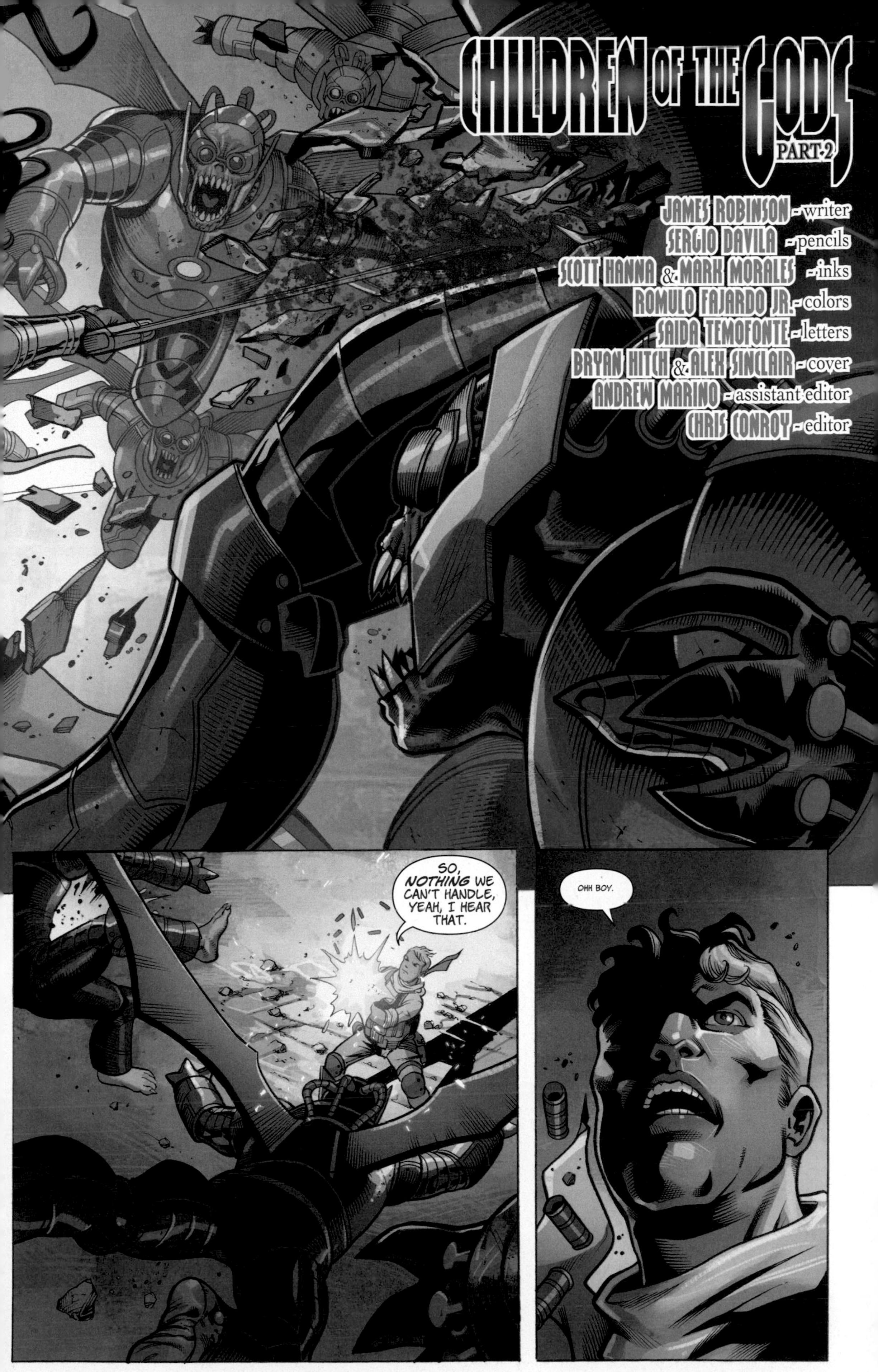
CHILDREN OF THE GODS
PART 2
JAMES ROBINSON - writer
SERGIO DAVILA - pencils
SCOTT HANNA & MARK MORALES - inks
ROMULO FAJARDO JR. - colors
SAIDA TEMOFONTE - letters
BRYAN HITCH & ALEX SINCLAIR - cover
ANDREW MARINO - assistant editor
CHRIS CONROY - editor
SO, NOTHING WE CAN'T HANDLE, YEAH, I HEAR THAT.
OHH BOY.

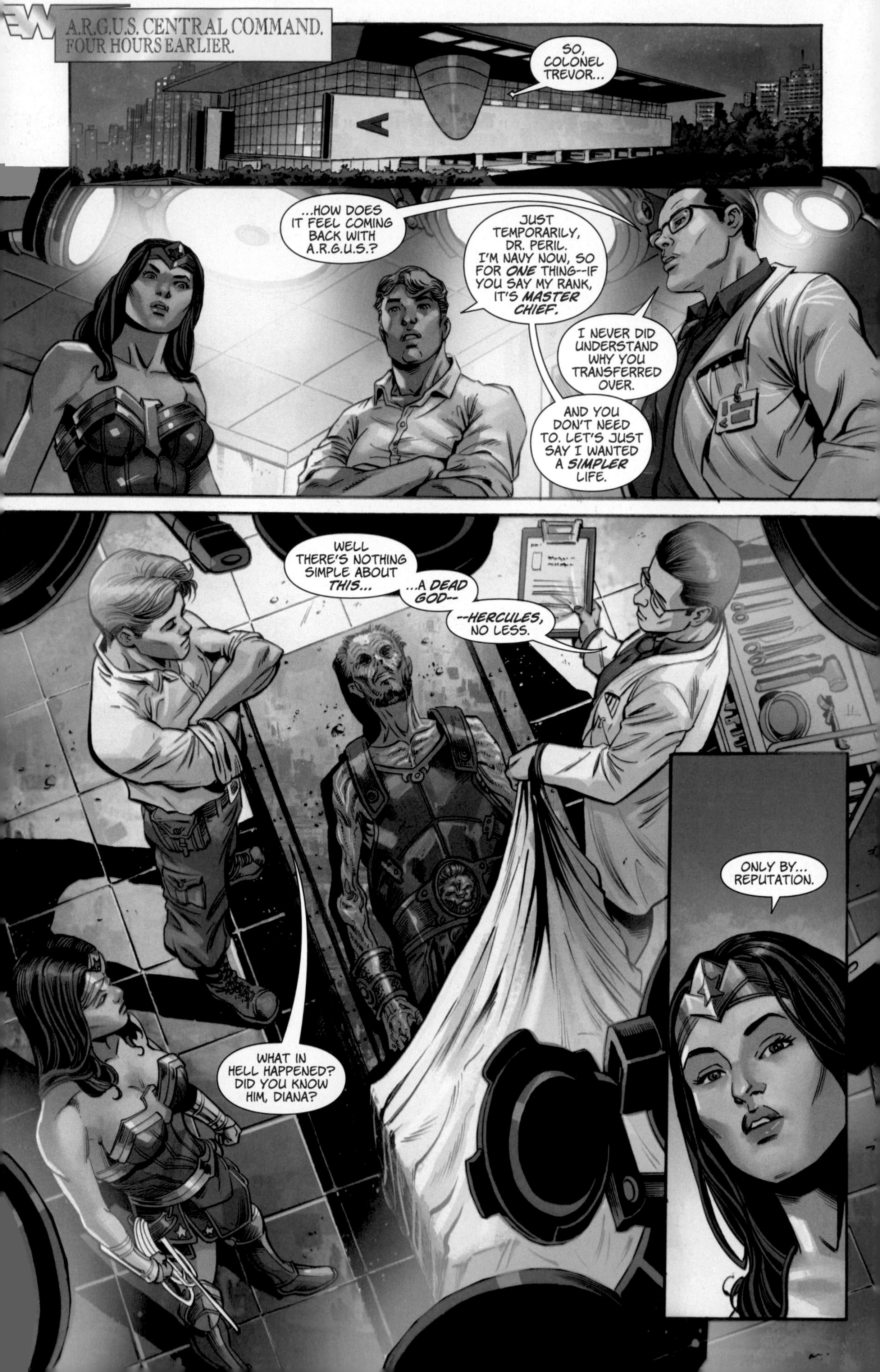
A.R.G.U.S. CENTRAL COMMAND. FOUR HOURS EARLIER.
SO, COLONEL TREVOR...
...HOW DOES IT FEEL COMING BACK WITH A.R.G.U.S.?
JUST TEMPORARILY, DR. PERIL. I'M NAVY NOW, SO FOR ONE THING--IF YOU SAY MY RANK, IT'S MASTER CHIEF.
I NEVER DID UNDERSTAND WHY YOU TRANSFERRED OVER.
AND YOU DON'T NEED TO. LET'S JUST SAY I WANTED A SIMPLER LIFE.
WELL THERE'S NOTHING SIMPLE ABOUT THIS...
...A DEAD GOD--
--HERCULES, NO LESS.
WHAT IN HELL HAPPENED? DID YOU KNOW HIM, DIANA?
ONLY BY... REPUTATION.

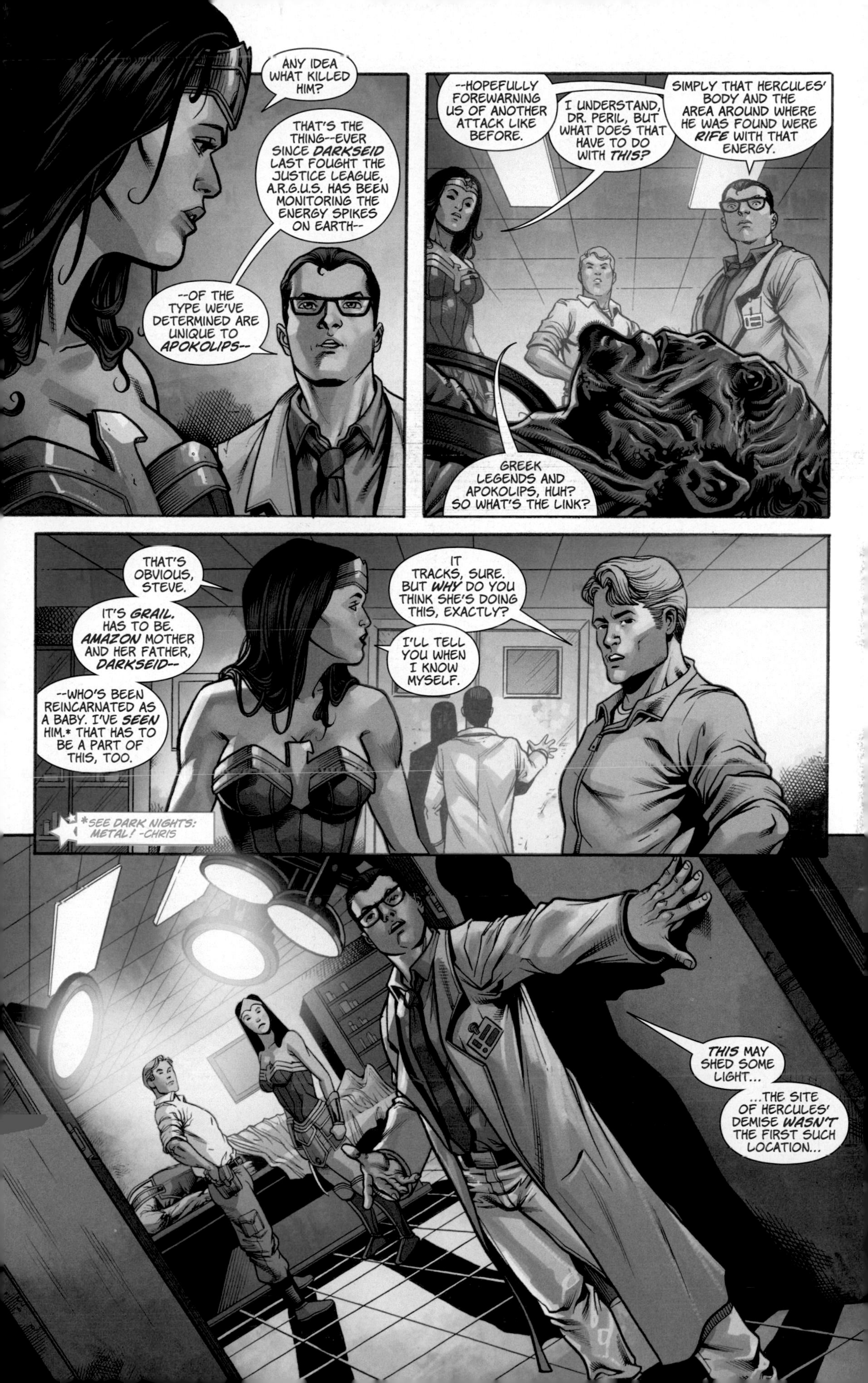
ANY IDEA WHAT KILLED HIM?
THAT'S THE THING--EVER SINCE DARKSEID LAST FOUGHT THE JUSTICE LEAGUE, A.R.G.U.S. HAS BEEN MONITORING THE ENERGY SPIKES ON EARTH--
--OF THE TYPE WE'VE DETERMINED ARE UNIQUE TO APOKOLIPS--
--HOPEFULLY FOREWARNING US OF ANOTHER ATTACK LIKE BEFORE.
I UNDERSTAND, DR. PERIL, BUT WHAT DOES THAT HAVE TO DO WITH THIS?
SIMPLY THAT HERCULES' BODY AND THE AREA AROUND WHERE HE WAS FOUND WERE RIFE WITH THAT ENERGY.
GREEK LEGENDS AND APOKOLIPS, HUH? SO WHAT'S THE LINK?
THAT'S OBVIOUS, STEVE.
IT'S GRAIL. HAS TO BE. AMAZON MOTHER AND HER FATHER, DARKSEID--
--WHO'S BEEN REINCARNATED AS A BABY. I'VE SEEN HIM.* THAT HAS TO BE A PART OF THIS, TOO.
IT TRACKS, SURE. BUT WHY DO YOU THINK SHE'S DOING THIS, EXACTLY?
I'LL TELL YOU WHEN I KNOW MYSELF.
*SEE DARK NIGHTS: METAL! -CHRIS
THIS MAY SHED SOME LIGHT...
...THE SITE OF HERCULES' DEMISE WASN'T THE FIRST SUCH LOCATION...

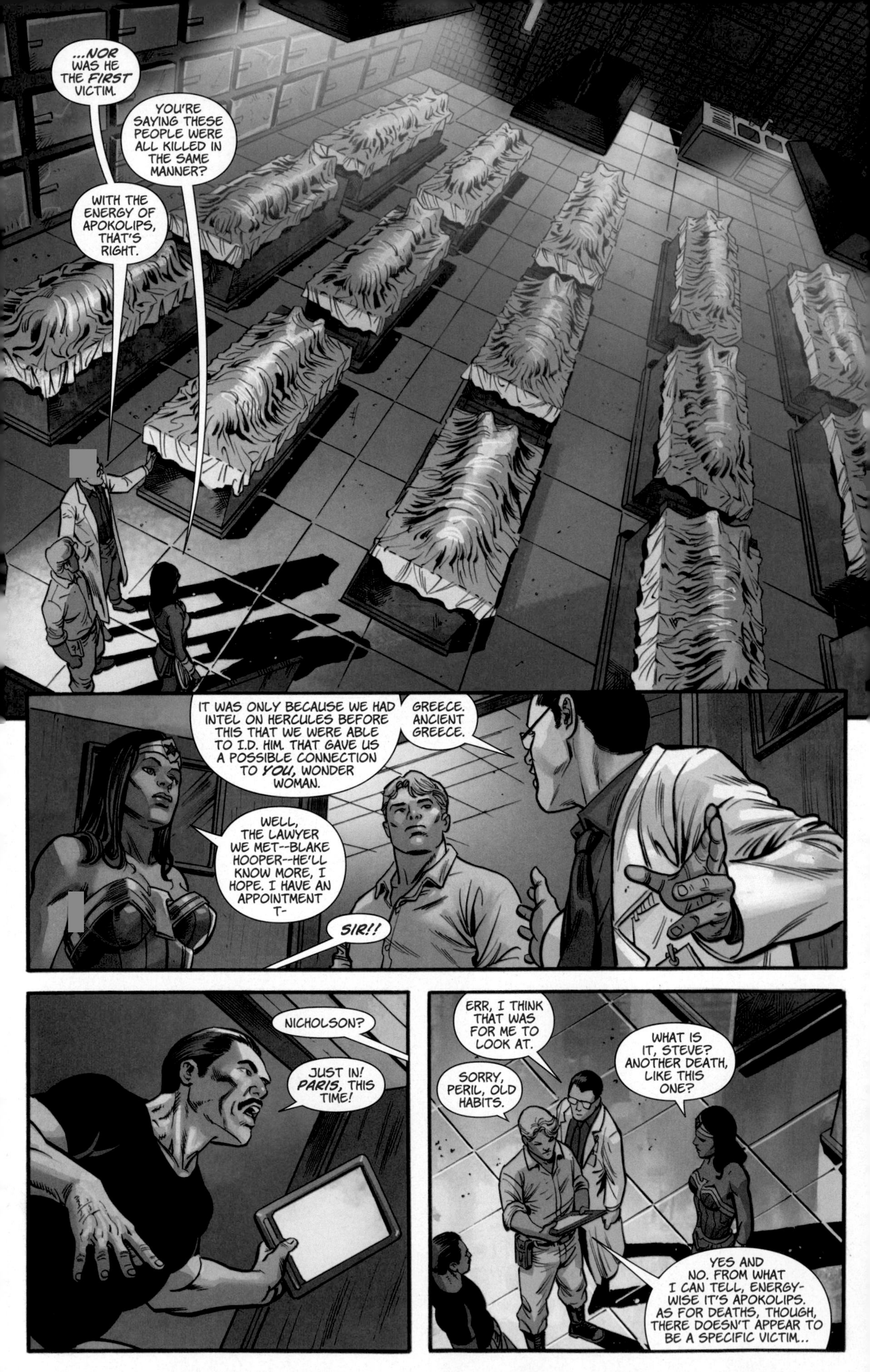
...NOR WAS HE THE FIRST VICTIM.
YOU'RE SAYING THESE PEOPLE WERE ALL KILLED IN THE SAME MANNER?
WITH THE ENERGY OF APOKOLIPS, THAT'S RIGHT.
IT WAS ONLY BECAUSE WE HAD INTEL ON HERCULES BEFORE THIS THAT WE WERE ABLE TO I.D. HIM. THAT GAVE US A POSSIBLE CONNECTION TO YOU, WONDER WOMAN.
GREECE. ANCIENT GREECE.
WELL, THE LAWYER WE MET--BLAKE HOOPER--HE'LL KNOW MORE, I HOPE. I HAVE AN APPOINTMENT T-
SIR!!
NICHOLSON?
JUST IN! PARIS, THIS TIME!
ERR, I THINK THAT WAS FOR ME TO LOOK AT.
SORRY, PERIL, OLD HABITS.
WHAT IS IT, STEVE? ANOTHER DEATH, LIKE THIS ONE?
YES AND NO. FROM WHAT I CAN TELL, ENERGY-WISE IT'S APOKOLIPS. AS FOR DEATHS, THOUGH, THERE DOESN'T APPEAR TO BE A SPECIFIC VICTIM..

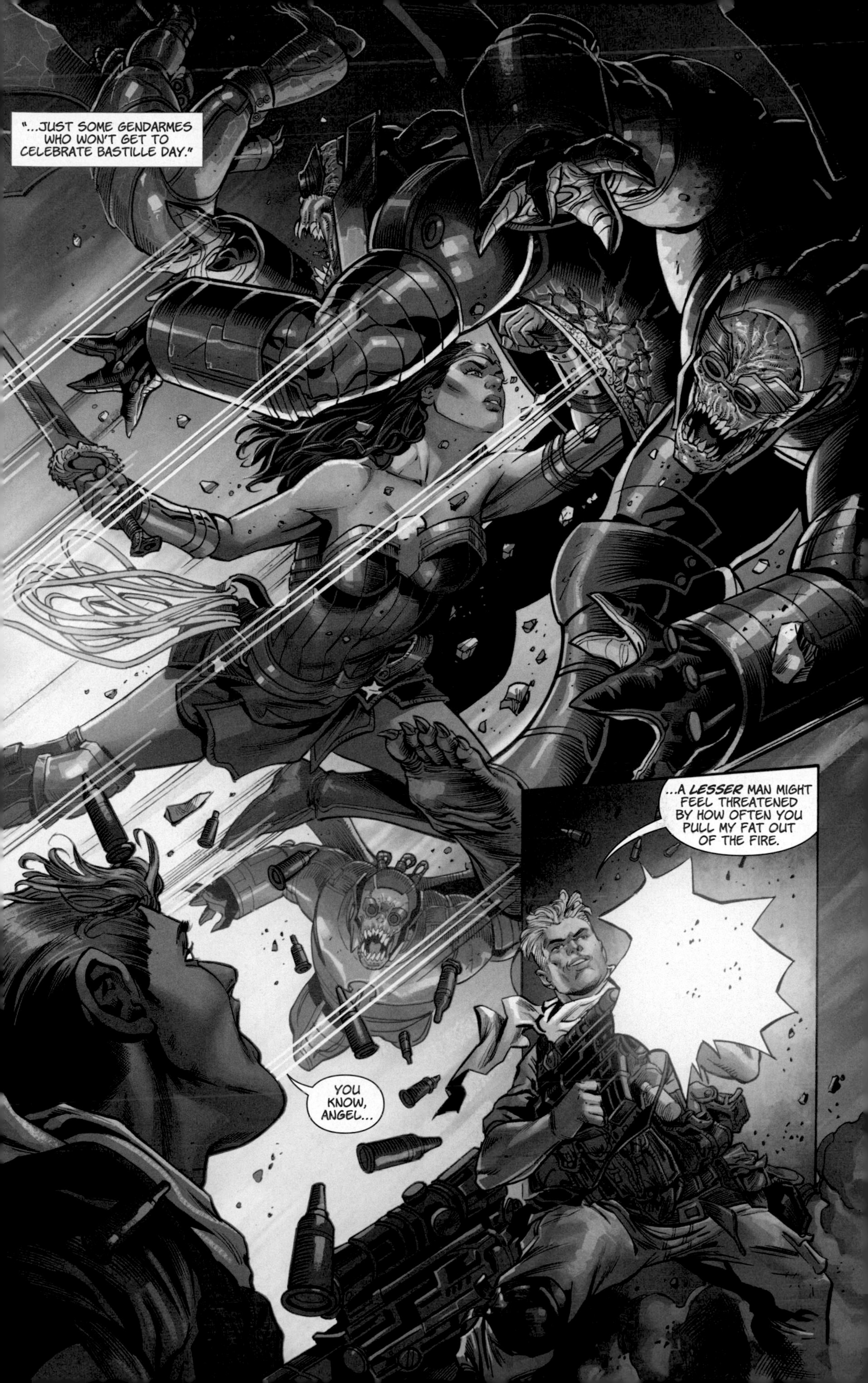
"...JUST SOME GENDARMES WHO WON'T GET TO CELEBRATE BASTILLE DAY."
YOU KNOW, ANGEL...
...A *LESSER* MAN MIGHT FEEL THREATENED BY HOW OFTEN YOU PULL MY FAT OUT OF THE FIRE.

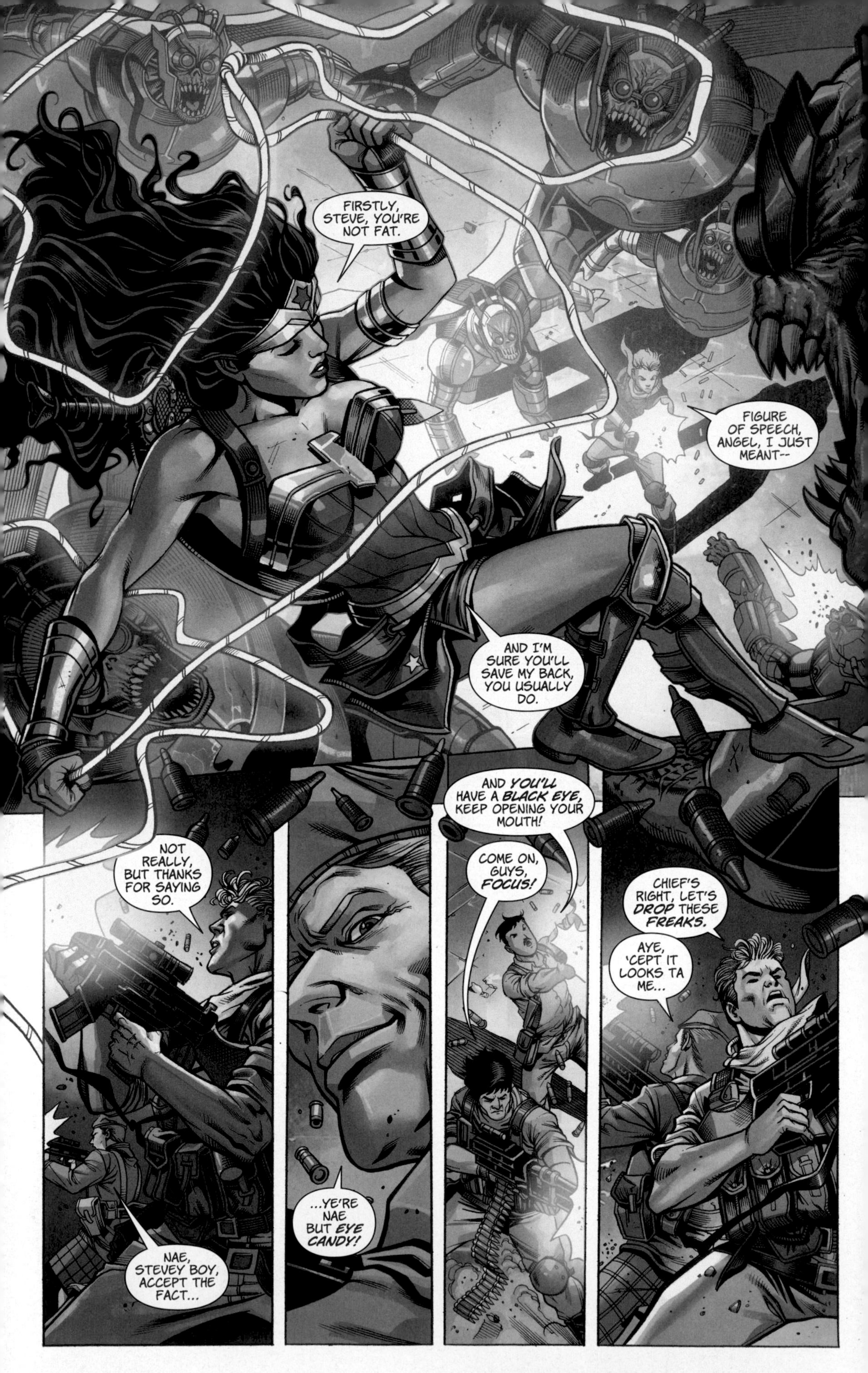
FIRSTLY, STEVE, YOU'RE NOT FAT.
FIGURE OF SPEECH, ANGEL, I JUST MEANT--
AND I'M SURE YOU'LL SAVE MY BACK, YOU USUALLY DO.
NOT REALLY, BUT THANKS FOR SAYING SO.
NAE, STEVEY BOY, ACCEPT THE FACT...
...YE'RE NAE BUT EYE CANDY!
AND YOU'LL HAVE A BLACK EYE, KEEP OPENING YOUR MOUTH!
COME ON, GUYS, FOCUS!
CHIEF'S RIGHT, LET'S DROP THESE FREAKS.
AYE, 'CEPT IT LOOKS TA ME...

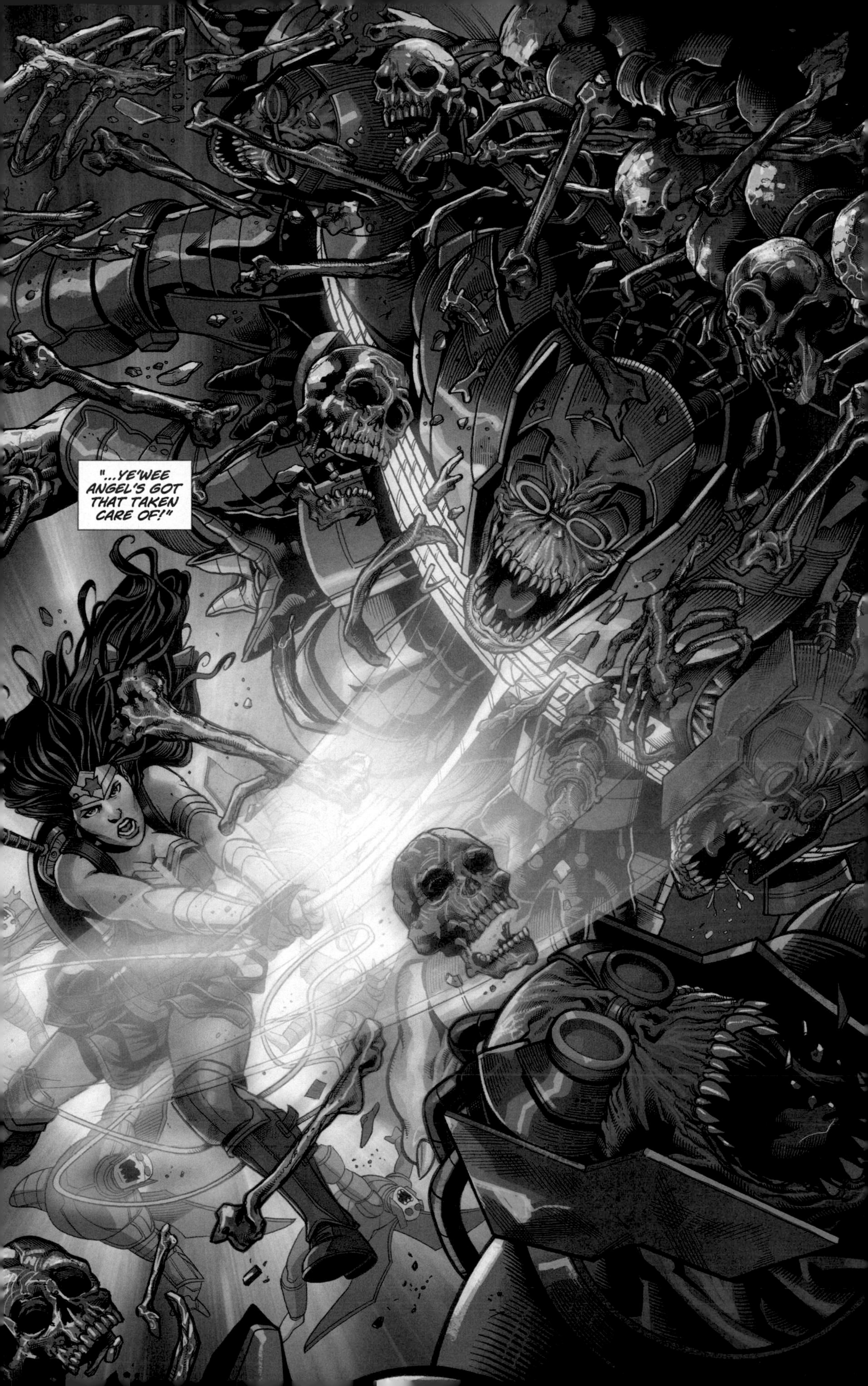
"...YE'WEE ANGEL'S GOT THAT TAKEN CARE OF!"

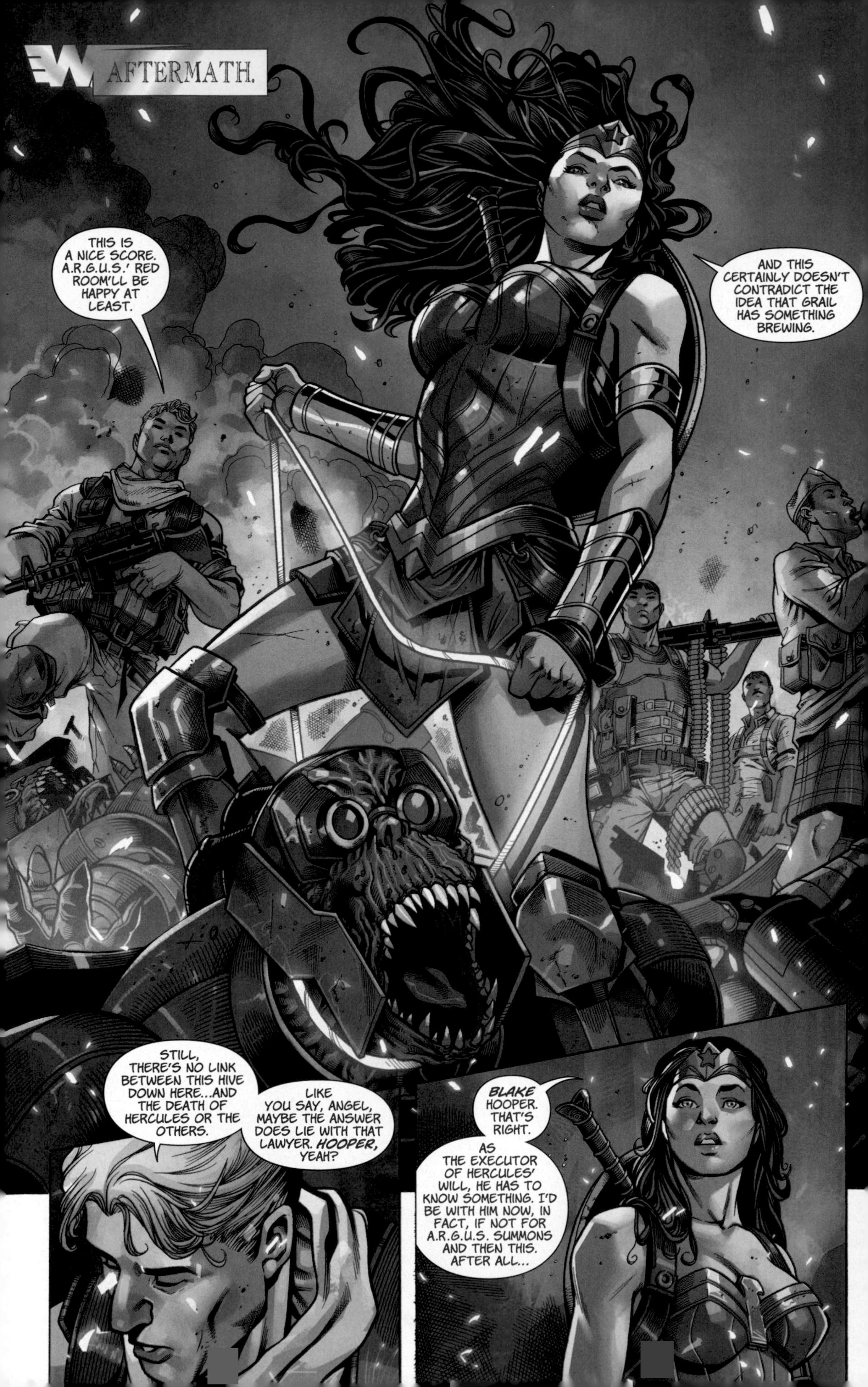
AFTERMATH.
THIS IS A NICE SCORE. A.R.G.U.S.' RED ROOM'LL BE HAPPY AT LEAST.
AND THIS CERTAINLY DOESN'T CONTRADICT THE IDEA THAT GRAIL HAS SOMETHING BREWING.
STILL, THERE'S NO LINK BETWEEN THIS HIVE DOWN HERE...AND THE DEATH OF HERCULES OR THE OTHERS.
LIKE YOU SAY, ANGEL, MAYBE THE ANSWER DOES LIE WITH THAT LAWYER. *HOOPER,* YEAH?
BLAKE HOOPER. THAT'S RIGHT.
AS THE EXECUTOR OF HERCULES' WILL, HE HAS TO KNOW SOMETHING. I'D BE WITH HIM NOW, IN FACT, IF NOT FOR A.R.G.U.S. SUMMONS AND THEN THIS. AFTER ALL...

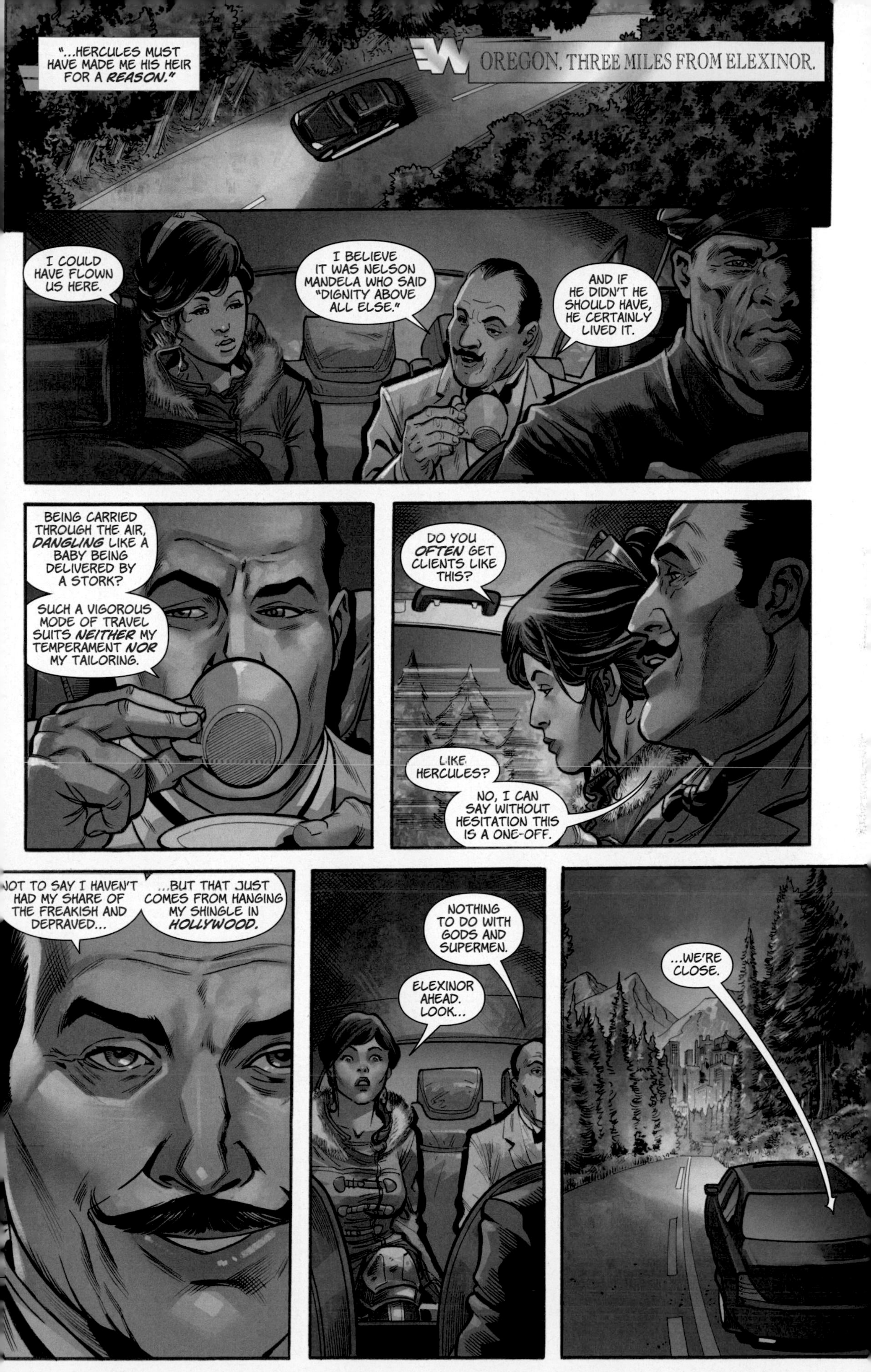
"...HERCULES MUST HAVE MADE ME HIS HEIR FOR A *REASON*."
OREGON. THREE MILES FROM ELEXINOR.
I COULD HAVE FLOWN US HERE.
I BELIEVE IT WAS NELSON MANDELA WHO SAID "DIGNITY ABOVE ALL ELSE."
AND IF HE DIDN'T HE SHOULD HAVE, HE CERTAINLY LIVED IT.
BEING CARRIED THROUGH THE AIR, *DANGLING* LIKE A BABY BEING DELIVERED BY A STORK?
SUCH A VIGOROUS MODE OF TRAVEL SUITS *NEITHER* MY TEMPERAMENT *NOR* MY TAILORING.
DO YOU *OFTEN* GET CLIENTS LIKE THIS?
LIKE HERCULES?
NO, I CAN SAY WITHOUT HESITATION THIS IS A ONE-OFF.
NOT TO SAY I HAVEN'T HAD MY SHARE OF THE FREAKISH AND DEPRAVED...
...BUT THAT JUST COMES FROM HANGING MY SHINGLE IN *HOLLYWOOD*.
NOTHING TO DO WITH GODS AND SUPERMEN.
ELEXINOR AHEAD. LOOK...
...WE'RE CLOSE.

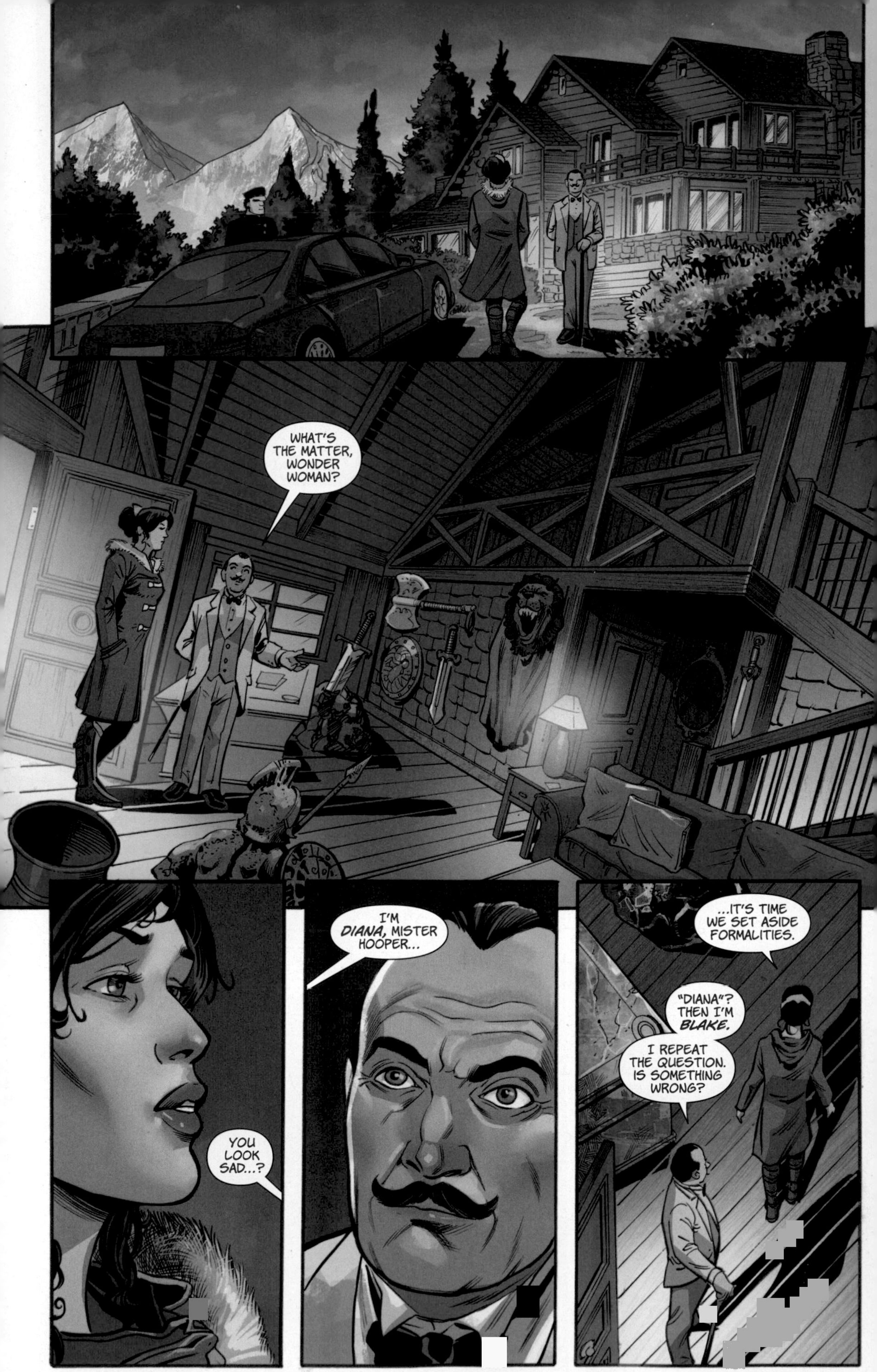
WHAT'S THE MATTER, WONDER WOMAN?
YOU LOOK SAD...?
I'M DIANA, MISTER HOOPER...
...IT'S TIME WE SET ASIDE FORMALITIES.
"DIANA"? THEN I'M BLAKE.
I REPEAT THE QUESTION. IS SOMETHING WRONG?

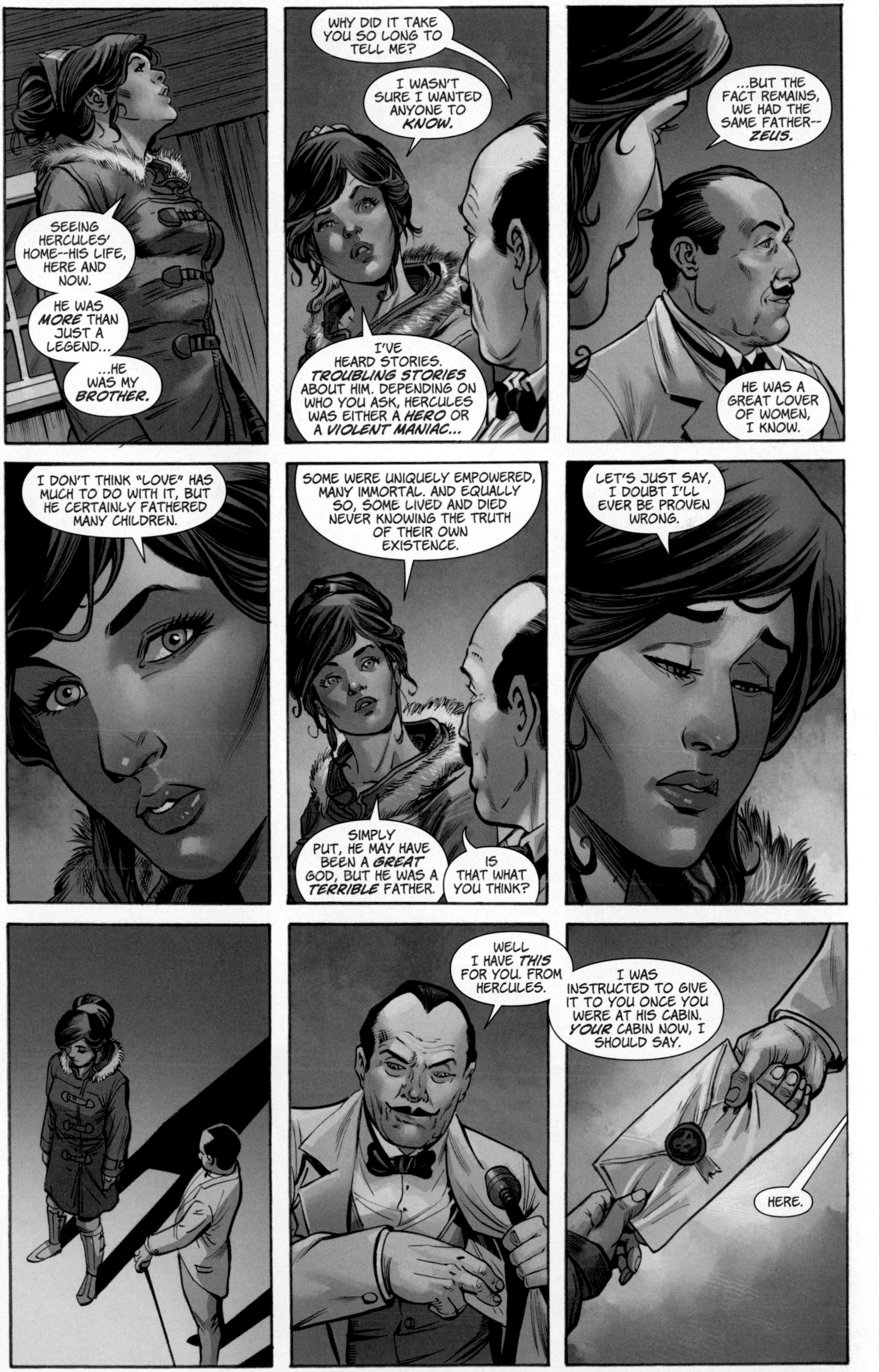

SEEING HERCULES' HOME--HIS LIFE, HERE AND NOW.
HE WAS MORE THAN JUST A LEGEND...
...HE WAS MY BROTHER.
WHY DID IT TAKE YOU SO LONG TO TELL ME?
I WASN'T SURE I WANTED ANYONE TO KNOW.
I'VE HEARD STORIES. TROUBLING STORIES ABOUT HIM. DEPENDING ON WHO YOU ASK, HERCULES WAS EITHER A HERO OR A VIOLENT MANIAC...
...BUT THE FACT REMAINS, WE HAD THE SAME FATHER--ZEUS.
HE WAS A GREAT LOVER OF WOMEN, I KNOW.
I DON'T THINK "LOVE" HAS MUCH TO DO WITH IT, BUT HE CERTAINLY FATHERED MANY CHILDREN.
SOME WERE UNIQUELY EMPOWERED, MANY IMMORTAL. AND EQUALLY SO, SOME LIVED AND DIED NEVER KNOWING THE TRUTH OF THEIR OWN EXISTENCE.
SIMPLY PUT, HE MAY HAVE BEEN A GREAT GOD, BUT HE WAS A TERRIBLE FATHER.
IS THAT WHAT YOU THINK?
LET'S JUST SAY, I DOUBT I'LL EVER BE PROVEN WRONG.
WELL I HAVE THIS FOR YOU. FROM HERCULES.
I WAS INSTRUCTED TO GIVE IT TO YOU ONCE YOU WERE AT HIS CABIN. YOUR CABIN NOW, I SHOULD SAY.
HERE.

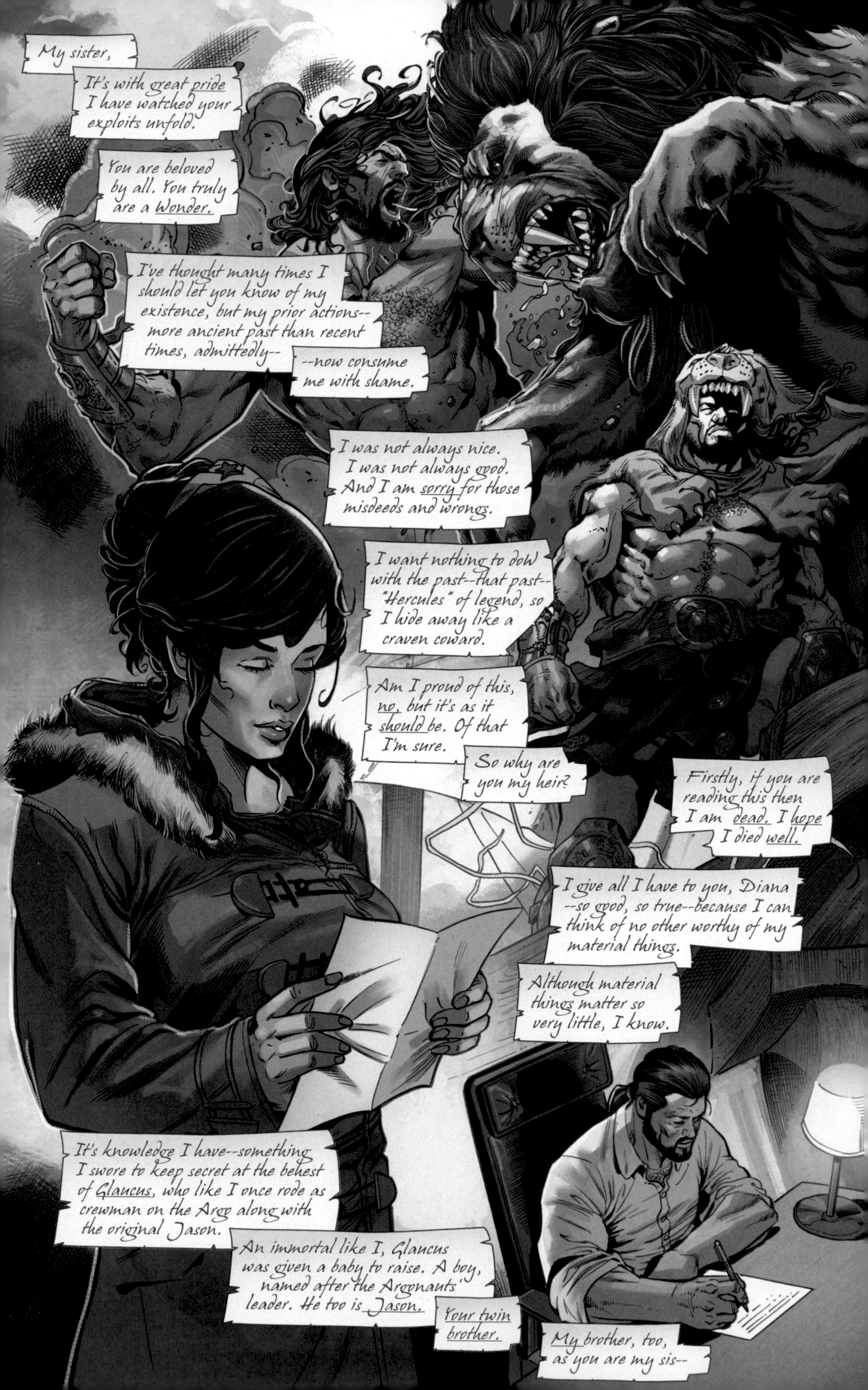

My sister,
It's with great pride I have watched your exploits unfold.
You are beloved by all. You truly are a Wonder.
I've thought many times I should let you know of my existence, but my prior actions--more ancient past than recent times, admittedly--
--now consume me with shame.
I was not always nice. I was not always good. And I am sorry for those misdeeds and wrongs.
I want nothing to dow with the past--that past--"Hercules" of legend, so I hide away like a craven coward.
Am I proud of this, no, but it's as it should be. Of that I'm sure.
So why are you my heir?
Firstly, if you are reading this then I am dead. I hope I died well.
I give all I have to you, Diana--so good, so true--because I can think of no other worthy of my material things.
Although material things matter so very little, I know.
It's knowledge I have--something I swore to keep secret at the behest of Glaucus, who like I once rode as crewman on the Argo along with the original Jason.
An immortal like I, Glaucus was given a baby to raise. A boy, named after the Argonauts' leader. He too is Jason.
Your twin brother.
My brother, too, as you are my sis--

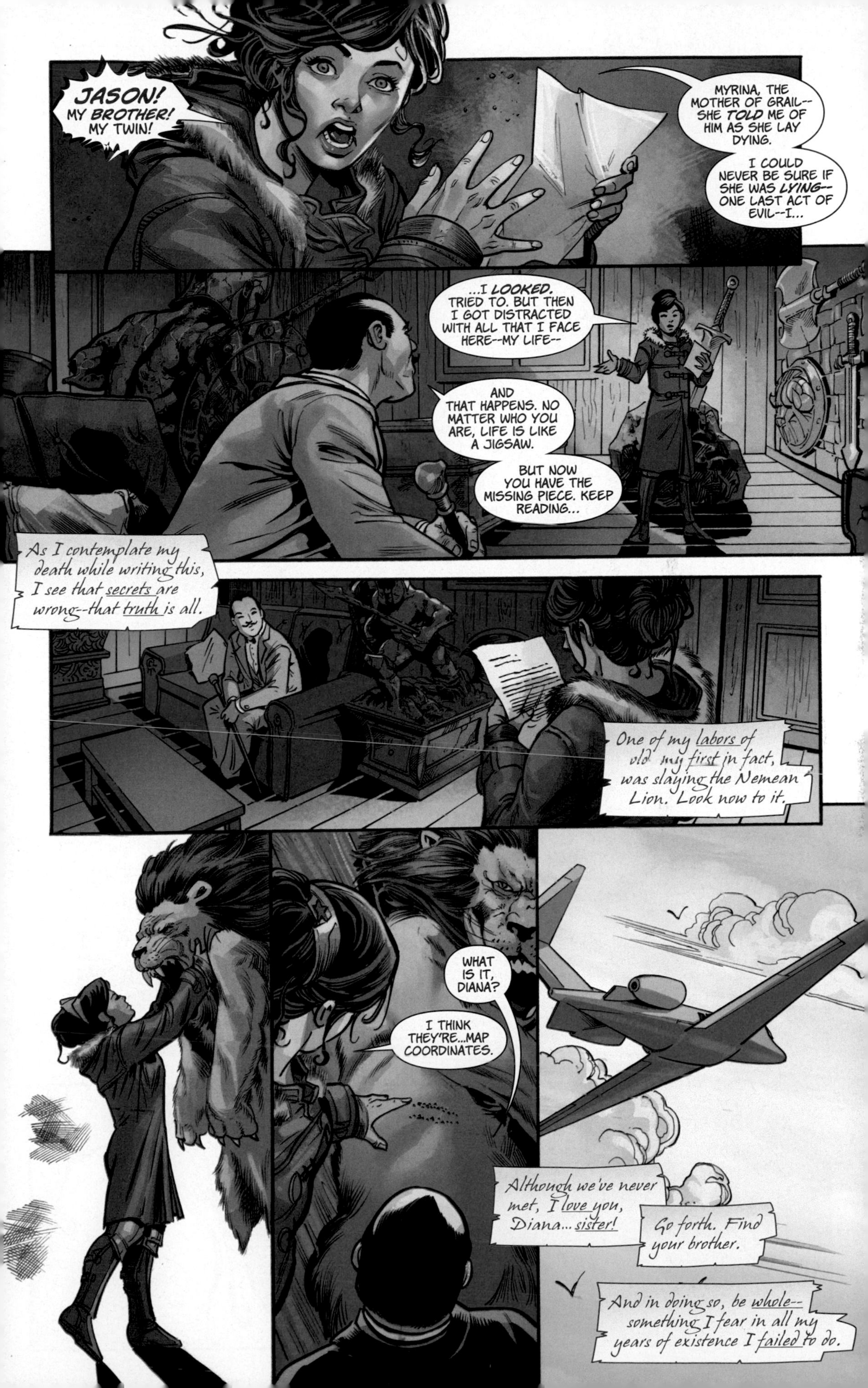

JASON! MY BROTHER! MY TWIN!
MYRINA, THE MOTHER OF GRAIL--SHE TOLD ME OF HIM AS SHE LAY DYING.
I COULD NEVER BE SURE IF SHE WAS LYING--ONE LAST ACT OF EVIL--I...
...I LOOKED. TRIED TO. BUT THEN I GOT DISTRACTED WITH ALL THAT I FACE HERE--MY LIFE--
AND THAT HAPPENS. NO MATTER WHO YOU ARE, LIFE IS LIKE A JIGSAW.
BUT NOW YOU HAVE THE MISSING PIECE. KEEP READING...
As I contemplate my death while writing this, I see that secrets are wrong--that truth is all.
One of my labors of old my first in fact, was slaying the Nemean Lion. Look now to it.
WHAT IS IT, DIANA?
I THINK THEY'RE...MAP COORDINATES.
Although we've never met, I love you, Diana... sister!
Go forth. Find your brother.
And in doing so, be whole--something I fear in all my years of existence I failed to do.

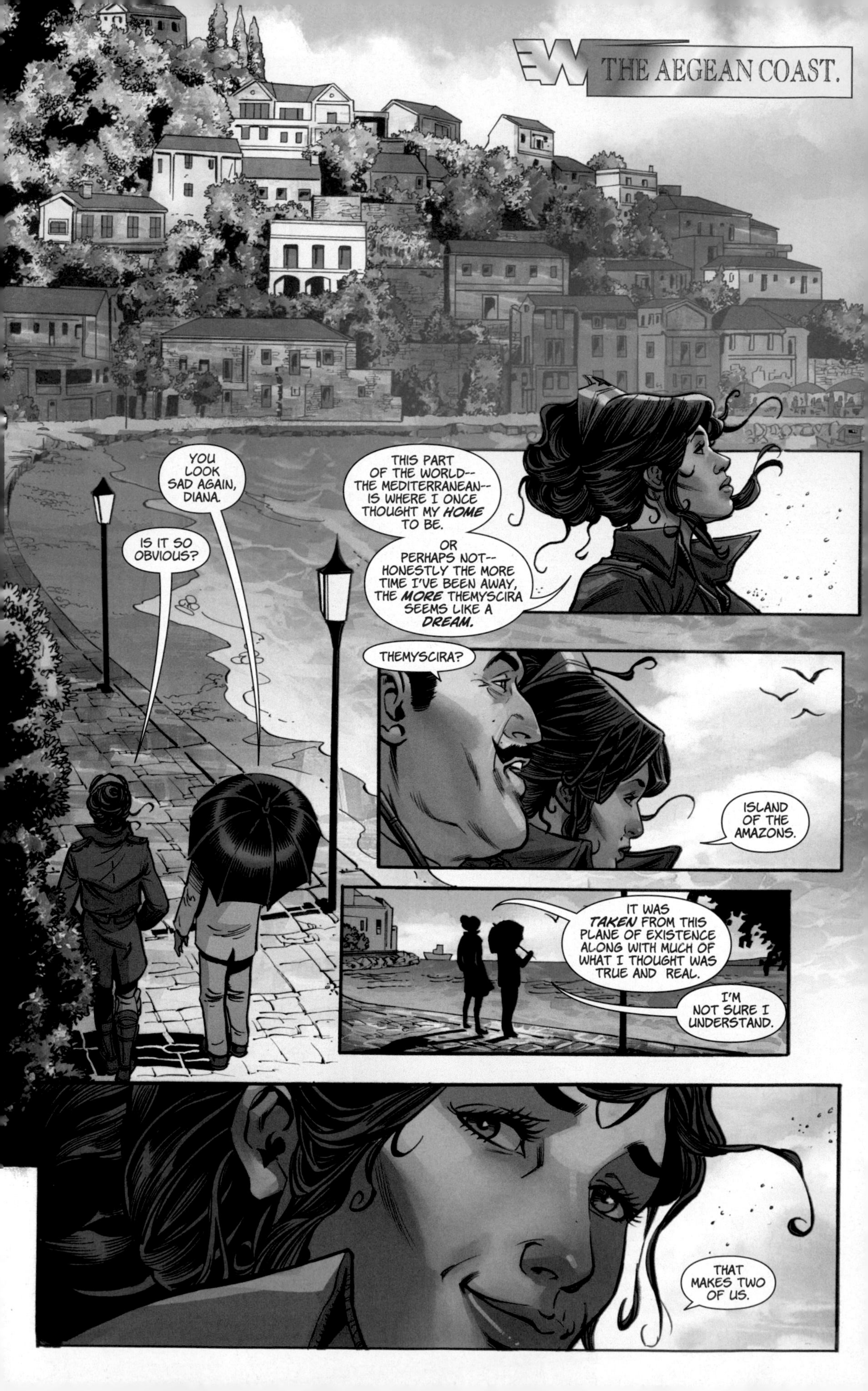
THE AEGEAN COAST.
YOU LOOK SAD AGAIN, DIANA.
IS IT SO OBVIOUS?
THIS PART OF THE WORLD--THE MEDITERRANEAN--IS WHERE I ONCE THOUGHT MY HOME TO BE.
OR PERHAPS NOT--HONESTLY THE MORE TIME I'VE BEEN AWAY, THE MORE THEMYSCIRA SEEMS LIKE A DREAM.
THEMYSCIRA?
ISLAND OF THE AMAZONS.
IT WAS TAKEN FROM THIS PLANE OF EXISTENCE ALONG WITH MUCH OF WHAT I THOUGHT WAS TRUE AND REAL.
I'M NOT SURE I UNDERSTAND.
THAT MAKES TWO OF US.

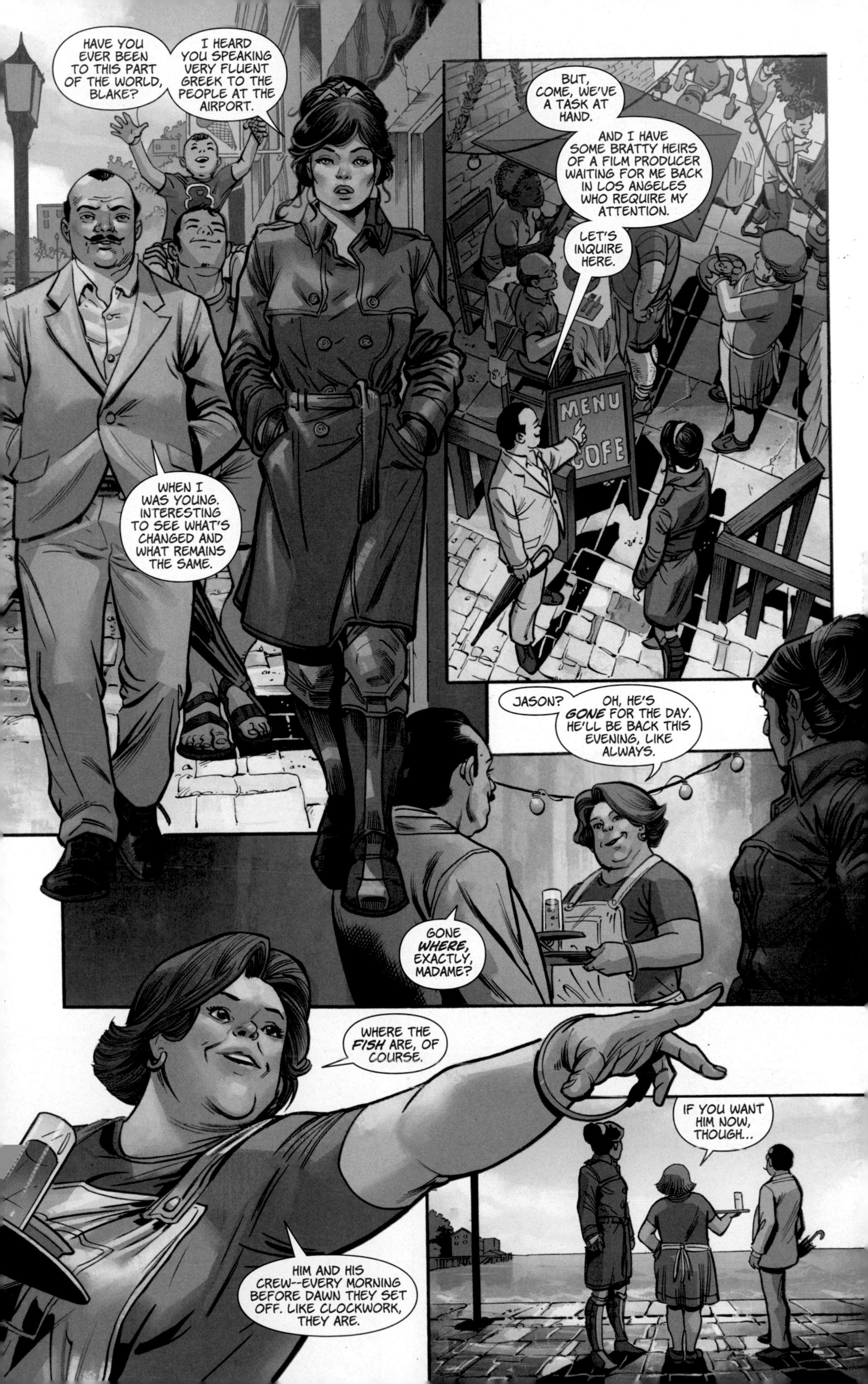
HAVE YOU EVER BEEN TO THIS PART OF THE WORLD, BLAKE?
I HEARD YOU SPEAKING VERY FLUENT GREEK TO THE PEOPLE AT THE AIRPORT.
WHEN I WAS YOUNG. INTERESTING TO SEE WHAT'S CHANGED AND WHAT REMAINS THE SAME.
BUT, COME, WE'VE A TASK AT HAND.
AND I HAVE SOME BRATTY HEIRS OF A FILM PRODUCER WAITING FOR ME BACK IN LOS ANGELES WHO REQUIRE MY ATTENTION.
LET'S INQUIRE HERE.
MENU
COFE
JASON?
OH, HE'S GONE FOR THE DAY. HE'LL BE BACK THIS EVENING, LIKE ALWAYS.
GONE WHERE, EXACTLY, MADAME?
WHERE THE FISH ARE, OF COURSE.
HIM AND HIS CREW--EVERY MORNING BEFORE DAWN THEY SET OFF. LIKE CLOCKWORK, THEY ARE.
IF YOU WANT HIM NOW, THOUGH...

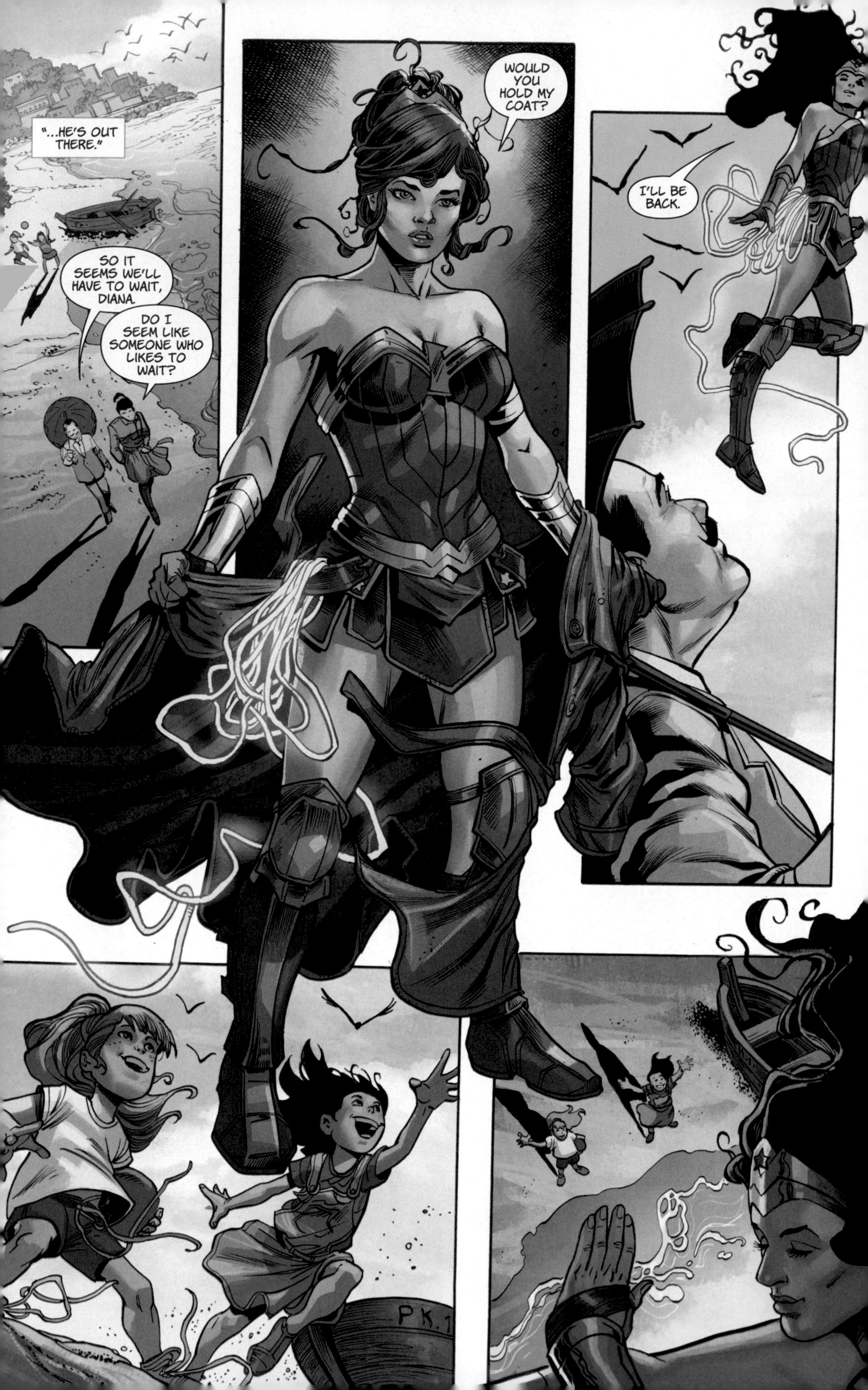
"...HE'S OUT THERE."
SO IT SEEMS WE'LL HAVE TO WAIT, DIANA.
DO I SEEM LIKE SOMEONE WHO LIKES TO WAIT?
WOULD YOU HOLD MY COAT?
I'LL BE BACK.
PK.1

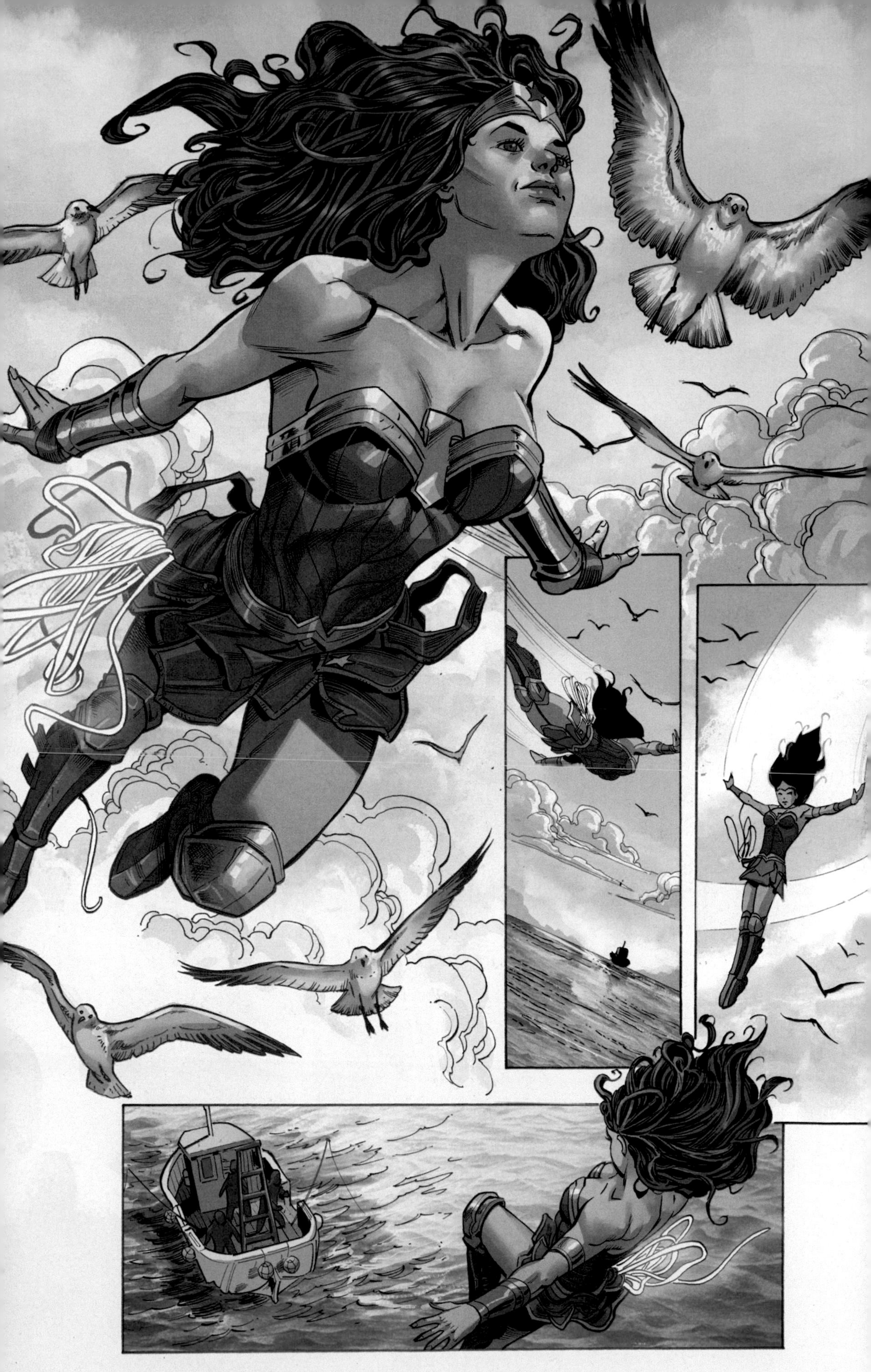

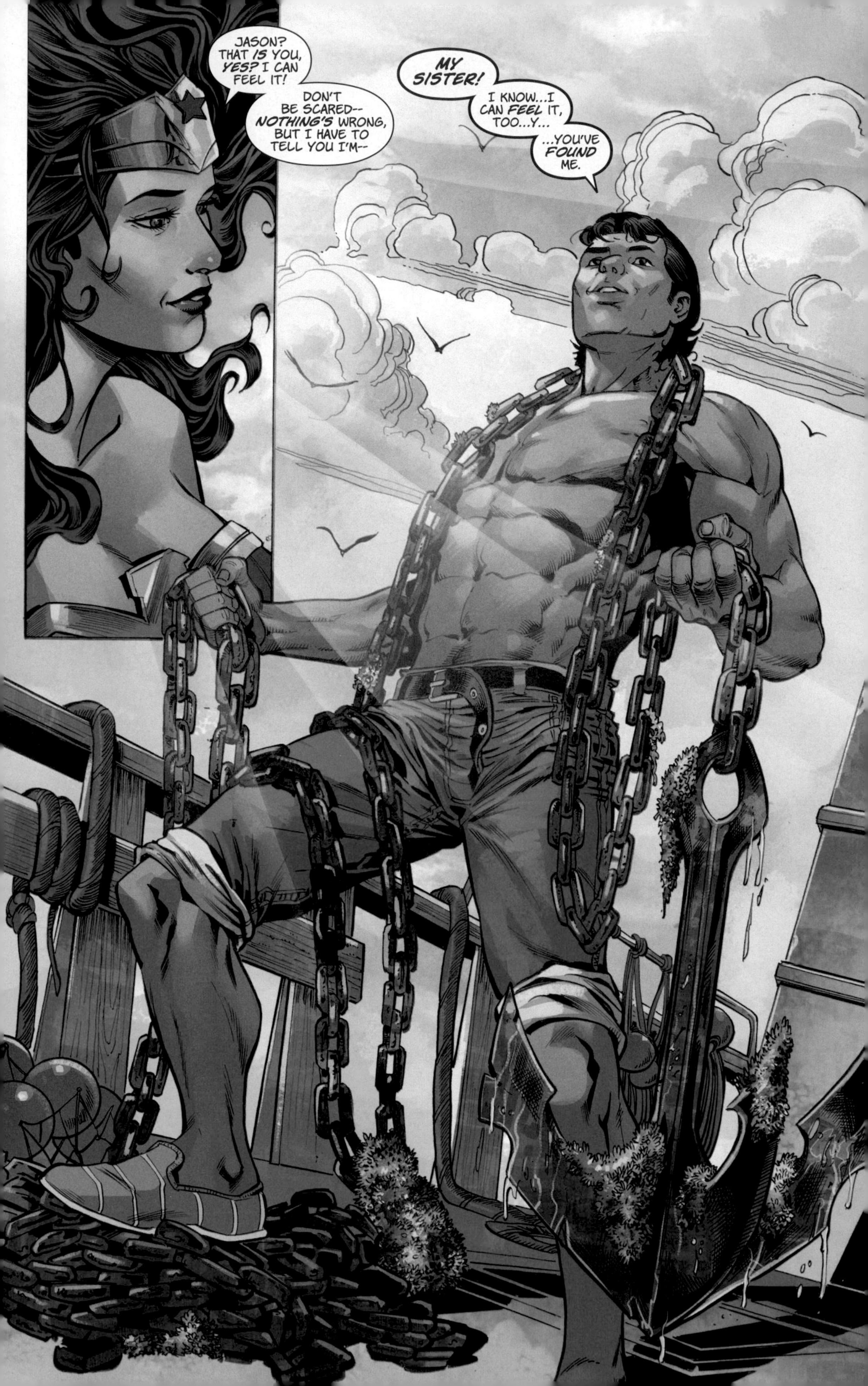
JASON? THAT IS YOU, YES? I CAN FEEL IT!
DON'T BE SCARED-- NOTHING'S WRONG, BUT I HAVE TO TELL YOU I'M--
MY SISTER!
I KNOW...I CAN FEEL IT, TOO...Y...
...YOU'VE FOUND ME.

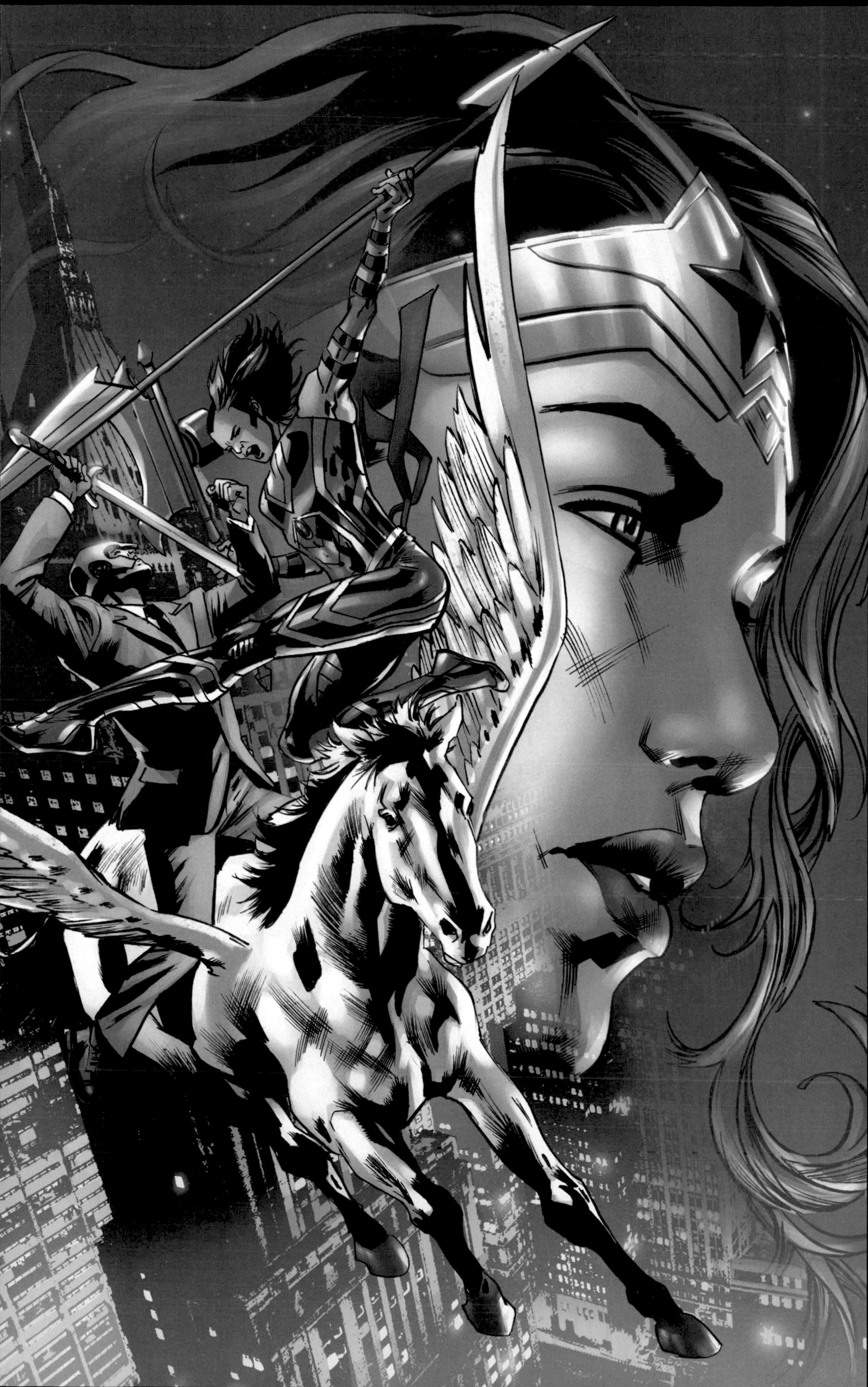

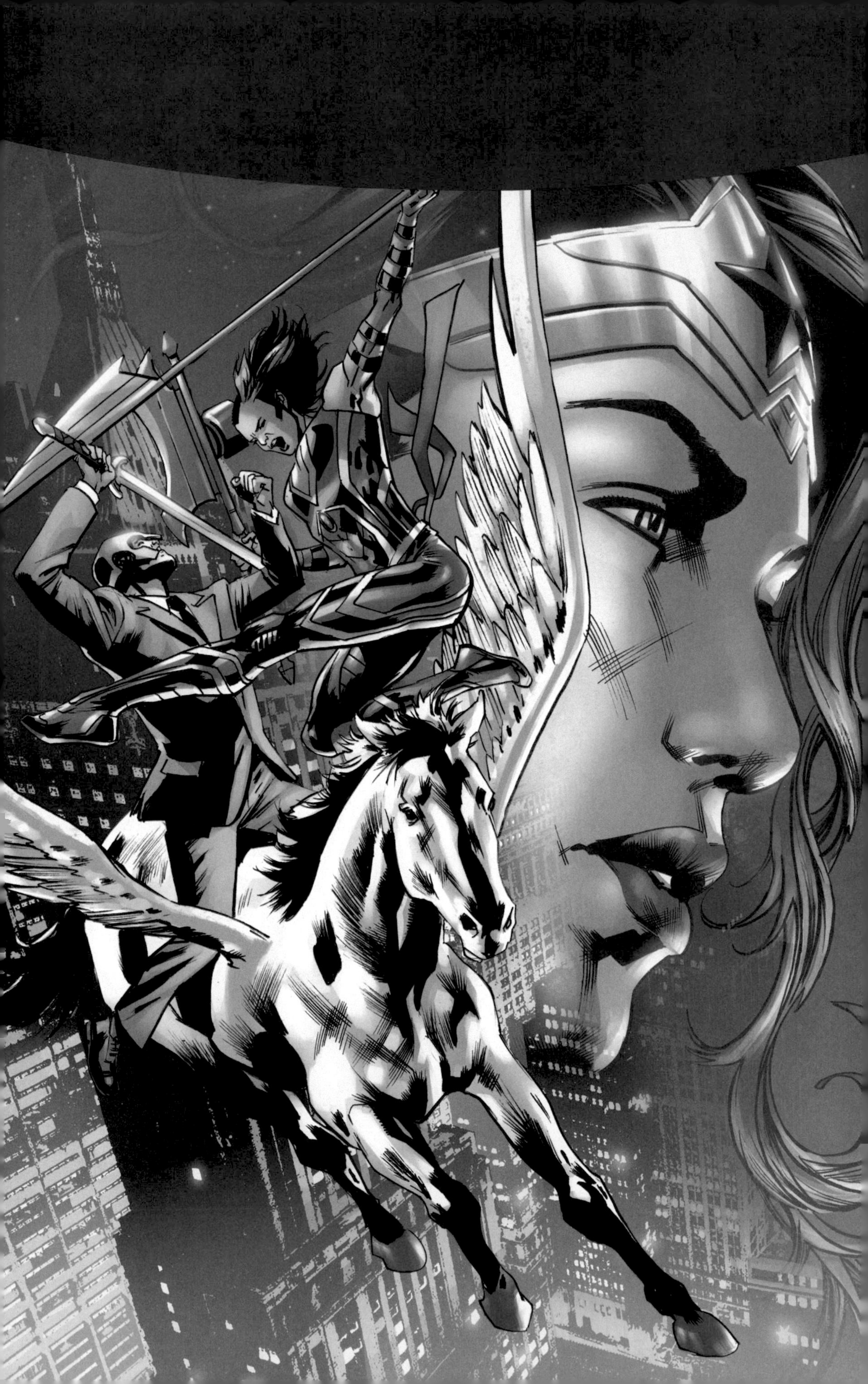

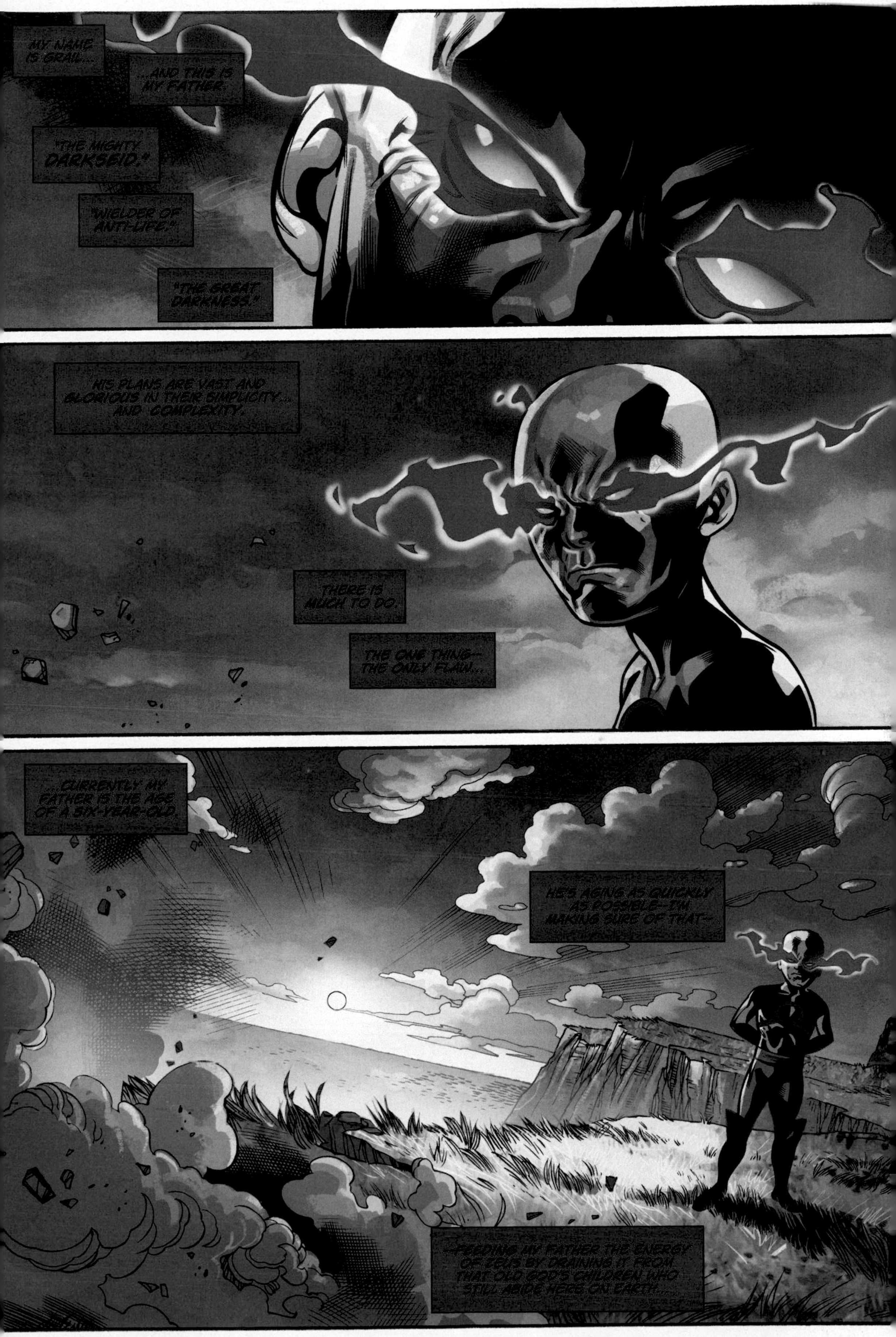
MY NAME IS GRAIL...
...AND THIS IS MY FATHER.
"THE MIGHTY DARKSEID."
"WIELDER OF ANTI-LIFE."
"THE GREAT DARKNESS."
HIS PLANS ARE VAST AND GLORIOUS IN THEIR SIMPLICITY... AND COMPLEXITY.
THERE IS MUCH TO DO.
THE ONE THING-- THE ONLY FLAW...
...CURRENTLY MY FATHER IS THE AGE OF A SIX-YEAR-OLD.
HE'S AGING AS QUICKLY AS POSSIBLE--I'M MAKING SURE OF THAT--
--FEEDING MY FATHER THE ENERGY OF ZEUS BY DRAINING IT FROM THAT OLD GOD'S CHILDREN WHO STILL ABIDE HERE ON EARTH...

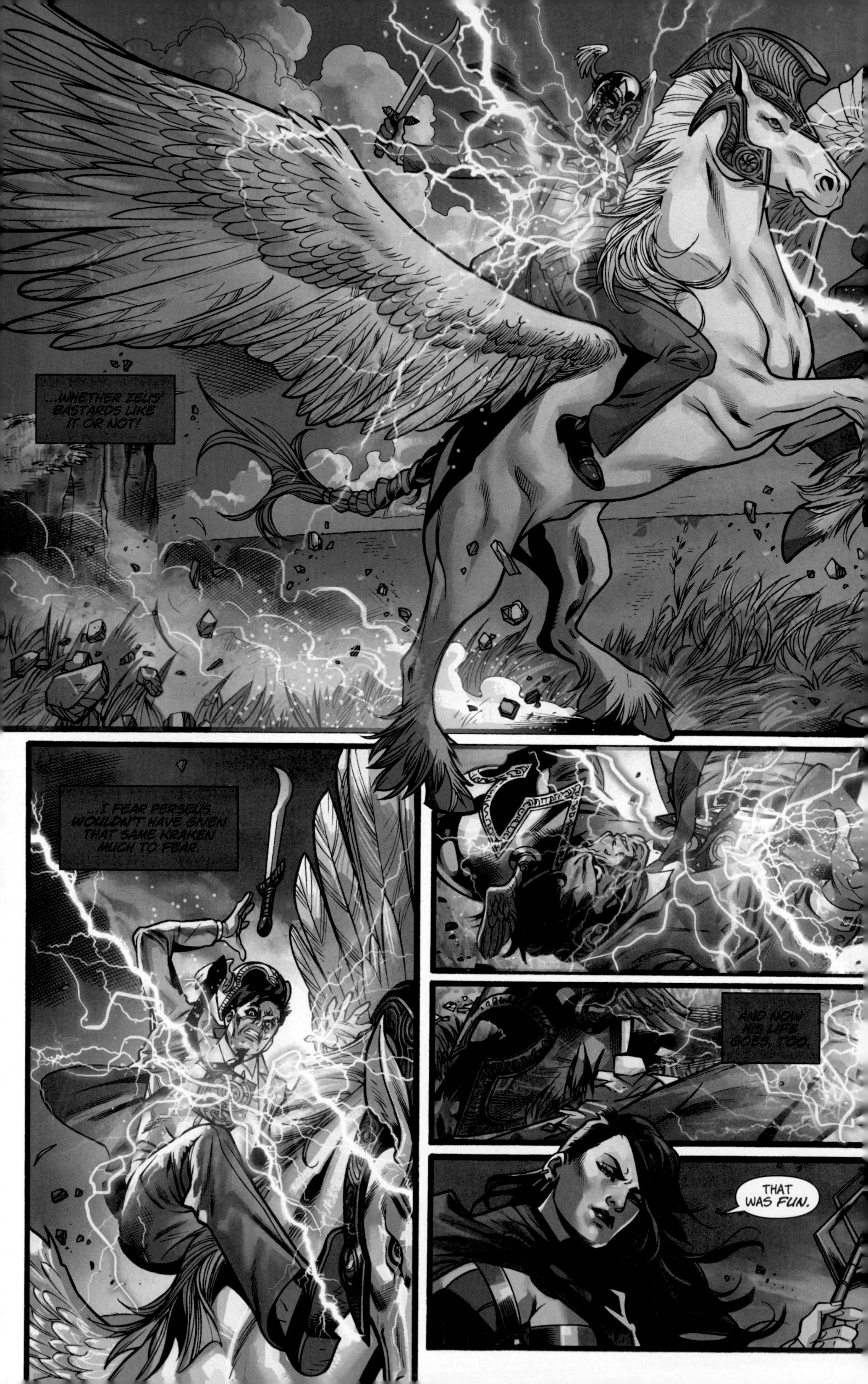
...WHETHER ZEUS' BASTARDS LIKE IT OR NOT!
...I FEAR PERSEUS WOULDN'T HAVE GIVEN THAT SAME KRAKEN MUCH TO FEAR.
AND NOW HIS LIFE GOES, TOO.
THAT WAS FUN.

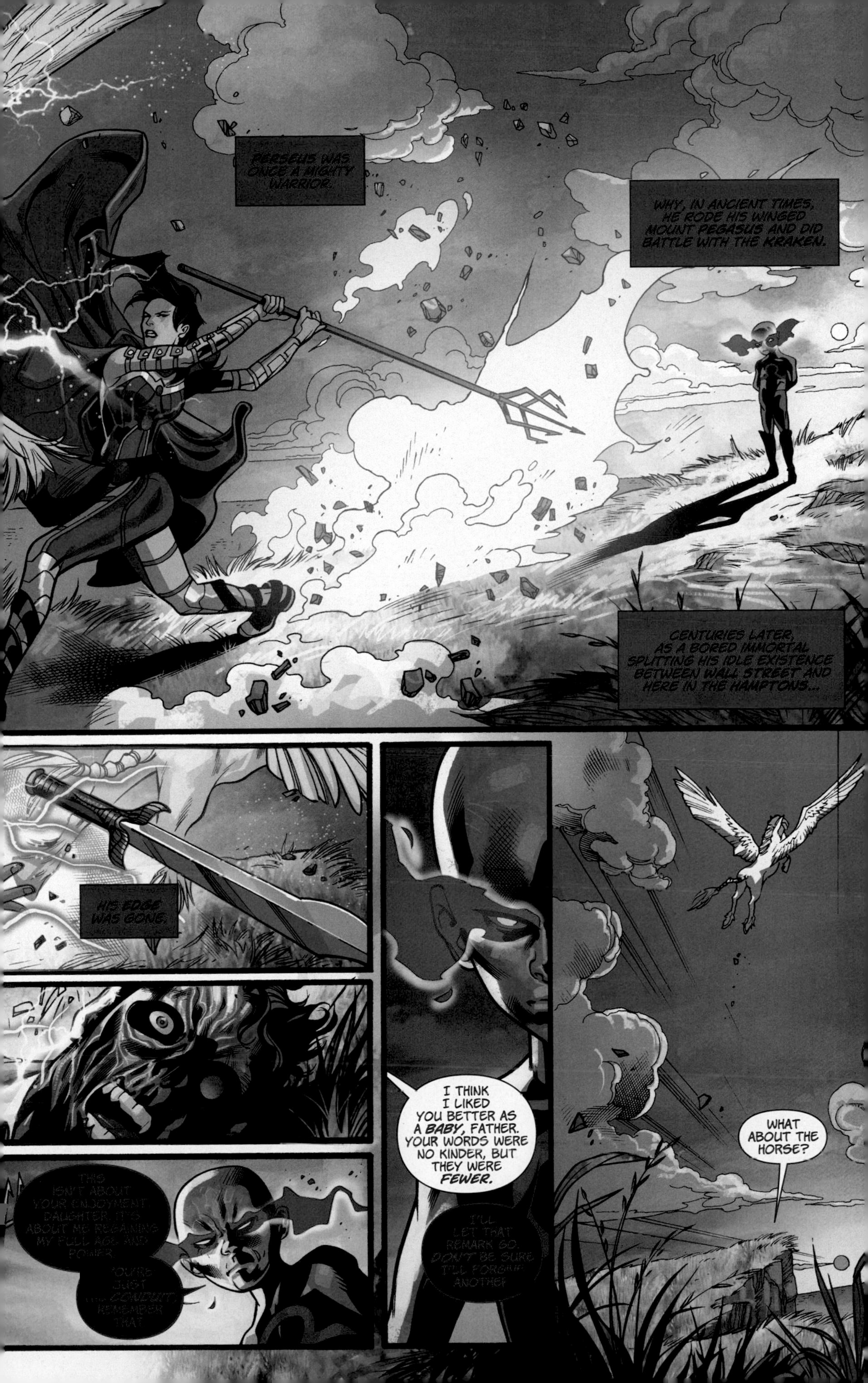
PERSEUS WAS ONCE A MIGHTY WARRIOR.
WHY, IN ANCIENT TIMES, HE RODE HIS WINGED MOUNT PEGASUS AND DID BATTLE WITH THE KRAKEN.
CENTURIES LATER, AS A BORED IMMORTAL SPLITTING HIS IDLE EXISTENCE BETWEEN WALL STREET AND HERE IN THE HAMPTONS...
HIS EDGE WAS GONE.
I THINK I LIKED YOU BETTER AS A *BABY*, FATHER. YOUR WORDS WERE NO KINDER, BUT THEY WERE *FEWER.*
THIS ISN'T ABOUT YOUR ENJOYMENT, DAUGHTER. IT'S ABOUT ME REGAINING MY FULL AGE AND POWER.
YOU'RE JUST THE *CONDUIT.* REMEMBER THAT.
I'LL LET THAT REMARK GO. *DON'T* BE SURE I'LL FORGIVE ANOTHER.
WHAT ABOUT THE HORSE?

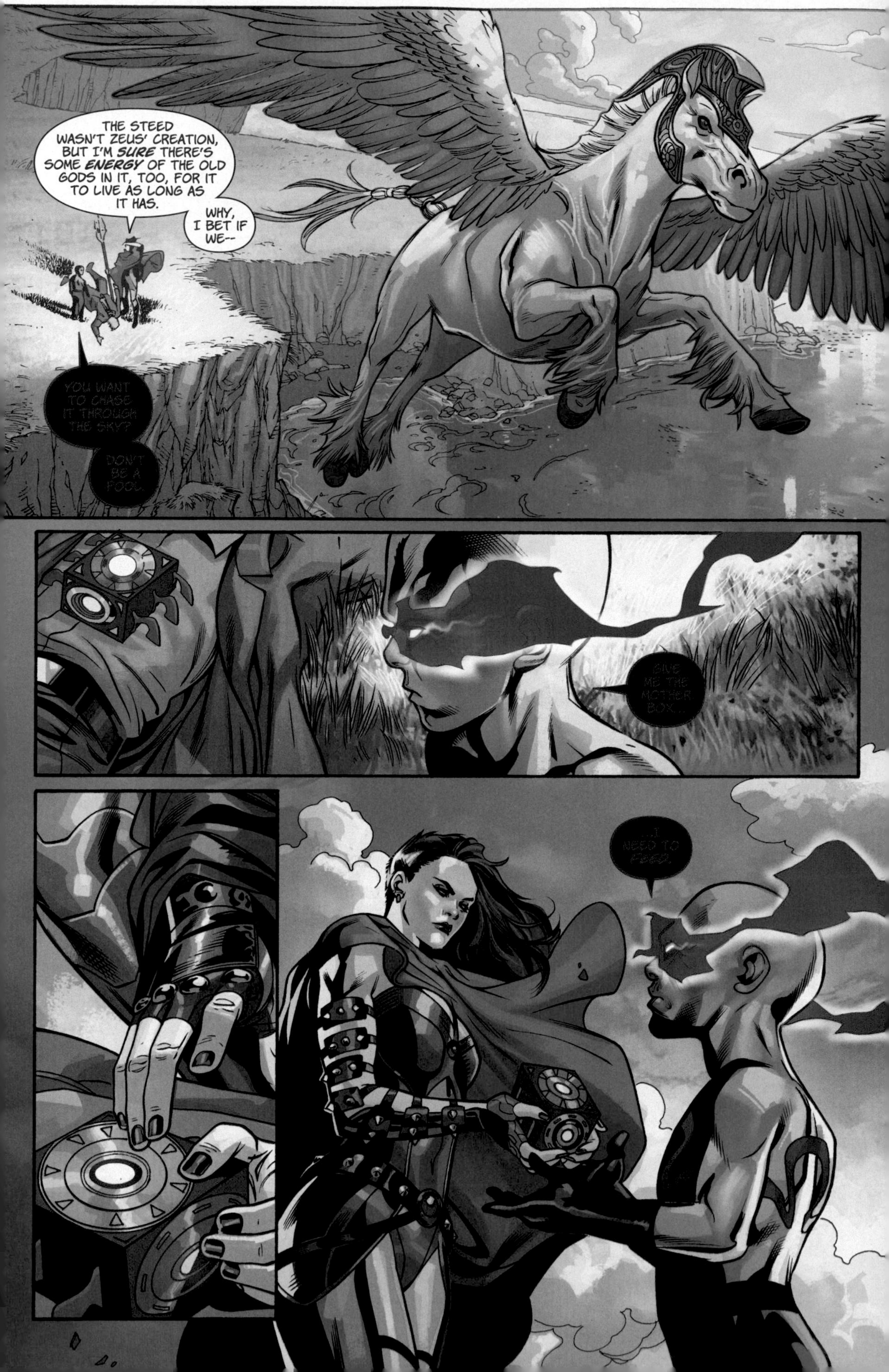
THE STEED WASN'T ZEUS' CREATION, BUT I'M *SURE* THERE'S SOME *ENERGY* OF THE OLD GODS IN IT, TOO, FOR IT TO LIVE AS LONG AS IT HAS.
WHY, I BET IF WE--
YOU WANT TO CHASE IT THROUGH THE SKY?
DON'T BE A FOOL.
GIVE ME THE MOTHER BOX...
...I NEED TO *FEED*.

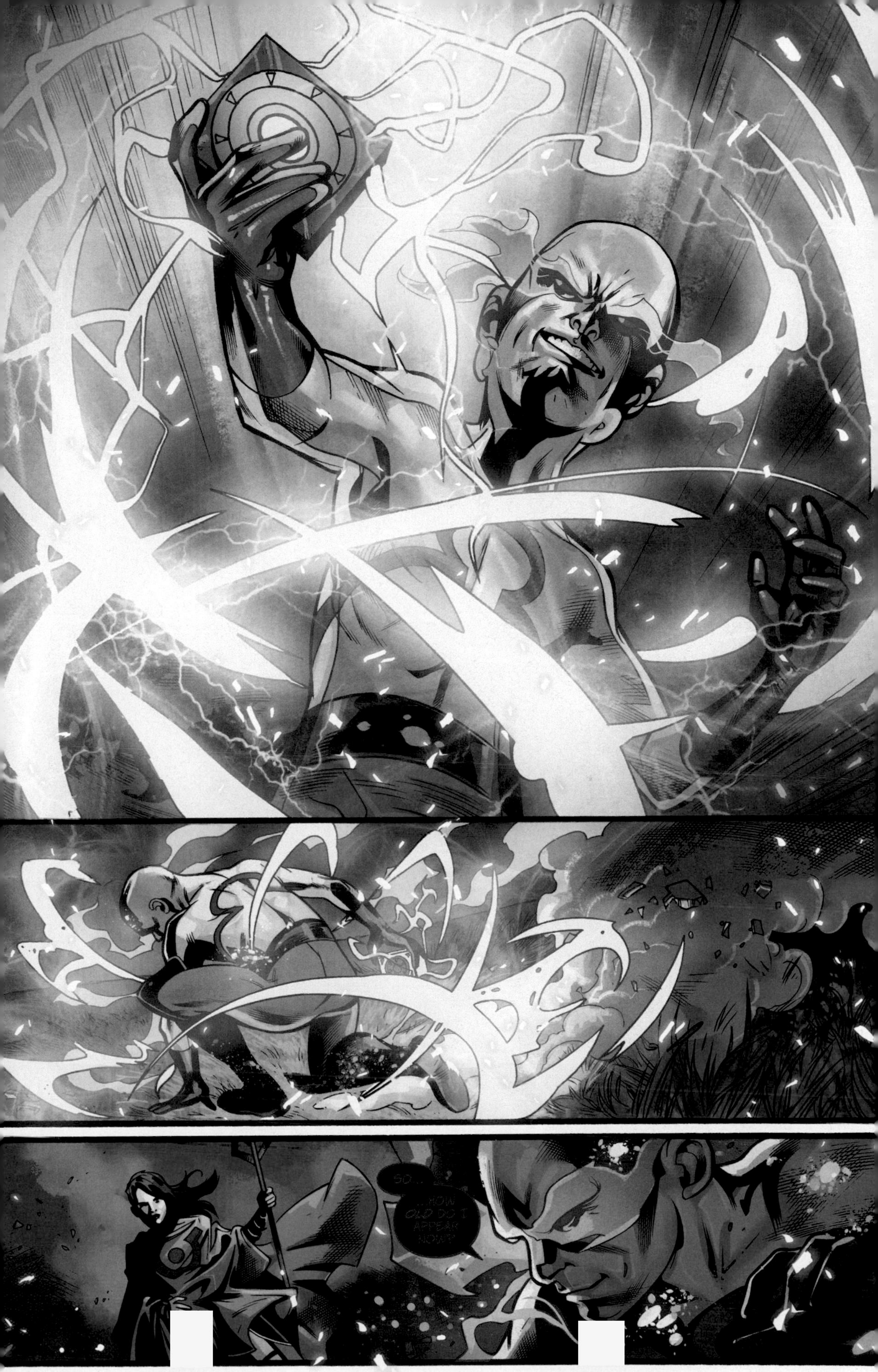
SO...
...HOW *OLD* DO I APPEAR NOW?

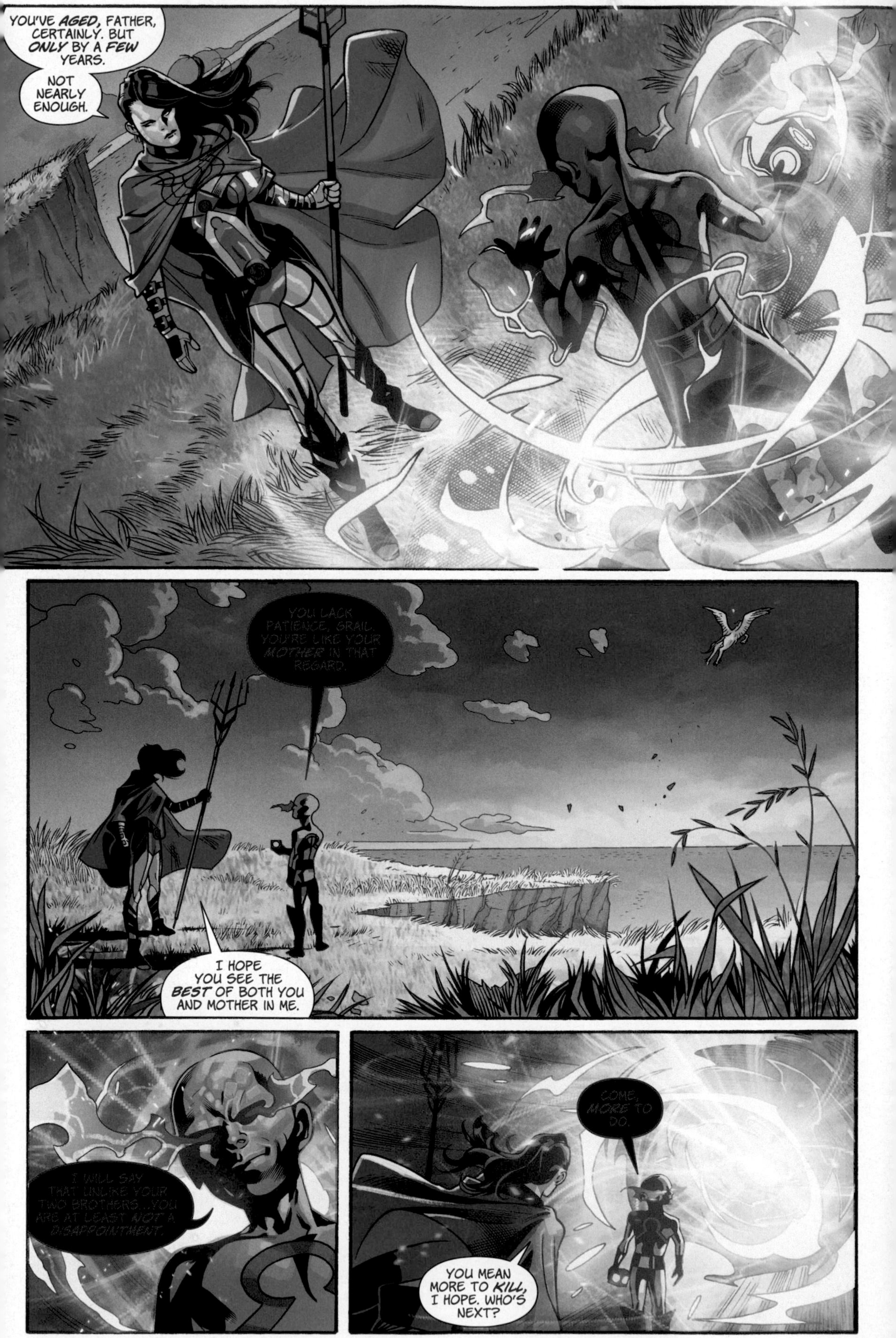
YOU'VE *AGED*, FATHER, CERTAINLY. BUT *ONLY* BY A *FEW* YEARS.
NOT NEARLY ENOUGH.
YOU LACK PATIENCE, GRAIL. YOU'RE LIKE YOUR *MOTHER* IN THAT REGARD.
I HOPE YOU SEE THE *BEST* OF BOTH YOU AND MOTHER IN ME.
I WILL SAY THAT UNLIKE YOUR TWO BROTHERS...YOU ARE AT LEAST *NOT* A *DISAPPOINTMENT*.
COME, *MORE* TO DO.
YOU MEAN MORE TO *KILL*, I HOPE. WHO'S NEXT?

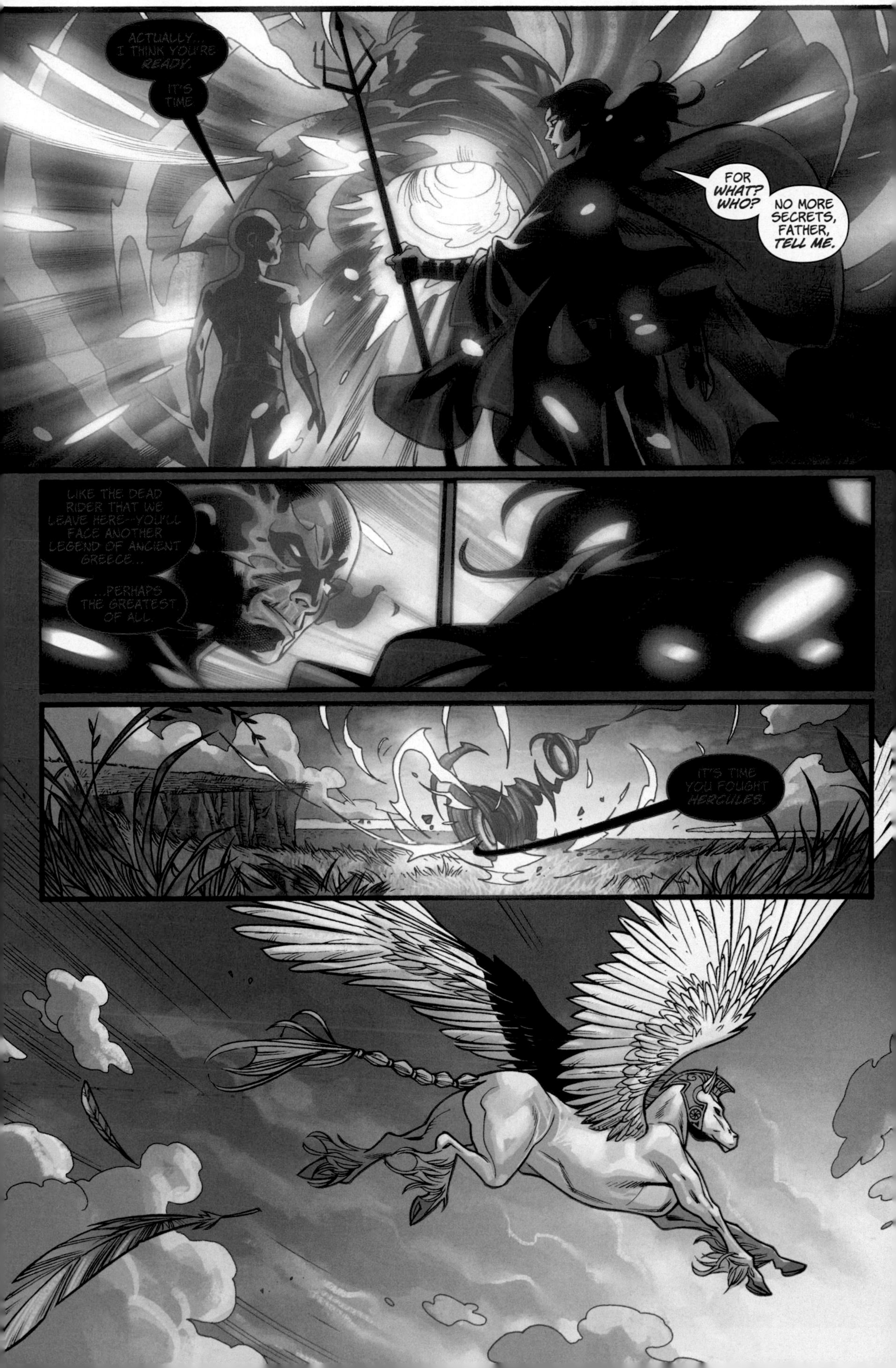
ACTUALLY... I THINK YOU'RE READY.
IT'S TIME
FOR WHAT? WHO?
NO MORE SECRETS, FATHER, TELL ME.
LIKE THE DEAD RIDER THAT WE LEAVE HERE--YOU'LL FACE ANOTHER LEGEND OF ANCIENT GREECE...
...PERHAPS THE GREATEST OF ALL.
IT'S TIME YOU FOUGHT HERCULES.

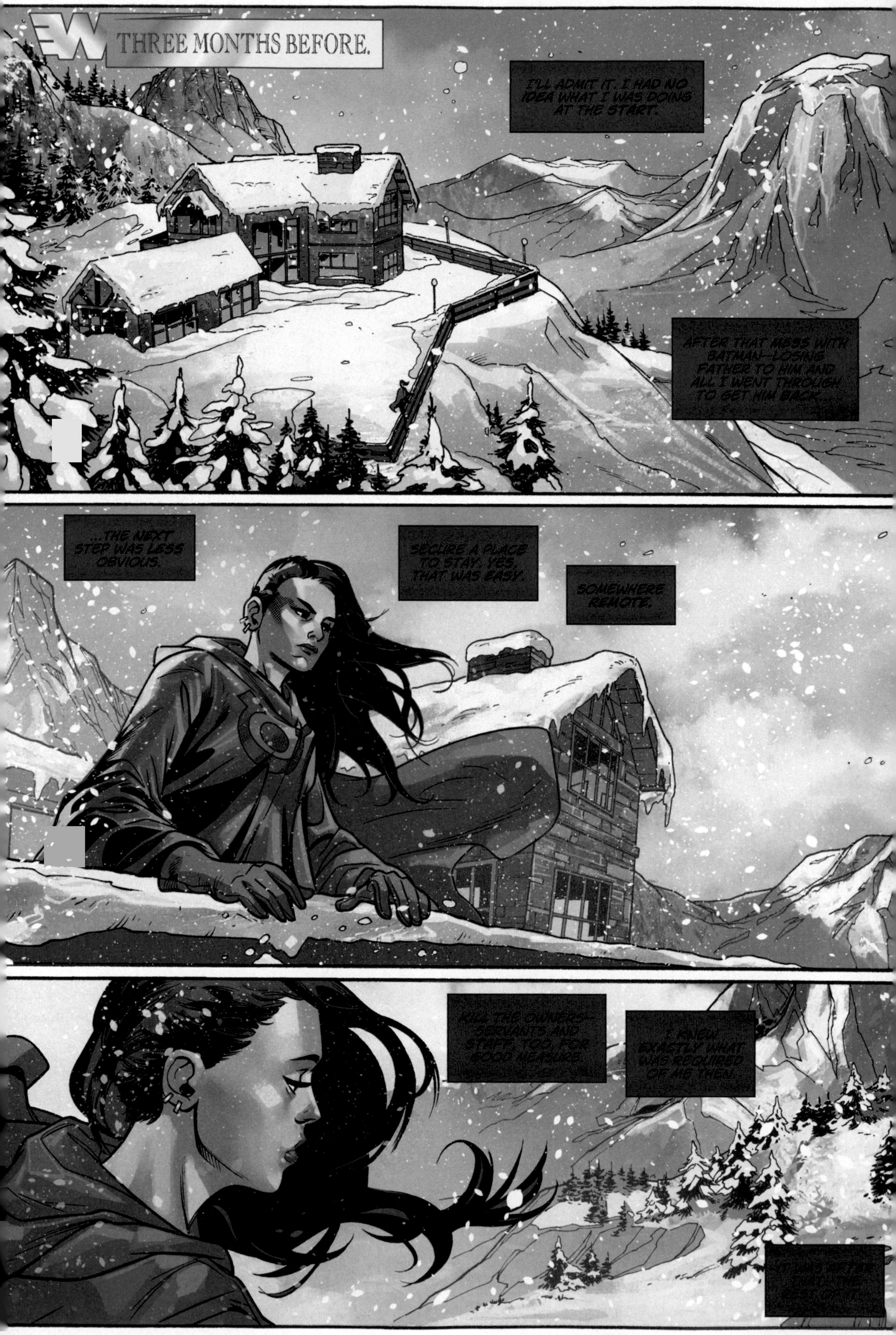

THREE MONTHS BEFORE.
I'LL ADMIT IT. I HAD NO IDEA WHAT I WAS DOING AT THE START.
AFTER THAT MESS WITH BATMAN--LOSING FATHER TO HIM AND ALL I WENT THROUGH TO GET HIM BACK...
...THE NEXT STEP WAS LESS OBVIOUS.
SECURE A PLACE TO STAY. YES, THAT WAS EASY.
SOMEWHERE REMOTE.
KILL THE OWNERS--SERVANTS AND STAFF, TOO, FOR GOOD MEASURE.
I KNEW EXACTLY WHAT WAS REQUIRED OF ME THEN.
[redacted]

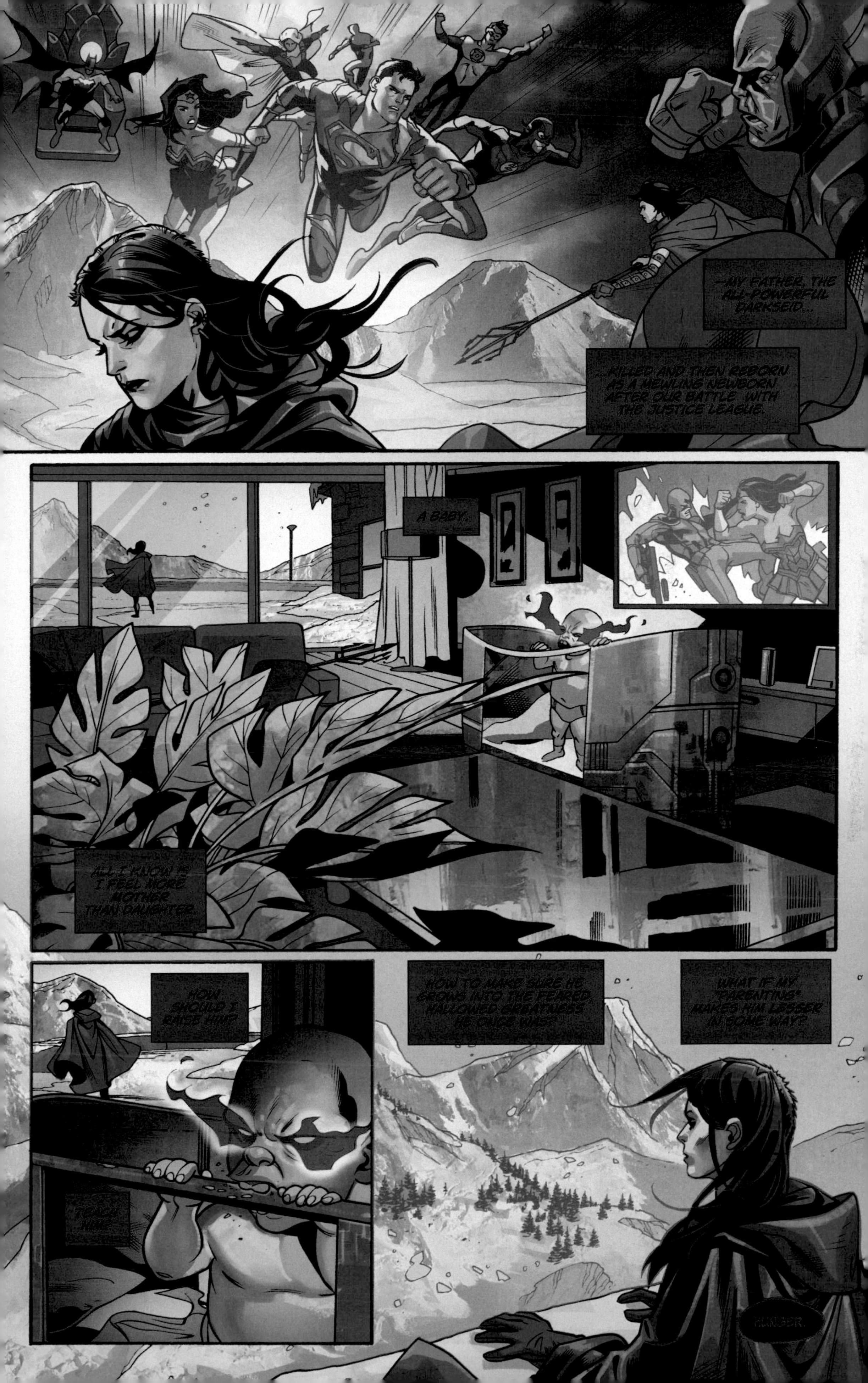
—MY FATHER, THE ALL-POWERFUL DARKSEID...
...KILLED AND THEN REBORN AS A MEWLING NEWBORN AFTER OUR BATTLE WITH THE JUSTICE LEAGUE.
A BABY.
ALL I KNOW IS I FEEL MORE MOTHER THAN DAUGHTER.
HOW SHOULD I RAISE HIM?
HOW TO MAKE SURE HE GROWS INTO THE FEARED, HALLOWED GREATNESS HE ONCE WAS?
WHAT IF MY "PARENTING" MAKES HIM LESSER IN SOME WAY?

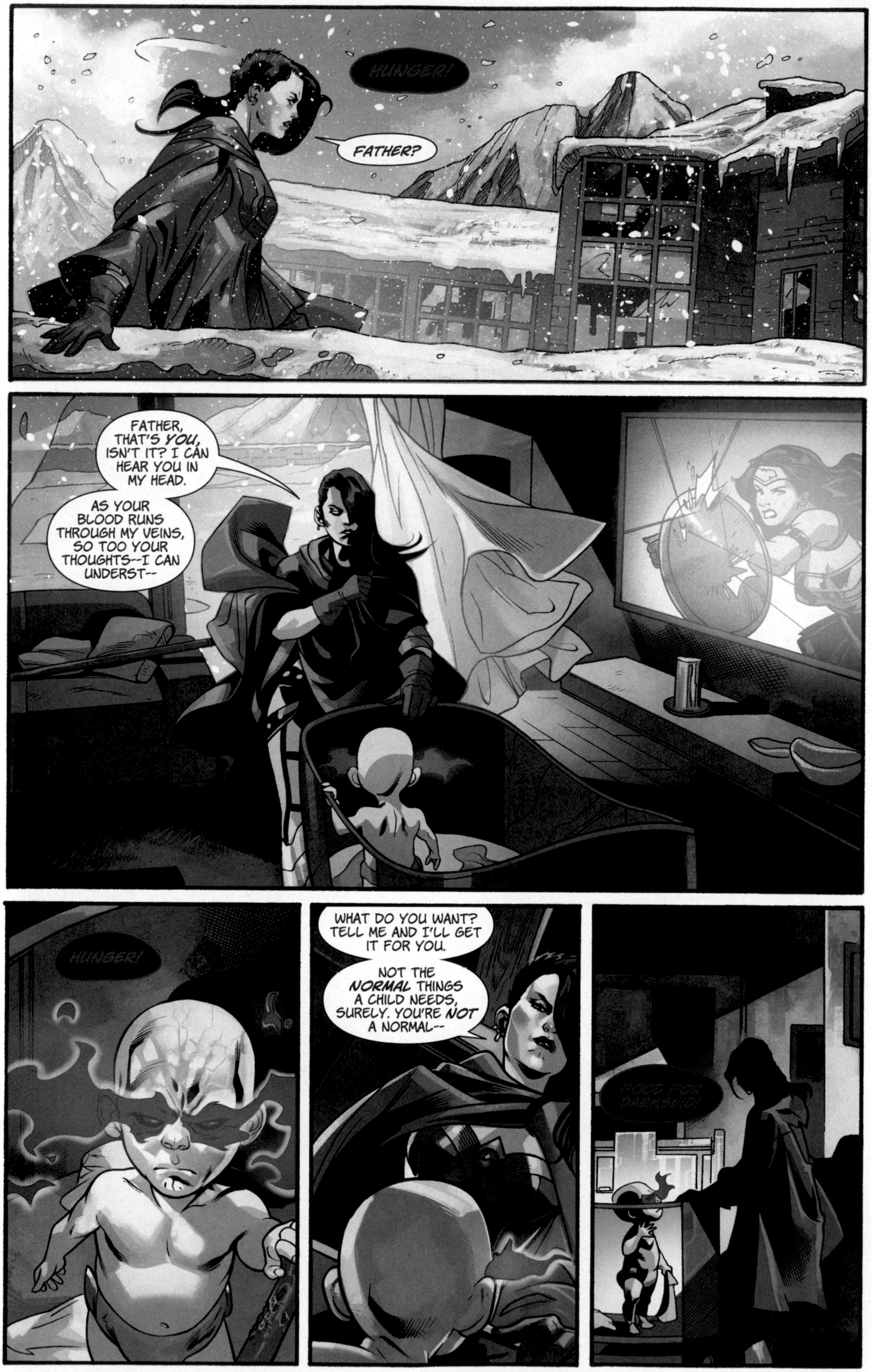
HUNGER!
FATHER?
FATHER, THAT'S YOU, ISN'T IT? I CAN HEAR YOU IN MY HEAD.
AS YOUR BLOOD RUNS THROUGH MY VEINS, SO TOO YOUR THOUGHTS--I CAN UNDERST--
HUNGER!
WHAT DO YOU WANT? TELL ME AND I'LL GET IT FOR YOU.
NOT THE NORMAL THINGS A CHILD NEEDS, SURELY. YOU'RE NOT A NORMAL--
FOOD FOR DARKSEID!

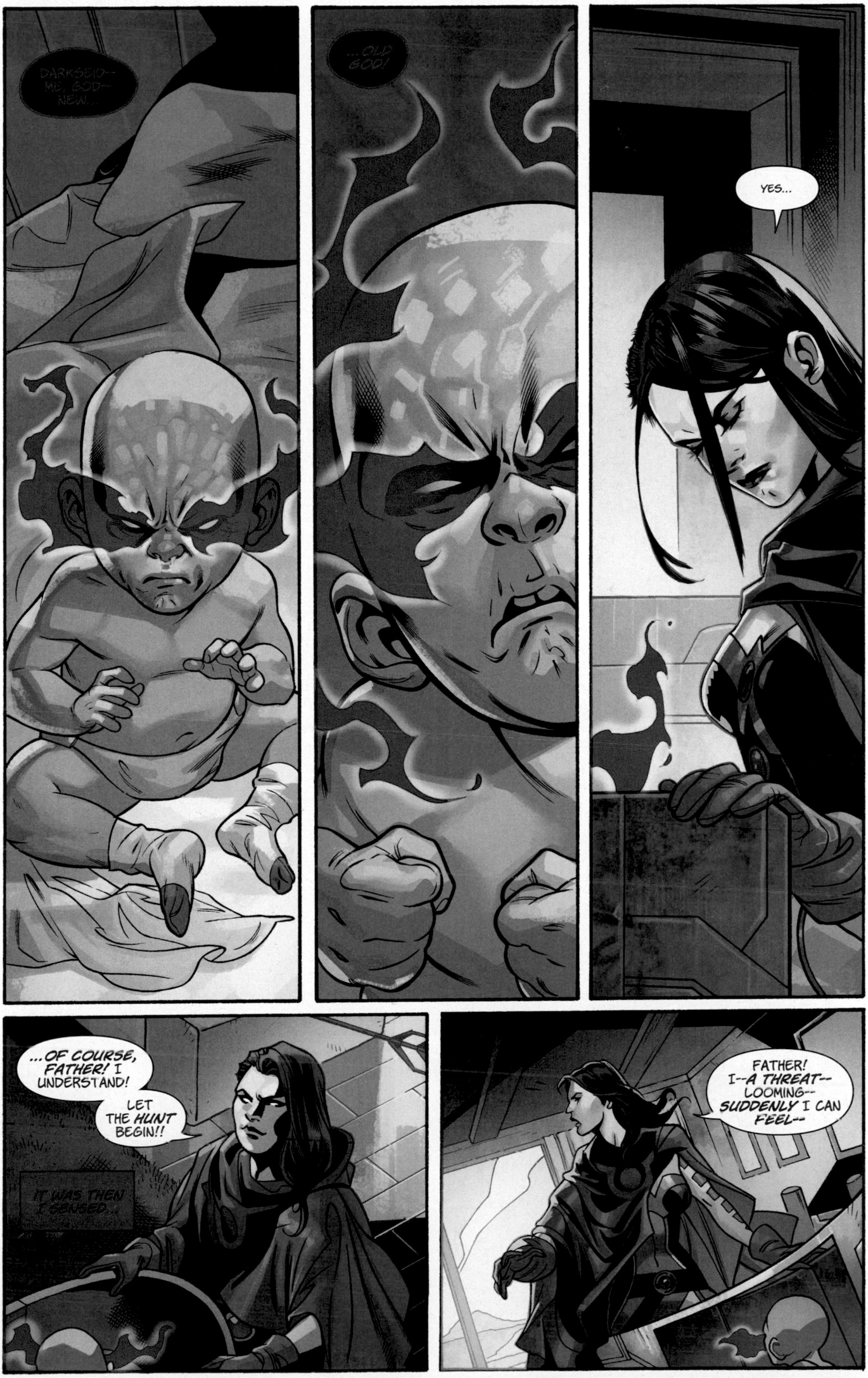
DARKSEID--
ME, GOD--
NEW...
...OLD GOD!
YES...
...OF COURSE, FATHER! I UNDERSTAND!
LET THE HUNT BEGIN!!
IT WAS THEN I SENSED...
FATHER! I--A THREAT-- LOOMING-- SUDDENLY I CAN FEEL--

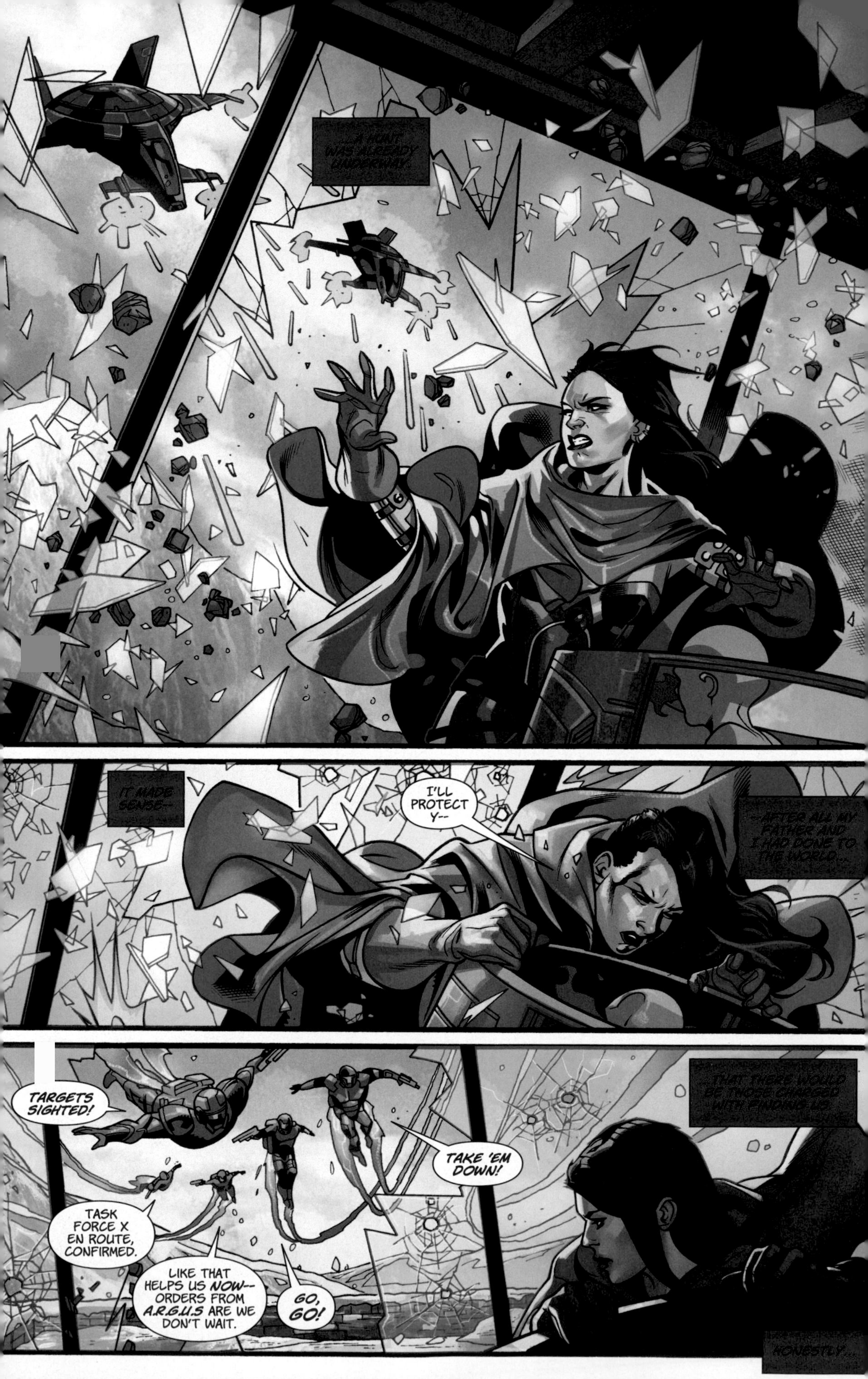
...A HUNT WAS ALREADY UNDERWAY.
IT MADE SENSE--
I'LL PROTECT Y--
--AFTER ALL MY FATHER AND I HAD DONE TO THE WORLD...
TARGETS SIGHTED!
TAKE 'EM DOWN!
TASK FORCE X EN ROUTE, CONFIRMED.
LIKE THAT HELPS US NOW--ORDERS FROM A.R.G.U.S ARE WE DON'T WAIT.
GO, GO!
...THAT THERE WOULD BE THOSE CHARGED WITH FINDING US.
HONESTLY...

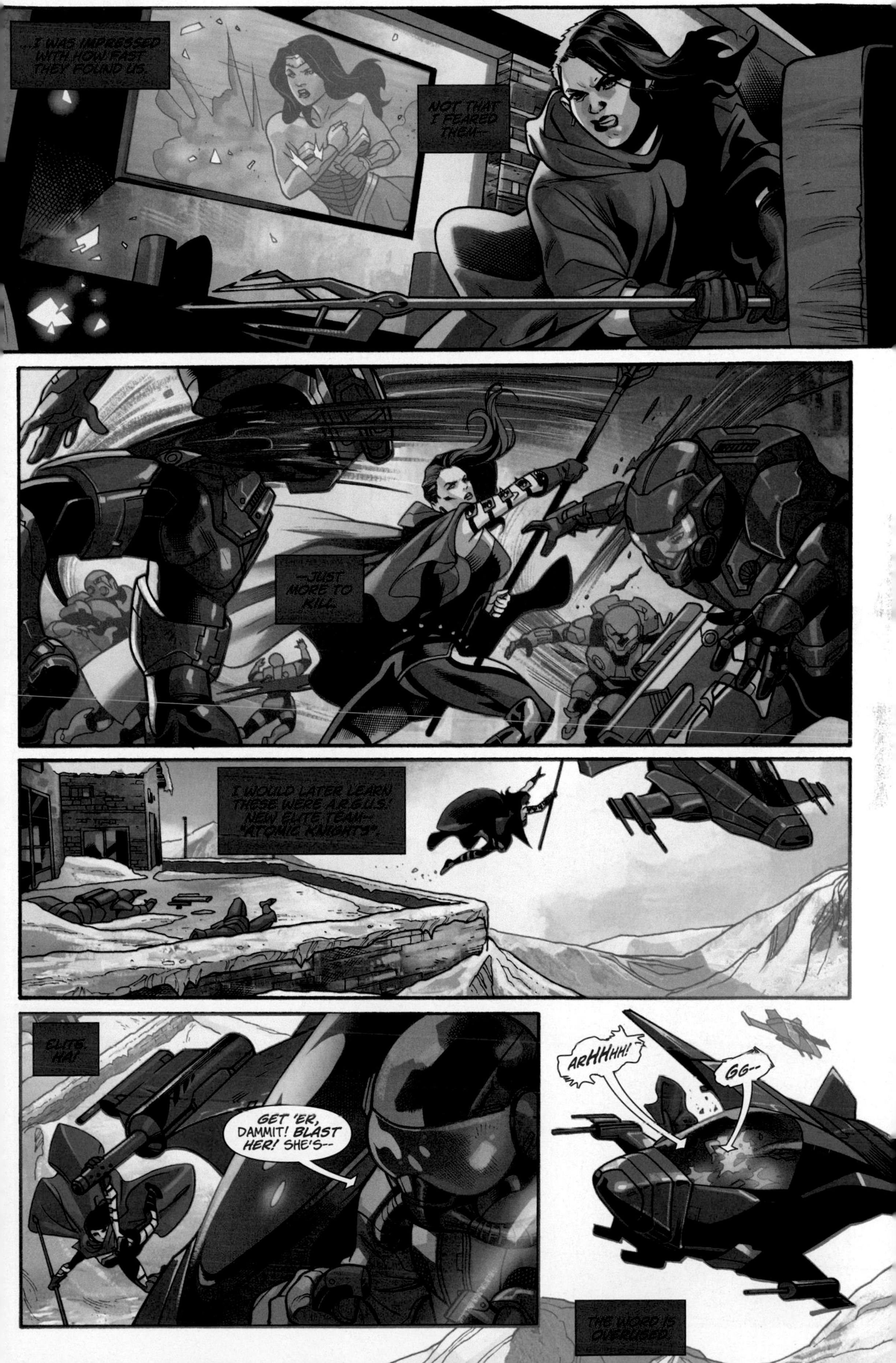
...I WAS IMPRESSED WITH HOW FAST THEY FOUND US.
NOT THAT I FEARED THEM--
--JUST MORE TO KILL.
I WOULD LATER LEARN THESE WERE A.R.G.U.S.' NEW ELITE TEAM-- "ATOMIC KNIGHTS".
ELITE. HA!
GET 'ER, DAMMIT! BLAST HER! SHE'S--
ARHHHH!
GG--
THE WORD IS OVERUSED.

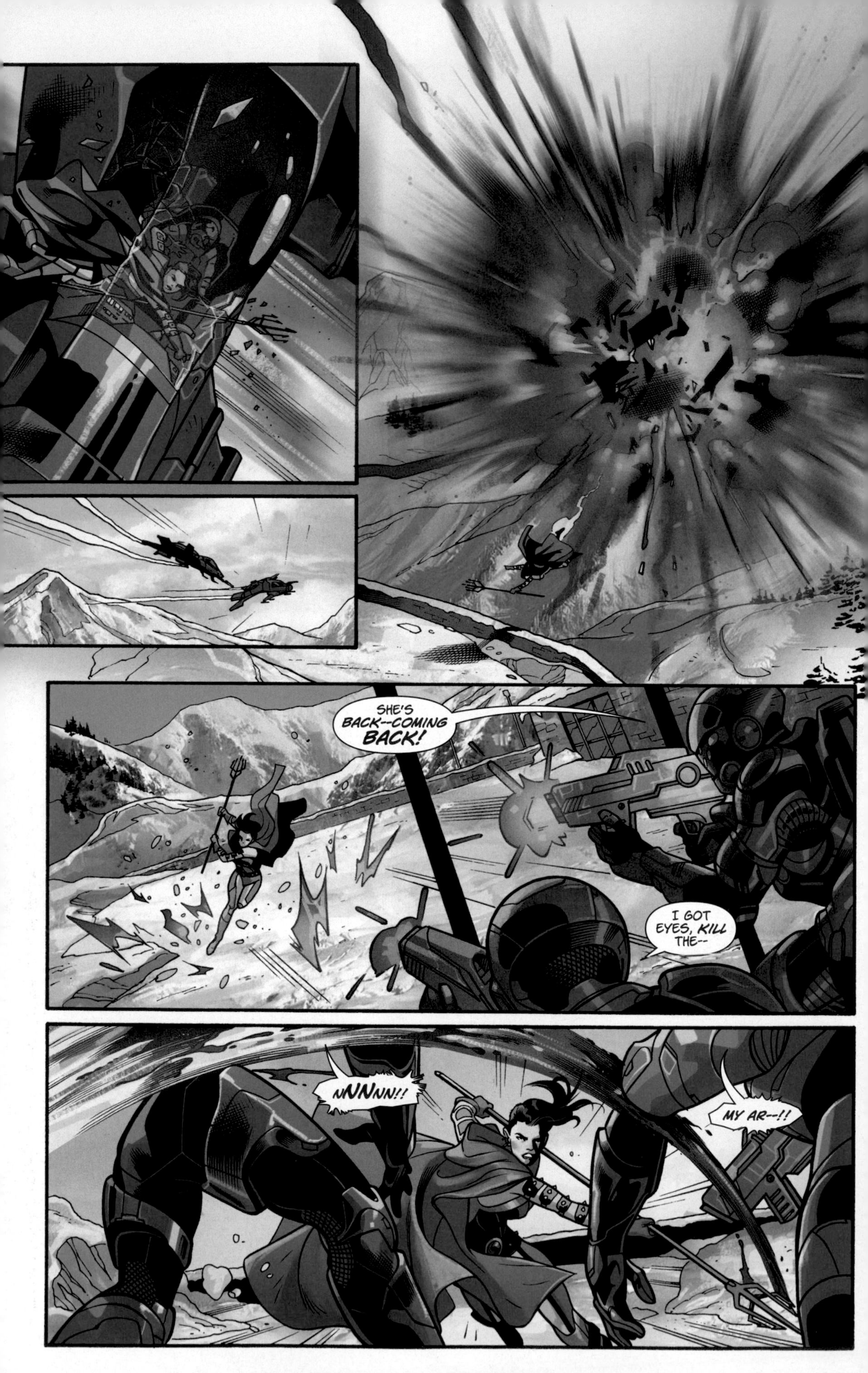
SHE'S BACK--COMING BACK!
I GOT EYES, KILL THE--
nNNnn!!
MY AR--!!

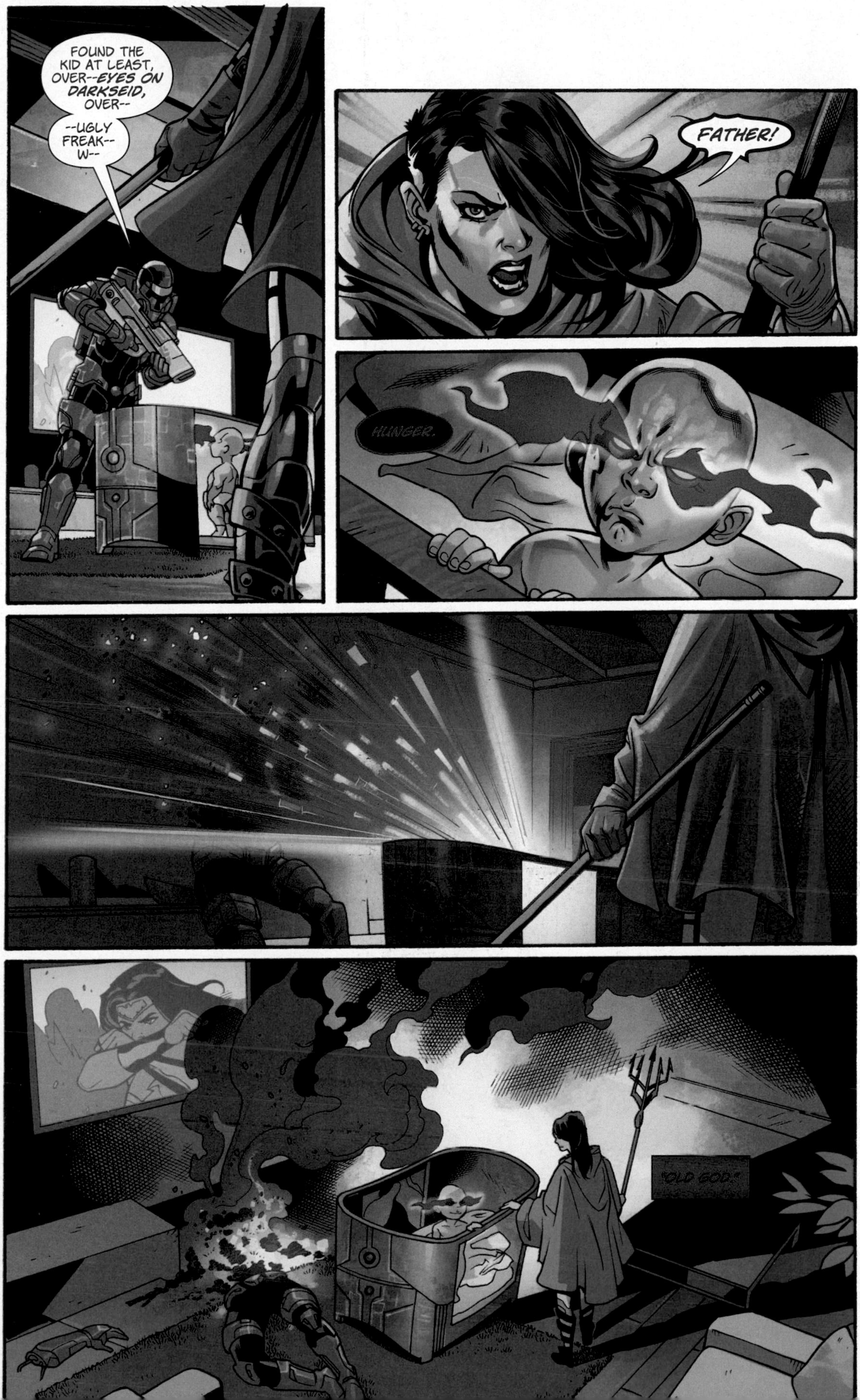
FOUND THE KID AT LEAST, OVER--EYES ON DARKSEID, OVER--
--UGLY FREAK-- W--
FATHER!
HUNGER.
"OLD GOD."

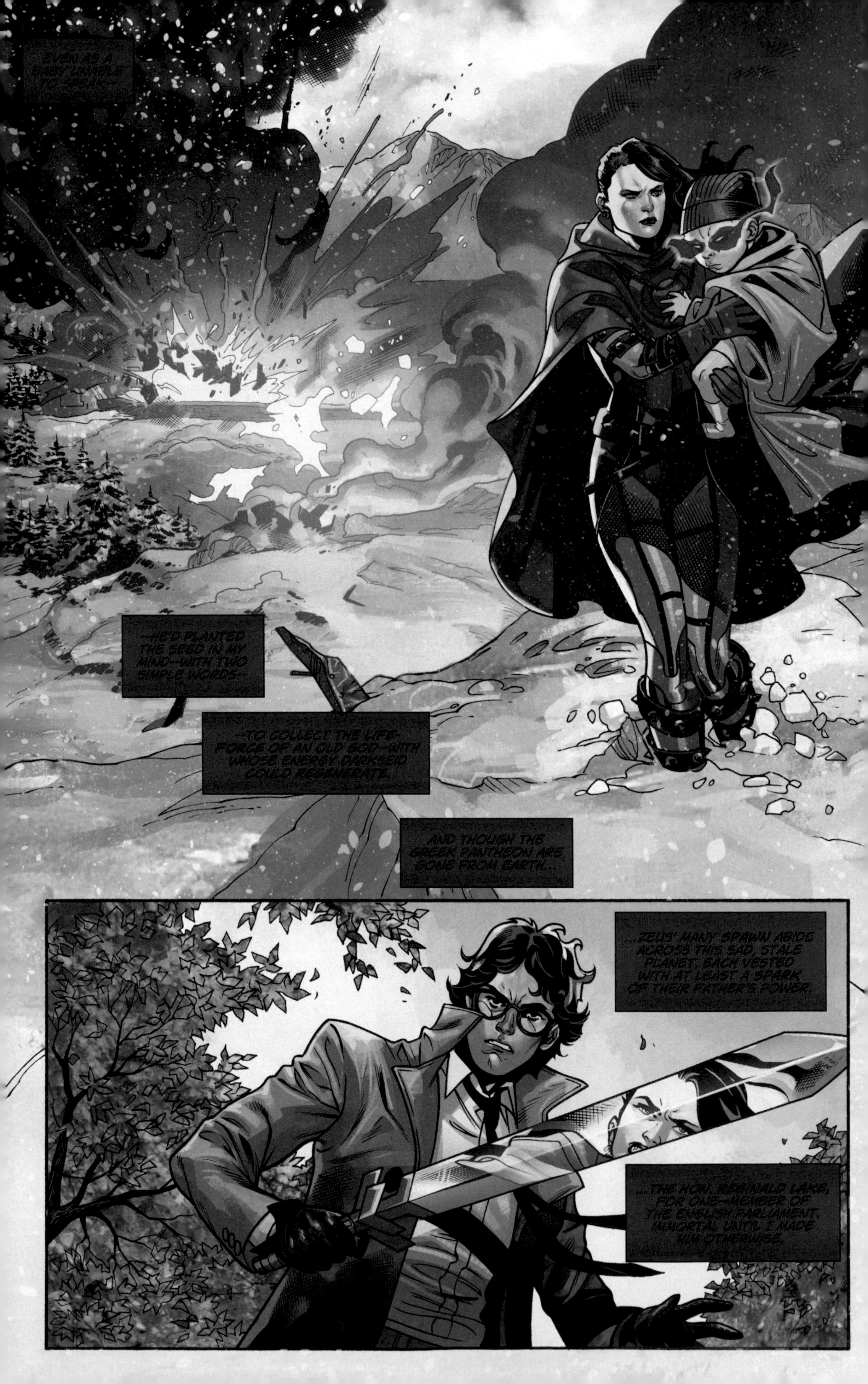
EVEN AS A
--HE'D PLANTED THE SEED IN MY MIND--WITH TWO SIMPLE WORDS--
--TO COLLECT THE LIFE-FORCE OF AN OLD GOD--WITH WHOSE ENERGY DARKSEID COULD REGENERATE.
AND THOUGH THE GREEK PANTHEON ARE GONE FROM EARTH...
...ZEUS' MANY SPAWN ABIDE ACROSS THIS SAD, STALE PLANET, EACH VESTED WITH AT LEAST A SPARK OF THEIR FATHER'S POWER.
...THE HON. REGINALD LAKE, FOR ONE--MEMBER OF THE ENGLISH PARLIAMENT, IMMORTAL UNTIL I MADE HIM OTHERWISE.

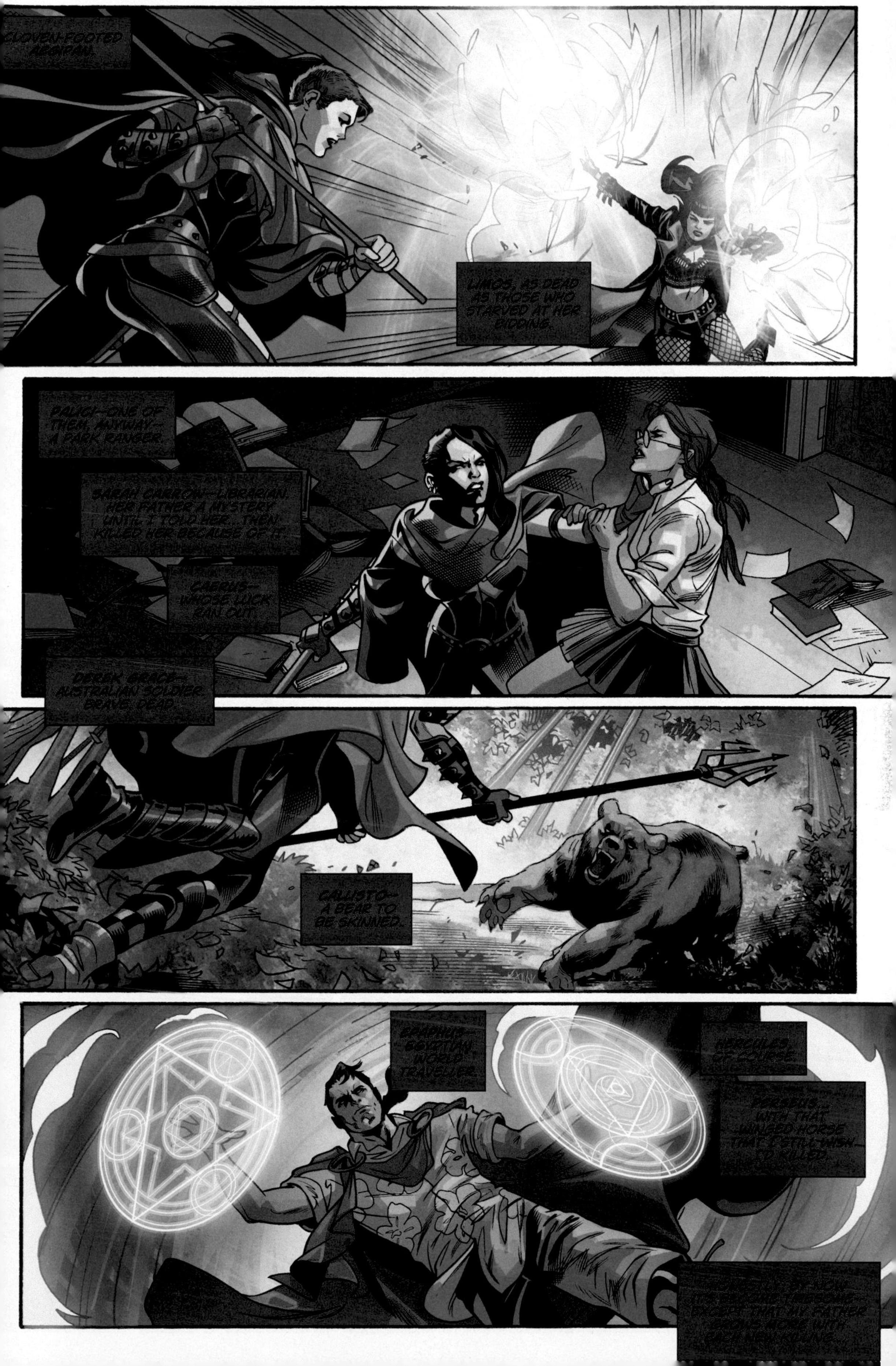

CLOVEN-FOOTED AEGIPAN.
LIMOS, AS DEAD AS THOSE WHO STARVED AT HER BIDDING.
PAUGI—ONE OF THEM, ANYWAY—A PARK RANGER.
SARAH CARROW—LIBRARIAN. HER FATHER A MYSTERY UNTIL I TOLD HER. THEN KILLED HER BECAUSE OF IT.
CAERUS—WHOSE LUCK RAN OUT.
DEREK GRACE—AUSTRALIAN SOLDIER. BRAVE. DEAD.
CALLISTO—A BEAR TO BE SKINNED.
EGYPTIAN WORLD TRAVELLER.
HERCULES, OF COURSE.
PERSEUS—WITH THAT WINGED HORSE THAT I STILL WISH I'D KILLED.

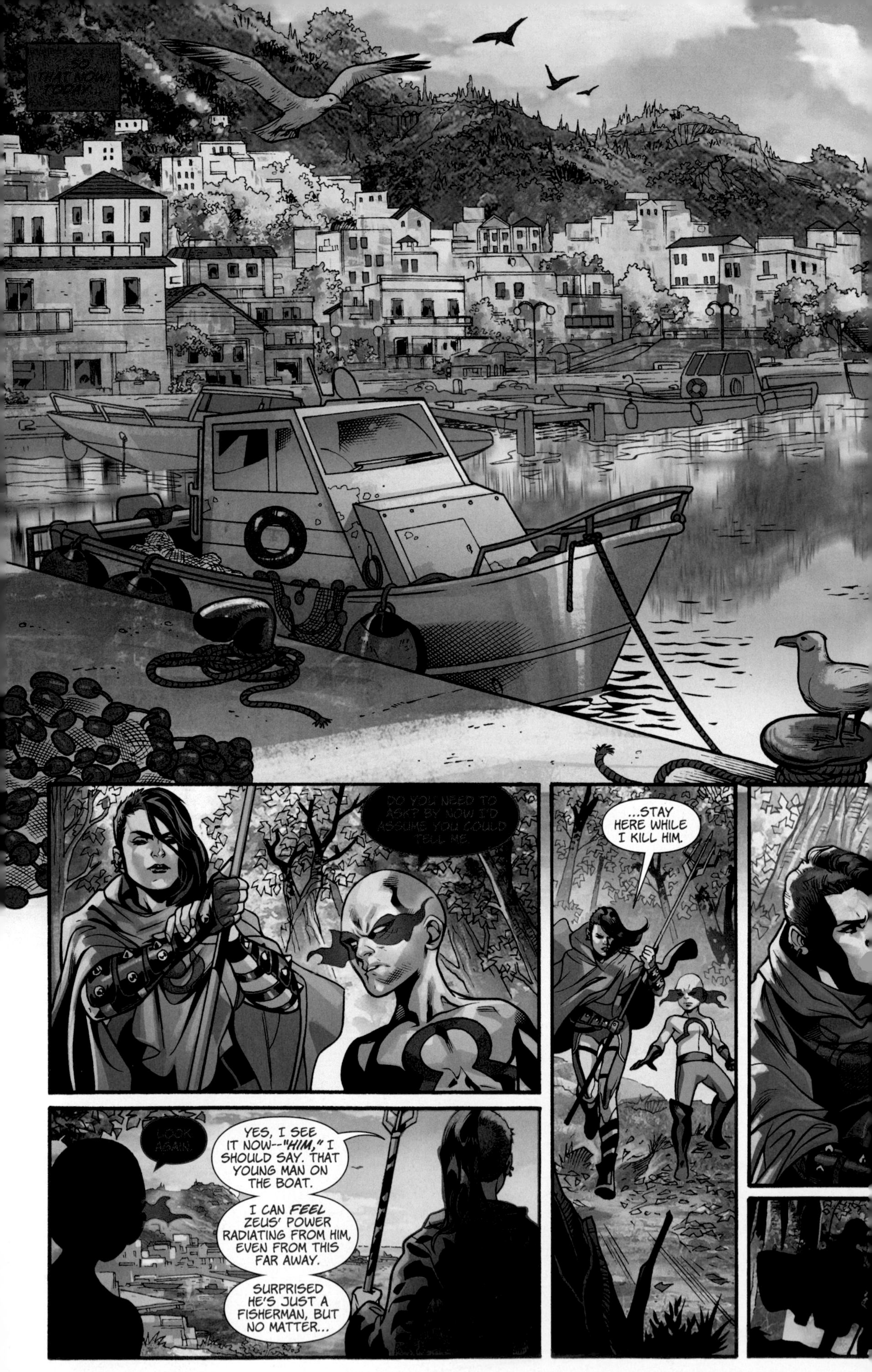
DO YOU NEED TO ASK? BY NOW I'D ASSUME YOU COULD TELL ME.
LOOK AGAIN.
YES, I SEE IT NOW--"HIM," I SHOULD SAY. THAT YOUNG MAN ON THE BOAT.
I CAN FEEL ZEUS' POWER RADIATING FROM HIM, EVEN FROM THIS FAR AWAY.
SURPRISED HE'S JUST A FISHERMAN, BUT NO MATTER...
...STAY HERE WHILE I KILL HIM.

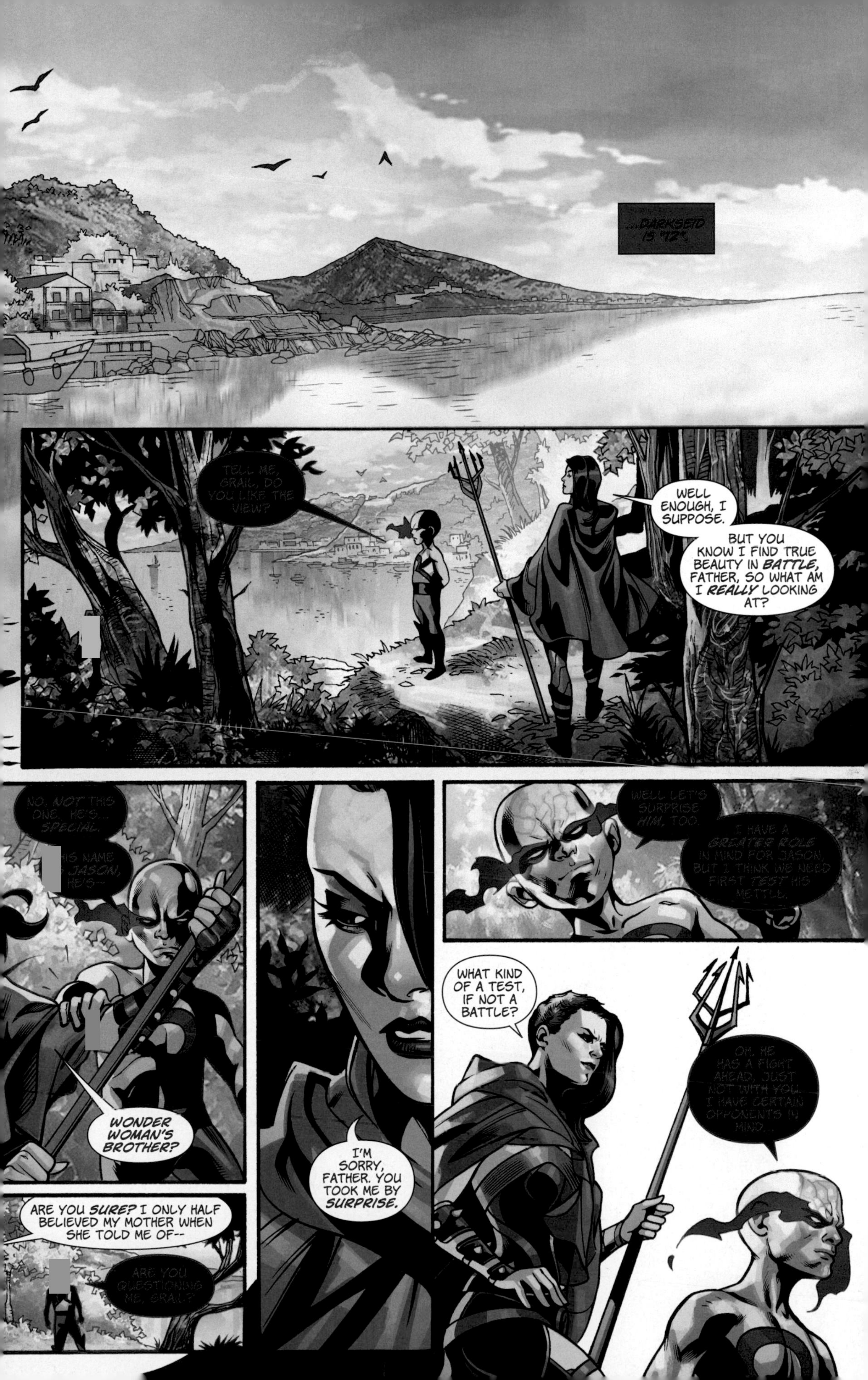
...DARKSEID IS "12".
TELL ME, GRAIL, DO YOU LIKE THE VIEW?
WELL ENOUGH, I SUPPOSE.
BUT YOU KNOW I FIND TRUE BEAUTY IN BATTLE, FATHER, SO WHAT AM I REALLY LOOKING AT?
NO, NOT THIS ONE. HE'S... SPECIAL.
HIS NAME
JASON, HE'S--
WONDER WOMAN'S BROTHER?
ARE YOU SURE? I ONLY HALF BELIEVED MY MOTHER WHEN SHE TOLD ME OF--
ARE YOU QUESTIONING ME, GRAIL?
I'M SORRY, FATHER. YOU TOOK ME BY SURPRISE.
WELL LET'S SURPRISE HIM, TOO.
I HAVE A GREATER ROLE IN MIND FOR JASON, BUT I THINK WE NEED FIRST TEST HIS METTLE.
WHAT KIND OF A TEST, IF NOT A BATTLE?
OH, HE HAS A FIGHT AHEAD, JUST NOT WITH YOU. I HAVE CERTAIN OPPONENTS IN MIND...

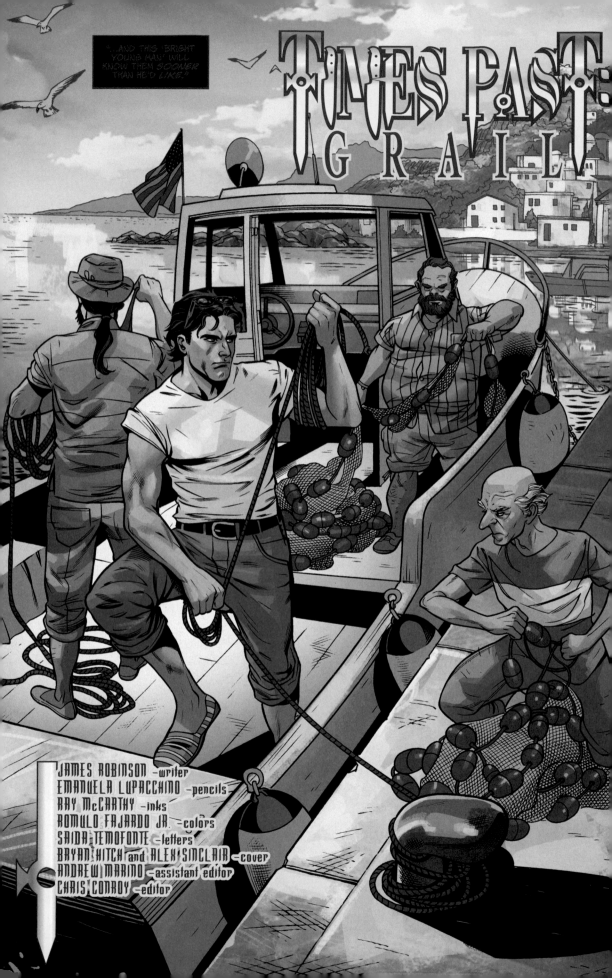

"...AND THIS 'BRIGHT YOUNG MAN' WILL KNOW THEM *SOONER* THAN HE'D *LIKE*."

TIMES PAST:
GRAIL

JAMES ROBINSON –writer
EMANUELA LUPACCHINO –pencils
RAY McCARTHY –inks
ROMULO FAJARDO JR. –colors
SAIDA TEMOFONTE –letters
BRYAN HITCH and ALEX SINCLAIR –cover
ANDREW MARINO –assistant editor
CHRIS CONROY –editor

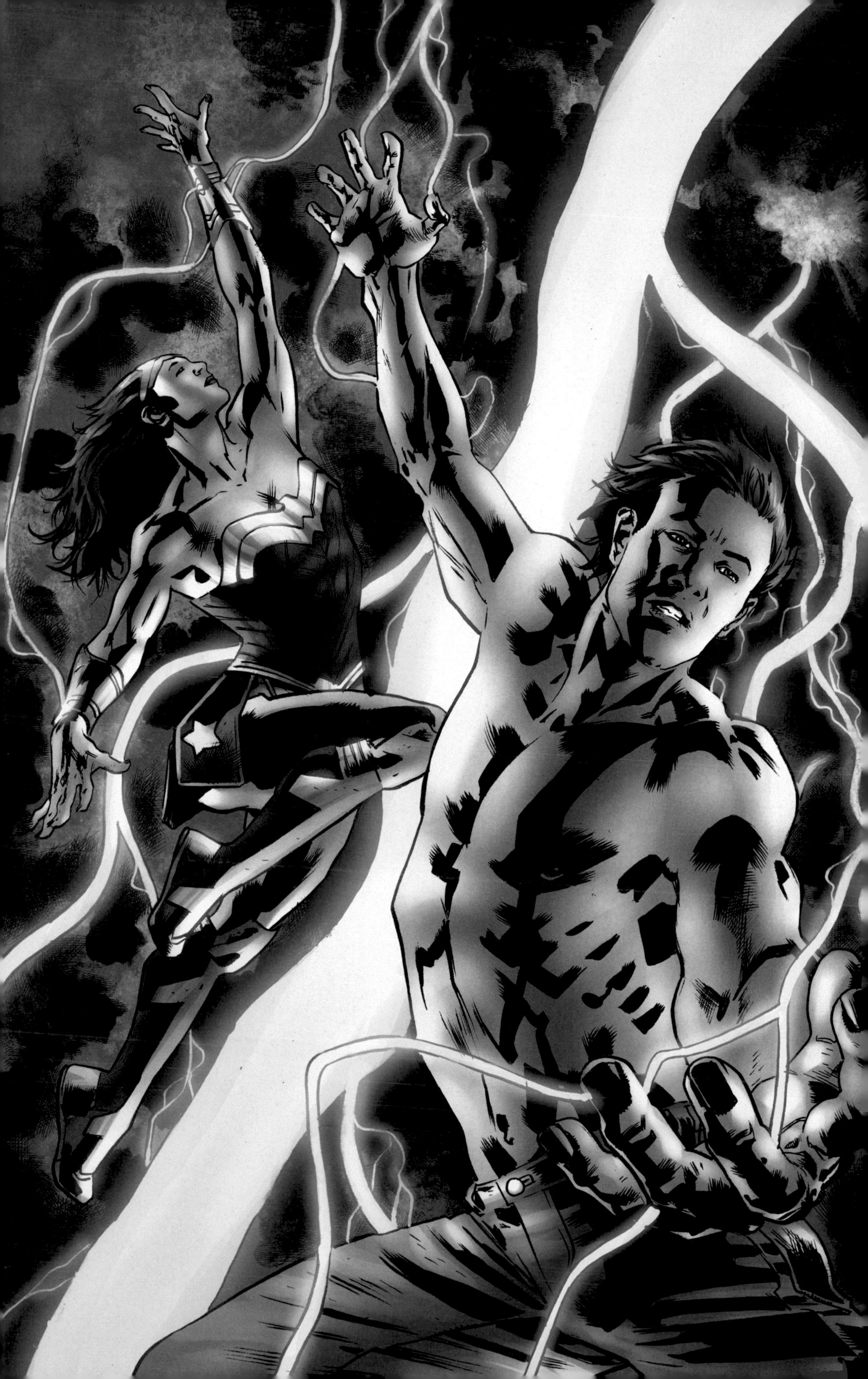

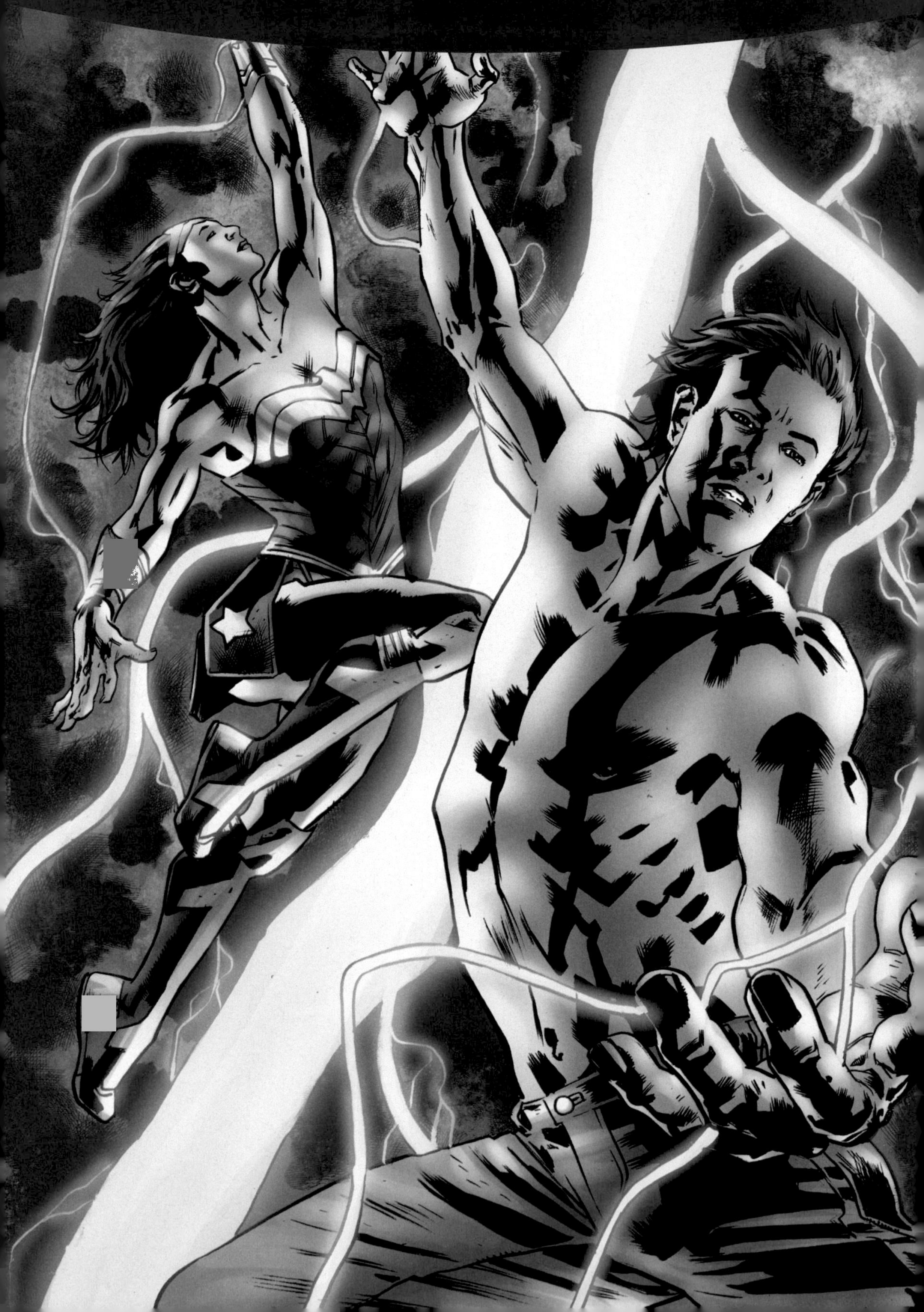

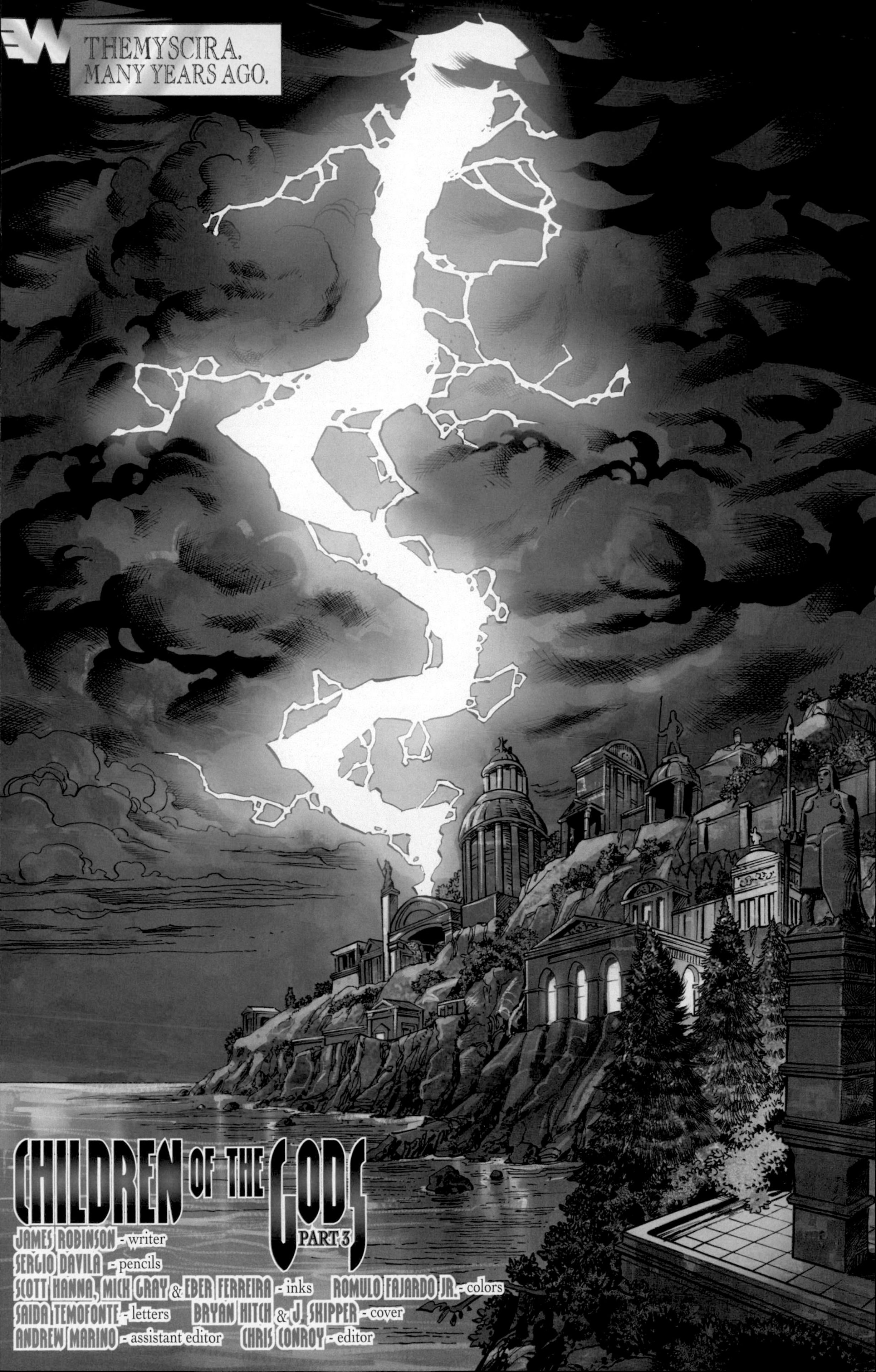
THEMYSCIRA. MANY YEARS AGO.
CHILDREN OF THE GODS
PART 3
JAMES ROBINSON - writer
SERGIO DAVILA - pencils
SCOTT HANNA, MICK GRAY & EBER FERREIRA - inks
ROMULO FAJARDO JR. - colors
SAIDA TEMOFONTE - letters
BRYAN HITCH & J. SKIPPER - cover
ANDREW MARINO - assistant editor
CHRIS CONROY - editor

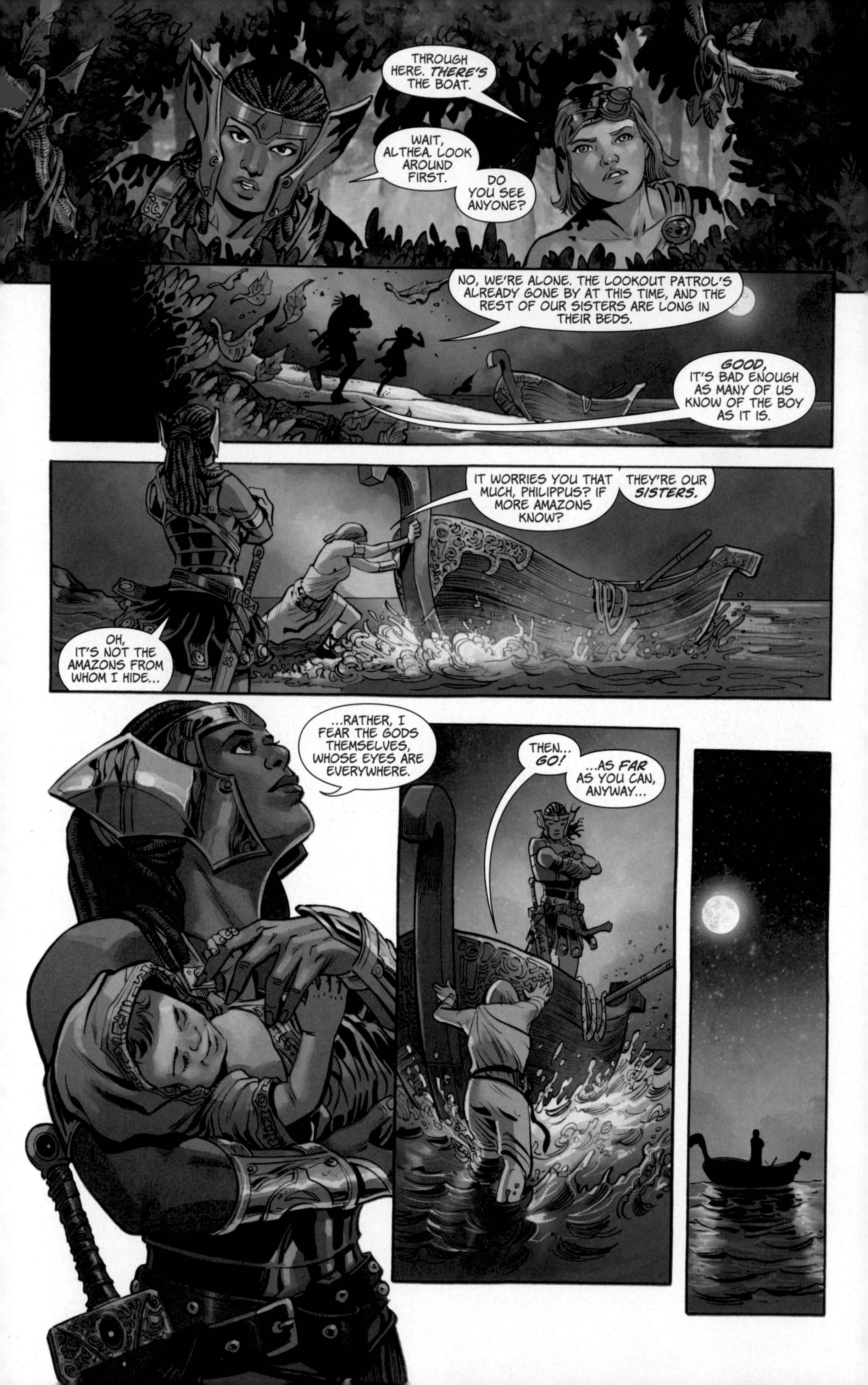
THROUGH HERE. *THERE'S* THE BOAT.
WAIT, ALTHEA. LOOK AROUND FIRST.
DO YOU SEE ANYONE?
NO, WE'RE ALONE. THE LOOKOUT PATROL'S ALREADY GONE BY AT THIS TIME, AND THE REST OF OUR SISTERS ARE LONG IN THEIR BEDS.
GOOD, IT'S BAD ENOUGH AS MANY OF US KNOW OF THE BOY AS IT IS.
IT WORRIES YOU THAT MUCH, PHILIPPUS? IF MORE AMAZONS KNOW?
THEY'RE OUR *SISTERS.*
OH, IT'S NOT THE AMAZONS FROM WHOM I HIDE...
...RATHER, I FEAR THE GODS THEMSELVES, WHOSE EYES ARE EVERYWHERE.
THEN... *GO!*
...AS *FAR* AS YOU CAN, ANYWAY...

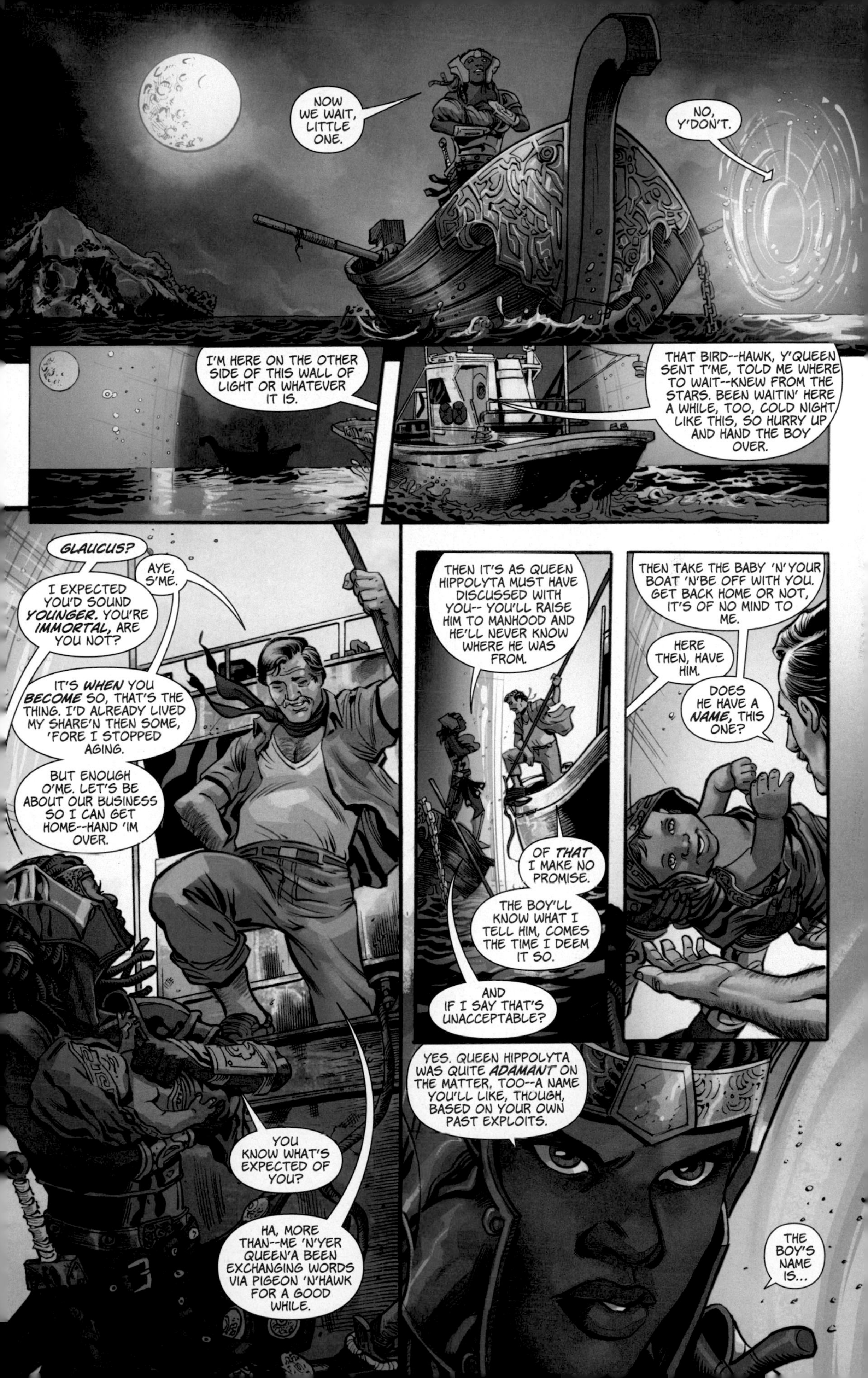
NOW WE WAIT, LITTLE ONE.
NO, Y'DON'T.
I'M HERE ON THE OTHER SIDE OF THIS WALL OF LIGHT OR WHATEVER IT IS.
THAT BIRD--HAWK, Y'QUEEN SENT T'ME, TOLD ME WHERE TO WAIT--KNEW FROM THE STARS. BEEN WAITIN' HERE A WHILE, TOO, COLD NIGHT LIKE THIS, SO HURRY UP AND HAND THE BOY OVER.
GLAUCUS?
AYE, S'ME.
I EXPECTED YOU'D SOUND YOUNGER. YOU'RE IMMORTAL, ARE YOU NOT?
IT'S WHEN YOU BECOME SO, THAT'S THE THING. I'D ALREADY LIVED MY SHARE'N THEN SOME, 'FORE I STOPPED AGING.
BUT ENOUGH O'ME. LET'S BE ABOUT OUR BUSINESS SO I CAN GET HOME--HAND 'IM OVER.
YOU KNOW WHAT'S EXPECTED OF YOU?
HA, MORE THAN--ME 'N'YER QUEEN'A BEEN EXCHANGING WORDS VIA PIGEON 'N'HAWK FOR A GOOD WHILE.
THEN IT'S AS QUEEN HIPPOLYTA MUST HAVE DISCUSSED WITH YOU-- YOU'LL RAISE HIM TO MANHOOD AND HE'LL NEVER KNOW WHERE HE WAS FROM.
OF THAT I MAKE NO PROMISE.
THE BOY'LL KNOW WHAT I TELL HIM, COMES THE TIME I DEEM IT SO.
AND IF I SAY THAT'S UNACCEPTABLE?
THEN TAKE THE BABY 'N' YOUR BOAT 'N'BE OFF WITH YOU. GET BACK HOME OR NOT, IT'S OF NO MIND TO ME.
HERE THEN, HAVE HIM.
DOES HE HAVE A NAME, THIS ONE?
YES. QUEEN HIPPOLYTA WAS QUITE ADAMANT ON THE MATTER, TOO--A NAME YOU'LL LIKE, THOUGH, BASED ON YOUR OWN PAST EXPLOITS.
THE BOY'S NAME IS...

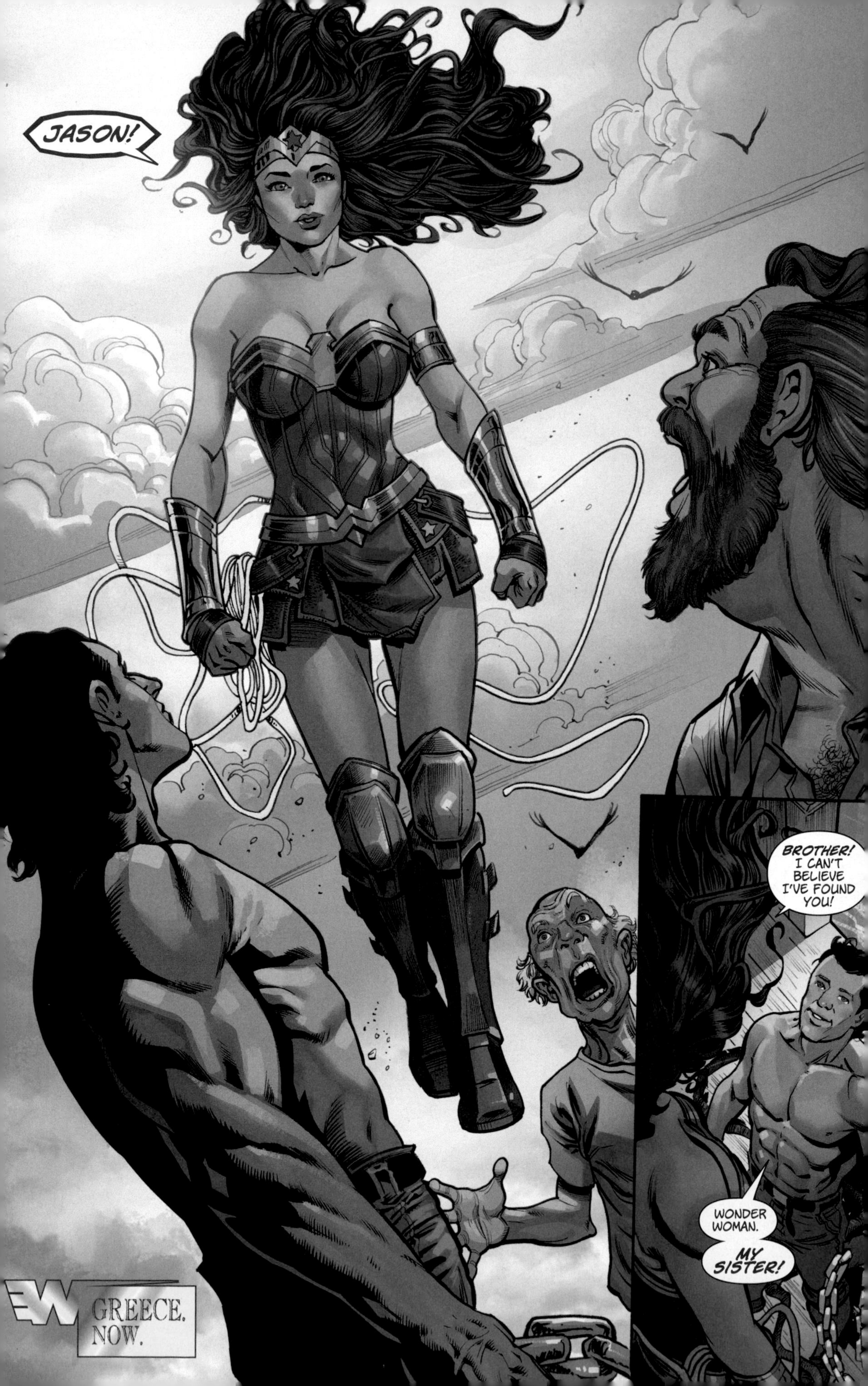
JASON!
BROTHER! I CAN'T BELIEVE I'VE FOUND YOU!
WONDER WOMAN.
MY SISTER!
GREECE. NOW.

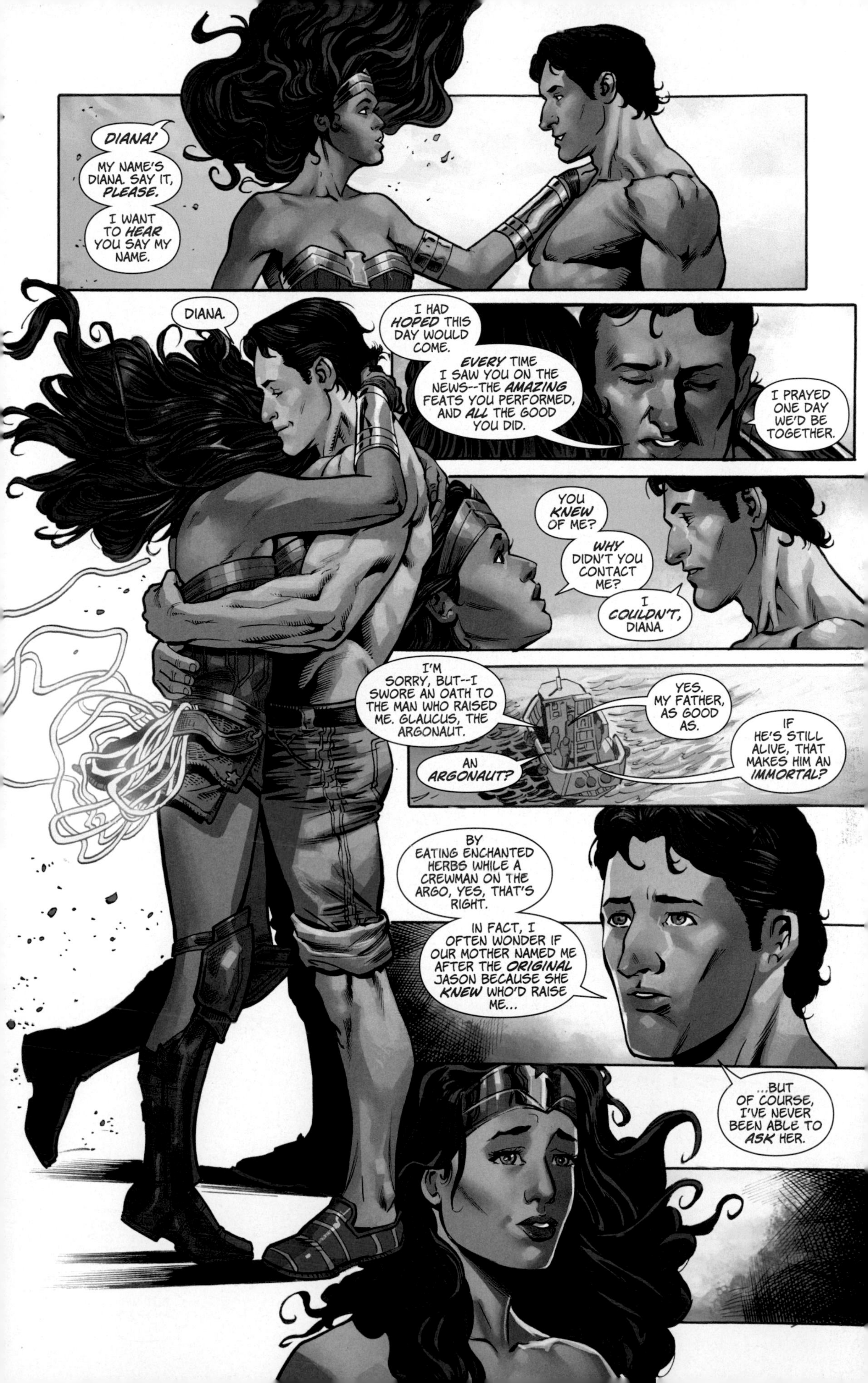
DIANA!
MY NAME'S DIANA. SAY IT, PLEASE.
I WANT TO HEAR YOU SAY MY NAME.
DIANA.
I HAD HOPED THIS DAY WOULD COME.
EVERY TIME I SAW YOU ON THE NEWS--THE AMAZING FEATS YOU PERFORMED, AND ALL THE GOOD YOU DID.
I PRAYED ONE DAY WE'D BE TOGETHER.
YOU KNEW OF ME?
WHY DIDN'T YOU CONTACT ME?
I COULDN'T, DIANA.
I'M SORRY, BUT--I SWORE AN OATH TO THE MAN WHO RAISED ME. GLAUCUS, THE ARGONAUT.
AN ARGONAUT?
YES. MY FATHER, AS GOOD AS.
IF HE'S STILL ALIVE, THAT MAKES HIM AN IMMORTAL?
BY EATING ENCHANTED HERBS WHILE A CREWMAN ON THE ARGO, YES, THAT'S RIGHT.
IN FACT, I OFTEN WONDER IF OUR MOTHER NAMED ME AFTER THE ORIGINAL JASON BECAUSE SHE KNEW WHO'D RAISE ME...
...BUT OF COURSE, I'VE NEVER BEEN ABLE TO ASK HER.

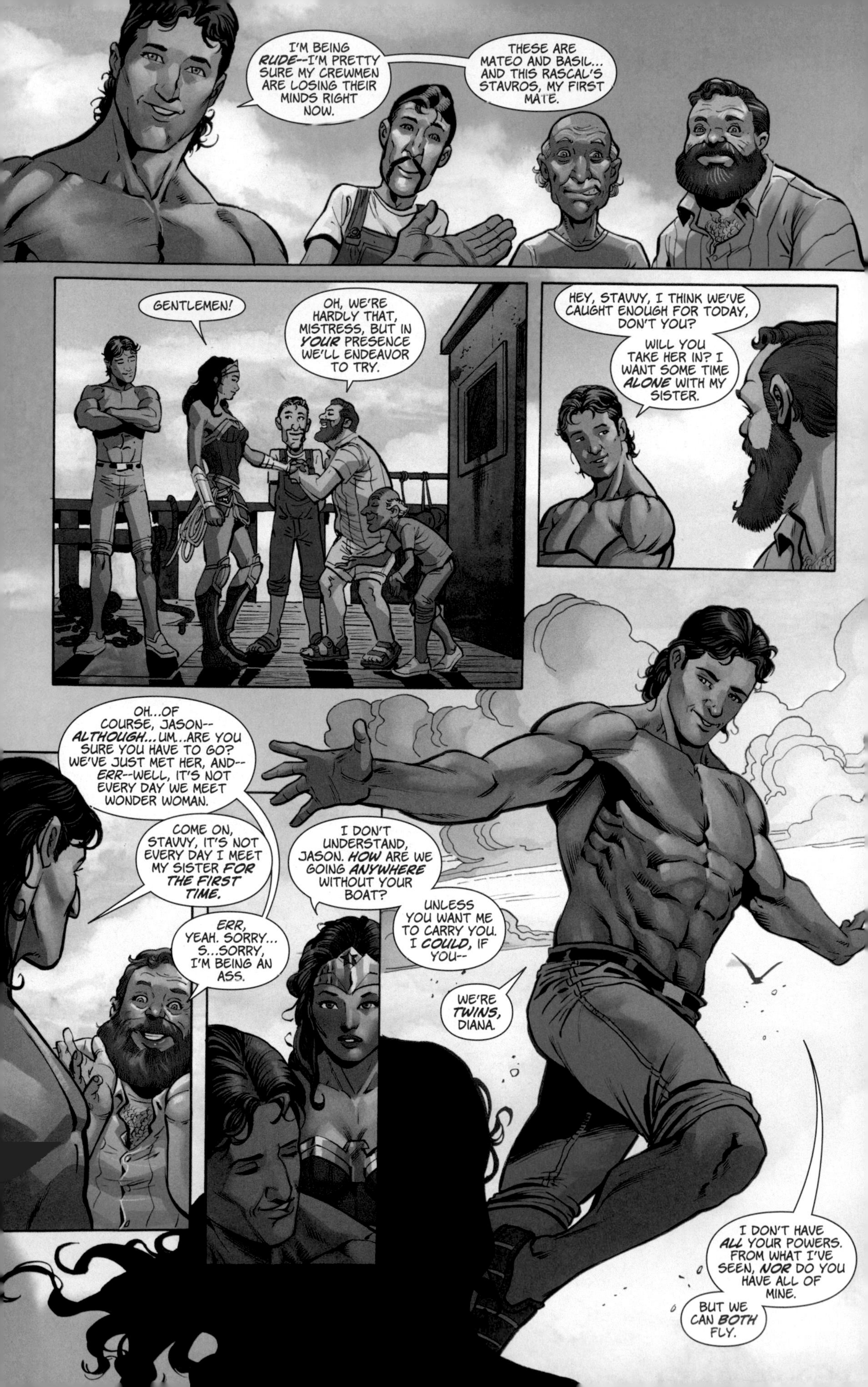
I'M BEING RUDE--I'M PRETTY SURE MY CREWMEN ARE LOSING THEIR MINDS RIGHT NOW.
THESE ARE MATEO AND BASIL... AND THIS RASCAL'S STAVROS, MY FIRST MATE.
GENTLEMEN!
OH, WE'RE HARDLY THAT, MISTRESS, BUT IN YOUR PRESENCE WE'LL ENDEAVOR TO TRY.
HEY, STAVVY, I THINK WE'VE CAUGHT ENOUGH FOR TODAY, DON'T YOU?
WILL YOU TAKE HER IN? I WANT SOME TIME ALONE WITH MY SISTER.
OH...OF COURSE, JASON-- ALTHOUGH...UM...ARE YOU SURE YOU HAVE TO GO? WE'VE JUST MET HER, AND-- ERR--WELL, IT'S NOT EVERY DAY WE MEET WONDER WOMAN.
COME ON, STAVVY, IT'S NOT EVERY DAY I MEET MY SISTER FOR THE FIRST TIME.
ERR, YEAH. SORRY... S...SORRY, I'M BEING AN ASS.
I DON'T UNDERSTAND, JASON. HOW ARE WE GOING ANYWHERE WITHOUT YOUR BOAT?
UNLESS YOU WANT ME TO CARRY YOU. I COULD, IF YOU--
WE'RE TWINS, DIANA.
I DON'T HAVE ALL YOUR POWERS. FROM WHAT I'VE SEEN, NOR DO YOU HAVE ALL OF MINE.
BUT WE CAN BOTH FLY.

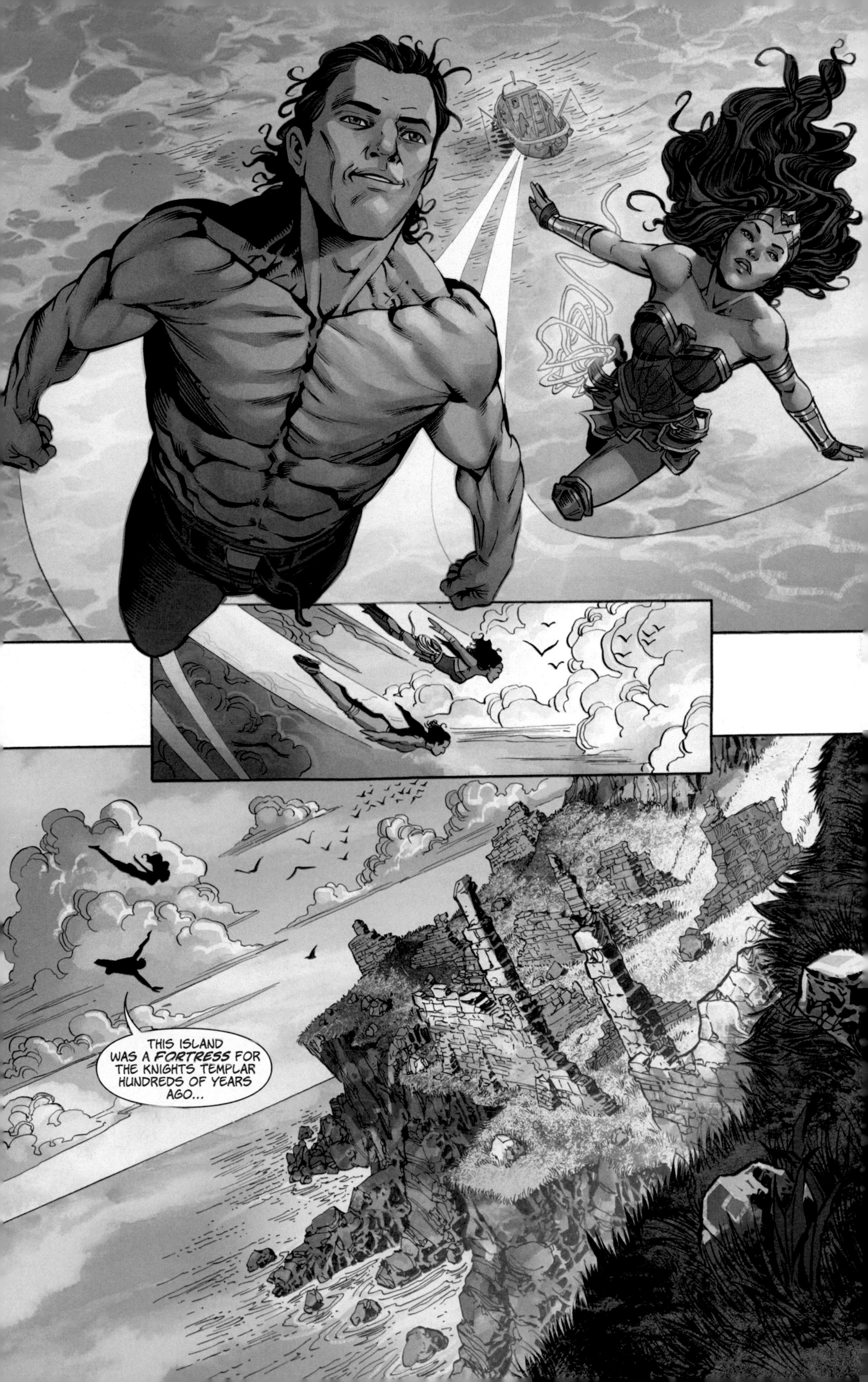
THIS ISLAND WAS A FORTRESS FOR THE KNIGHTS TEMPLAR HUNDREDS OF YEARS AGO...

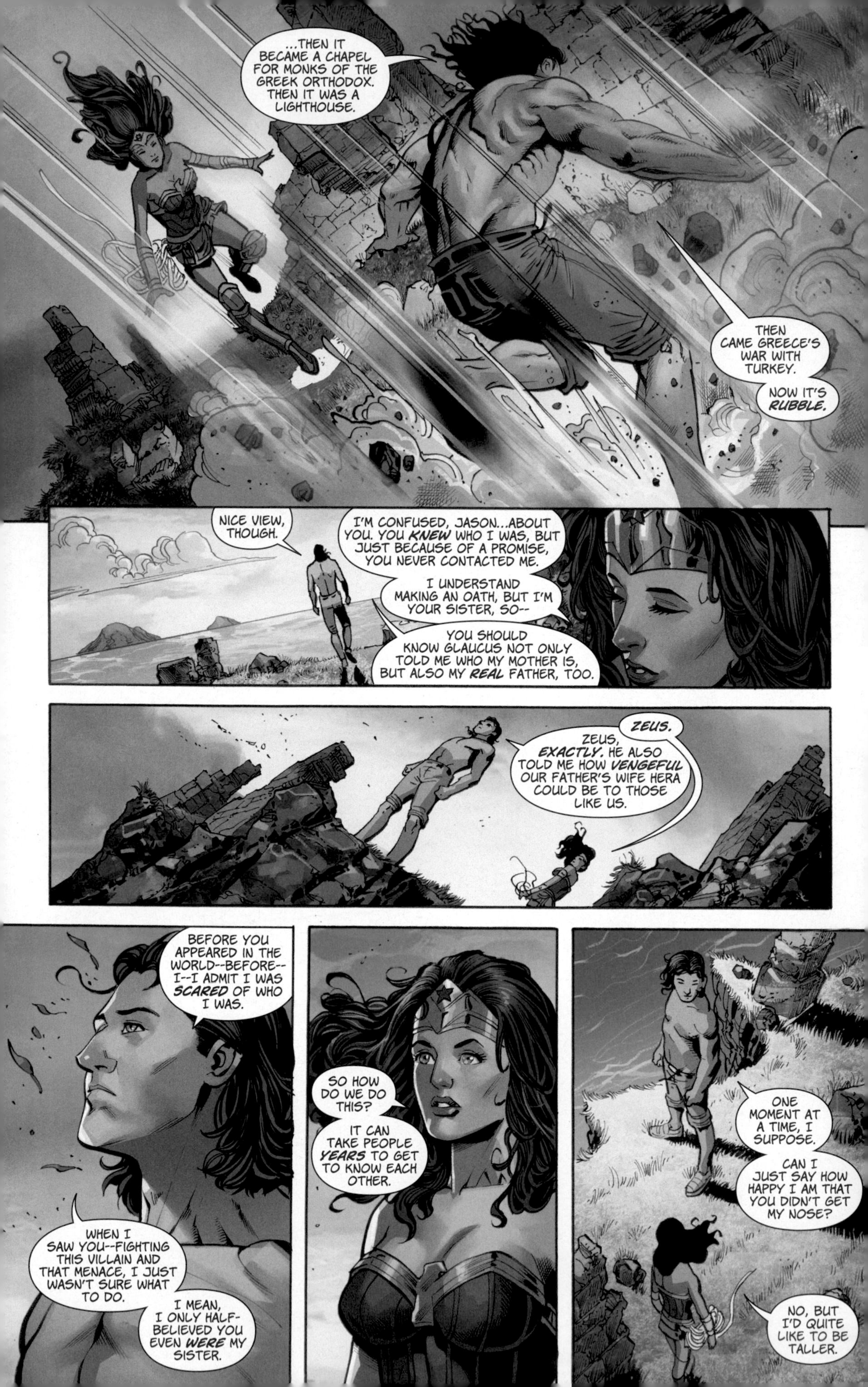

...THEN IT BECAME A CHAPEL FOR MONKS OF THE GREEK ORTHODOX. THEN IT WAS A LIGHTHOUSE.
THEN CAME GREECE'S WAR WITH TURKEY.
NOW IT'S RUBBLE.
NICE VIEW, THOUGH.
I'M CONFUSED, JASON...ABOUT YOU. YOU KNEW WHO I WAS, BUT JUST BECAUSE OF A PROMISE, YOU NEVER CONTACTED ME.
I UNDERSTAND MAKING AN OATH, BUT I'M YOUR SISTER, SO--
YOU SHOULD KNOW GLAUCUS NOT ONLY TOLD ME WHO MY MOTHER IS, BUT ALSO MY REAL FATHER, TOO.
ZEUS.
ZEUS, EXACTLY. HE ALSO TOLD ME HOW VENGEFUL OUR FATHER'S WIFE HERA COULD BE TO THOSE LIKE US.
BEFORE YOU APPEARED IN THE WORLD--BEFORE--I--I ADMIT I WAS SCARED OF WHO I WAS.
WHEN I SAW YOU--FIGHTING THIS VILLAIN AND THAT MENACE, I JUST WASN'T SURE WHAT TO DO.
I MEAN, I ONLY HALF-BELIEVED YOU EVEN WERE MY SISTER.
SO HOW DO WE DO THIS?
IT CAN TAKE PEOPLE YEARS TO GET TO KNOW EACH OTHER.
ONE MOMENT AT A TIME, I SUPPOSE.
CAN I JUST SAY HOW HAPPY I AM THAT YOU DIDN'T GET MY NOSE?
NO, BUT I'D QUITE LIKE TO BE TALLER.

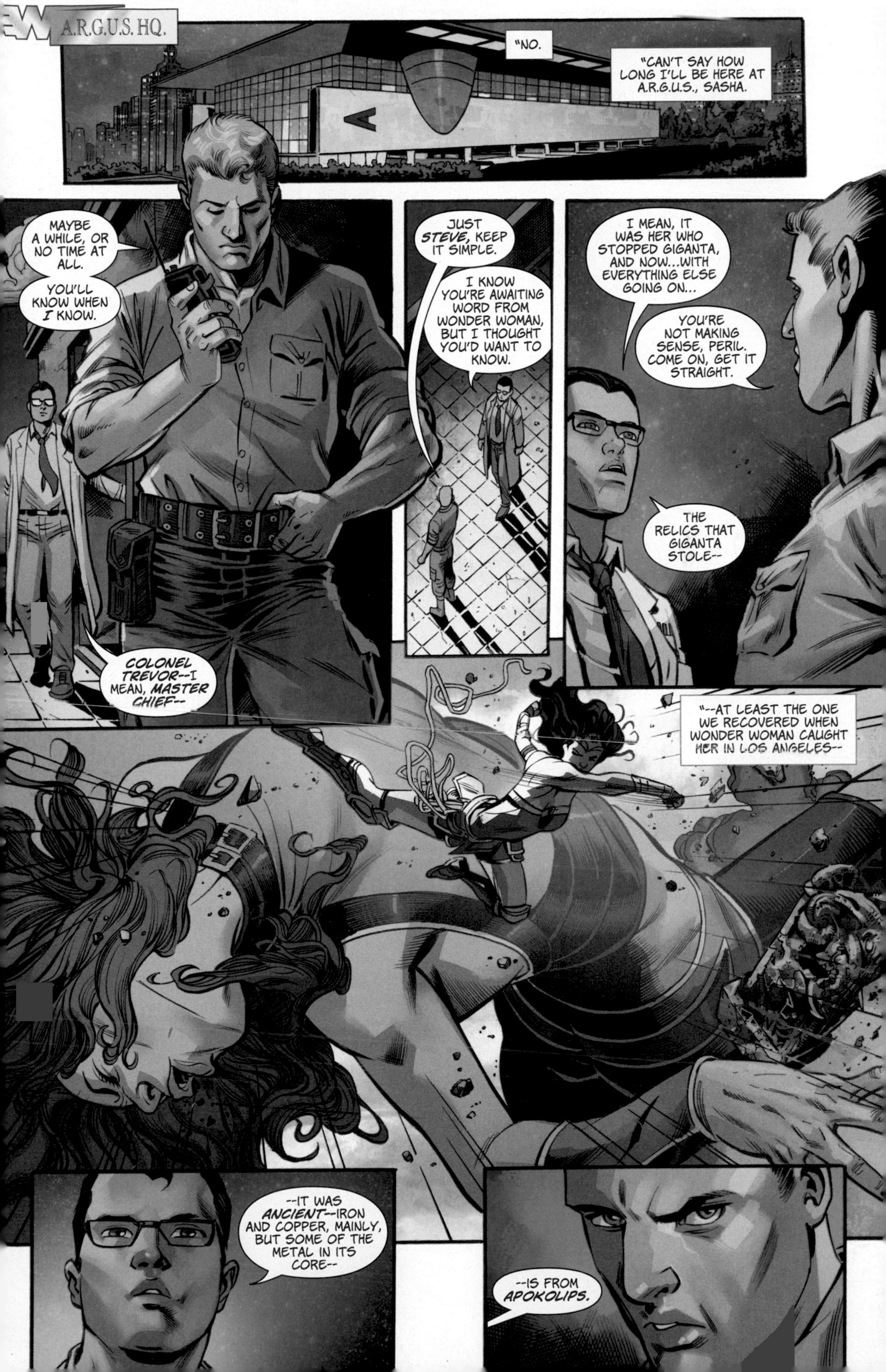
A.R.G.U.S. HQ.
"NO.
"CAN'T SAY HOW LONG I'LL BE HERE AT A.R.G.U.S., SASHA.
MAYBE A WHILE, OR NO TIME AT ALL.
YOU'LL KNOW WHEN I KNOW.
COLONEL TREVOR--I MEAN, MASTER CHIEF--
JUST STEVE, KEEP IT SIMPLE.
I KNOW YOU'RE AWAITING WORD FROM WONDER WOMAN, BUT I THOUGHT YOU'D WANT TO KNOW.
I MEAN, IT WAS HER WHO STOPPED GIGANTA, AND NOW...WITH EVERYTHING ELSE GOING ON...
YOU'RE NOT MAKING SENSE, PERIL. COME ON, GET IT STRAIGHT.
THE RELICS THAT GIGANTA STOLE--
"--AT LEAST THE ONE WE RECOVERED WHEN WONDER WOMAN CAUGHT HER IN LOS ANGELES--
--IT WAS ANCIENT--IRON AND COPPER, MAINLY, BUT SOME OF THE METAL IN ITS CORE--
--IS FROM APOKOLIPS.

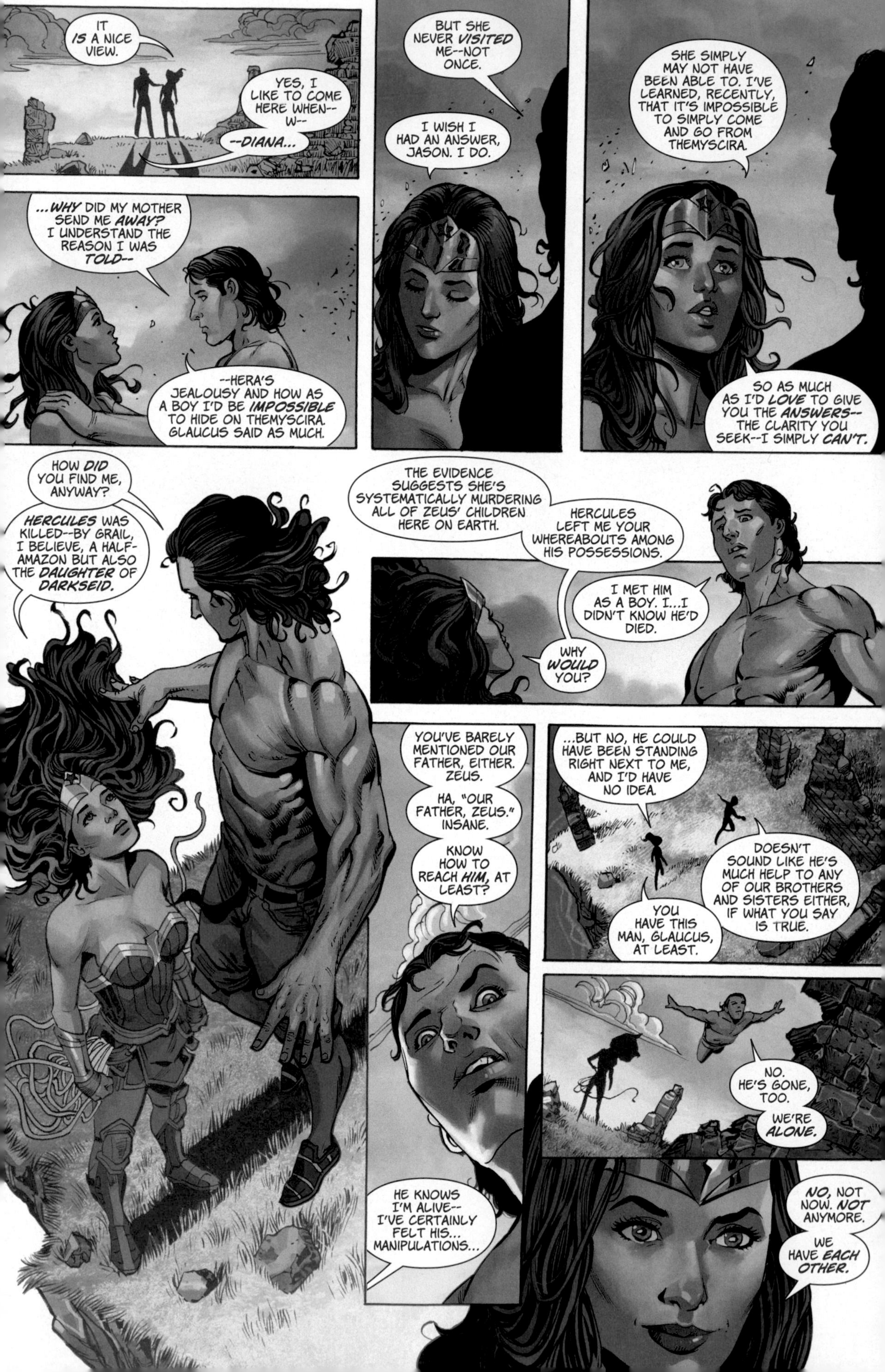
IT IS A NICE VIEW.
YES, I LIKE TO COME HERE WHEN-- W--
--DIANA...
BUT SHE NEVER VISITED ME--NOT ONCE.
I WISH I HAD AN ANSWER, JASON. I DO.
SHE SIMPLY MAY NOT HAVE BEEN ABLE TO. I'VE LEARNED, RECENTLY, THAT IT'S IMPOSSIBLE TO SIMPLY COME AND GO FROM THEMYSCIRA.
...WHY DID MY MOTHER SEND ME AWAY? I UNDERSTAND THE REASON I WAS TOLD--
--HERA'S JEALOUSY AND HOW AS A BOY I'D BE IMPOSSIBLE TO HIDE ON THEMYSCIRA. GLAUCUS SAID AS MUCH.
SO AS MUCH AS I'D LOVE TO GIVE YOU THE ANSWERS-- THE CLARITY YOU SEEK--I SIMPLY CAN'T.
HOW DID YOU FIND ME, ANYWAY?
HERCULES WAS KILLED--BY GRAIL, I BELIEVE, A HALF-AMAZON BUT ALSO THE DAUGHTER OF DARKSEID.
THE EVIDENCE SUGGESTS SHE'S SYSTEMATICALLY MURDERING ALL OF ZEUS' CHILDREN HERE ON EARTH.
HERCULES LEFT ME YOUR WHEREABOUTS AMONG HIS POSSESSIONS.
I MET HIM AS A BOY. I...I DIDN'T KNOW HE'D DIED.
WHY WOULD YOU?
YOU'VE BARELY MENTIONED OUR FATHER, EITHER. ZEUS.
HA, "OUR FATHER, ZEUS." INSANE.
KNOW HOW TO REACH HIM, AT LEAST?
HE KNOWS I'M ALIVE-- I'VE CERTAINLY FELT HIS... MANIPULATIONS...
...BUT NO, HE COULD HAVE BEEN STANDING RIGHT NEXT TO ME, AND I'D HAVE NO IDEA.
YOU HAVE THIS MAN, GLAUCUS, AT LEAST.
DOESN'T SOUND LIKE HE'S MUCH HELP TO ANY OF OUR BROTHERS AND SISTERS EITHER, IF WHAT YOU SAY IS TRUE.
NO. HE'S GONE, TOO.
WE'RE ALONE.
NO, NOT NOW. NOT ANYMORE.
WE HAVE EACH OTHER.

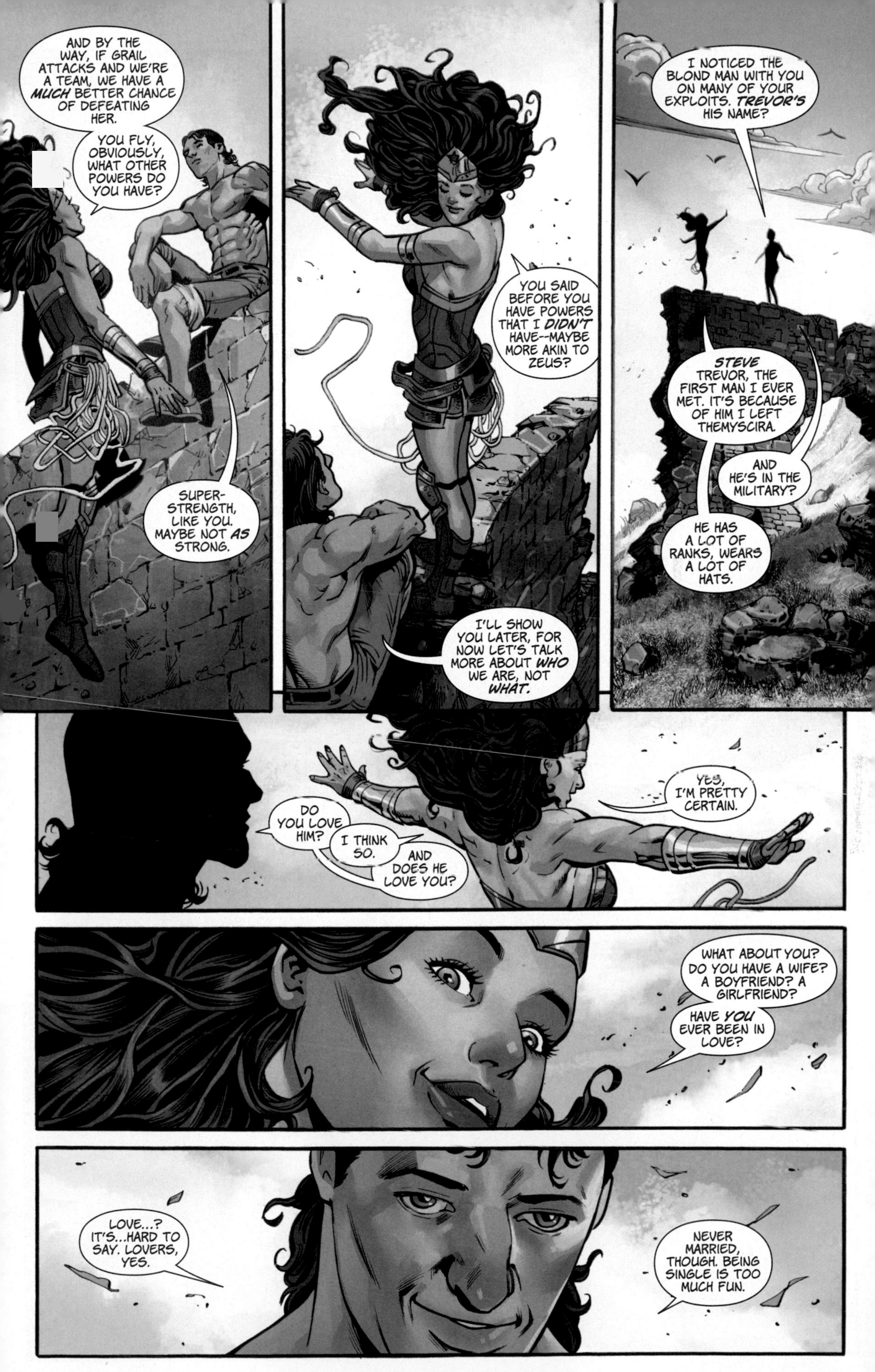
AND BY THE WAY, IF GRAIL ATTACKS AND WE'RE A TEAM, WE HAVE A *MUCH* BETTER CHANCE OF DEFEATING HER.
YOU FLY, OBVIOUSLY, WHAT OTHER POWERS DO YOU HAVE?
SUPER-STRENGTH, LIKE YOU. MAYBE NOT *AS* STRONG.
YOU SAID BEFORE YOU HAVE POWERS THAT I *DIDN'T* HAVE--MAYBE MORE AKIN TO ZEUS?
I'LL SHOW YOU LATER, FOR NOW LET'S TALK MORE ABOUT *WHO* WE ARE, NOT *WHAT.*
I NOTICED THE BLOND MAN WITH YOU ON MANY OF YOUR EXPLOITS. *TREVOR'S* HIS NAME?
STEVE TREVOR, THE FIRST MAN I EVER MET. IT'S BECAUSE OF HIM I LEFT THEMYSCIRA.
AND HE'S IN THE MILITARY?
HE HAS A LOT OF RANKS, WEARS A LOT OF HATS.
DO YOU LOVE HIM?
I THINK SO.
AND DOES HE LOVE YOU?
YES, I'M PRETTY CERTAIN.
WHAT ABOUT YOU? DO YOU HAVE A WIFE? A BOYFRIEND? A GIRLFRIEND?
HAVE *YOU* EVER BEEN IN LOVE?
LOVE...? IT'S...HARD TO SAY. LOVERS, YES.
NEVER MARRIED, THOUGH. BEING SINGLE IS TOO MUCH FUN.

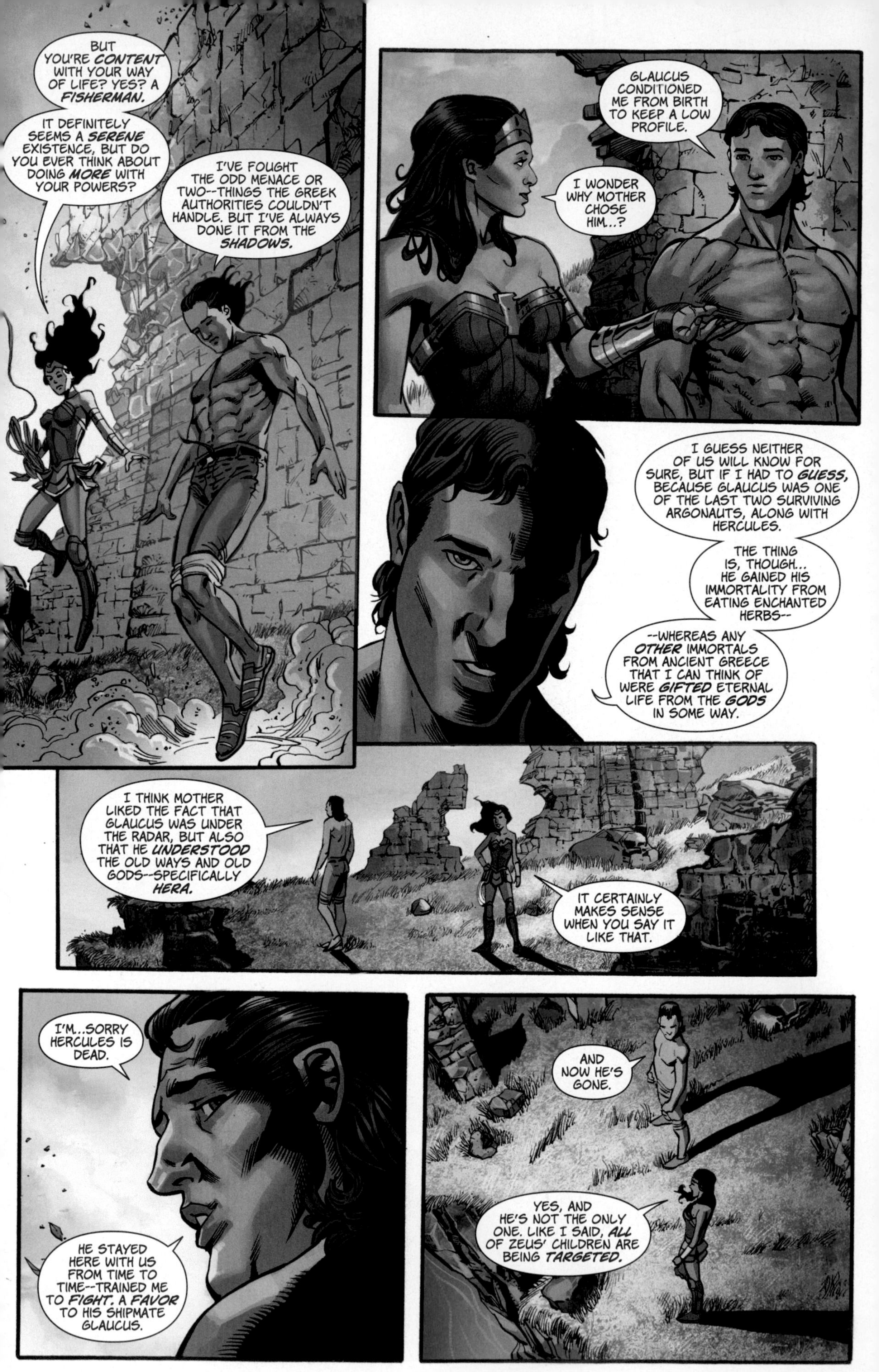
BUT YOU'RE CONTENT WITH YOUR WAY OF LIFE? YES? A FISHERMAN.
IT DEFINITELY SEEMS A SERENE EXISTENCE, BUT DO YOU EVER THINK ABOUT DOING MORE WITH YOUR POWERS?
I'VE FOUGHT THE ODD MENACE OR TWO--THINGS THE GREEK AUTHORITIES COULDN'T HANDLE. BUT I'VE ALWAYS DONE IT FROM THE SHADOWS.
GLAUCUS CONDITIONED ME FROM BIRTH TO KEEP A LOW PROFILE.
I WONDER WHY MOTHER CHOSE HIM...?
I GUESS NEITHER OF US WILL KNOW FOR SURE, BUT IF I HAD TO GUESS, BECAUSE GLAUCUS WAS ONE OF THE LAST TWO SURVIVING ARGONAUTS, ALONG WITH HERCULES.
THE THING IS, THOUGH... HE GAINED HIS IMMORTALITY FROM EATING ENCHANTED HERBS--
--WHEREAS ANY OTHER IMMORTALS FROM ANCIENT GREECE THAT I CAN THINK OF WERE GIFTED ETERNAL LIFE FROM THE GODS IN SOME WAY.
I THINK MOTHER LIKED THE FACT THAT GLAUCUS WAS UNDER THE RADAR, BUT ALSO THAT HE UNDERSTOOD THE OLD WAYS AND OLD GODS--SPECIFICALLY HERA.
IT CERTAINLY MAKES SENSE WHEN YOU SAY IT LIKE THAT.
I'M...SORRY HERCULES IS DEAD.
HE STAYED HERE WITH US FROM TIME TO TIME--TRAINED ME TO FIGHT. A FAVOR TO HIS SHIPMATE GLAUCUS.
AND NOW HE'S GONE.
YES, AND HE'S NOT THE ONLY ONE. LIKE I SAID, ALL OF ZEUS' CHILDREN ARE BEING TARGETED.

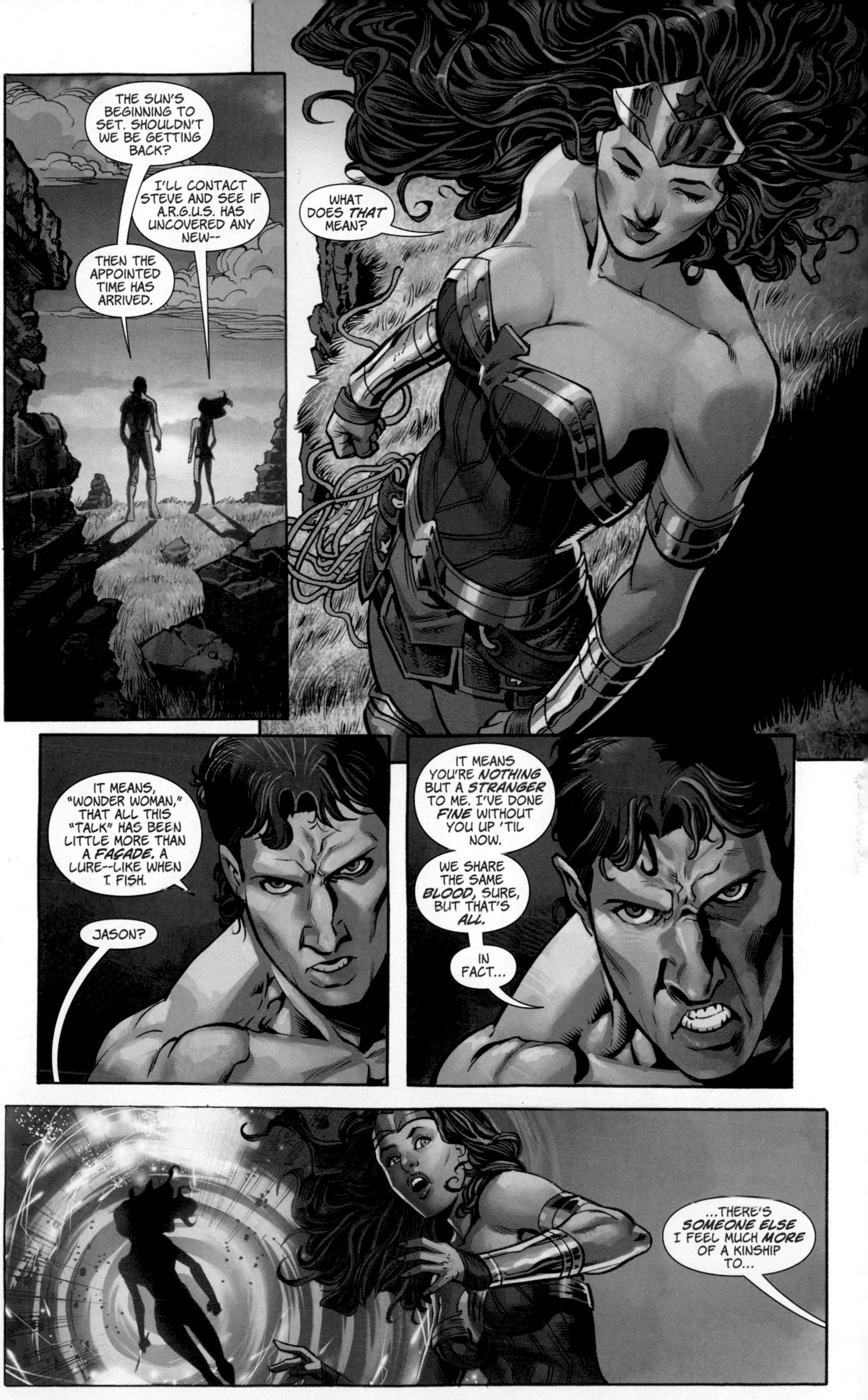
THE SUN'S BEGINNING TO SET. SHOULDN'T WE BE GETTING BACK?
I'LL CONTACT STEVE AND SEE IF A.R.G.U.S. HAS UNCOVERED ANY NEW--
THEN THE APPOINTED TIME HAS ARRIVED.
WHAT DOES THAT MEAN?
IT MEANS, "WONDER WOMAN," THAT ALL THIS "TALK" HAS BEEN LITTLE MORE THAN A FAÇADE. A LURE--LIKE WHEN I FISH.
JASON?
IT MEANS YOU'RE NOTHING BUT A STRANGER TO ME. I'VE DONE FINE WITHOUT YOU UP 'TIL NOW.
WE SHARE THE SAME BLOOD, SURE, BUT THAT'S ALL.
IN FACT...
...THERE'S SOMEONE ELSE I FEEL MUCH MORE OF A KINSHIP TO...

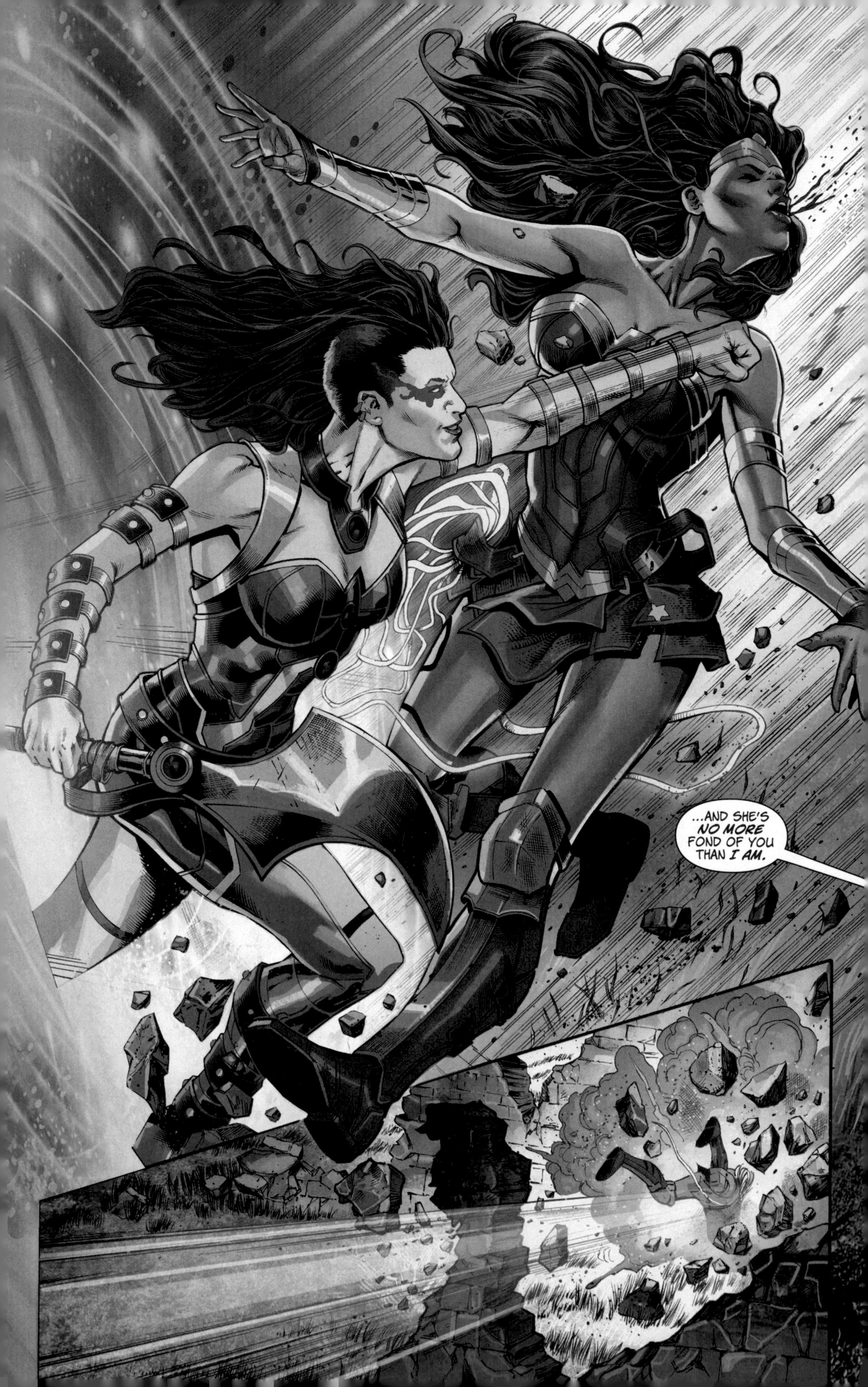
...AND SHE'S *NO MORE* FOND OF YOU THAN *I AM.*

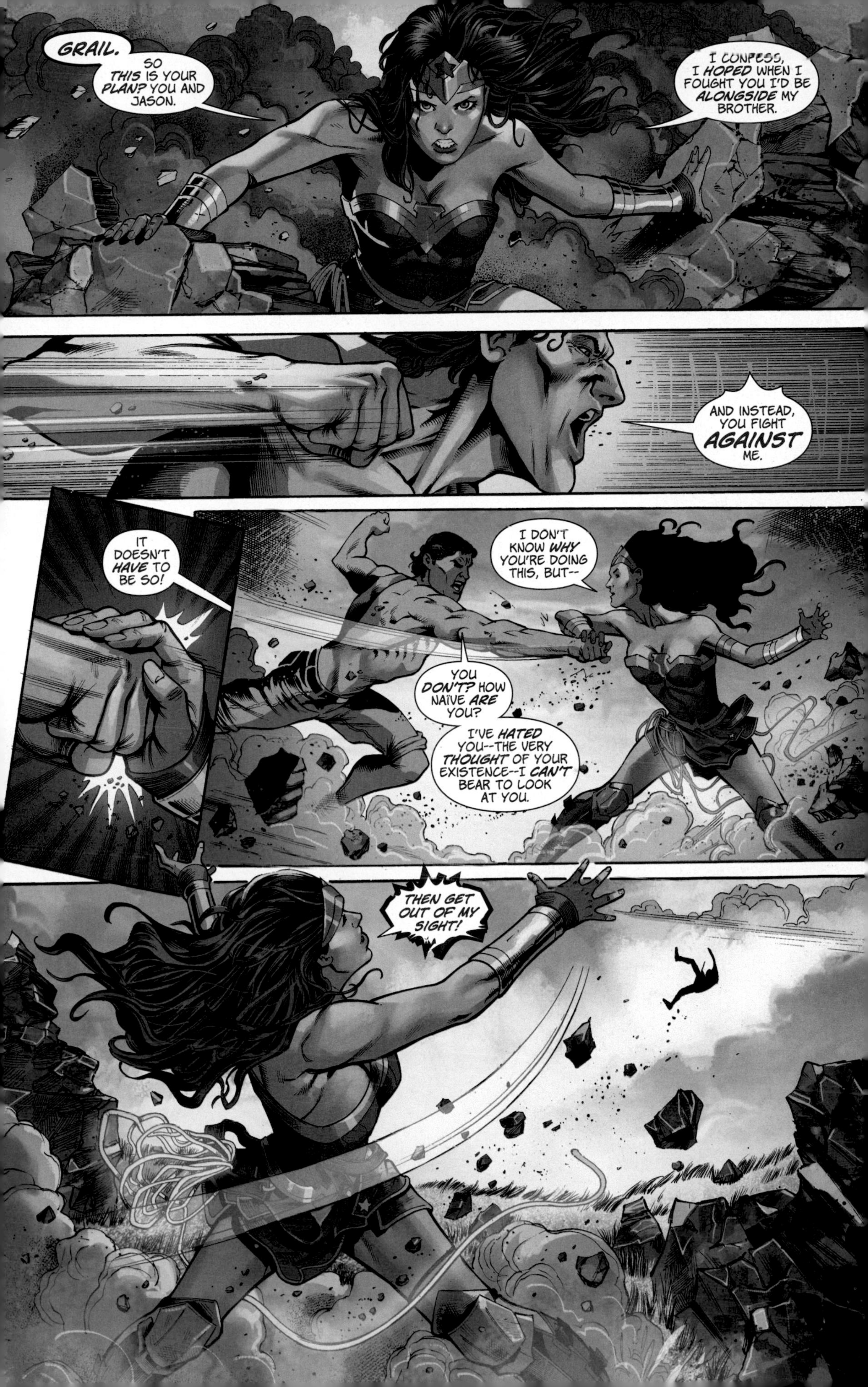
GRAIL.
SO THIS IS YOUR PLAN? YOU AND JASON.
I CONFESS, I HOPED WHEN I FOUGHT YOU I'D BE ALONGSIDE MY BROTHER.
AND INSTEAD, YOU FIGHT AGAINST ME.
IT DOESN'T HAVE TO BE SO!
I DON'T KNOW WHY YOU'RE DOING THIS, BUT--
YOU DON'T? HOW NAÏVE ARE YOU?
I'VE HATED YOU--THE VERY THOUGHT OF YOUR EXISTENCE--I CAN'T BEAR TO LOOK AT YOU.
THEN GET OUT OF MY SIGHT!

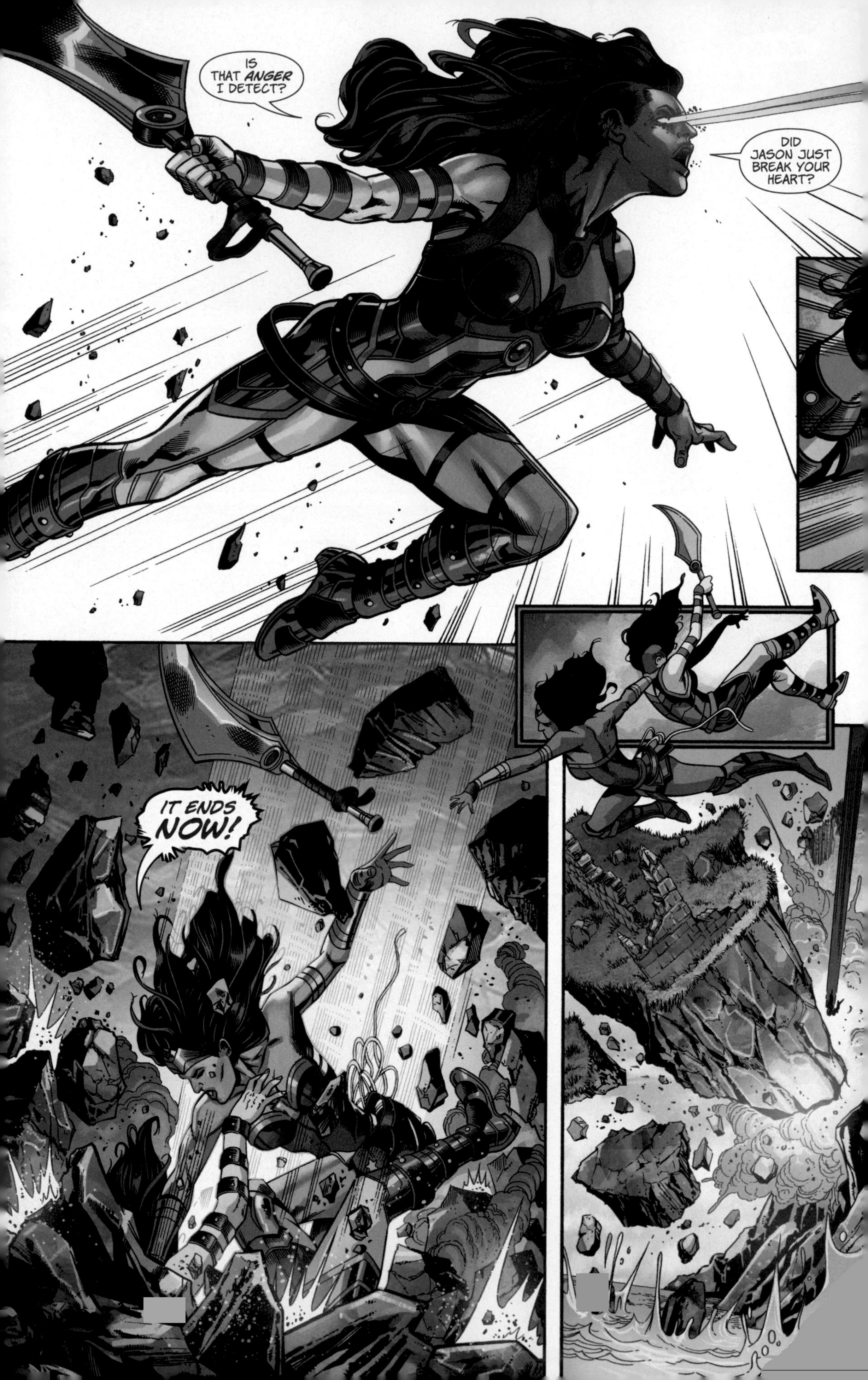
IS THAT ANGER I DETECT?
DID JASON JUST BREAK YOUR HEART?
IT ENDS NOW!

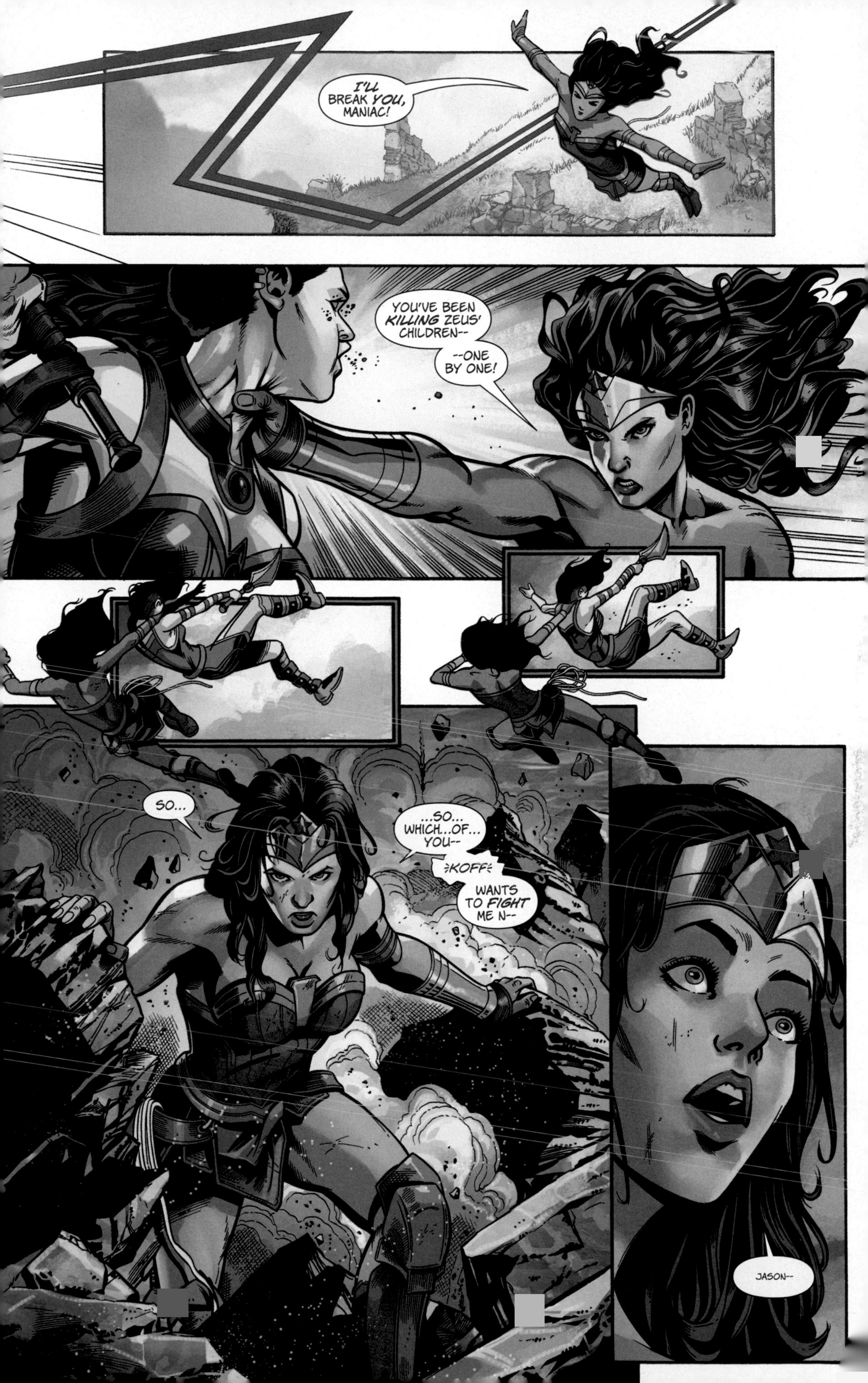
I'LL BREAK YOU, MANIAC!
YOU'VE BEEN KILLING ZEUS' CHILDREN--
--ONE BY ONE!
SO...
...SO... WHICH...OF... YOU--
KOFF
WANTS TO FIGHT ME N--
JASON--

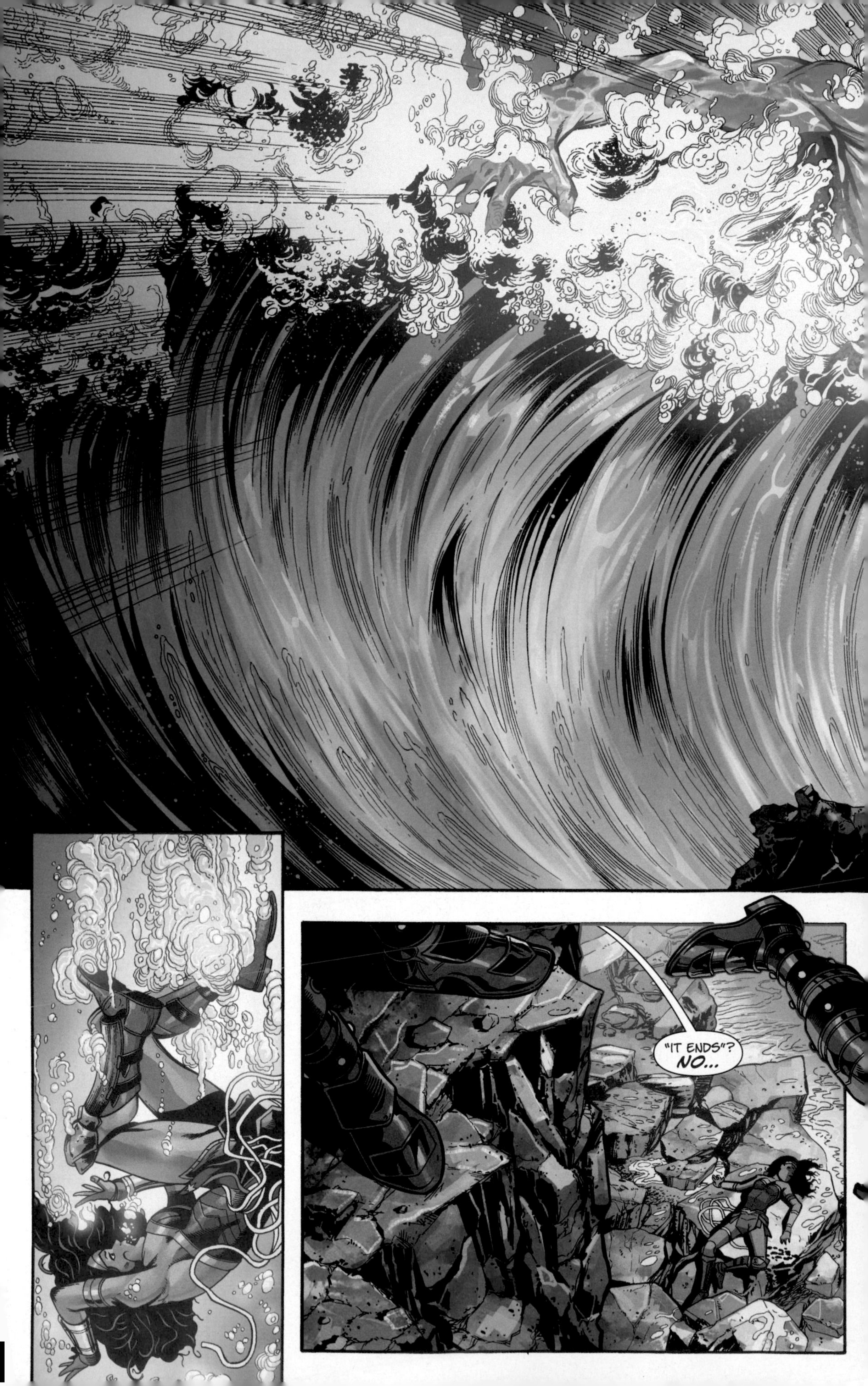
"IT ENDS"? NO...

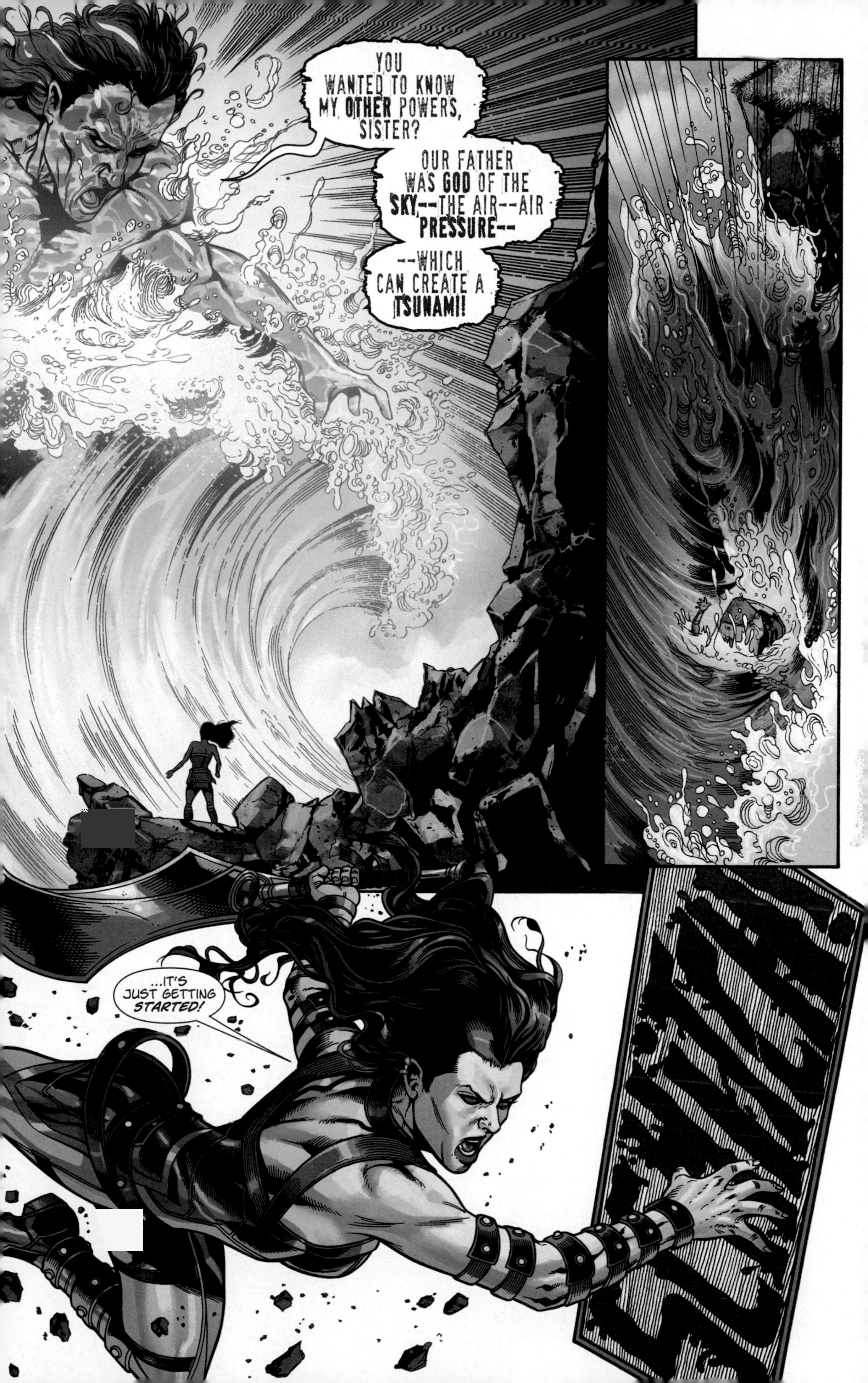
YOU WANTED TO KNOW MY OTHER POWERS, SISTER?
OUR FATHER WAS GOD OF THE SKY--THE AIR--AIR PRESSURE--
--WHICH CAN CREATE A TSUNAMI!
...IT'S JUST GETTING STARTED!

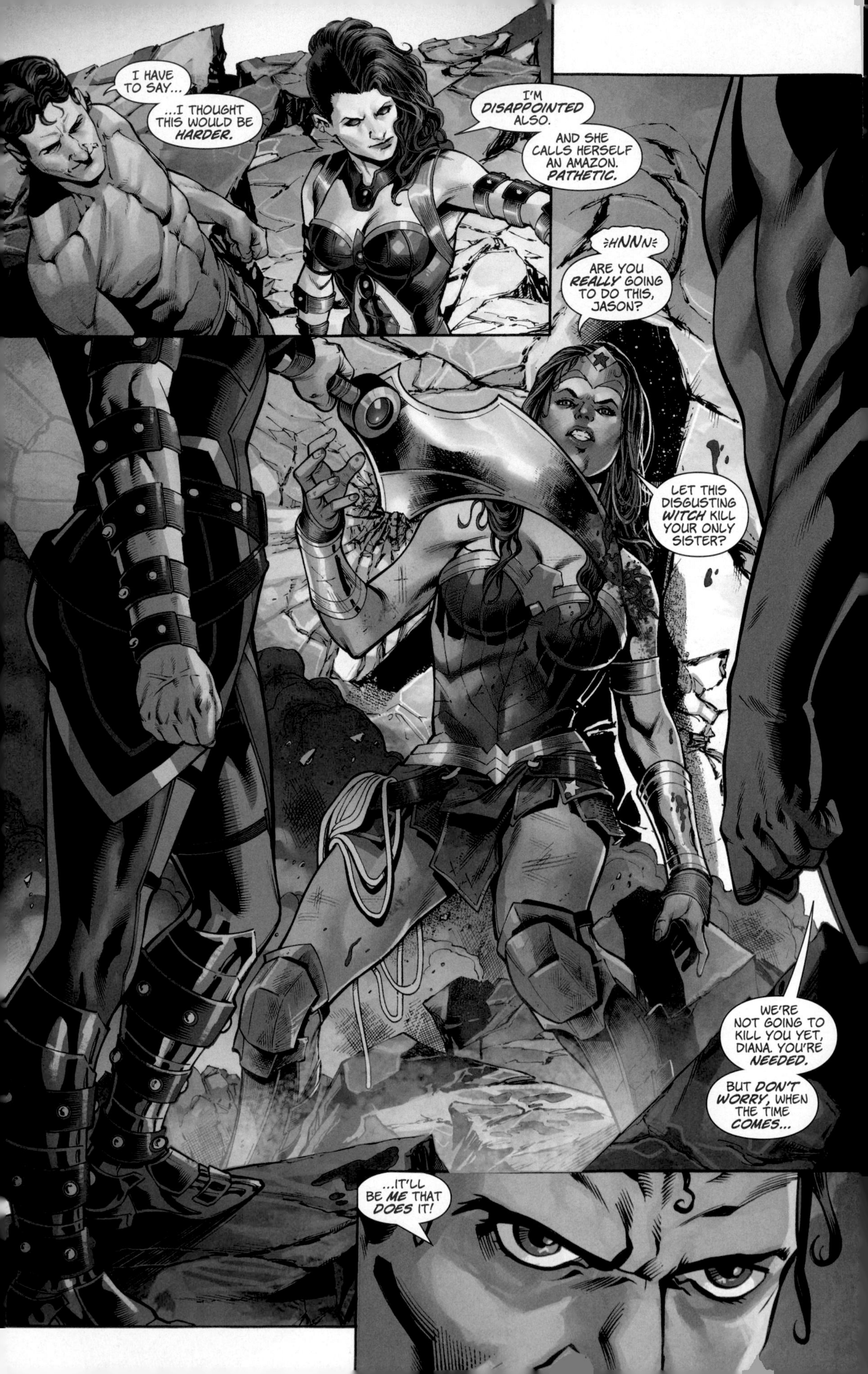

I HAVE TO SAY...
...I THOUGHT THIS WOULD BE HARDER.
I'M DISAPPOINTED ALSO.
AND SHE CALLS HERSELF AN AMAZON. PATHETIC.
HNNN
ARE YOU REALLY GOING TO DO THIS, JASON?
LET THIS DISGUSTING WITCH KILL YOUR ONLY SISTER?
WE'RE NOT GOING TO KILL YOU YET, DIANA. YOU'RE NEEDED.
BUT DON'T WORRY, WHEN THE TIME COMES...
...IT'LL BE ME THAT DOES IT!

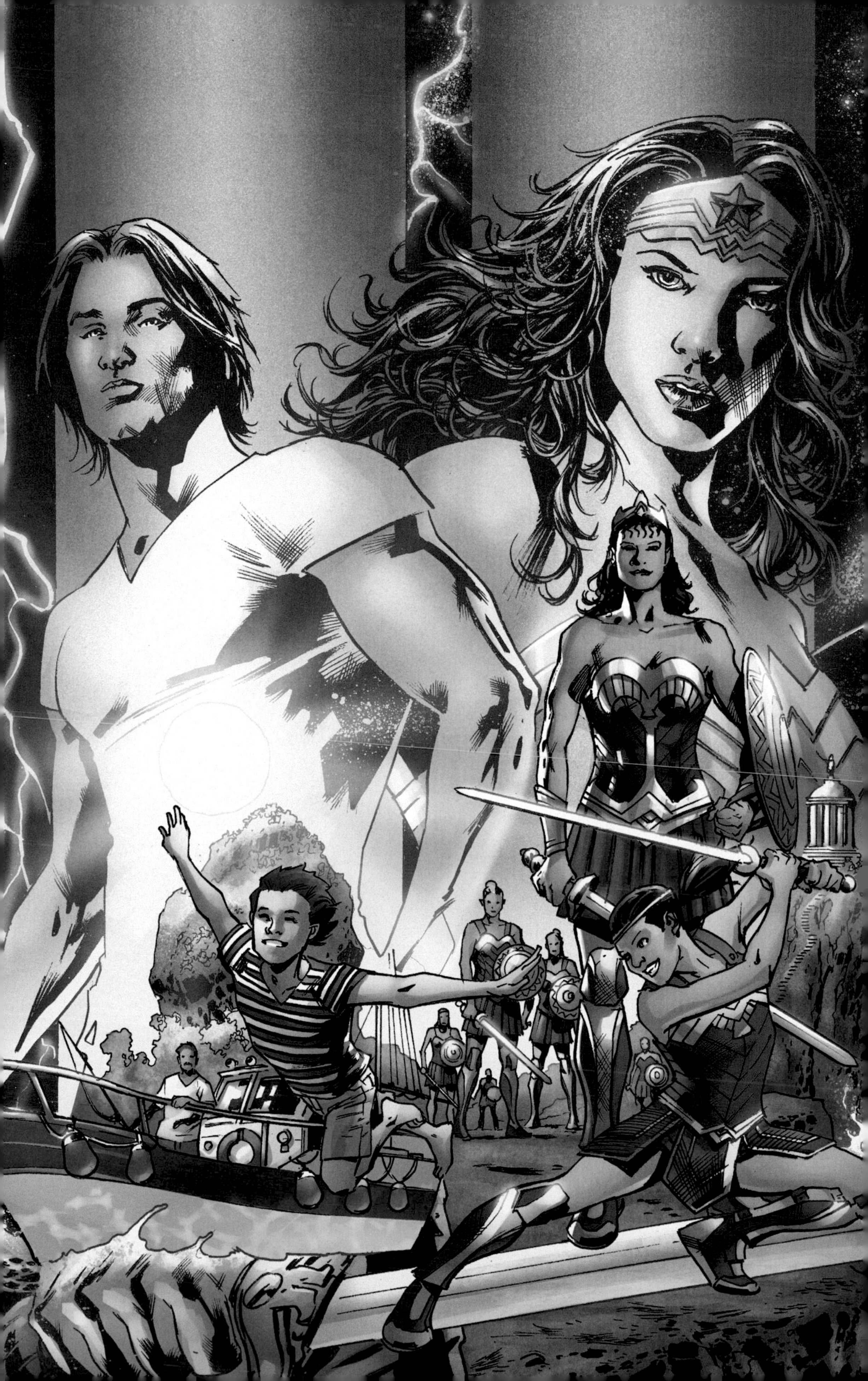

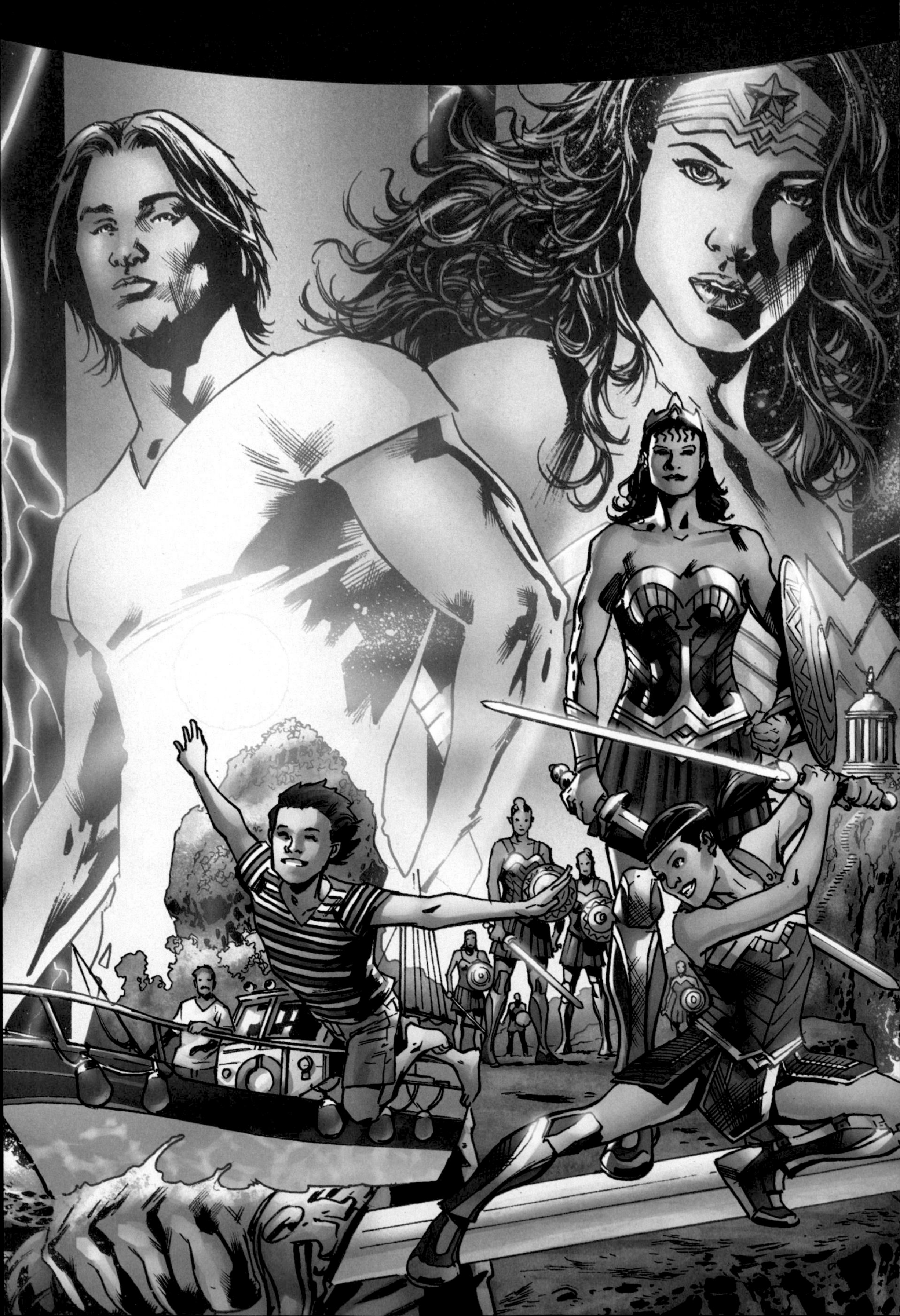

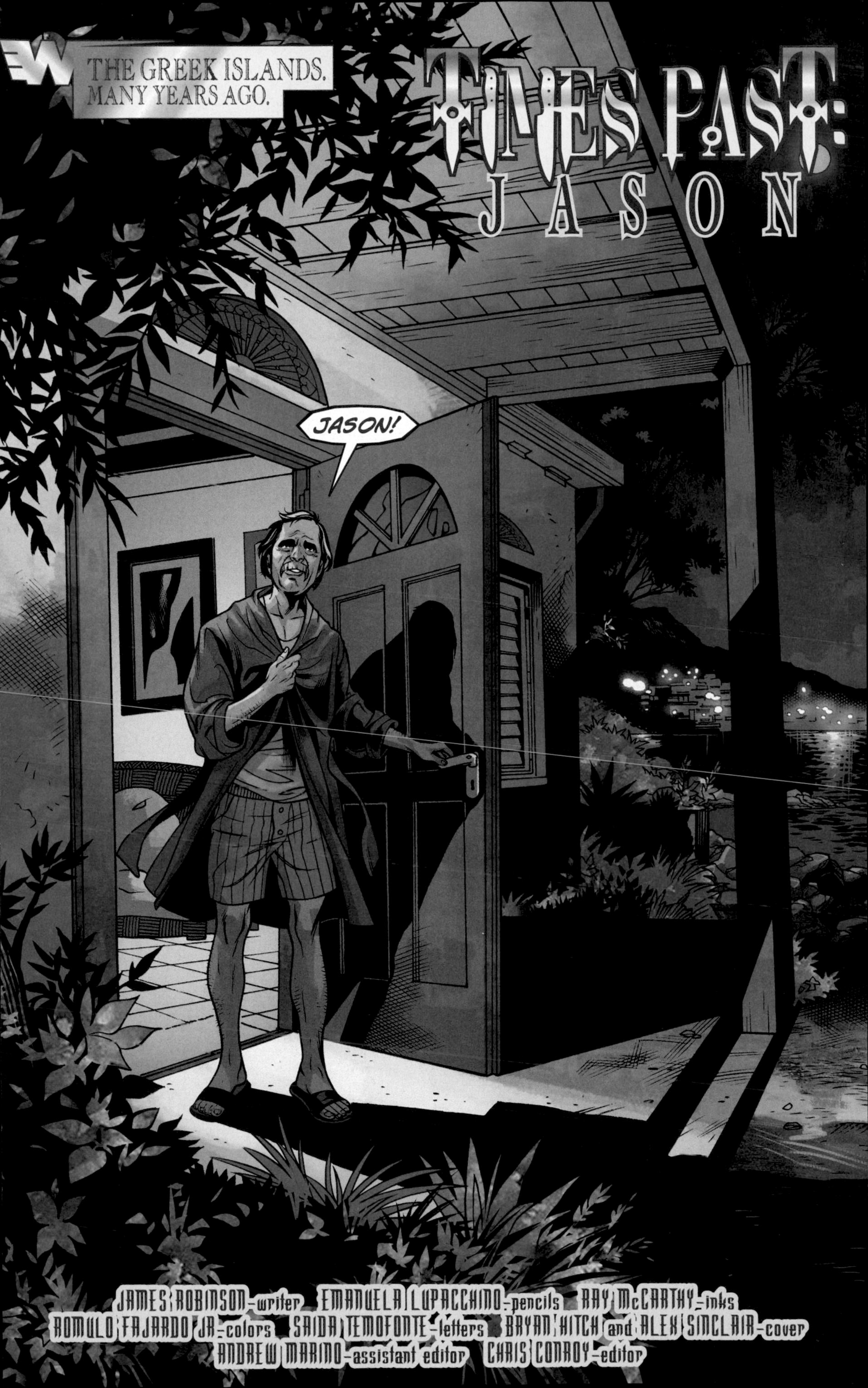

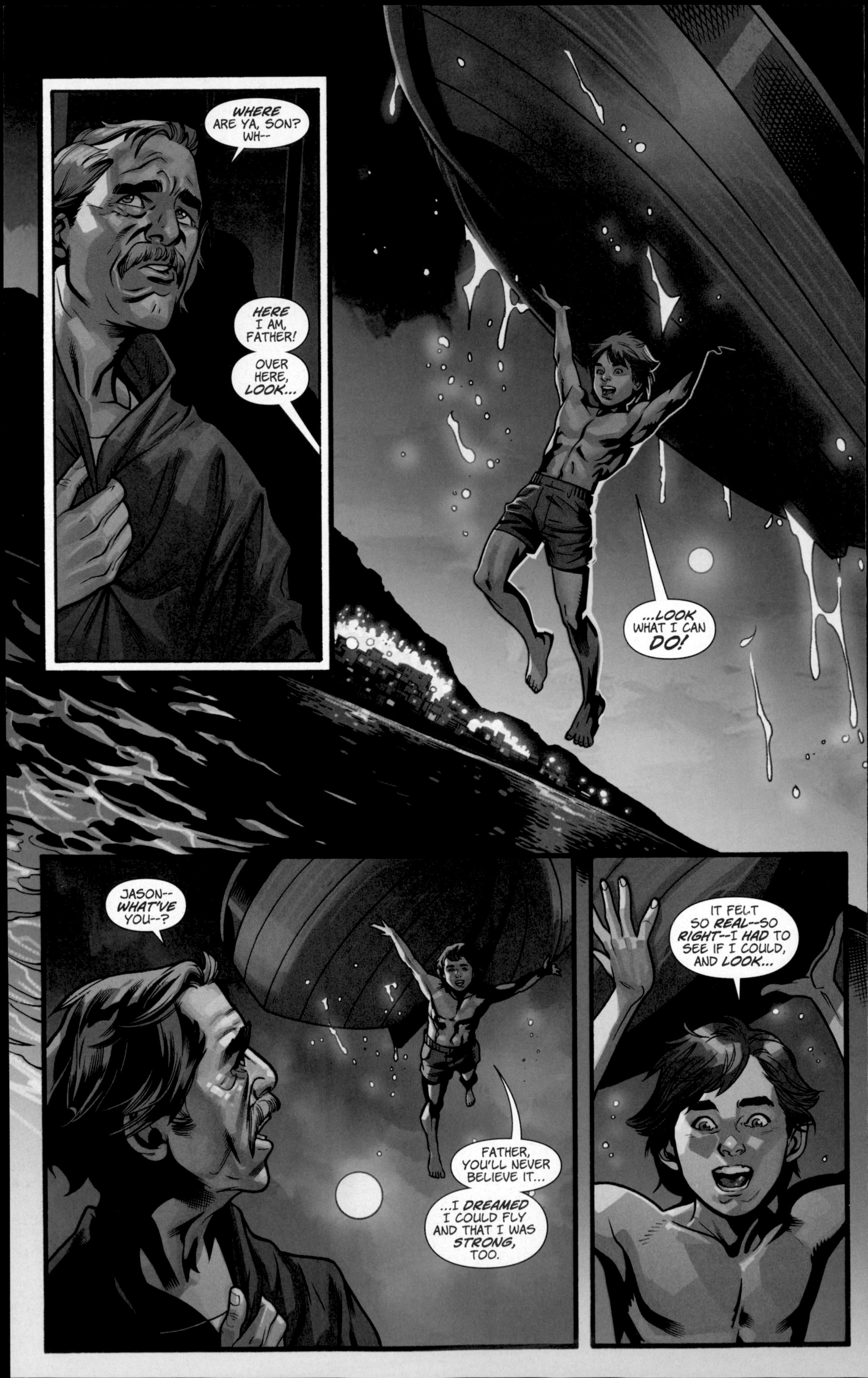
WHERE ARE YA, SON? WH--
HERE I AM, FATHER!
OVER HERE, LOOK...
...LOOK WHAT I CAN DO!
JASON-- WHAT'VE YOU--?
FATHER, YOU'LL NEVER BELIEVE IT...
...I DREAMED I COULD FLY AND THAT I WAS STRONG, TOO.
IT FELT SO REAL--SO RIGHT--I HAD TO SEE IF I COULD, AND LOOK...

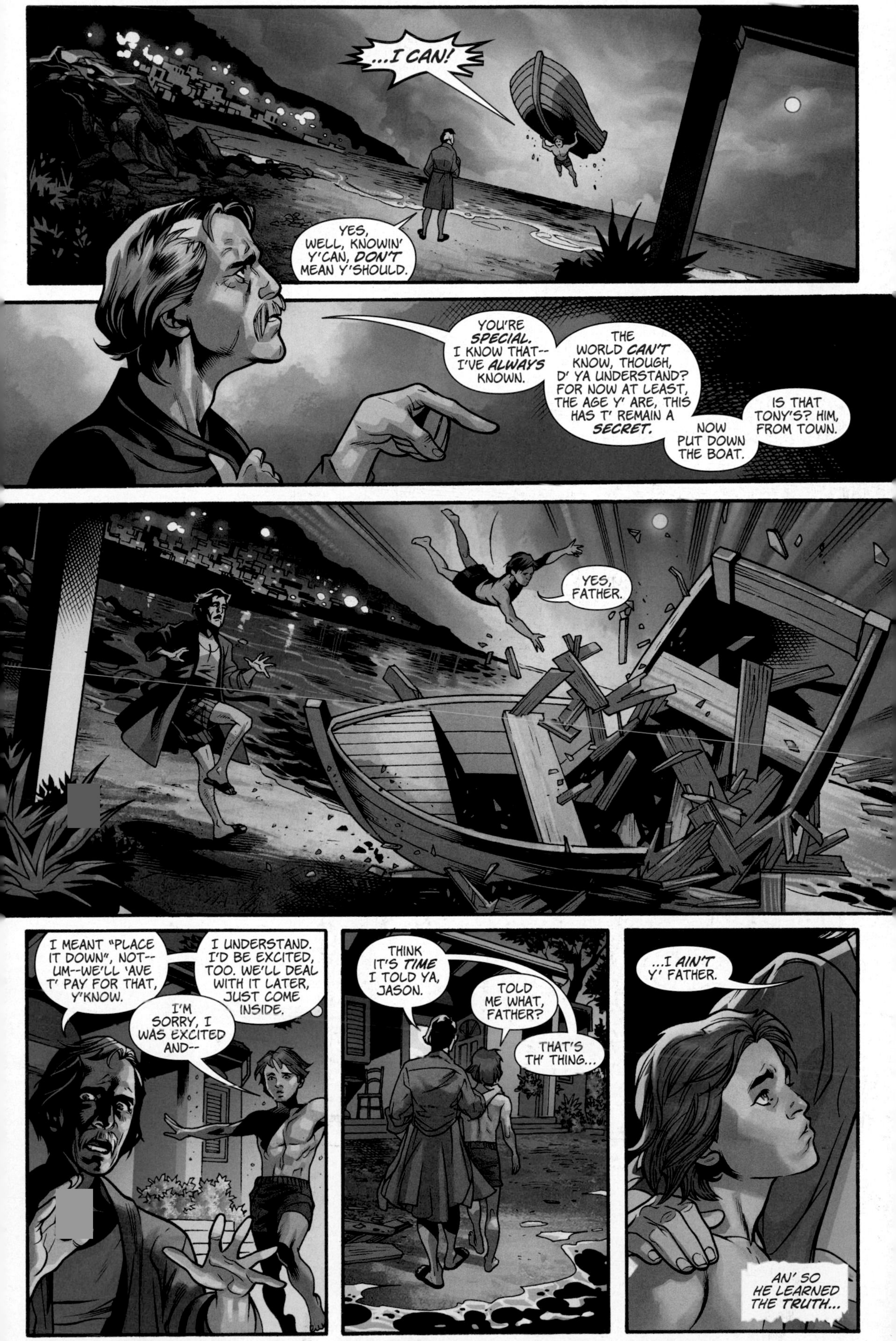
...I CAN!
YES, WELL, KNOWIN' Y'CAN, DON'T MEAN Y'SHOULD.
YOU'RE SPECIAL. I KNOW THAT-- I'VE ALWAYS KNOWN.
THE WORLD CAN'T KNOW, THOUGH, D' YA UNDERSTAND? FOR NOW AT LEAST, THE AGE Y' ARE, THIS HAS T' REMAIN A SECRET.
NOW PUT DOWN THE BOAT.
IS THAT TONY'S? HIM, FROM TOWN.
YES, FATHER.
I MEANT "PLACE IT DOWN", NOT-- UM--WE'LL 'AVE T' PAY FOR THAT, Y'KNOW.
I'M SORRY, I WAS EXCITED AND--
I UNDERSTAND. I'D BE EXCITED, TOO. WE'LL DEAL WITH IT LATER, JUST COME INSIDE.
THINK IT'S TIME I TOLD YA, JASON.
TOLD ME WHAT, FATHER?
THAT'S TH' THING...
...I AIN'T Y' FATHER.
AN' SO HE LEARNED THE TRUTH...

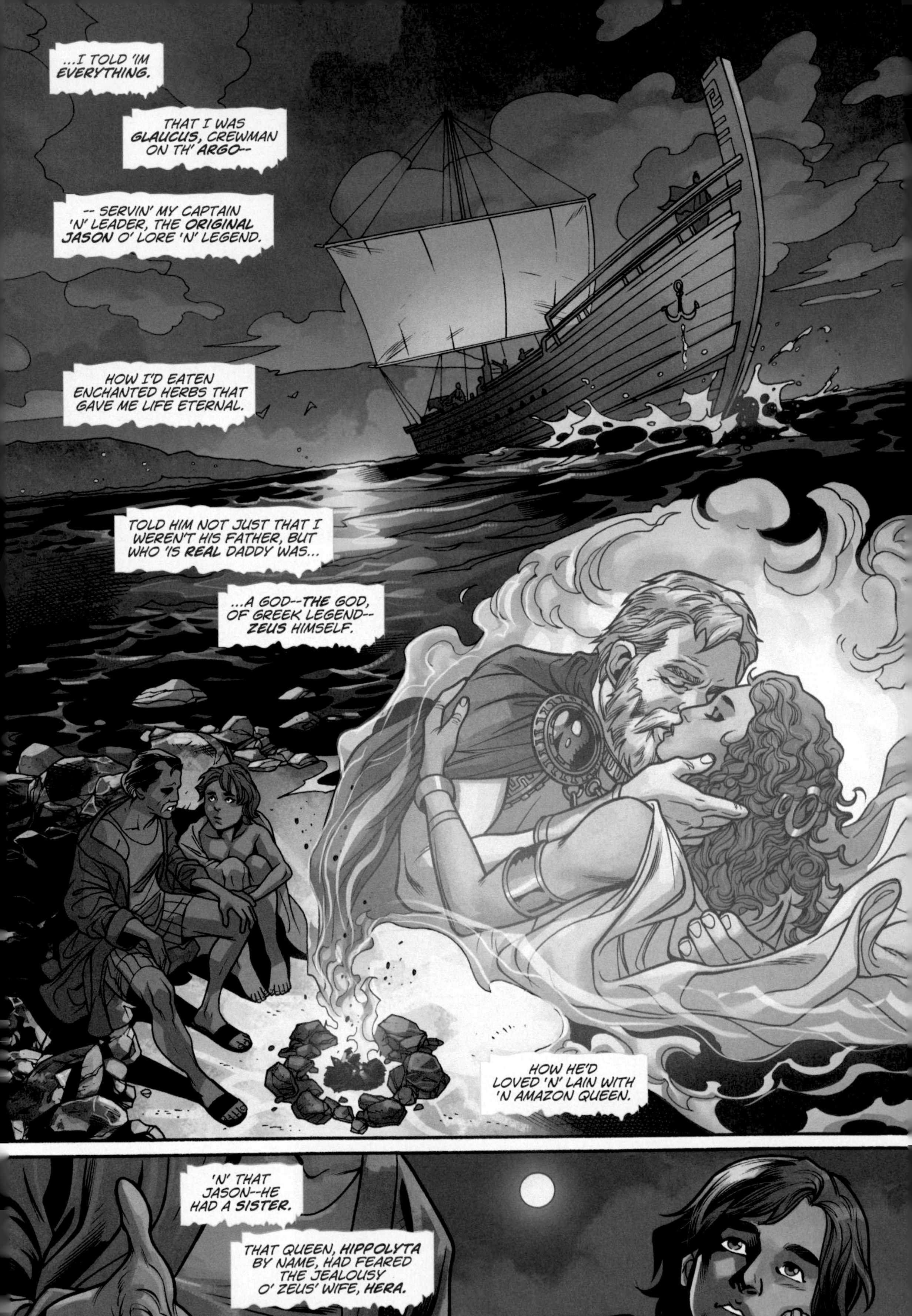
...I TOLD 'IM EVERYTHING.
THAT I WAS GLAUCUS, CREWMAN ON TH' ARGO--
-- SERVIN' MY CAPTAIN 'N' LEADER, THE ORIGINAL JASON O' LORE 'N' LEGEND.
HOW I'D EATEN ENCHANTED HERBS THAT GAVE ME LIFE ETERNAL.
TOLD HIM NOT JUST THAT I WEREN'T HIS FATHER, BUT WHO 'IS REAL DADDY WAS...
...A GOD--THE GOD, OF GREEK LEGEND-- ZEUS HIMSELF.
HOW HE'D LOVED 'N' LAIN WITH 'N AMAZON QUEEN.

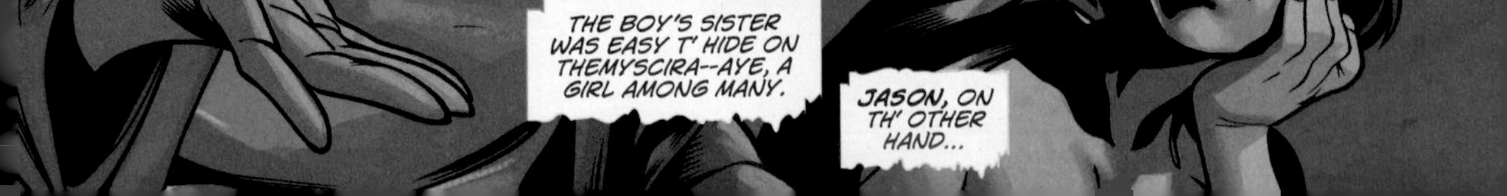
'N' THAT JASON--HE HAD A SISTER.
THAT QUEEN, HIPPOLYTA BY NAME, HAD FEARED THE JEALOUSY O' ZEUS' WIFE, HERA.
THE BOY'S SISTER WAS EASY T' HIDE ON THEMYSCIRA--AYE, A GIRL AMONG MANY.
JASON, ON TH' OTHER HAND...

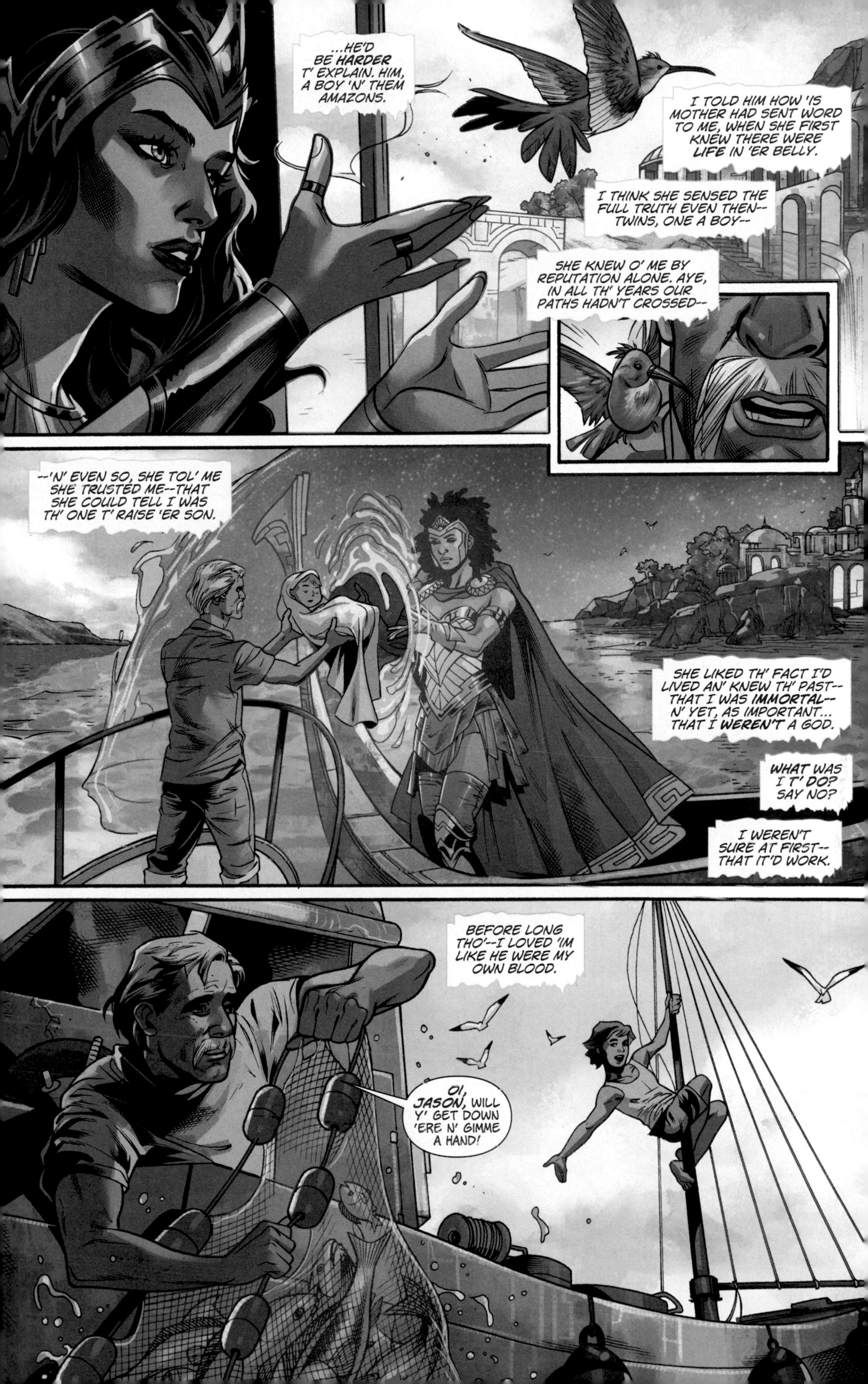
...HE'D BE HARDER T' EXPLAIN. HIM, A BOY 'N' THEM AMAZONS.
I TOLD HIM HOW 'IS MOTHER HAD SENT WORD TO ME, WHEN SHE FIRST KNEW THERE WERE LIFE IN 'ER BELLY.
I THINK SHE SENSED THE FULL TRUTH EVEN THEN--TWINS, ONE A BOY--
SHE KNEW O' ME BY REPUTATION ALONE. AYE, IN ALL TH' YEARS OUR PATHS HADN'T CROSSED--
--'N' EVEN SO, SHE TOL' ME SHE TRUSTED ME--THAT SHE COULD TELL I WAS TH' ONE T' RAISE 'ER SON.
SHE LIKED TH' FACT I'D LIVED AN' KNEW TH' PAST--THAT I WAS IMMORTAL--N' YET, AS IMPORTANT... THAT I WEREN'T A GOD.
WHAT WAS I T' DO? SAY NO?
I WEREN'T SURE AT FIRST--THAT IT'D WORK.
BEFORE LONG THO'--I LOVED 'IM LIKE HE WERE MY OWN BLOOD.
OI, JASON, WILL Y' GET DOWN 'ERE N' GIMME A HAND!

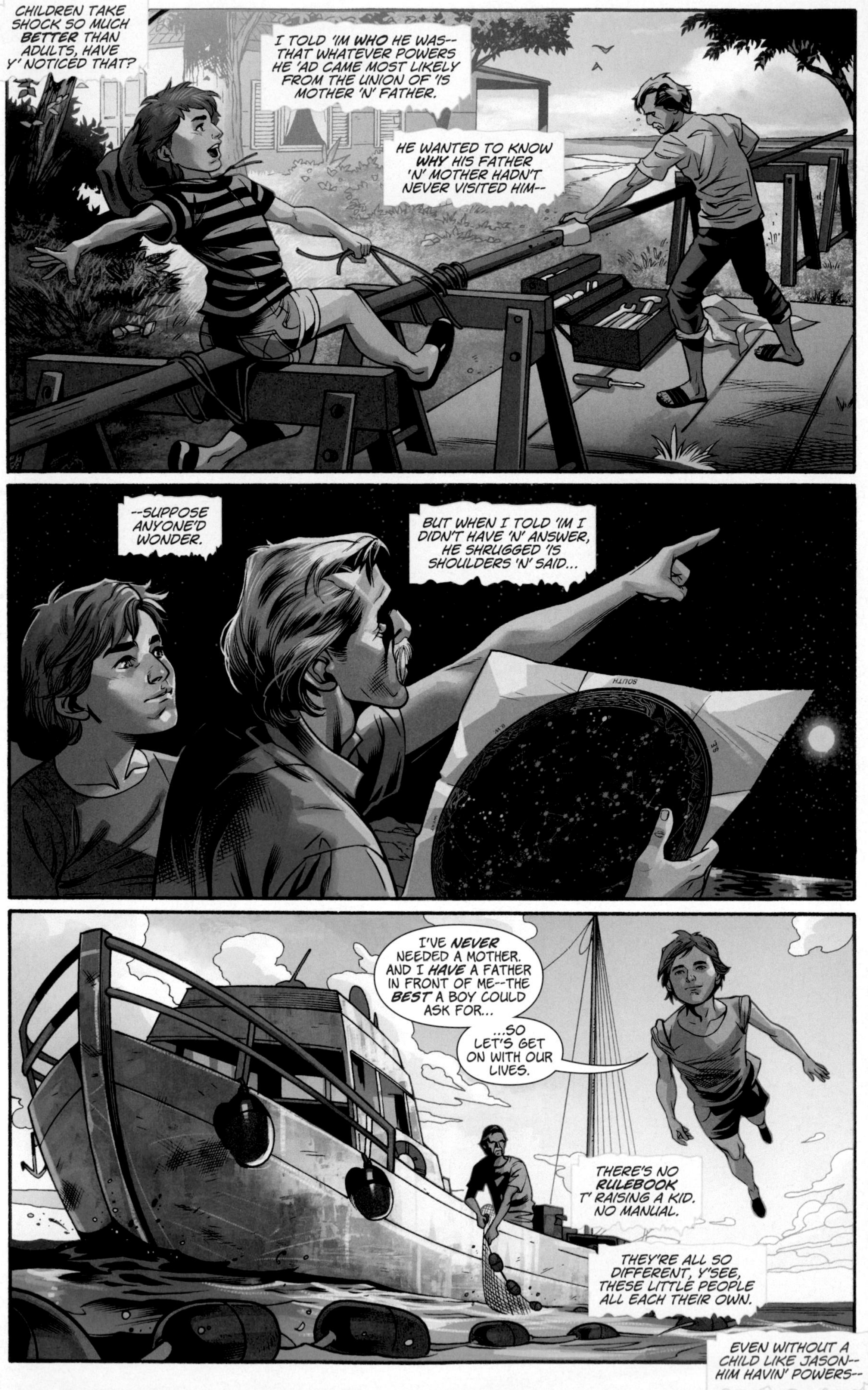
CHILDREN TAKE SHOCK SO MUCH BETTER THAN ADULTS, HAVE Y' NOTICED THAT?
I TOLD 'IM WHO HE WAS-- THAT WHATEVER POWERS HE 'AD CAME MOST LIKELY FROM THE UNION OF 'IS MOTHER 'N' FATHER.
HE WANTED TO KNOW WHY HIS FATHER 'N' MOTHER HADN'T NEVER VISITED HIM--
--SUPPOSE ANYONE'D WONDER.
BUT WHEN I TOLD 'IM I DIDN'T HAVE 'N' ANSWER, HE SHRUGGED 'IS SHOULDERS 'N' SAID...
I'VE NEVER NEEDED A MOTHER. AND I HAVE A FATHER IN FRONT OF ME--THE BEST A BOY COULD ASK FOR...
...SO LET'S GET ON WITH OUR LIVES.
THERE'S NO RULEBOOK T' RAISING A KID. NO MANUAL.
THEY'RE ALL SO DIFFERENT, Y'SEE, THESE LITTLE PEOPLE ALL EACH THEIR OWN.
EVEN WITHOUT A CHILD LIKE JASON-- HIM HAVIN' POWERS--

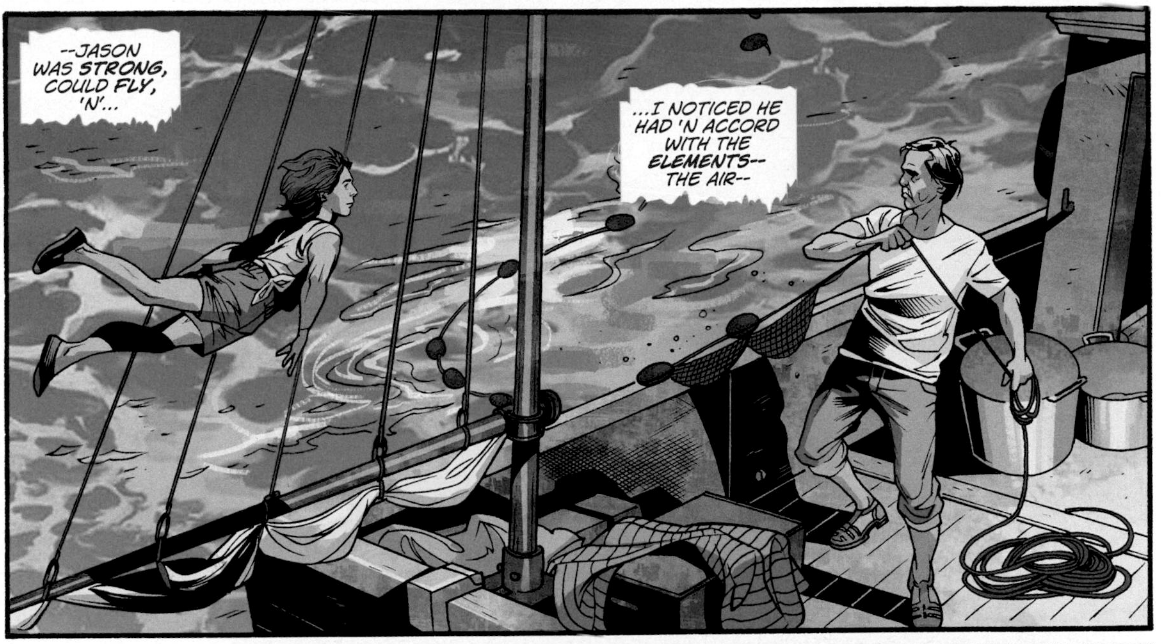
--JASON WAS STRONG, COULD FLY, 'N'...
...I NOTICED HE HAD 'N ACCORD WITH THE ELEMENTS-- THE AIR--

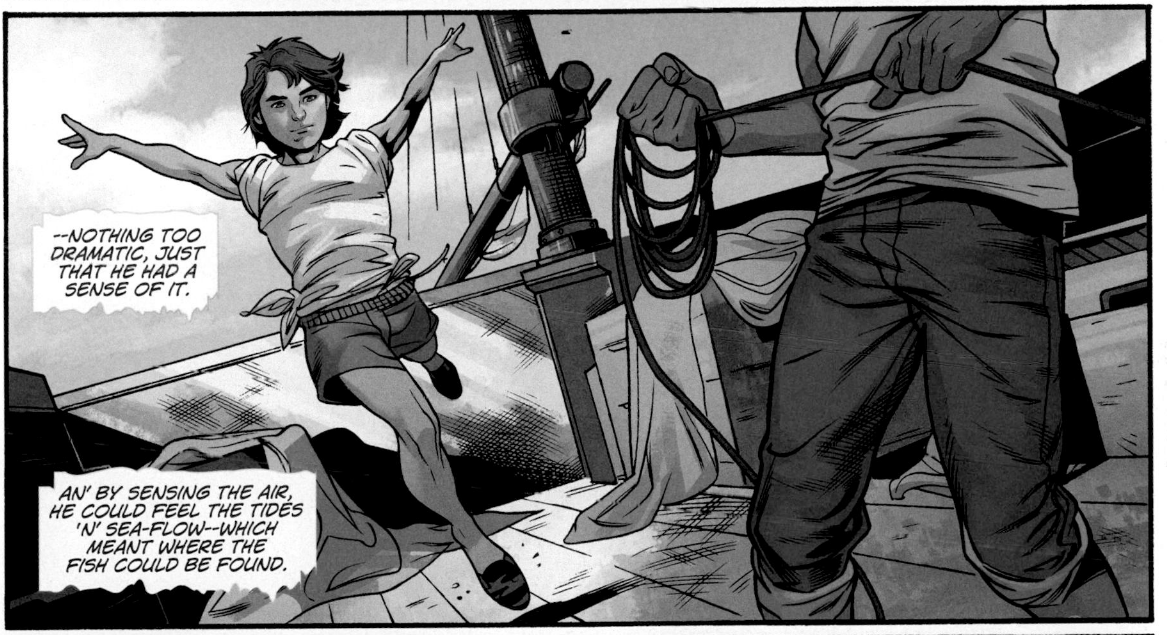
--NOTHING TOO DRAMATIC, JUST THAT HE HAD A SENSE OF IT.
AN' BY SENSING THE AIR, HE COULD FEEL THE TIDES 'N' SEA-FLOW--WHICH MEANT WHERE THE FISH COULD BE FOUND.

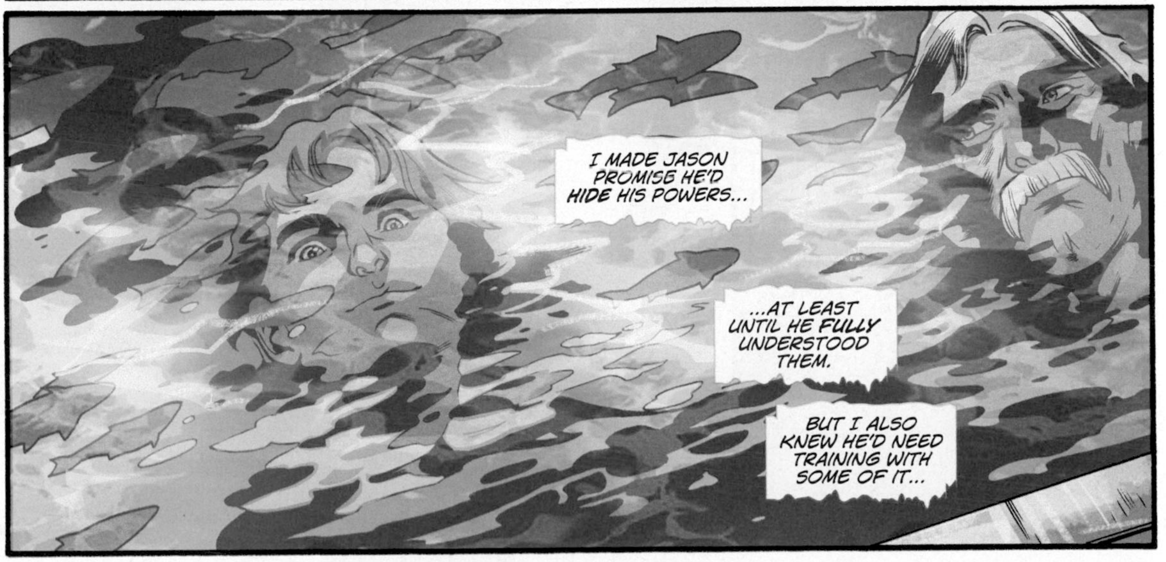
I MADE JASON PROMISE HE'D HIDE HIS POWERS...
...AT LEAST UNTIL HE FULLY UNDERSTOOD THEM.
BUT I ALSO KNEW HE'D NEED TRAINING WITH SOME OF IT...

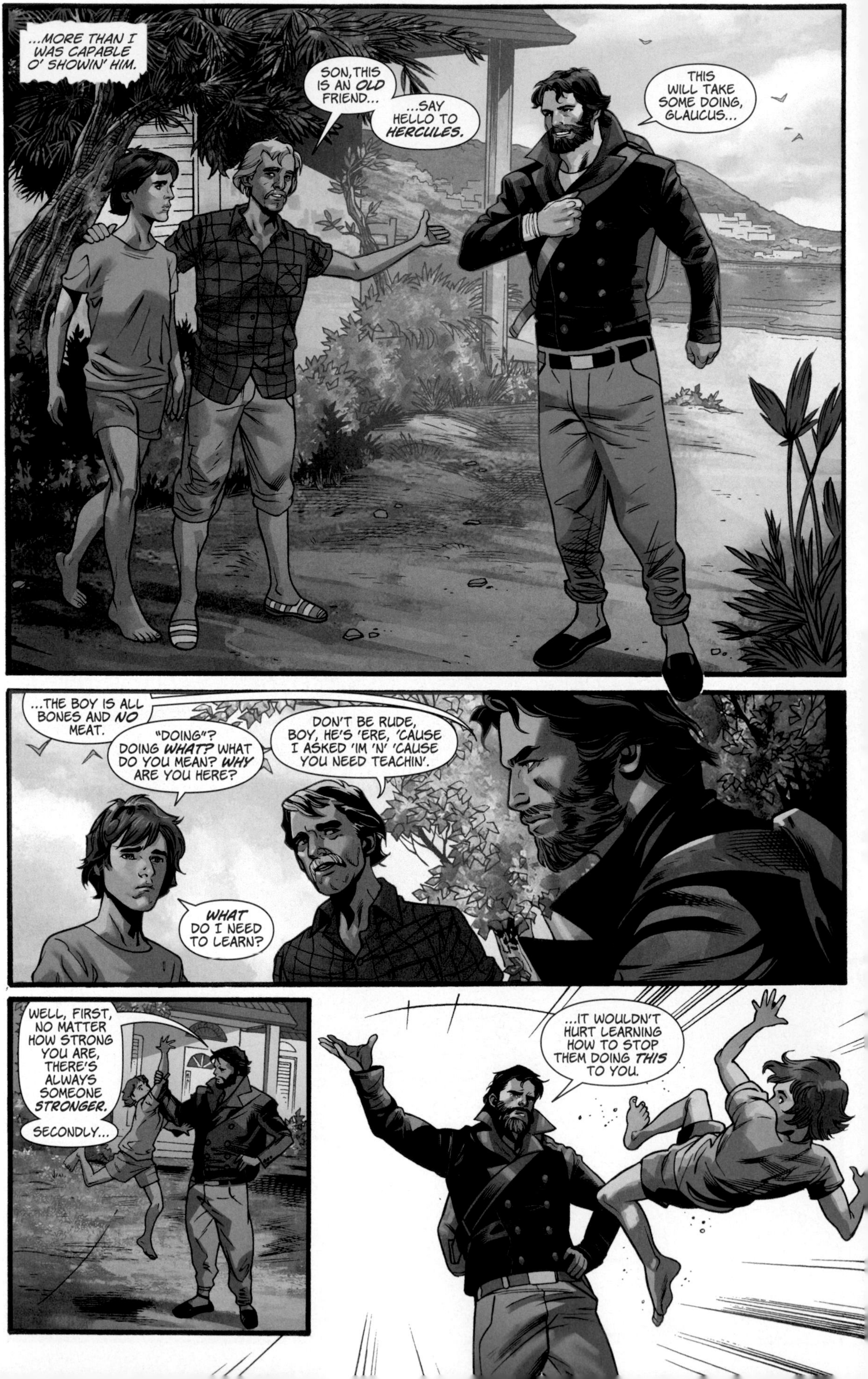
...MORE THAN I WAS CAPABLE O' SHOWIN' HIM.
SON, THIS IS AN OLD FRIEND...
...SAY HELLO TO HERCULES.
THIS WILL TAKE SOME DOING, GLAUCUS...
...THE BOY IS ALL BONES AND NO MEAT.
"DOING"? DOING WHAT? WHAT DO YOU MEAN? WHY ARE YOU HERE?
DON'T BE RUDE, BOY, HE'S 'ERE, 'CAUSE I ASKED 'IM 'N' 'CAUSE YOU NEED TEACHIN'.
WHAT DO I NEED TO LEARN?
WELL, FIRST, NO MATTER HOW STRONG YOU ARE, THERE'S ALWAYS SOMEONE STRONGER.
SECONDLY...
...IT WOULDN'T HURT LEARNING HOW TO STOP THEM DOING THIS TO YOU.

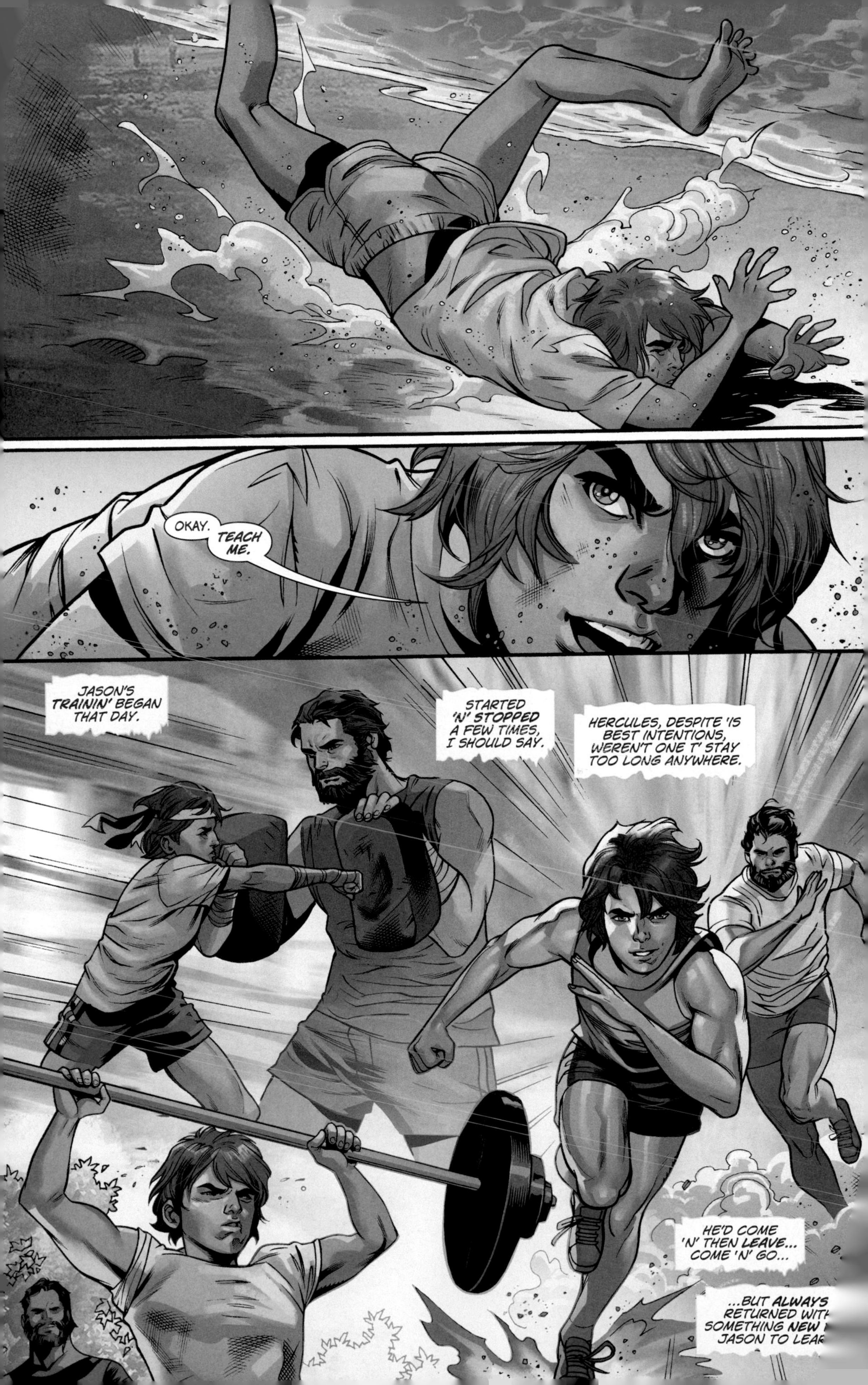
OKAY. TEACH ME.
JASON'S TRAININ' BEGAN THAT DAY.
STARTED 'N' STOPPED A FEW TIMES, I SHOULD SAY.
HERCULES, DESPITE 'IS BEST INTENTIONS, WEREN'T ONE T' STAY TOO LONG ANYWHERE.
HE'D COME 'N' THEN LEAVE... COME 'N' GO...
...BUT ALWAYS RETURNED WITH SOMETHING NEW FOR JASON TO LEARN.

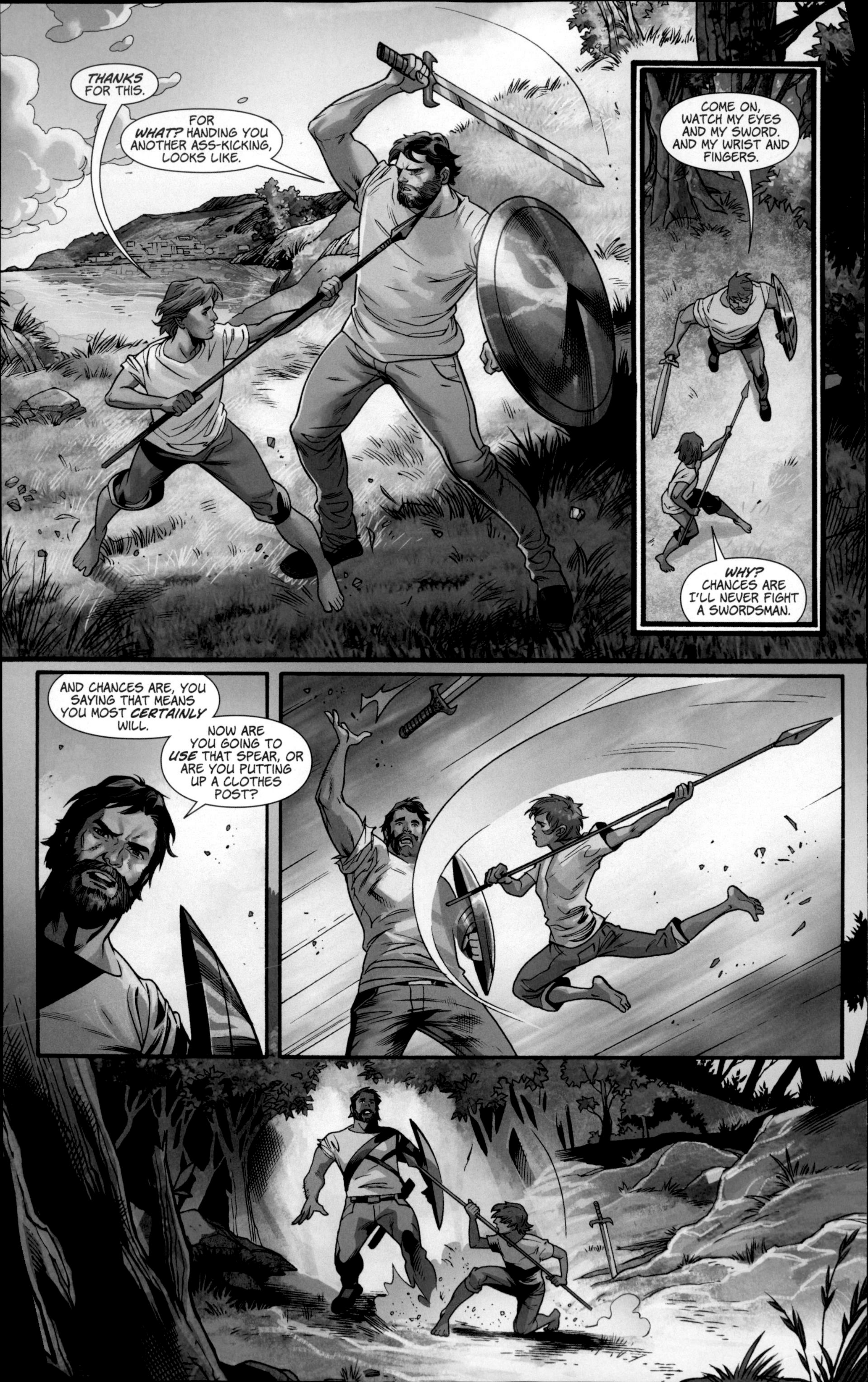
THANKS FOR THIS.
FOR WHAT? HANDING YOU ANOTHER ASS-KICKING, LOOKS LIKE.
COME ON, WATCH MY EYES AND MY SWORD. AND MY WRIST AND FINGERS.
WHY? CHANCES ARE I'LL NEVER FIGHT A SWORDSMAN.
AND CHANCES ARE, YOU SAYING THAT MEANS YOU MOST CERTAINLY WILL.
NOW ARE YOU GOING TO USE THAT SPEAR, OR ARE YOU PUTTING UP A CLOTHES POST?

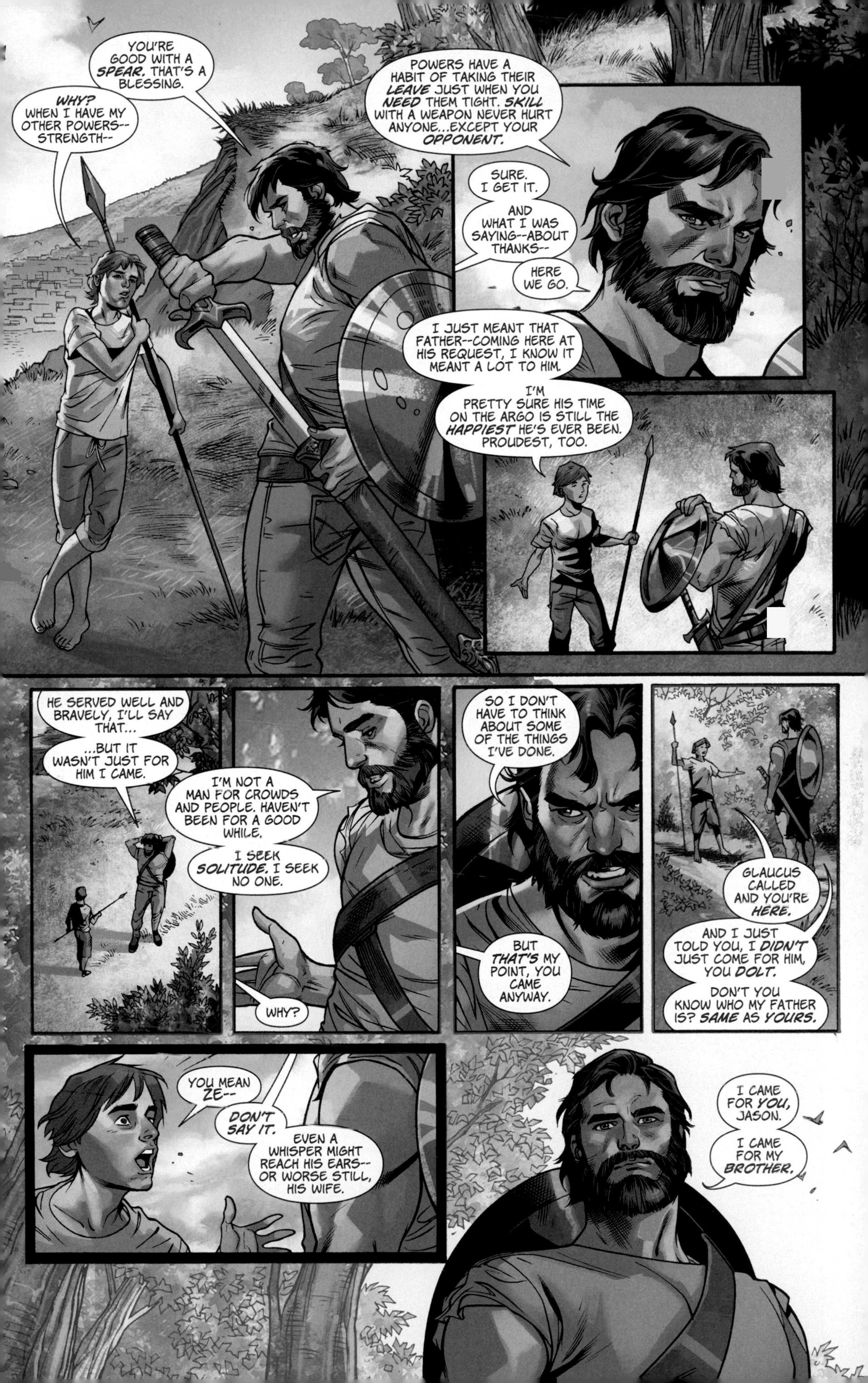

WHY? WHEN I HAVE MY OTHER POWERS--STRENGTH--
YOU'RE GOOD WITH A SPEAR. THAT'S A BLESSING.
POWERS HAVE A HABIT OF TAKING THEIR LEAVE JUST WHEN YOU NEED THEM TIGHT. SKILL WITH A WEAPON NEVER HURT ANYONE...EXCEPT YOUR OPPONENT.
SURE. I GET IT.
AND WHAT I WAS SAYING--ABOUT THANKS--
HERE WE GO.
I JUST MEANT THAT FATHER--COMING HERE AT HIS REQUEST, I KNOW IT MEANT A LOT TO HIM.
I'M PRETTY SURE HIS TIME ON THE ARGO IS STILL THE HAPPIEST HE'S EVER BEEN. PROUDEST, TOO.
HE SERVED WELL AND BRAVELY, I'LL SAY THAT...
...BUT IT WASN'T JUST FOR HIM I CAME.
I'M NOT A MAN FOR CROWDS AND PEOPLE. HAVEN'T BEEN FOR A GOOD WHILE.
I SEEK SOLITUDE. I SEEK NO ONE.
WHY?
SO I DON'T HAVE TO THINK ABOUT SOME OF THE THINGS I'VE DONE.
BUT THAT'S MY POINT, YOU CAME ANYWAY.
GLAUCUS CALLED AND YOU'RE HERE.
AND I JUST TOLD YOU, I DIDN'T JUST COME FOR HIM, YOU DOLT.
DON'T YOU KNOW WHO MY FATHER IS? SAME AS YOURS.
YOU MEAN ZE--
DON'T SAY IT.
EVEN A WHISPER MIGHT REACH HIS EARS--OR WORSE STILL, HIS WIFE.
I CAME FOR YOU, JASON.
I CAME FOR MY BROTHER.

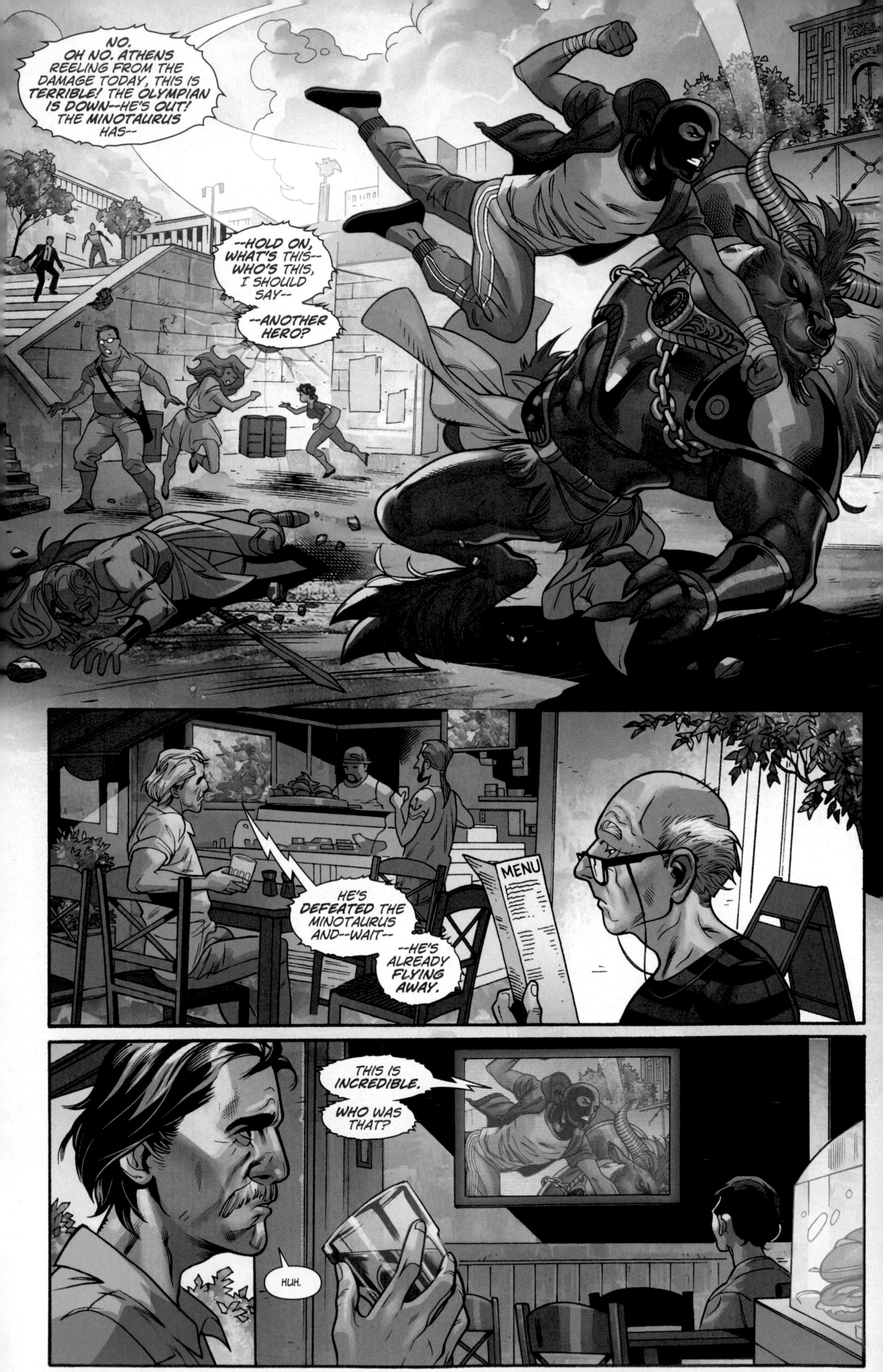
NO. OH NO. ATHENS REELING FROM THE DAMAGE TODAY, THIS IS TERRIBLE! THE OLYMPIAN IS DOWN--HE'S OUT! THE MINOTAURUS HAS--
--HOLD ON, WHAT'S THIS-- WHO'S THIS, I SHOULD SAY--
--ANOTHER HERO?
HE'S DEFEATED THE MINOTAURUS AND--WAIT--
--HE'S ALREADY FLYING AWAY.
MENU
THIS IS INCREDIBLE.
WHO WAS THAT?
HUH.

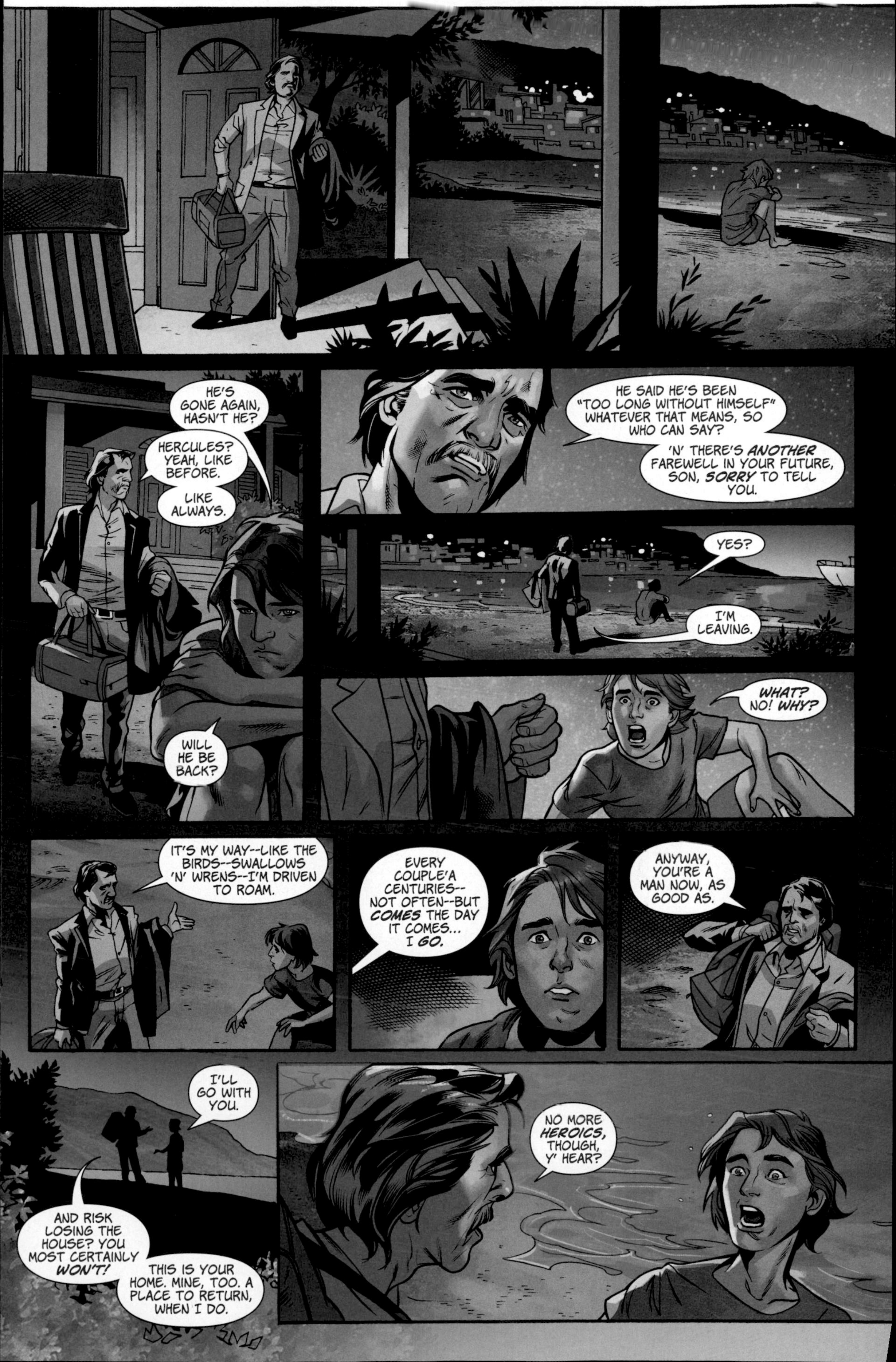
HE'S GONE AGAIN, HASN'T HE?
HERCULES? YEAH, LIKE BEFORE.
LIKE ALWAYS.
WILL HE BE BACK?
HE SAID HE'S BEEN "TOO LONG WITHOUT HIMSELF" WHATEVER THAT MEANS, SO WHO CAN SAY?
'N' THERE'S ANOTHER FAREWELL IN YOUR FUTURE, SON, SORRY TO TELL YOU.
YES?
I'M LEAVING.
WHAT? NO! WHY?
IT'S MY WAY--LIKE THE BIRDS--SWALLOWS 'N' WRENS--I'M DRIVEN TO ROAM.
EVERY COUPLE'A CENTURIES--NOT OFTEN--BUT COMES THE DAY IT COMES... I GO.
ANYWAY, YOU'RE A MAN NOW, AS GOOD AS.
I'LL GO WITH YOU.
AND RISK LOSING THE HOUSE? YOU MOST CERTAINLY WON'T!
THIS IS YOUR HOME. MINE, TOO. A PLACE TO RETURN, WHEN I DO.
NO MORE HEROICS, THOUGH, Y' HEAR?

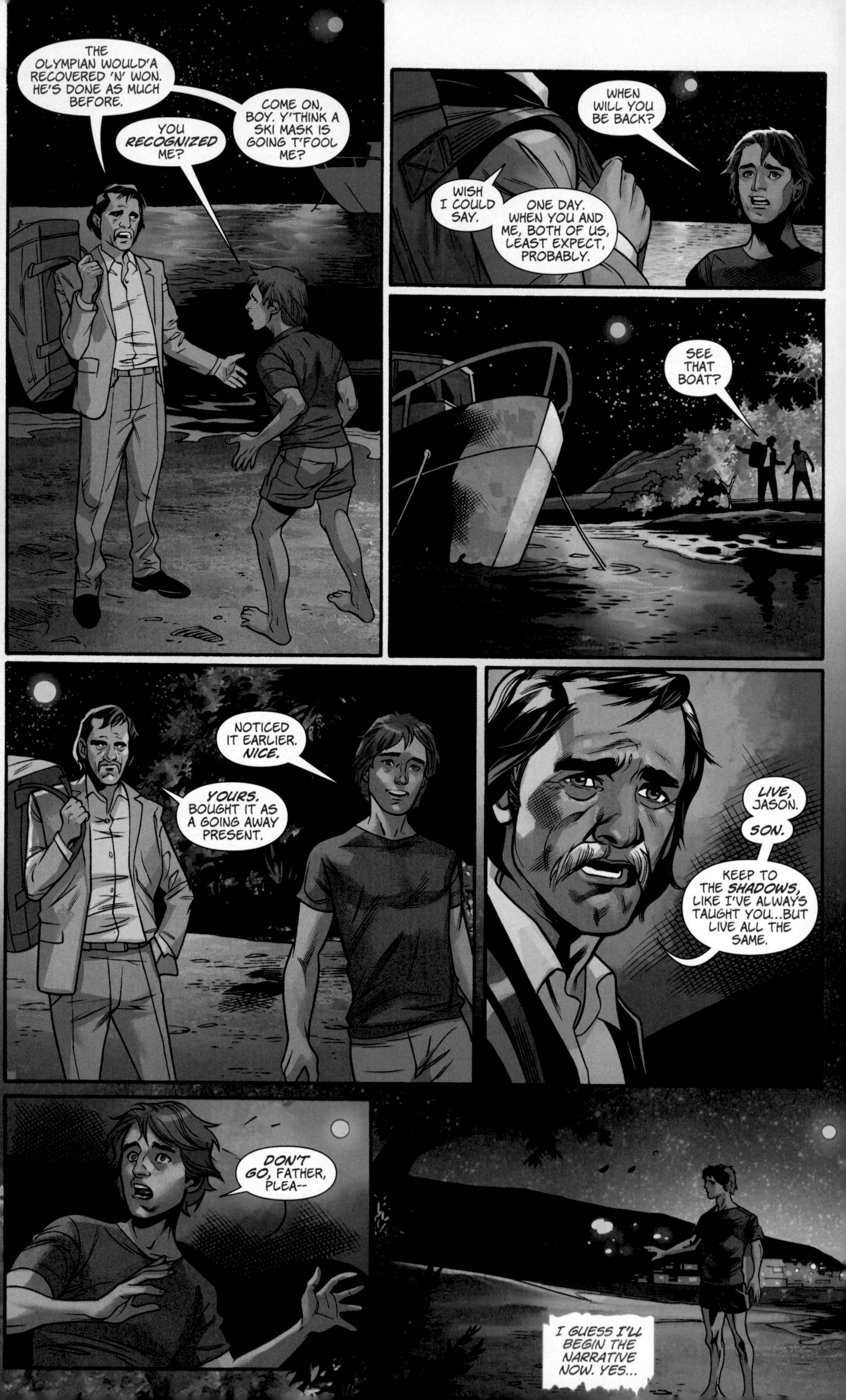
THE OLYMPIAN WOULD'A RECOVERED 'N' WON. HE'S DONE AS MUCH BEFORE.
YOU RECOGNIZED ME?
COME ON, BOY. Y'THINK A SKI MASK IS GOING T'FOOL ME?
WHEN WILL YOU BE BACK?
WISH I COULD SAY.
ONE DAY. WHEN YOU AND ME, BOTH OF US, LEAST EXPECT, PROBABLY.
SEE THAT BOAT?
NOTICED IT EARLIER. NICE.
YOURS. BOUGHT IT AS A GOING AWAY PRESENT.
LIVE, JASON.
SON.
KEEP TO THE SHADOWS, LIKE I'VE ALWAYS TAUGHT YOU...BUT LIVE ALL THE SAME.
DON'T GO, FATHER, PLEA--
I GUESS I'LL BEGIN THE NARRATIVE NOW. YES...

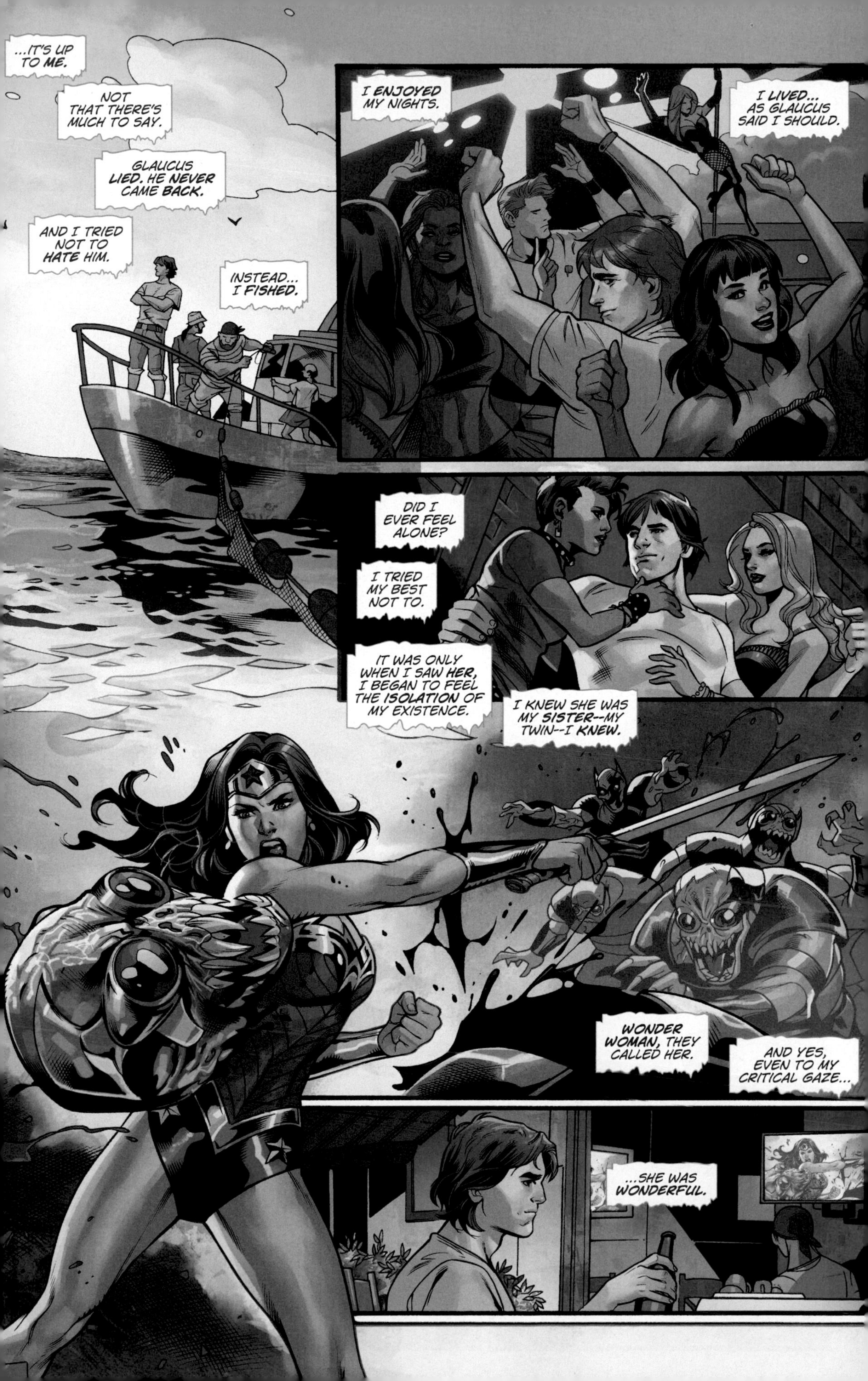
...IT'S UP TO ME.
NOT THAT THERE'S MUCH TO SAY.
GLAUCUS LIED. HE NEVER CAME BACK.
AND I TRIED NOT TO HATE HIM.
INSTEAD... I FISHED.
I ENJOYED MY NIGHTS.
I LIVED... AS GLAUCUS SAID I SHOULD.
DID I EVER FEEL ALONE?
I TRIED MY BEST NOT TO.
IT WAS ONLY WHEN I SAW HER, I BEGAN TO FEEL THE ISOLATION OF MY EXISTENCE.
I KNEW SHE WAS MY SISTER--MY TWIN--I KNEW.
WONDER WOMAN, THEY CALLED HER.
AND YES, EVEN TO MY CRITICAL GAZE...
...SHE WAS WONDERFUL.

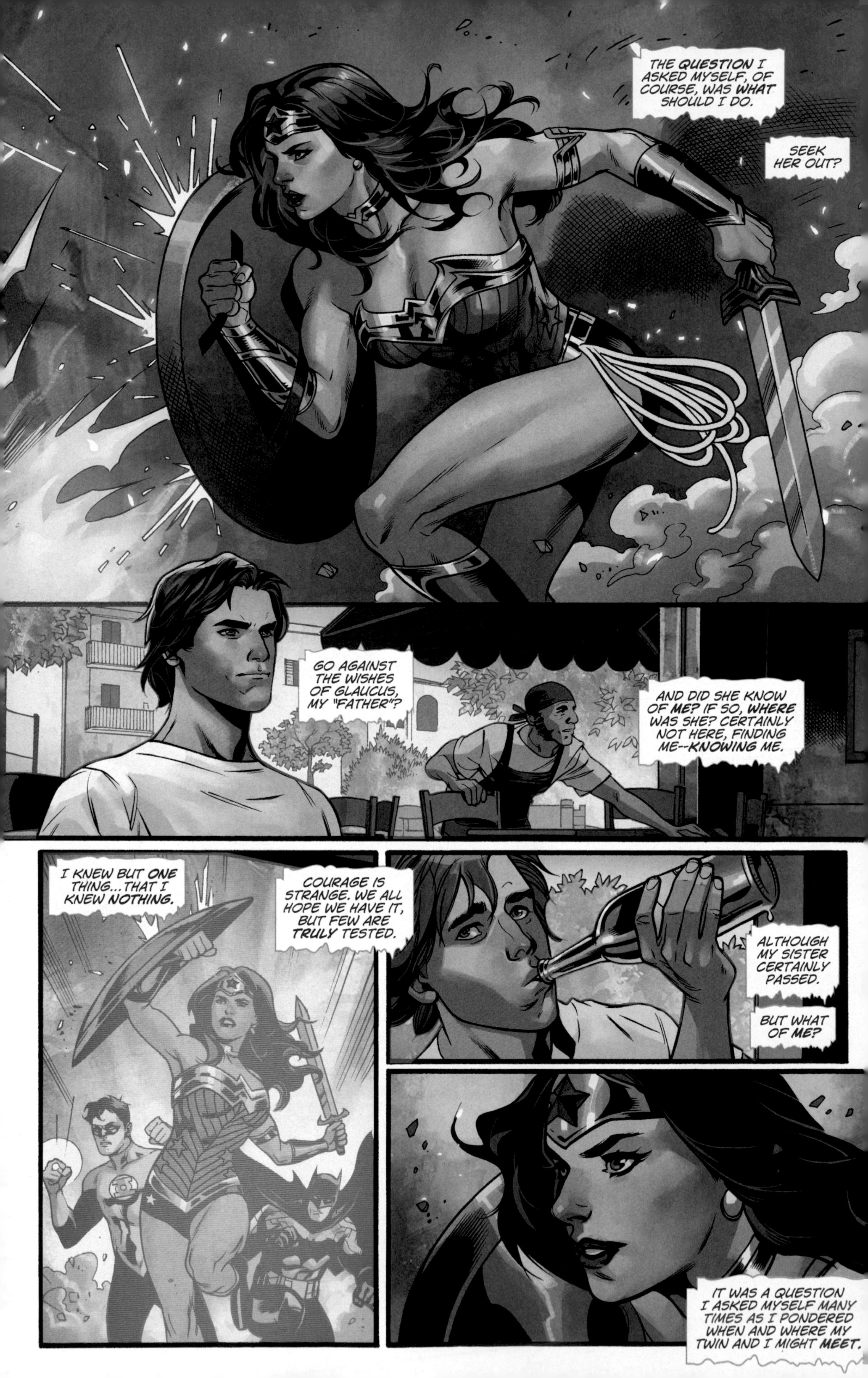
THE QUESTION I ASKED MYSELF, OF COURSE, WAS WHAT SHOULD I DO.
SEEK HER OUT?
GO AGAINST THE WISHES OF GLAUCUS, MY "FATHER"?
AND DID SHE KNOW OF ME? IF SO, WHERE WAS SHE? CERTAINLY NOT HERE, FINDING ME--KNOWING ME.
I KNEW BUT ONE THING... THAT I KNEW NOTHING.
COURAGE IS STRANGE. WE ALL HOPE WE HAVE IT, BUT FEW ARE TRULY TESTED.
ALTHOUGH MY SISTER CERTAINLY PASSED.
BUT WHAT OF ME?
IT WAS A QUESTION I ASKED MYSELF MANY TIMES AS I PONDERED WHEN AND WHERE MY TWIN AND I MIGHT MEET.

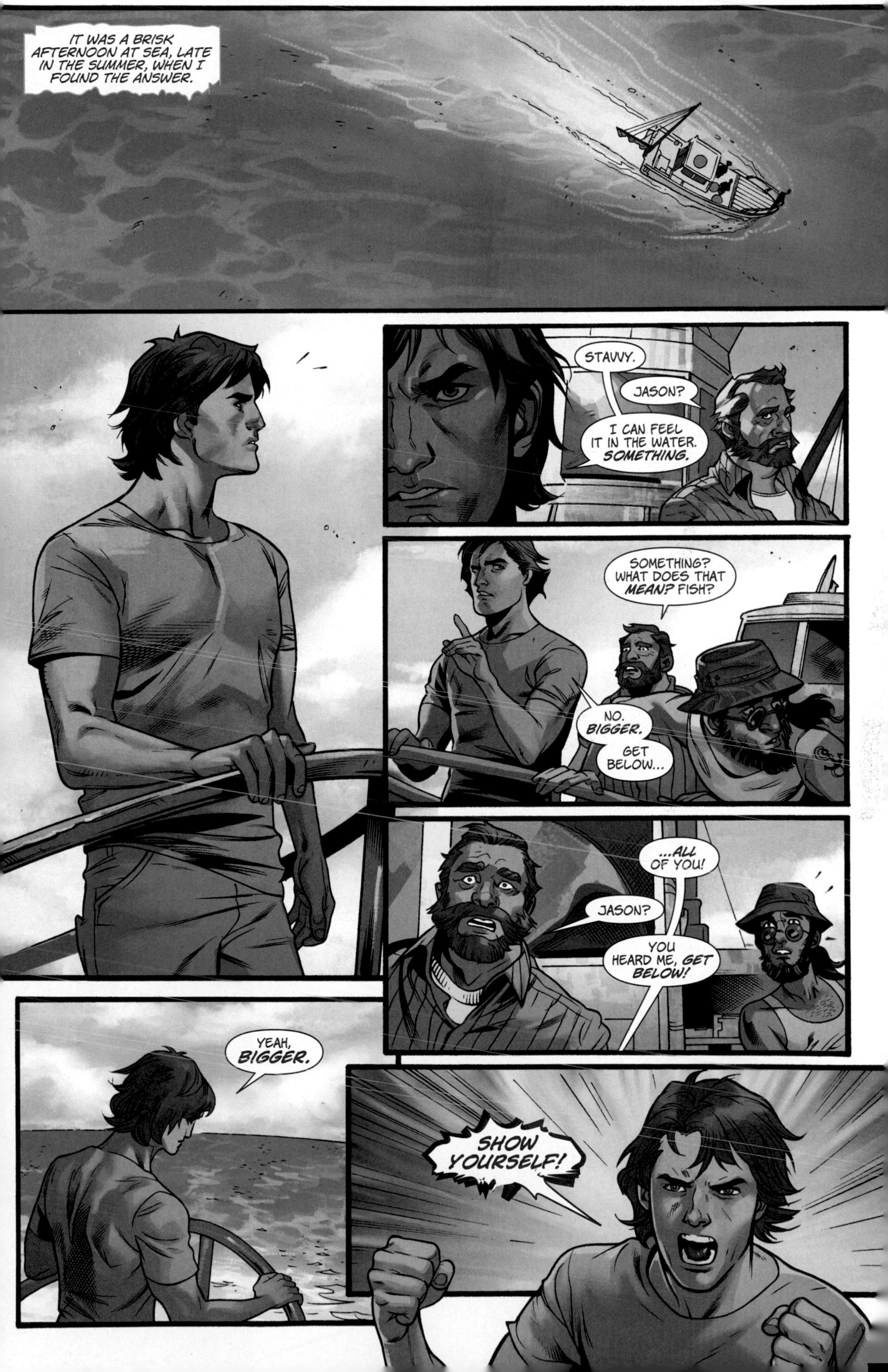
IT WAS A BRISK AFTERNOON AT SEA, LATE IN THE SUMMER, WHEN I FOUND THE ANSWER.
STAVVY.
JASON?
I CAN FEEL IT IN THE WATER. SOMETHING.
SOMETHING? WHAT DOES THAT MEAN? FISH?
NO. BIGGER.
GET BELOW...
...ALL OF YOU!
JASON?
YOU HEARD ME, GET BELOW!
YEAH, BIGGER.
SHOW YOURSELF!

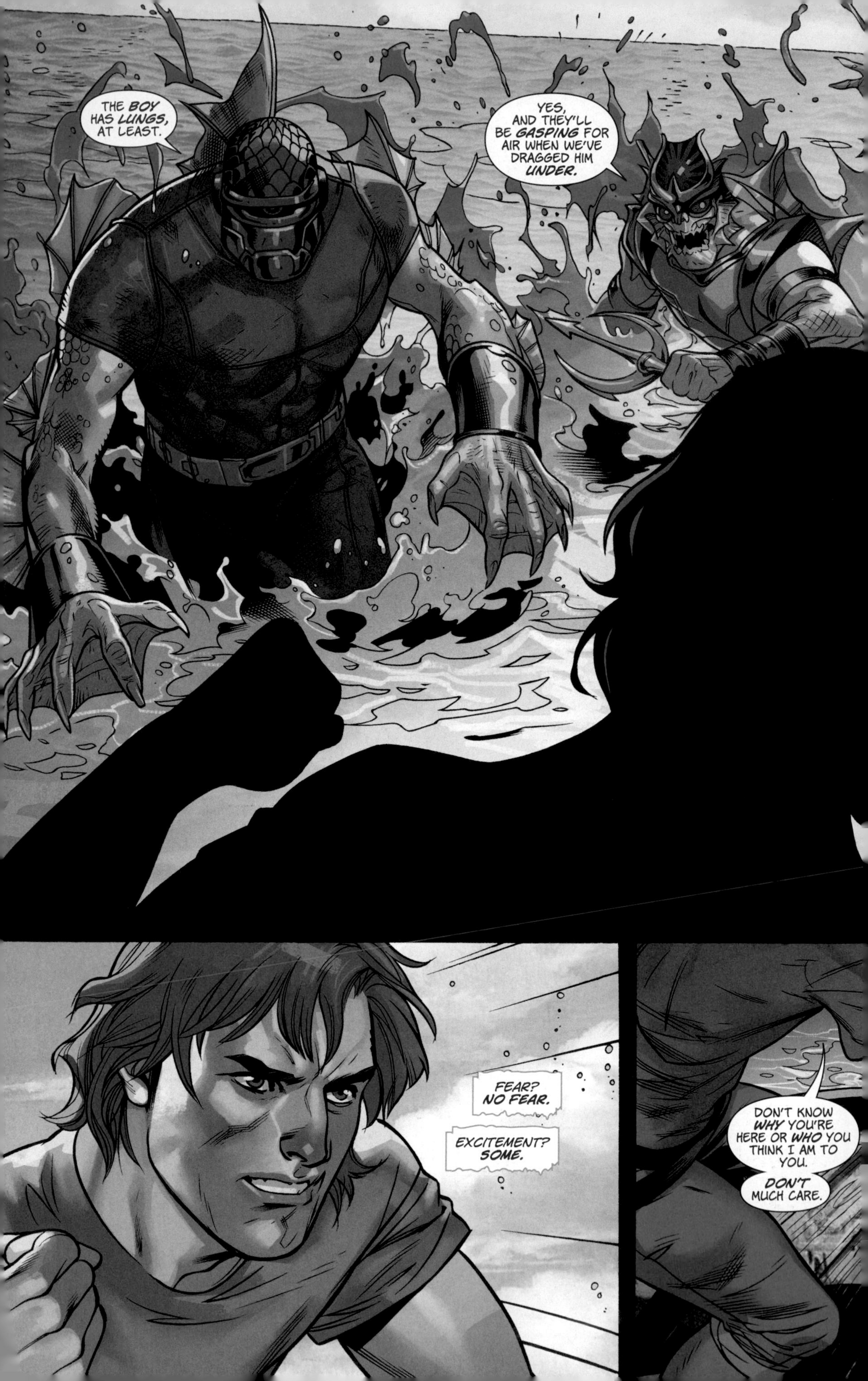
THE BOY HAS LUNGS, AT LEAST.
YES, AND THEY'LL BE GASPING FOR AIR WHEN WE'VE DRAGGED HIM UNDER.
FEAR? NO FEAR.
EXCITEMENT? SOME.
DON'T KNOW WHY YOU'RE HERE OR WHO YOU THINK I AM TO YOU.
DON'T MUCH CARE.

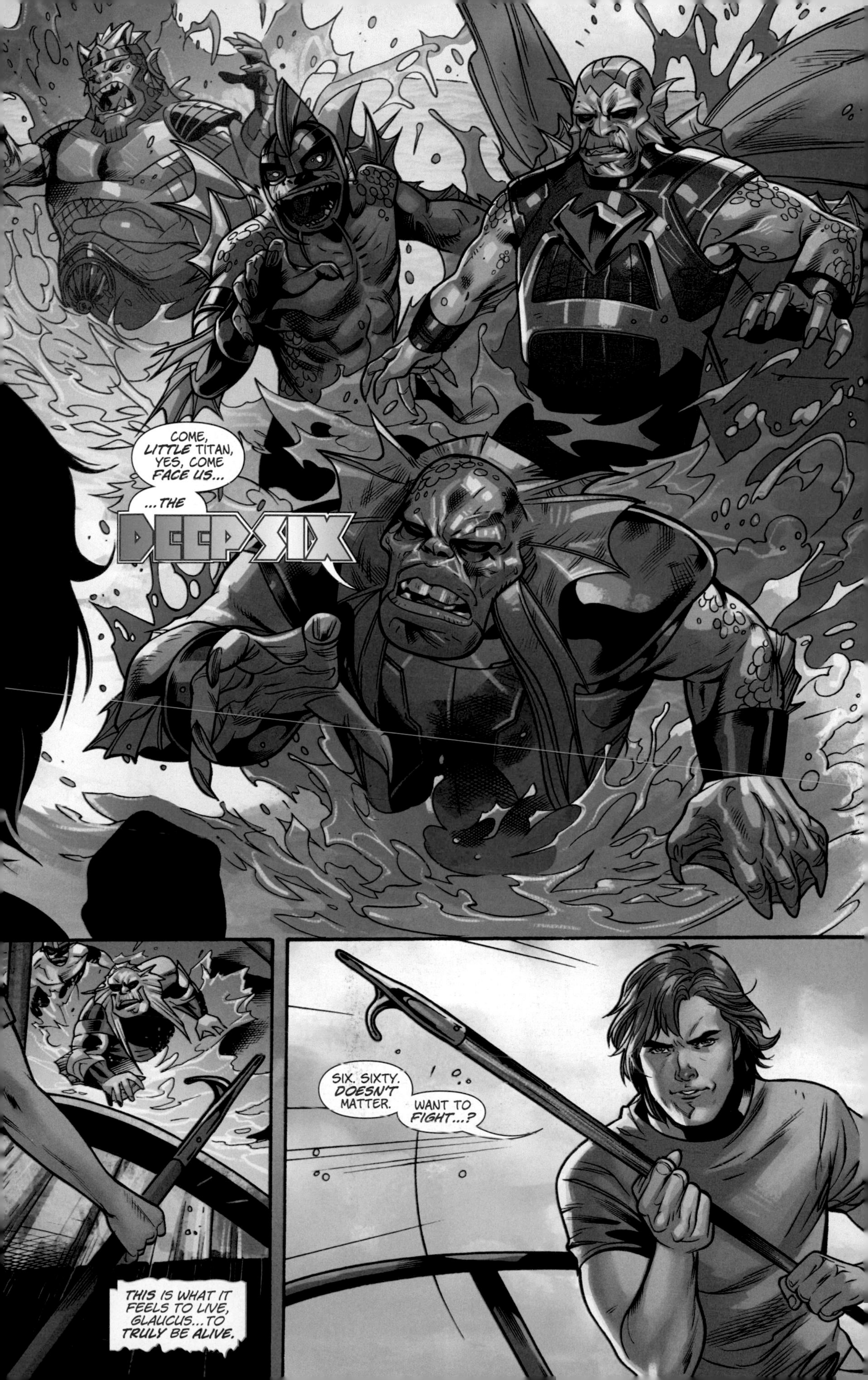
COME, LITTLE TITAN, YES, COME FACE US...
...THE
DEEP SIX
SIX. SIXTY. DOESN'T MATTER.
WANT TO FIGHT...?
THIS IS WHAT IT FEELS TO LIVE, GLAUCUS...TO TRULY BE ALIVE.

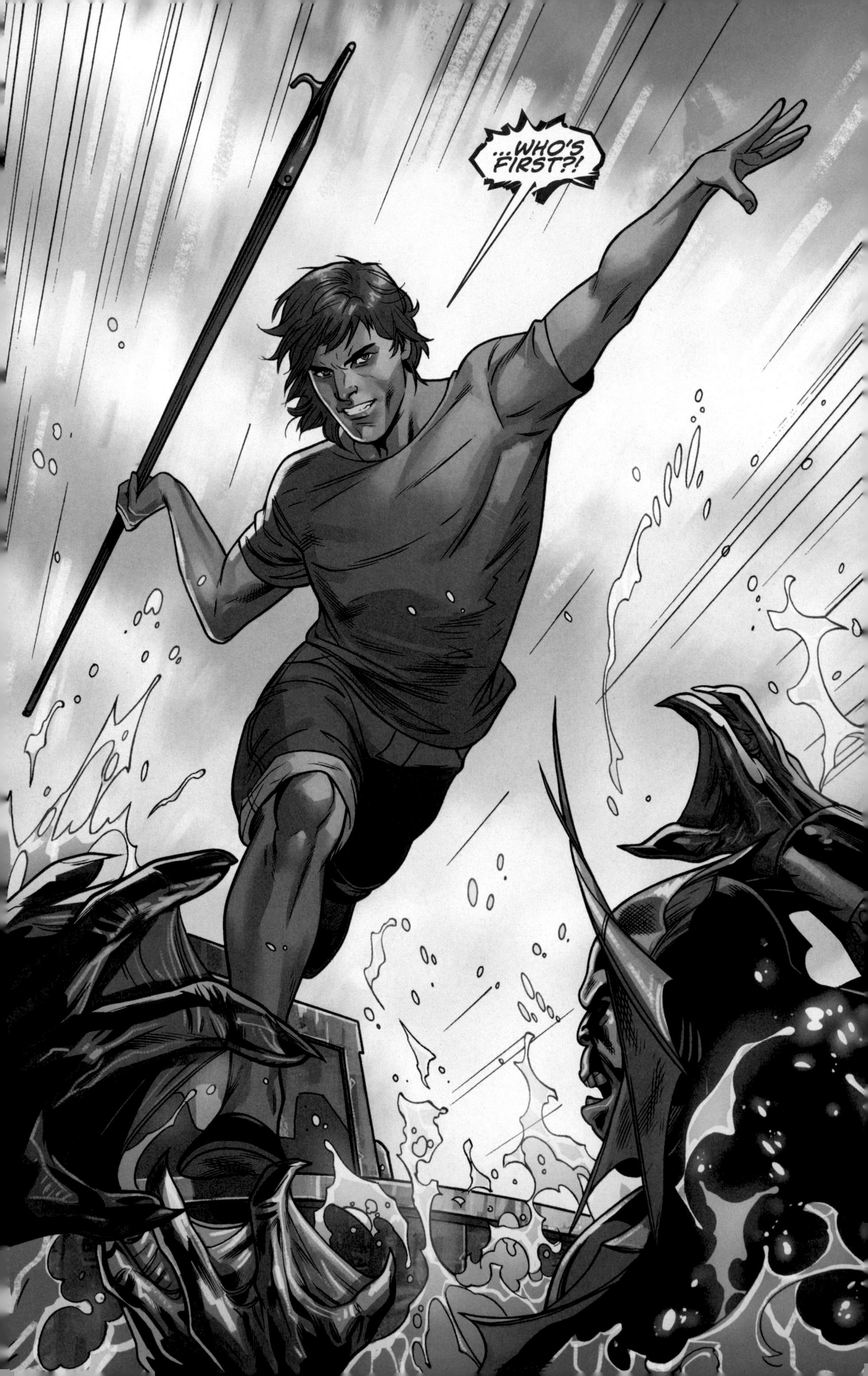
...WHO'S FIRST?!

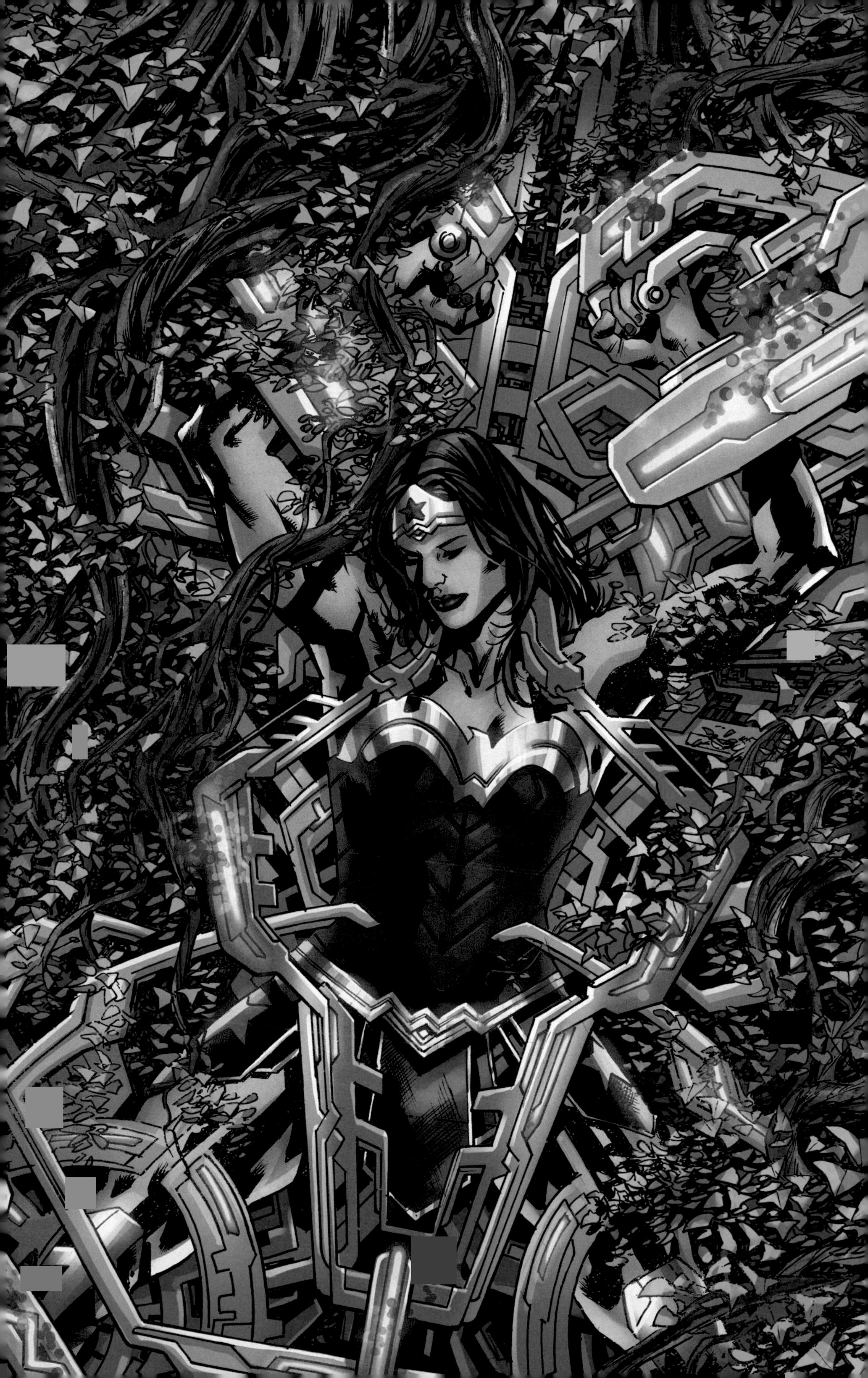

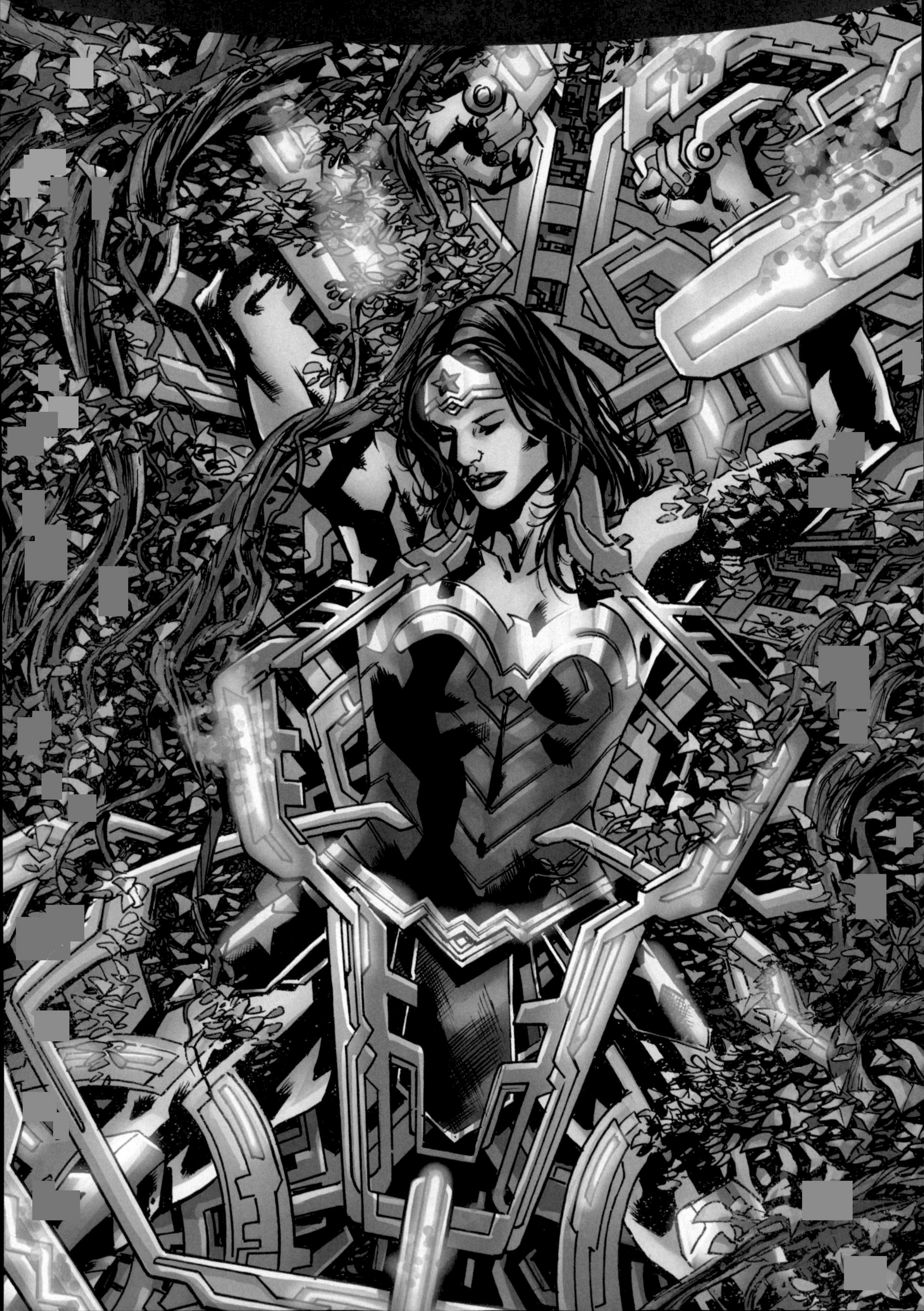

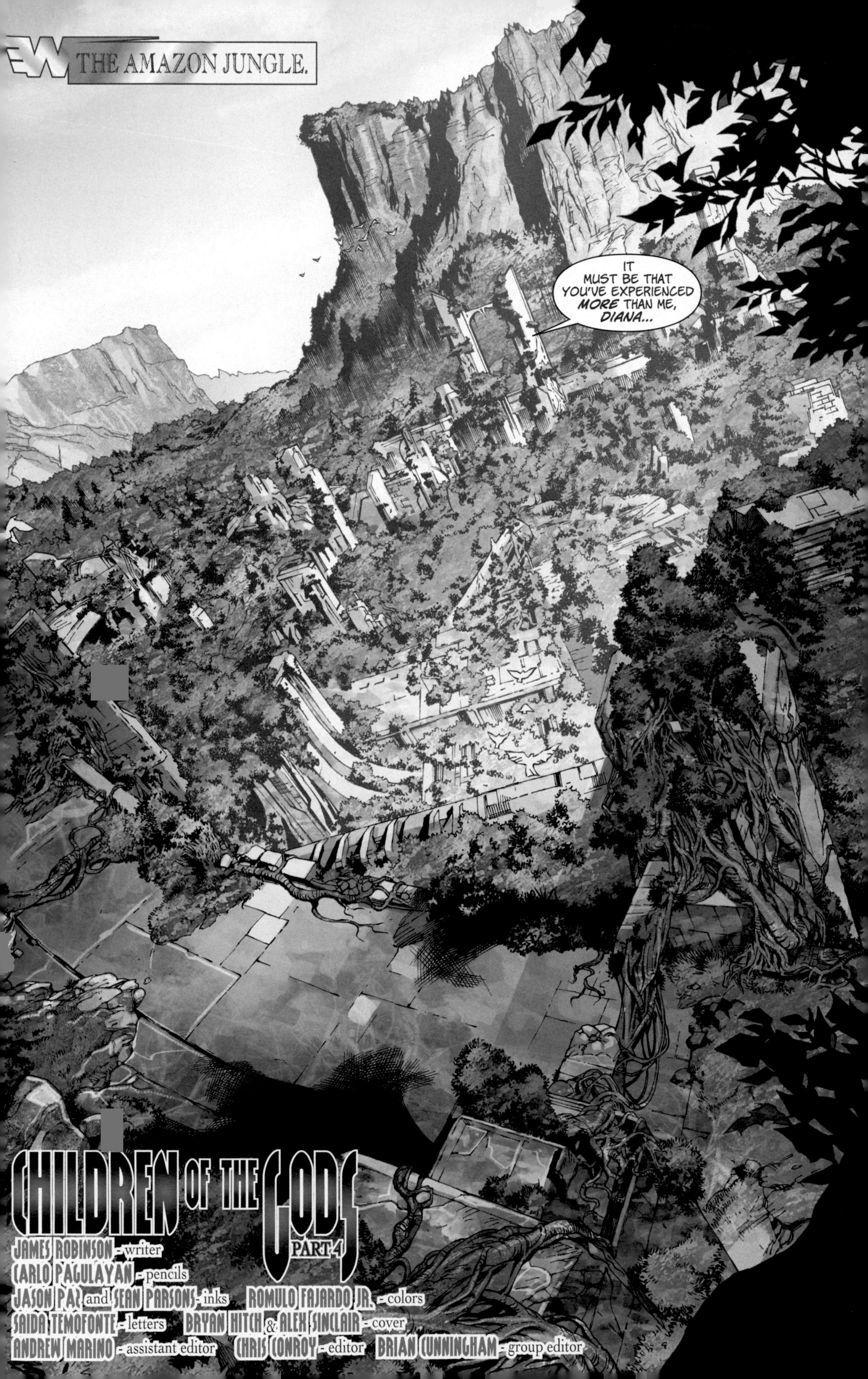

THE AMAZON JUNGLE.
IT MUST BE THAT YOU'VE EXPERIENCED MORE THAN ME, DIANA...
CHILDREN OF THE GODS
PART 4
JAMES ROBINSON - writer
CARLO PAGULAYAN - pencils
JASON PAZ and SEAN PARSONS - inks ROMULO FAJARDO JR. - colors
SAIDA TEMOFONTE - letters BRYAN HITCH & ALEX SINCLAIR - cover
ANDREW MARINO - assistant editor CHRIS CONROY - editor BRIAN CUNNINGHAM - group editor

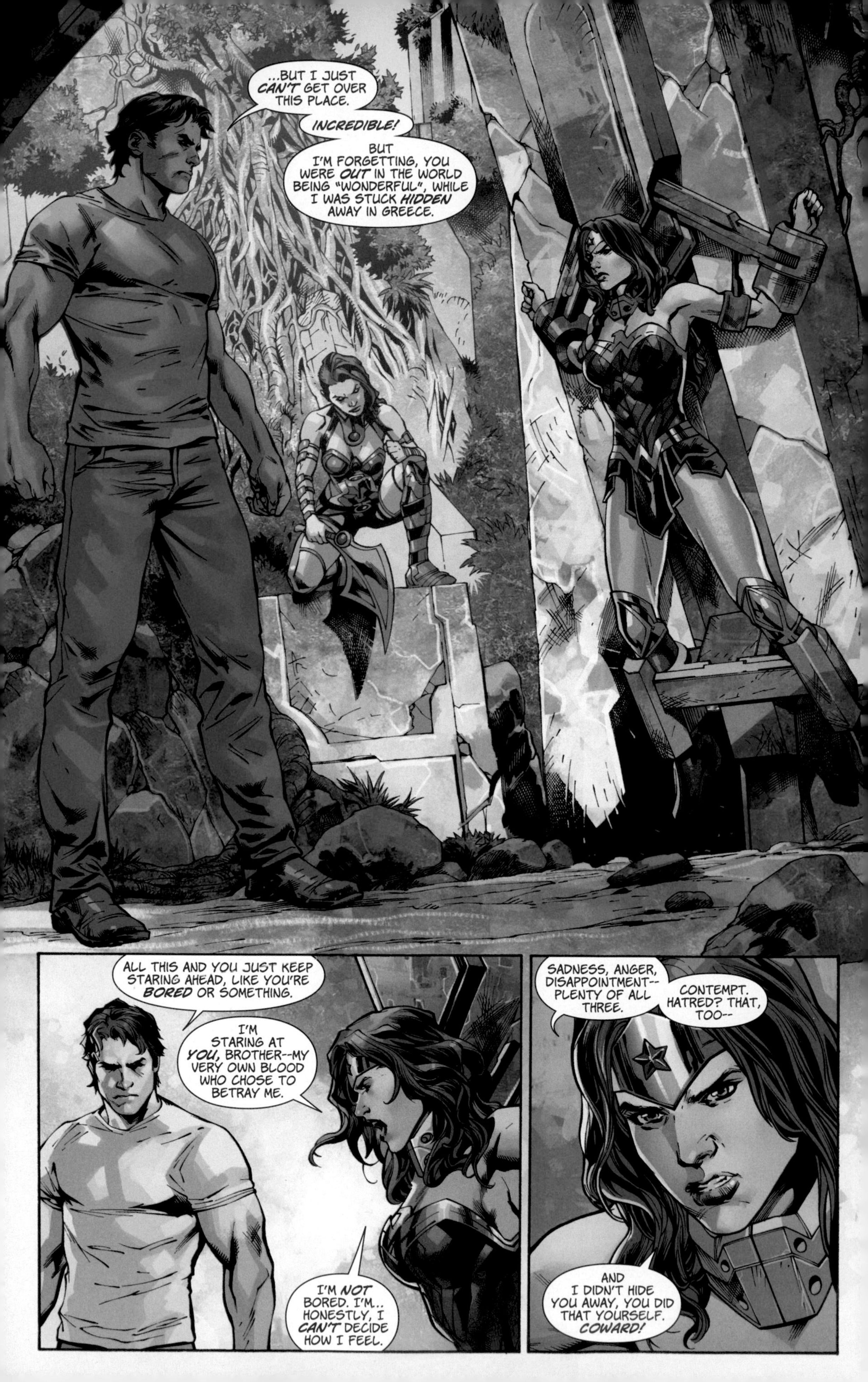
...BUT I JUST CAN'T GET OVER THIS PLACE.
INCREDIBLE!
BUT I'M FORGETTING, YOU WERE OUT IN THE WORLD BEING "WONDERFUL", WHILE I WAS STUCK HIDDEN AWAY IN GREECE.
ALL THIS AND YOU JUST KEEP STARING AHEAD, LIKE YOU'RE BORED OR SOMETHING.
I'M STARING AT YOU, BROTHER--MY VERY OWN BLOOD WHO CHOSE TO BETRAY ME.
I'M NOT BORED. I'M.. HONESTLY, I CAN'T DECIDE HOW I FEEL.
SADNESS, ANGER, DISAPPOINTMENT--PLENTY OF ALL THREE.
CONTEMPT. HATRED? THAT, TOO--
AND I DIDN'T HIDE YOU AWAY, YOU DID THAT YOURSELF. COWARD!

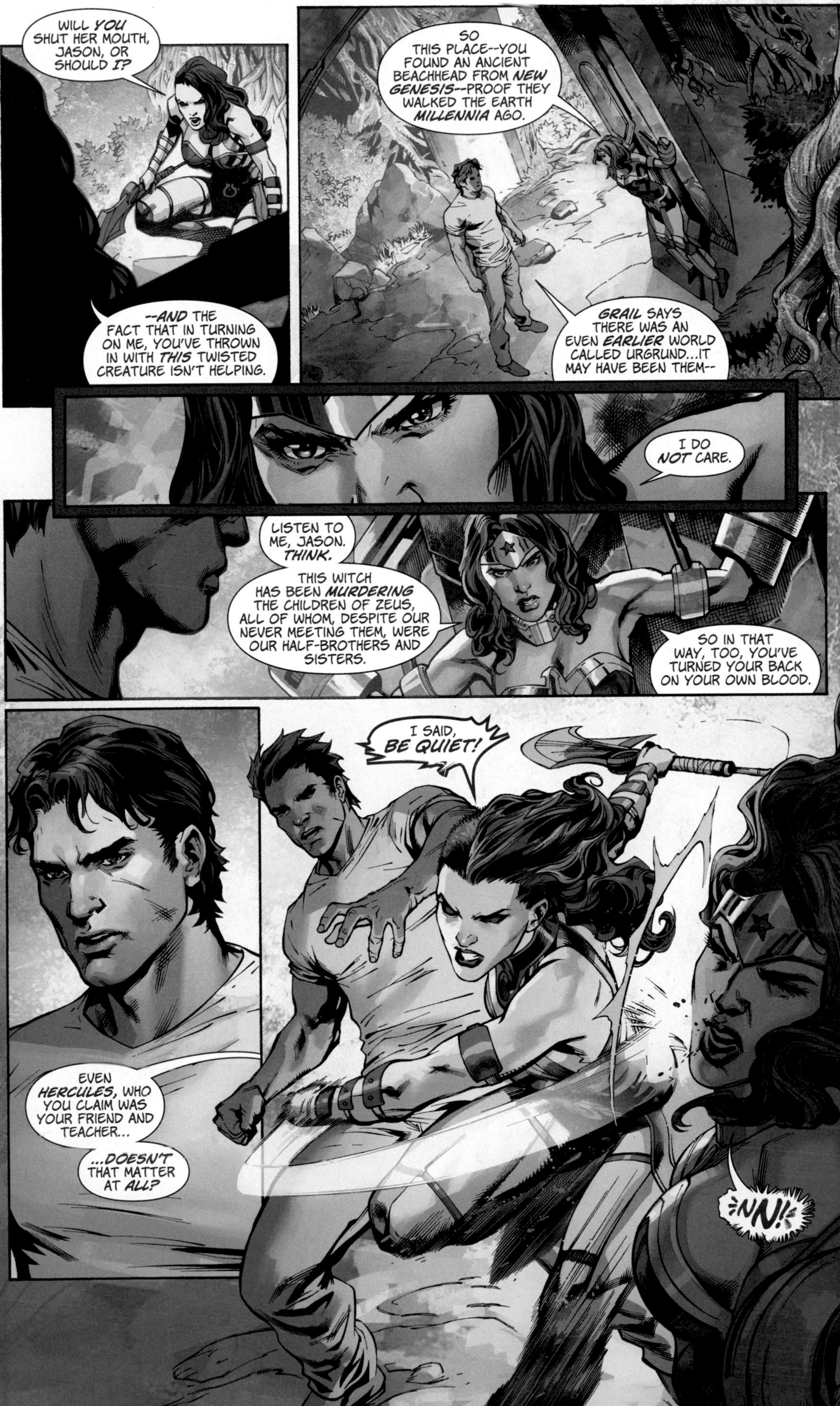
WILL YOU SHUT HER MOUTH, JASON, OR SHOULD I?
SO THIS PLACE--YOU FOUND AN ANCIENT BEACHHEAD FROM NEW GENESIS--PROOF THEY WALKED THE EARTH MILLENNIA AGO.
--AND THE FACT THAT IN TURNING ON ME, YOU'VE THROWN IN WITH THIS TWISTED CREATURE ISN'T HELPING.
GRAIL SAYS THERE WAS AN EVEN EARLIER WORLD CALLED URGRUND...IT MAY HAVE BEEN THEM--
I DO NOT CARE.
LISTEN TO ME, JASON. THINK.
THIS WITCH HAS BEEN MURDERING THE CHILDREN OF ZEUS, ALL OF WHOM, DESPITE OUR NEVER MEETING THEM, WERE OUR HALF-BROTHERS AND SISTERS.
SO IN THAT WAY, TOO, YOU'VE TURNED YOUR BACK ON YOUR OWN BLOOD.
EVEN HERCULES, WHO YOU CLAIM WAS YOUR FRIEND AND TEACHER...
...DOESN'T THAT MATTER AT ALL?
I SAID, BE QUIET!
NN!

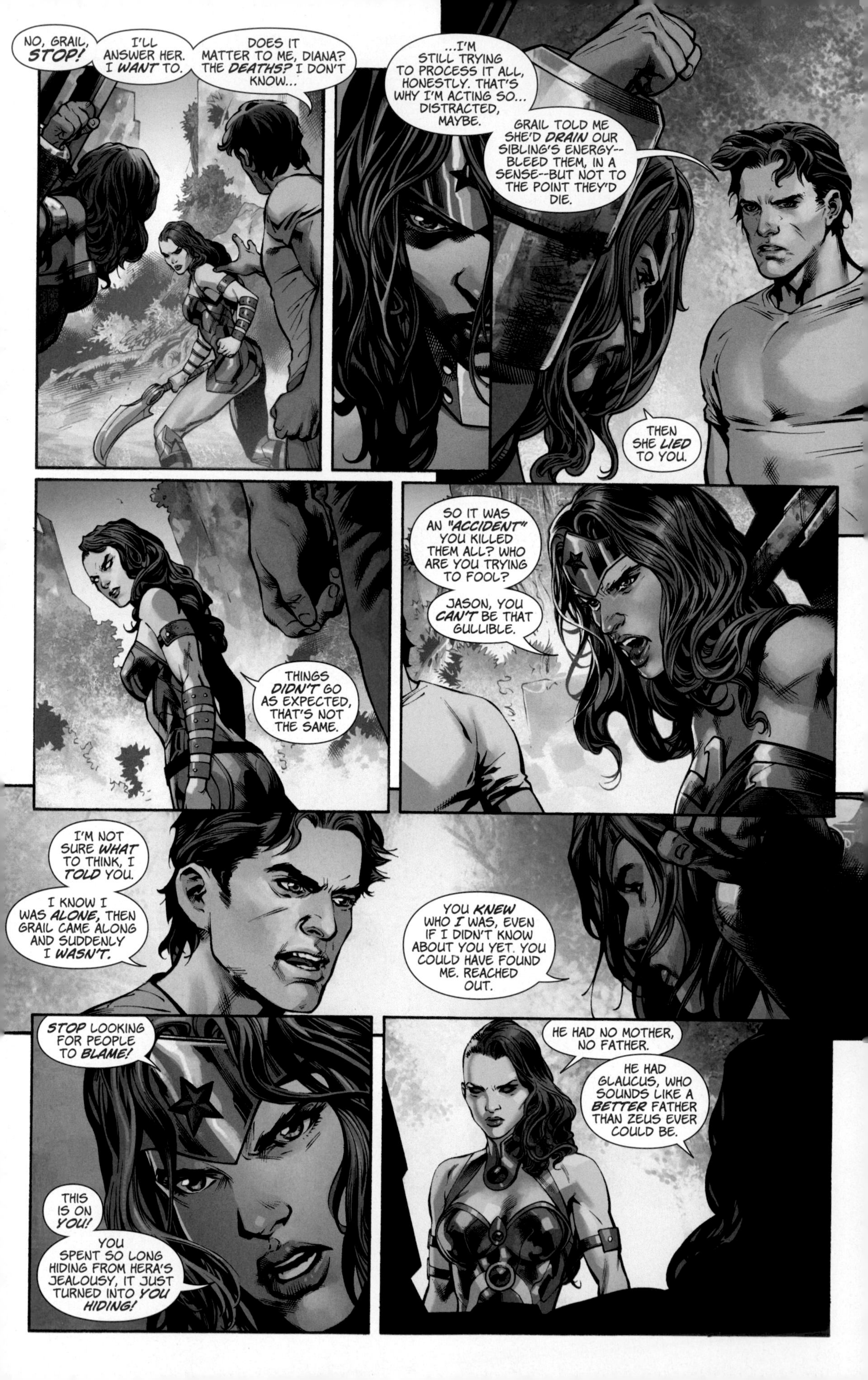

NO, GRAIL, STOP!
I'LL ANSWER HER. I WANT TO.
DOES IT MATTER TO ME, DIANA? THE DEATHS? I DON'T KNOW...
...I'M STILL TRYING TO PROCESS IT ALL, HONESTLY. THAT'S WHY I'M ACTING SO... DISTRACTED, MAYBE.
GRAIL TOLD ME SHE'D DRAIN OUR SIBLING'S ENERGY--BLEED THEM, IN A SENSE--BUT NOT TO THE POINT THEY'D DIE.
THEN SHE LIED TO YOU.
THINGS DIDN'T GO AS EXPECTED, THAT'S NOT THE SAME.
SO IT WAS AN "ACCIDENT" YOU KILLED THEM ALL? WHO ARE YOU TRYING TO FOOL?
JASON, YOU CAN'T BE THAT GULLIBLE.
I'M NOT SURE WHAT TO THINK, I TOLD YOU.
I KNOW I WAS ALONE, THEN GRAIL CAME ALONG AND SUDDENLY I WASN'T.
YOU KNEW WHO I WAS, EVEN IF I DIDN'T KNOW ABOUT YOU YET. YOU COULD HAVE FOUND ME. REACHED OUT.
STOP LOOKING FOR PEOPLE TO BLAME!
THIS IS ON YOU!
YOU SPENT SO LONG HIDING FROM HERA'S JEALOUSY, IT JUST TURNED INTO YOU HIDING!
HE HAD NO MOTHER, NO FATHER.
HE HAD GLAUCUS, WHO SOUNDS LIKE A BETTER FATHER THAN ZEUS EVER COULD BE.

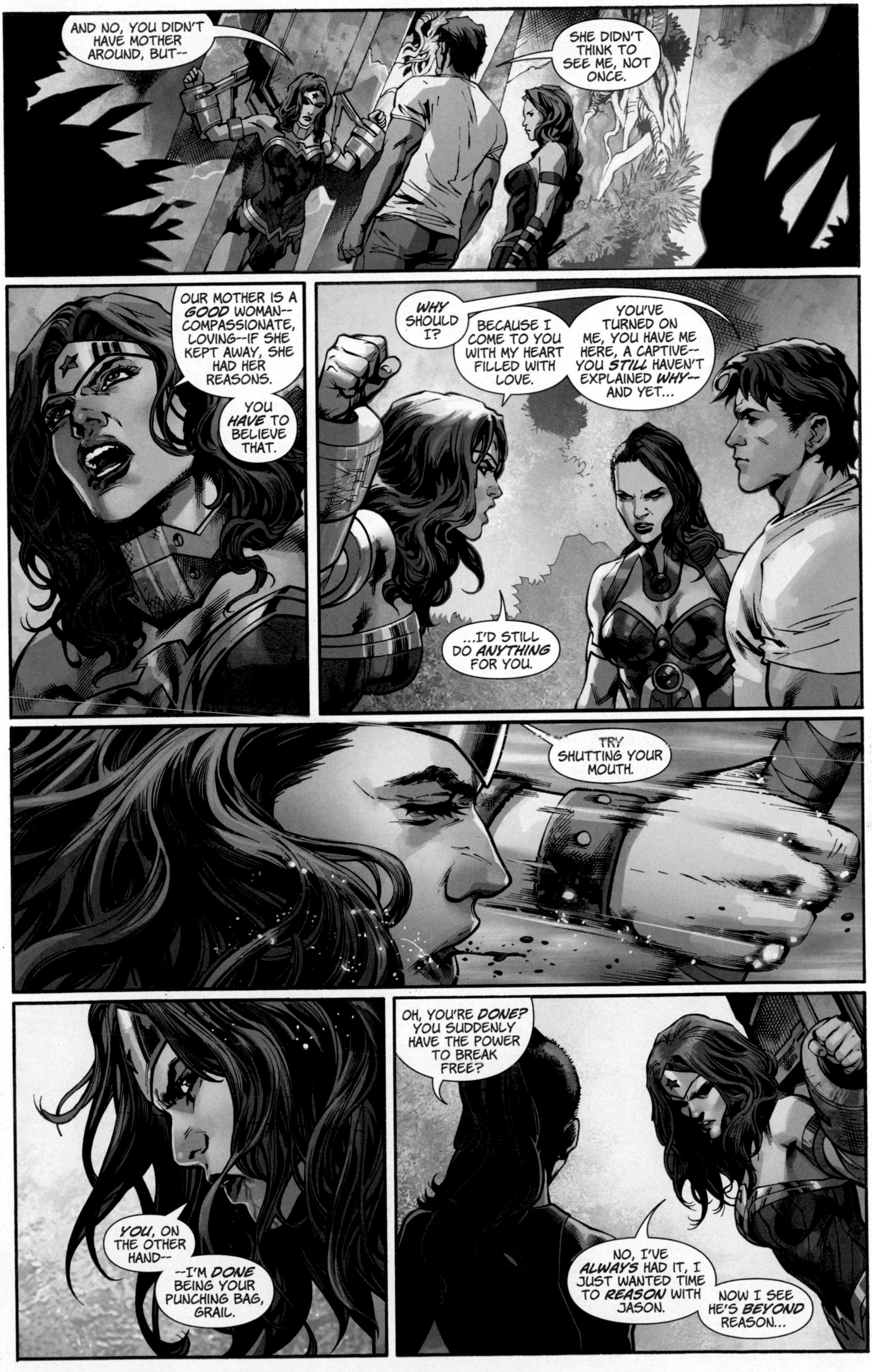

AND NO, YOU DIDN'T HAVE MOTHER AROUND, BUT--
SHE DIDN'T THINK TO SEE ME, NOT ONCE.
OUR MOTHER IS A *GOOD* WOMAN-- COMPASSIONATE, LOVING--IF SHE KEPT AWAY, SHE HAD HER REASONS.
YOU *HAVE* TO BELIEVE THAT.
WHY SHOULD I?
BECAUSE I COME TO YOU WITH MY HEART FILLED WITH LOVE.
YOU'VE TURNED ON ME, YOU HAVE ME HERE, A CAPTIVE-- YOU *STILL* HAVEN'T EXPLAINED *WHY*-- AND YET...
...I'D STILL DO *ANYTHING* FOR YOU.
TRY SHUTTING YOUR MOUTH.
YOU, ON THE OTHER HAND--
--I'M *DONE* BEING YOUR PUNCHING BAG, GRAIL.
OH, YOU'RE *DONE*? YOU SUDDENLY HAVE THE POWER TO BREAK FREE?
NO, I'VE *ALWAYS* HAD IT, I JUST WANTED TIME TO *REASON* WITH JASON.
NOW I SEE HE'S *BEYOND* REASON...

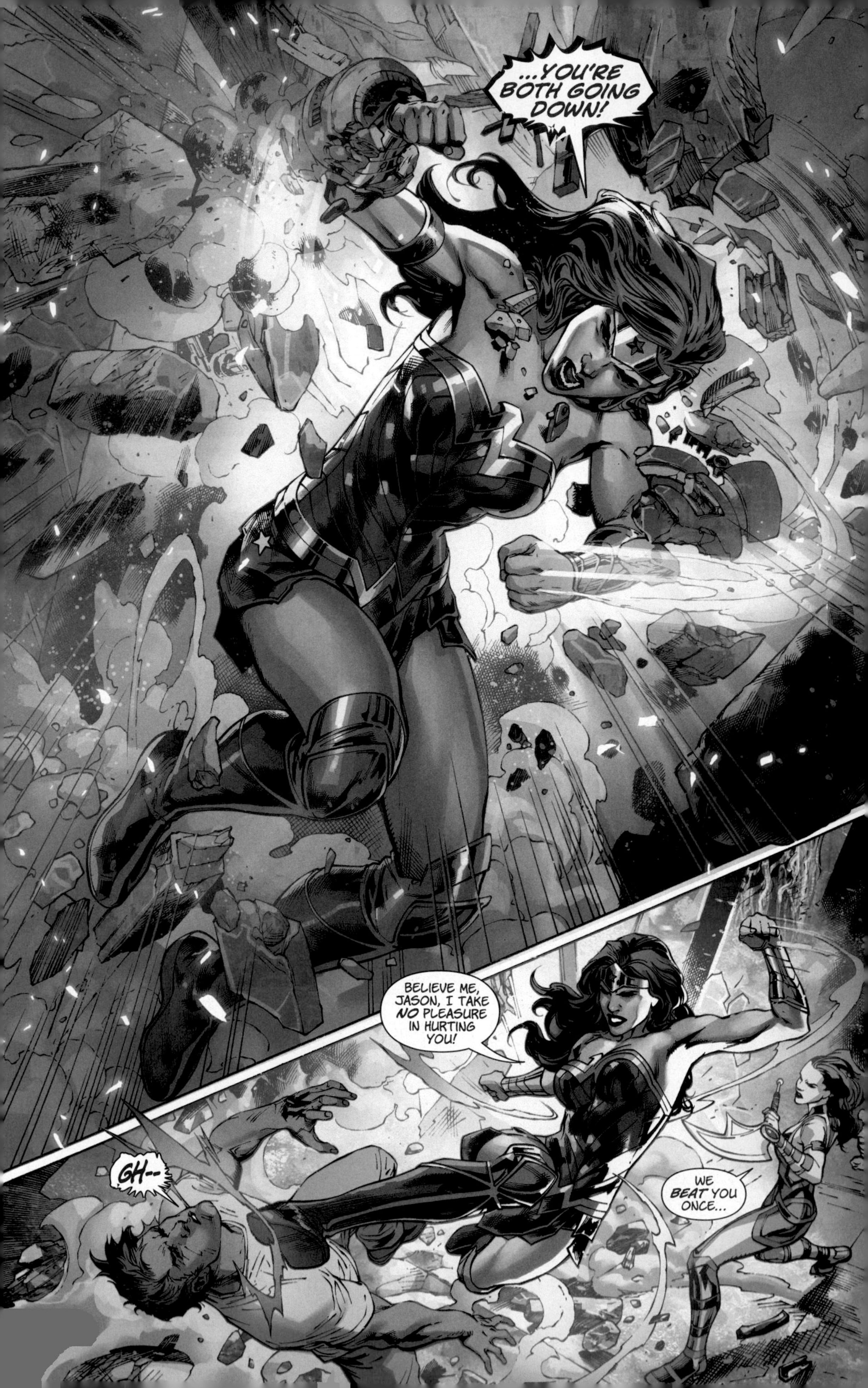
...YOU'RE BOTH GOING DOWN!
BELIEVE ME, JASON, I TAKE NO PLEASURE IN HURTING YOU!
GH--
WE BEAT YOU ONCE...

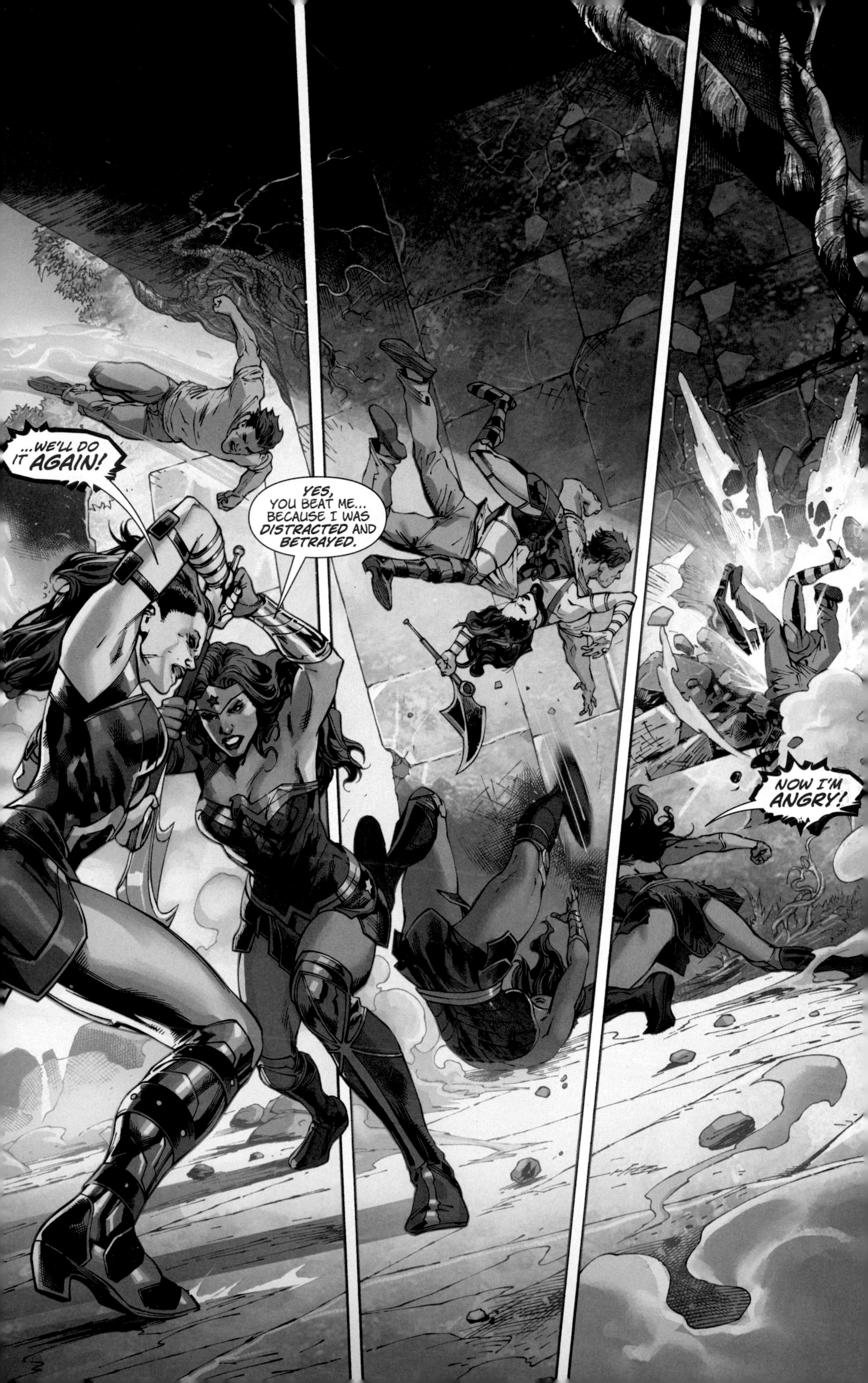
...WE'LL DO IT AGAIN!
YES, YOU BEAT ME... BECAUSE I WAS DISTRACTED AND BETRAYED.
NOW I'M ANGRY!

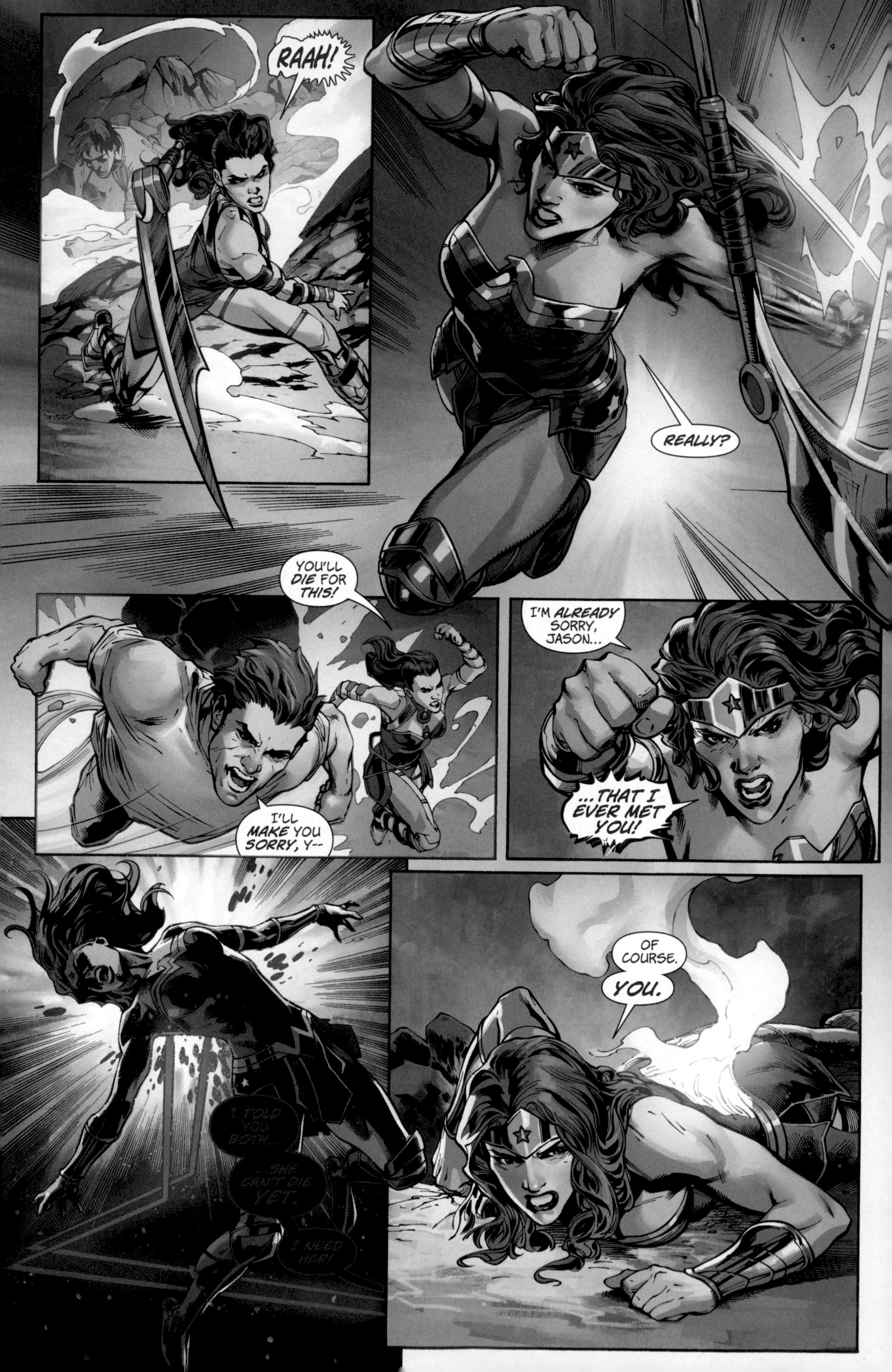
RAAH!
REALLY?
YOU'LL DIE FOR THIS!
I'LL MAKE YOU SORRY, Y--
I'M ALREADY SORRY, JASON...
...THAT I EVER MET YOU!
I TOLD YOU BOTH...
...SHE CAN'T DIE YET.
I NEED HER!
OF COURSE.
YOU.

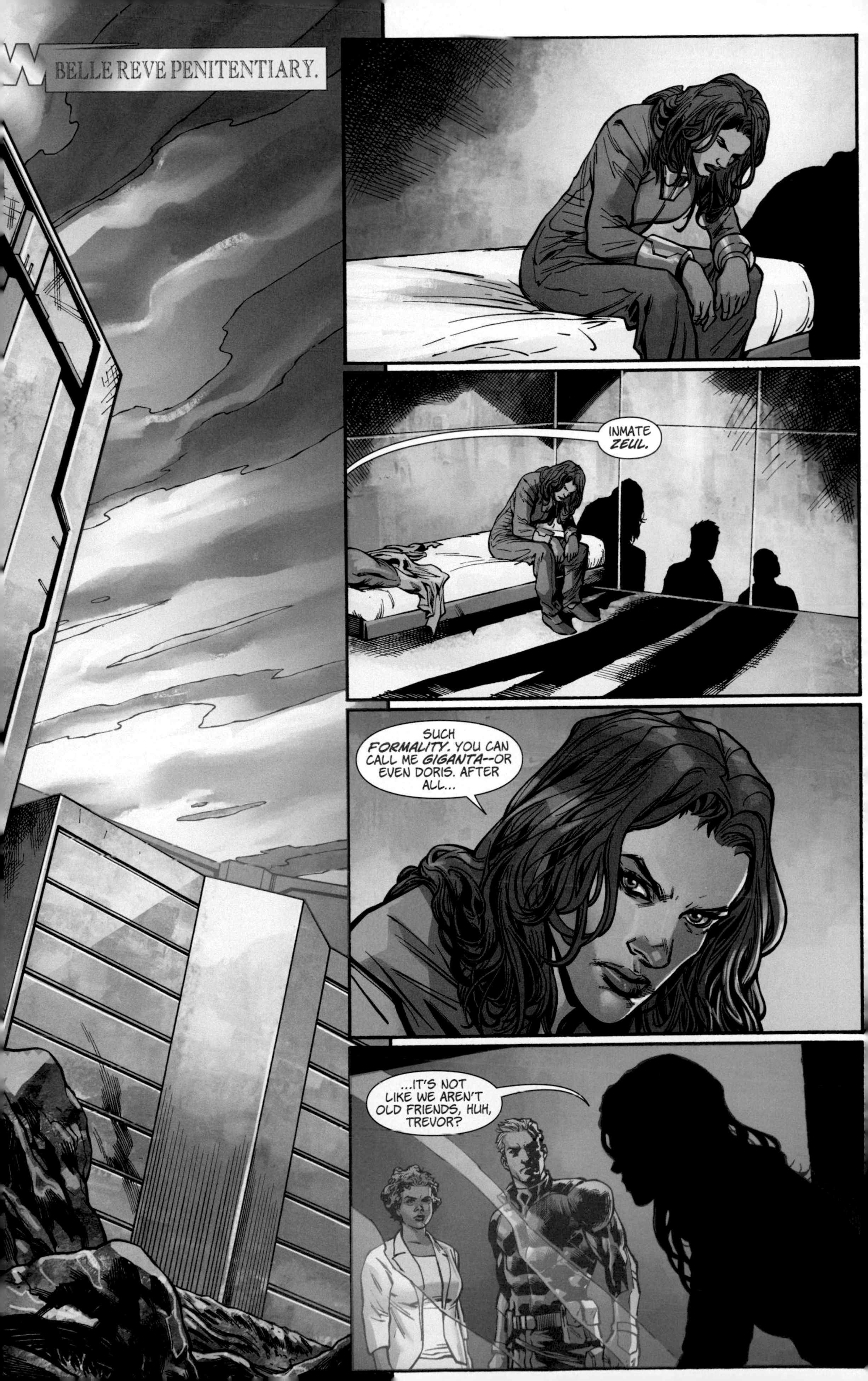
BELLE REVE PENITENTIARY.
INMATE ZEUL.
SUCH FORMALITY. YOU CAN CALL ME GIGANTA--OR EVEN DORIS. AFTER ALL...
...IT'S NOT LIKE WE AREN'T OLD FRIENDS, HUH, TREVOR?

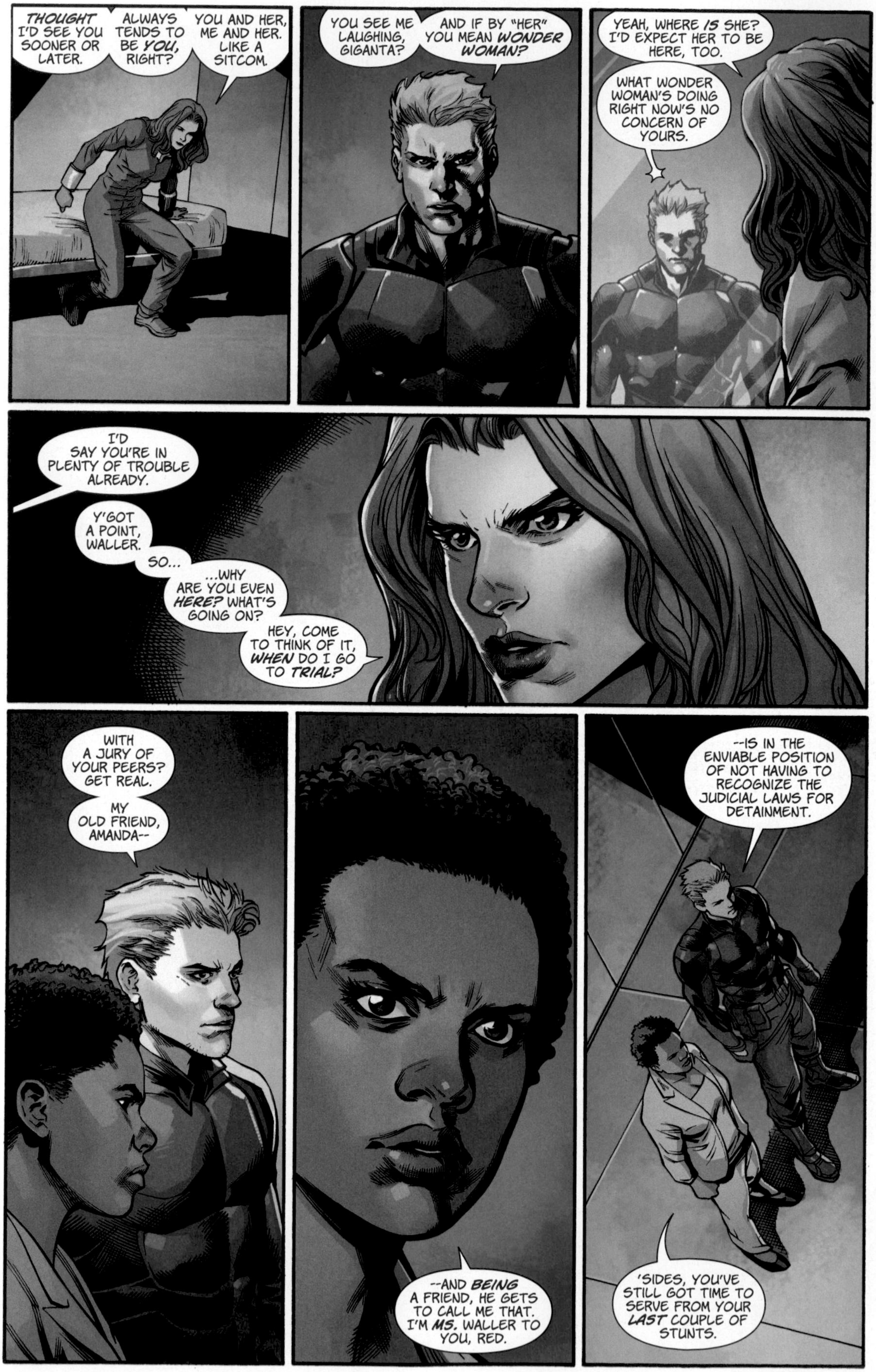
THOUGHT I'D SEE YOU SOONER OR LATER.
ALWAYS TENDS TO BE YOU, RIGHT?
YOU AND HER, ME AND HER. LIKE A SITCOM.
YOU SEE ME LAUGHING, GIGANTA?
AND IF BY "HER" YOU MEAN WONDER WOMAN?
YEAH, WHERE IS SHE? I'D EXPECT HER TO BE HERE, TOO.
WHAT WONDER WOMAN'S DOING RIGHT NOW'S NO CONCERN OF YOURS.
I'D SAY YOU'RE IN PLENTY OF TROUBLE ALREADY.
Y'GOT A POINT, WALLER.
SO...
...WHY ARE YOU EVEN HERE? WHAT'S GOING ON?
HEY, COME TO THINK OF IT, WHEN DO I GO TO TRIAL?
WITH A JURY OF YOUR PEERS? GET REAL.
MY OLD FRIEND, AMANDA--
--AND BEING A FRIEND, HE GETS TO CALL ME THAT. I'M MS. WALLER TO YOU, RED.
--IS IN THE ENVIABLE POSITION OF NOT HAVING TO RECOGNIZE THE JUDICIAL LAWS FOR DETAINMENT.
'SIDES, YOU'VE STILL GOT TIME TO SERVE FROM YOUR LAST COUPLE OF STUNTS.

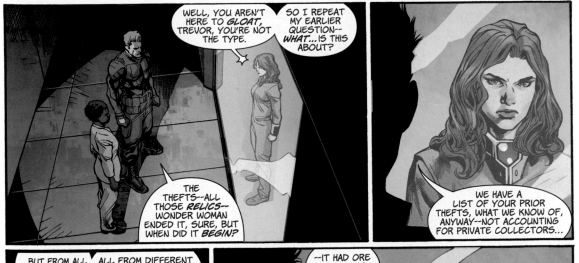

WELL, YOU AREN'T HERE TO *GLOAT,* TREVOR, YOU'RE NOT THE TYPE.

SO I REPEAT MY EARLIER QUESTION-- *WHAT...*IS THIS ABOUT?

THE THEFTS--ALL THOSE *RELICS*-- WONDER WOMAN ENDED IT, SURE, BUT WHEN DID IT *BEGIN?*

WE HAVE A LIST OF YOUR PRIOR THEFTS, WHAT WE KNOW OF, ANYWAY--NOT ACCOUNTING FOR PRIVATE COLLECTORS...

...BUT FROM ALL WE CAN TELL, THEY HAVE NOTHING IN COMMON.

ALL FROM DIFFERENT PARTS OF THE WORLD, ERAS, EMPIRES AND ANCIENT RELIGIONS. EGYPTIAN, MAYAN, MESOPOTAMIAN.

HELL, ONE WAS REPORTEDLY EVEN USED BY ARION, BACK IN ATLANTIS.

THING IS, THE *LAST* RELIC-- THE ONE WONDER WOMAN STOPPED YOU FROM TAKING--

--IT HAD ORE AMONG ITS COMPOSITION *NOT* OF *EARTH.*

MORE SPECIFICALLY, FROM A CERTAIN PLANET-- SOLAR SYSTEM--DIMENSION. WE'RE STILL TRYING TO DETERMINE WHICH *EXACTLY.*

ALL WE DO KNOW IS IT'S CALLED *APOKOLIPS,* AND BAD THINGS LIVE THERE.

SO...

YEAH?

ASSUMING YOU WEREN'T JUST COLLECTING KNICK-KNACKS FOR YOUR APARTMENT, SOMEONE HAD TO HAVE HIRED YOU.

A *NAME.*

Y'KNOW, HE NEVER ACTUALLY *SAID* HIS NAME, BUT ONE LOOK AT HIM..

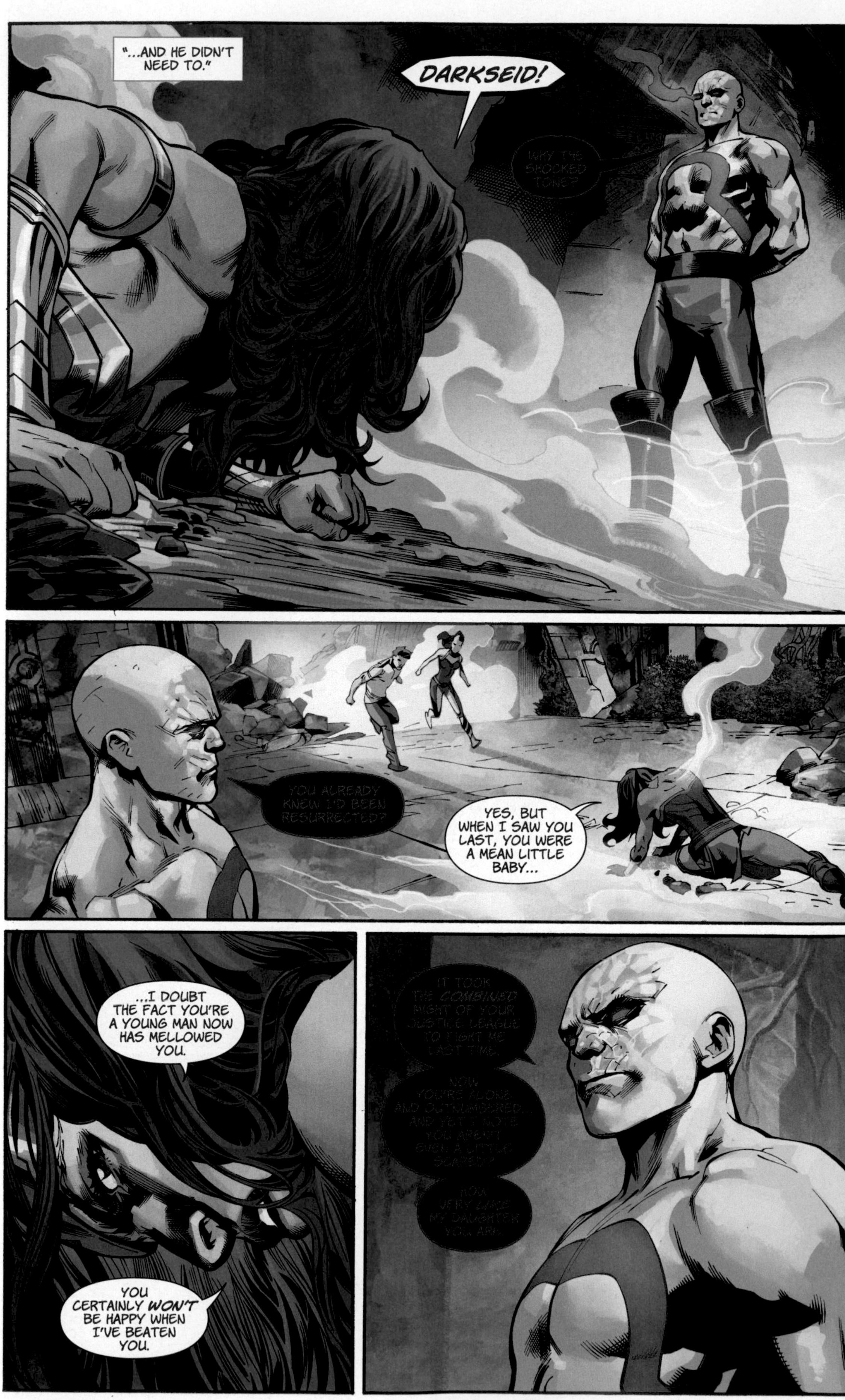
"...AND HE DIDN'T NEED TO."
DARKSEID!
WHY THE SHOCKED TONE?
YOU ALREADY KNEW I'D BEEN RESURRECTED?
YES, BUT WHEN I SAW YOU LAST, YOU WERE A MEAN LITTLE BABY...
...I DOUBT THE FACT YOU'RE A YOUNG MAN NOW HAS MELLOWED YOU.
IT TOOK THE *COMBINED* MIGHT OF YOUR JUSTICE LEAGUE TO FIGHT ME LAST TIME.
NOW YOU'RE ALONE AND OUTNUMBERED... AND YET I NOTE YOU AREN'T EVEN A LITTLE SCARED?
HOW VERY *LIKE* MY DAUGHTER YOU ARE.
YOU CERTAINLY *WON'T* BE HAPPY WHEN I'VE BEATEN YOU.

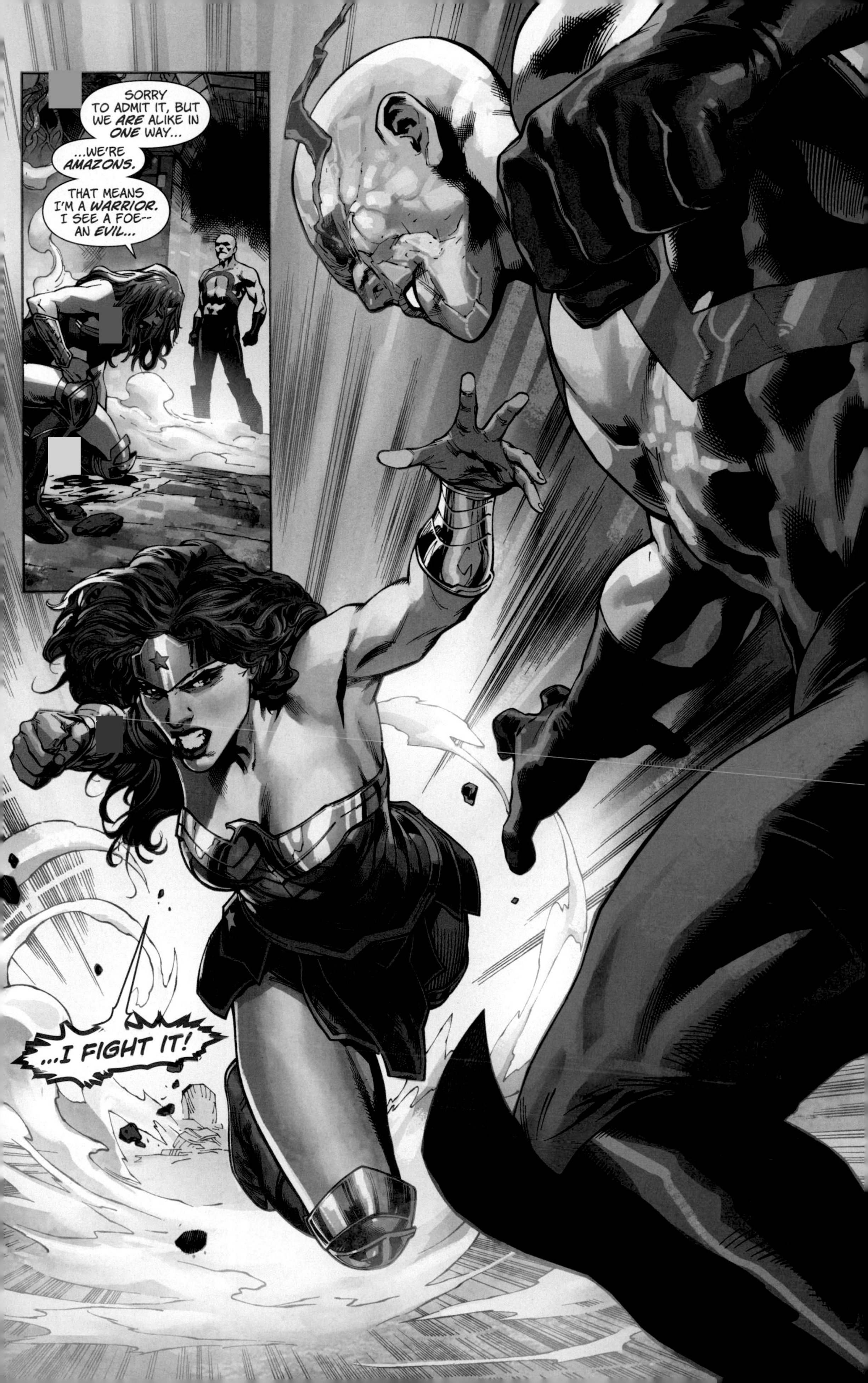
SORRY TO ADMIT IT, BUT WE ARE ALIKE IN ONE WAY...
...WE'RE AMAZONS.
THAT MEANS I'M A WARRIOR. I SEE A FOE-- AN EVIL...
...I FIGHT IT!

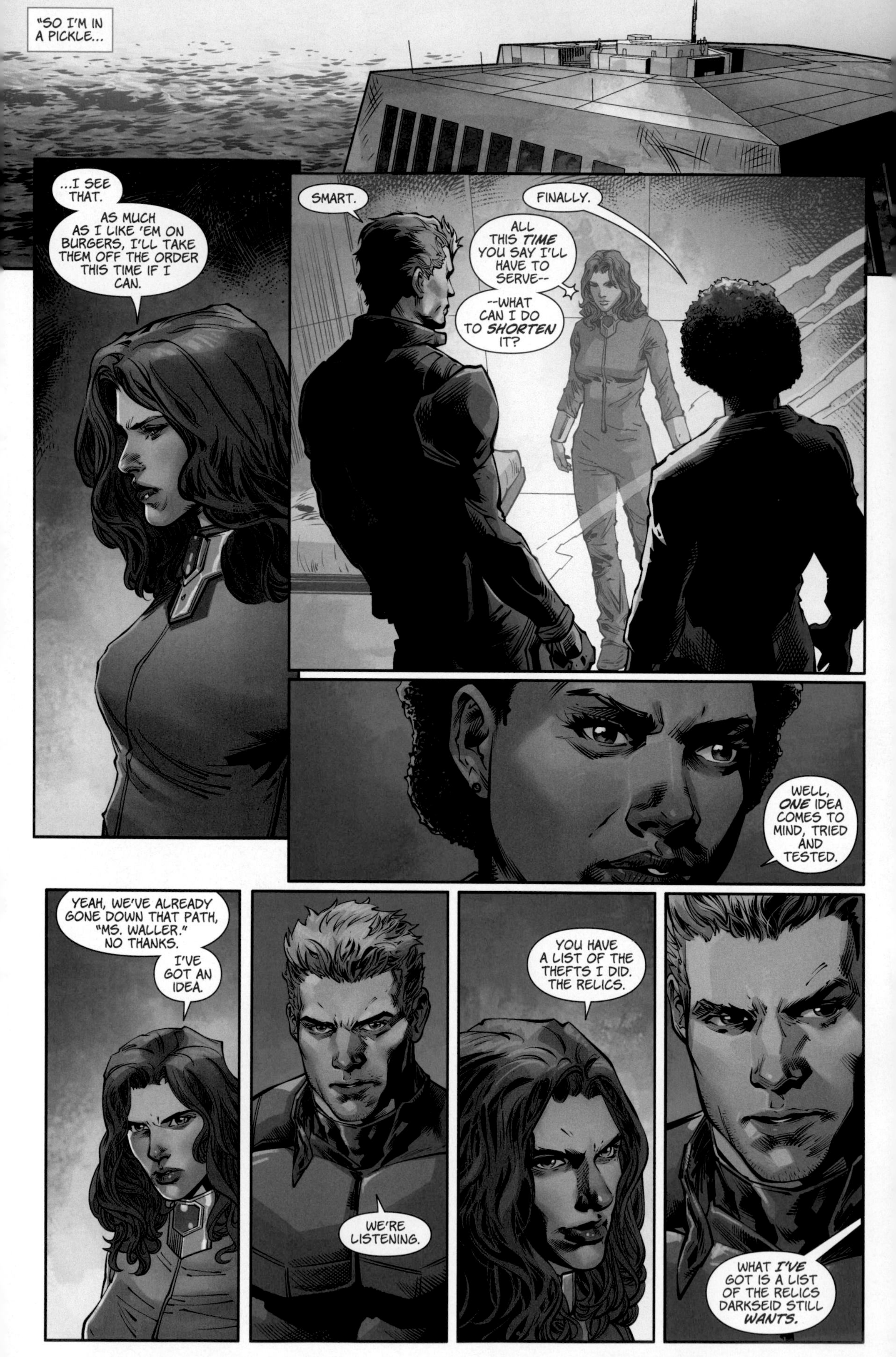
"SO I'M IN A PICKLE...
...I SEE THAT.
AS MUCH AS I LIKE 'EM ON BURGERS, I'LL TAKE THEM OFF THE ORDER THIS TIME IF I CAN.
SMART.
FINALLY.
ALL THIS TIME YOU SAY I'LL HAVE TO SERVE--
--WHAT CAN I DO TO SHORTEN IT?
WELL, ONE IDEA COMES TO MIND, TRIED AND TESTED.
YEAH, WE'VE ALREADY GONE DOWN THAT PATH, "MS. WALLER." NO THANKS.
I'VE GOT AN IDEA.
WE'RE LISTENING.
YOU HAVE A LIST OF THE THEFTS I DID. THE RELICS.
WHAT I'VE GOT IS A LIST OF THE RELICS DARKSEID STILL WANTS.

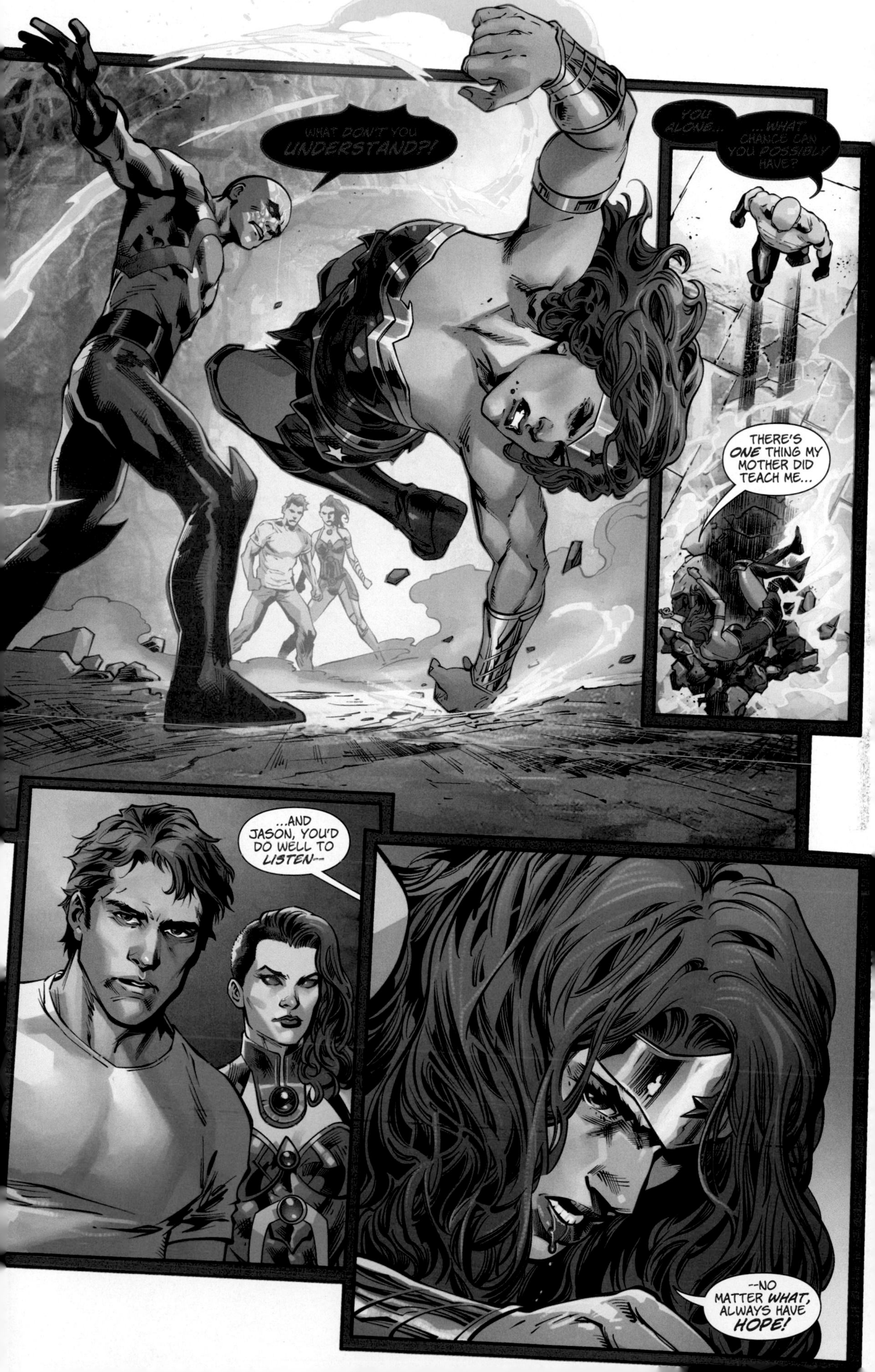
WHAT DON'T YOU UNDERSTAND?!
YOU ALONE...
...WHAT CHANCE CAN YOU POSSIBLY HAVE?
THERE'S ONE THING MY MOTHER DID TEACH ME...
...AND JASON, YOU'D DO WELL TO LISTEN--
--NO MATTER WHAT, ALWAYS HAVE HOPE!

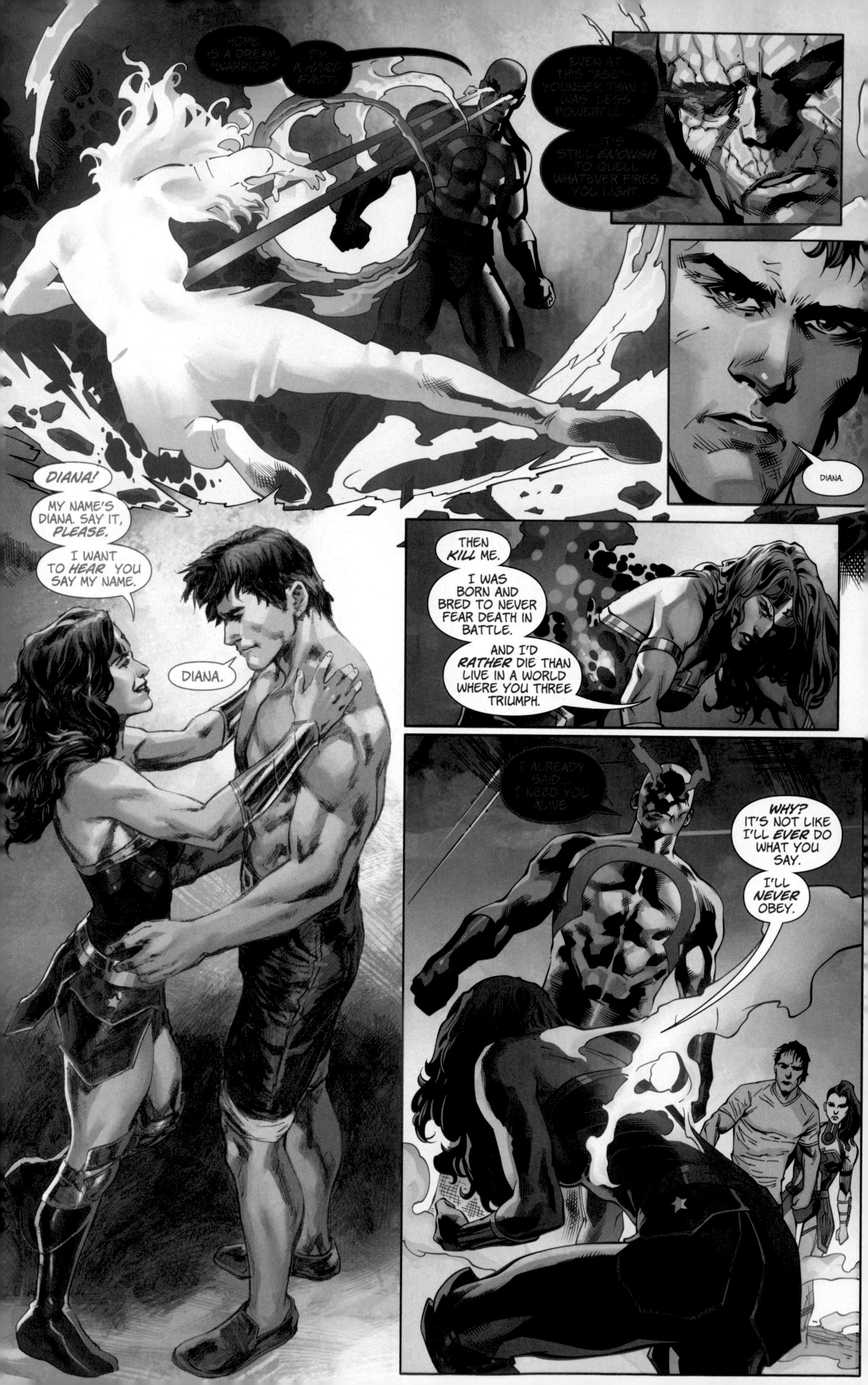
HOPE IS A DREAM, "WARRIOR."
I'M A HARD FAST.
EVEN AT THIS "AGE"--YOUNGER THAN I WAS, LESS POWERFUL...
...IT'S STILL ENOUGH TO QUELL WHATEVER FIRES YOU LIGHT.
DIANA.
DIANA!
MY NAME'S DIANA. SAY IT, PLEASE.
I WANT TO HEAR YOU SAY MY NAME.
DIANA.
THEN KILL ME.
I WAS BORN AND BRED TO NEVER FEAR DEATH IN BATTLE.
AND I'D RATHER DIE THAN LIVE IN A WORLD WHERE YOU THREE TRIUMPH.
I ALREADY SAID... I NEED YOU ALIVE.
WHY? IT'S NOT LIKE I'LL EVER DO WHAT YOU SAY.
I'LL NEVER OBEY.

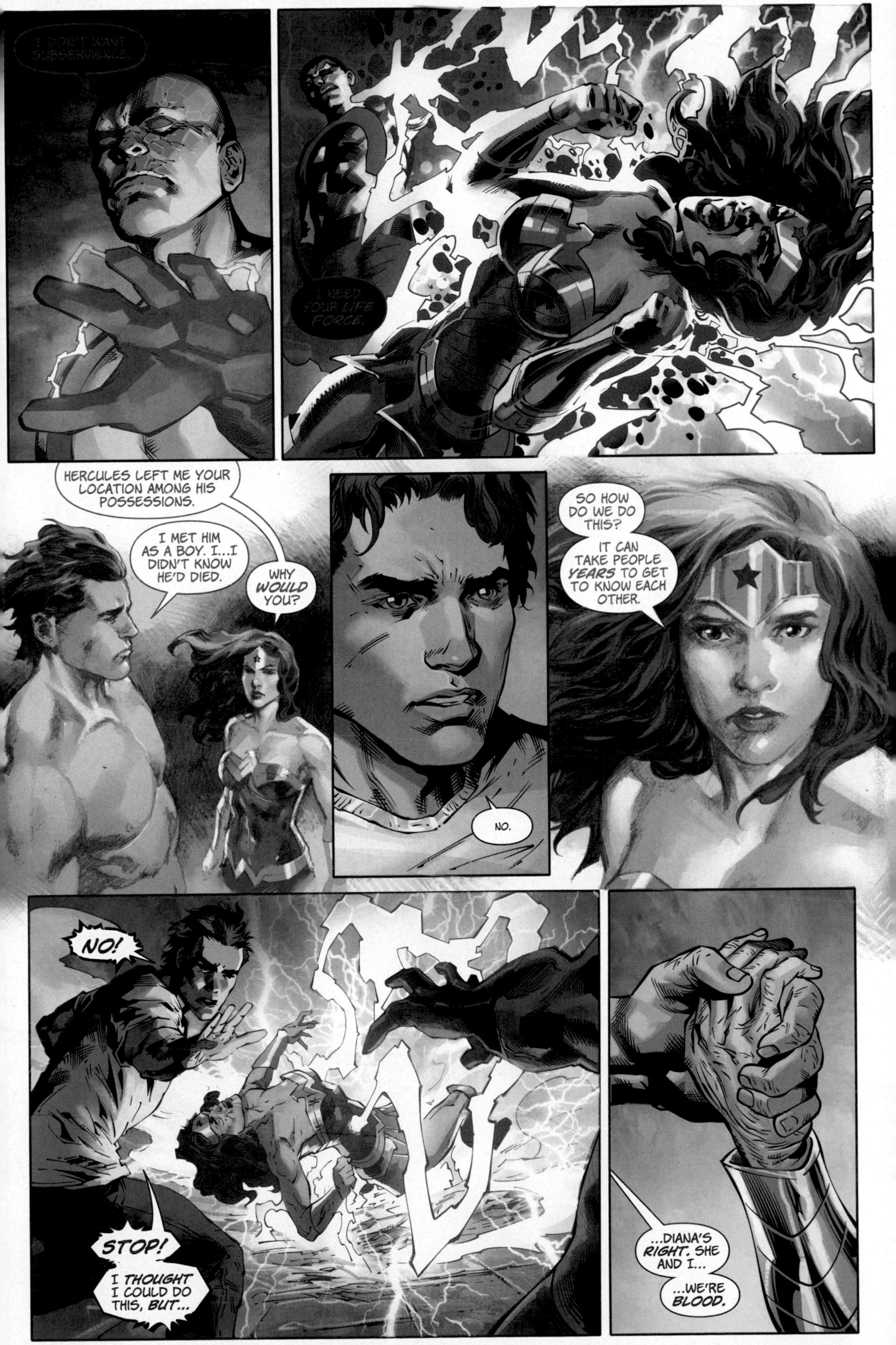

I DON'T WANT SUBSERVIENCE.
I NEED YOUR LIFE FORCE.
HERCULES LEFT ME YOUR LOCATION AMONG HIS POSSESSIONS.
I MET HIM AS A BOY. I...I DIDN'T KNOW HE'D DIED.
WHY WOULD YOU?
NO.
SO HOW DO WE DO THIS?
IT CAN TAKE PEOPLE YEARS TO GET TO KNOW EACH OTHER.
NO!
STOP!
I THOUGHT I COULD DO THIS, BUT...
...DIANA'S RIGHT. SHE AND I...
...WE'RE BLOOD.

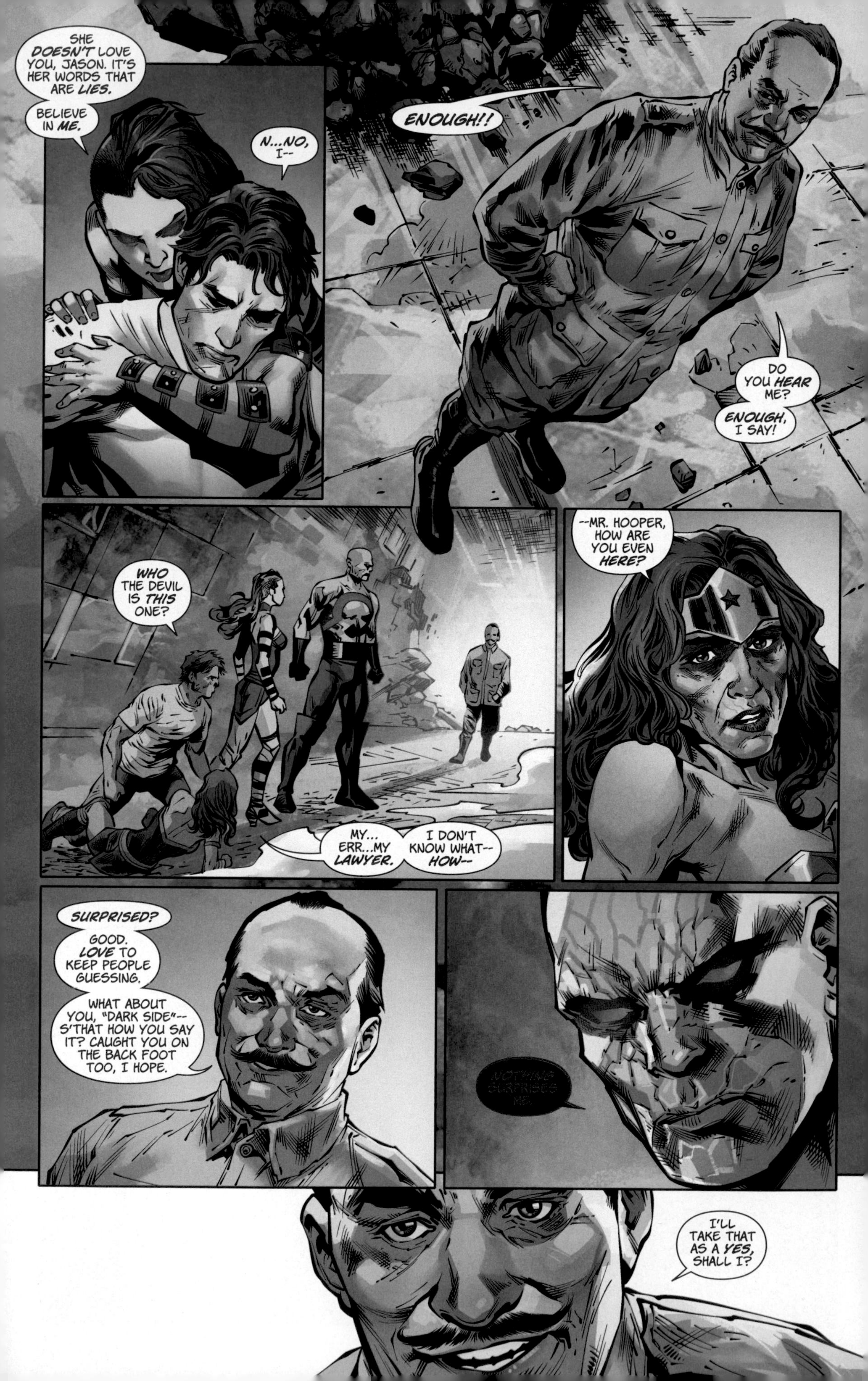
SHE DOESN'T LOVE YOU, JASON. IT'S HER WORDS THAT ARE LIES.
BELIEVE IN ME.
N...NO, I--
ENOUGH!!
DO YOU HEAR ME?
ENOUGH, I SAY!
WHO THE DEVIL IS THIS ONE?
MY... ERR...MY LAWYER.
I DON'T KNOW WHAT--HOW--
--MR. HOOPER, HOW ARE YOU EVEN HERE?
SURPRISED?
GOOD. LOVE TO KEEP PEOPLE GUESSING.
WHAT ABOUT YOU, "DARK SIDE"--S'THAT HOW YOU SAY IT? CAUGHT YOU ON THE BACK FOOT TOO, I HOPE.
NOTHING SURPRISES ME.
I'LL TAKE THAT AS A YES, SHALL I?

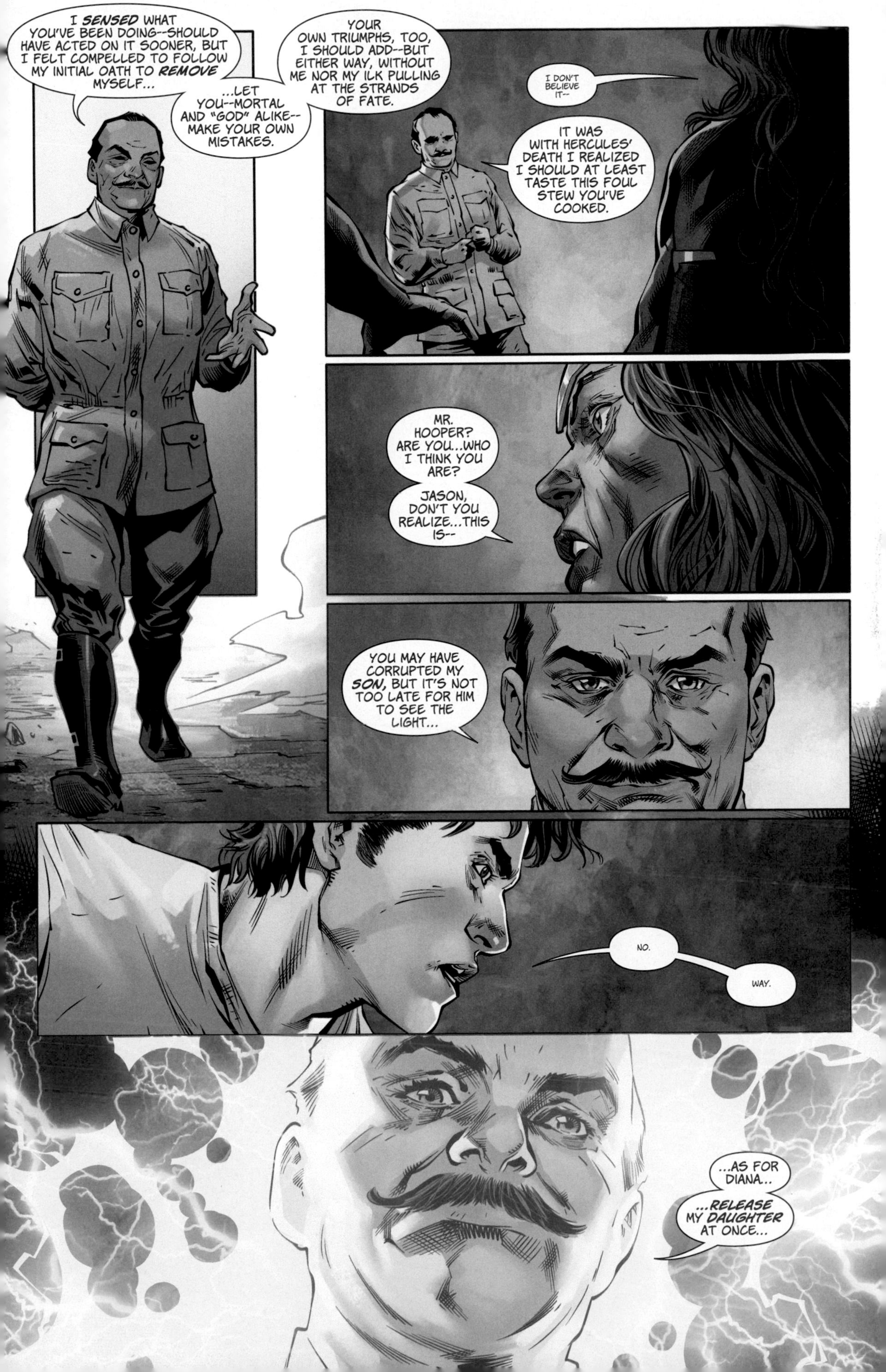
I SENSED WHAT YOU'VE BEEN DOING--SHOULD HAVE ACTED ON IT SOONER, BUT I FELT COMPELLED TO FOLLOW MY INITIAL OATH TO REMOVE MYSELF...
...LET YOU--MORTAL AND "GOD" ALIKE--MAKE YOUR OWN MISTAKES.
YOUR OWN TRIUMPHS, TOO, I SHOULD ADD--BUT EITHER WAY, WITHOUT ME NOR MY ILK PULLING AT THE STRANDS OF FATE.
I DON'T BELIEVE IT--
IT WAS WITH HERCULES' DEATH I REALIZED I SHOULD AT LEAST TASTE THIS FOUL STEW YOU'VE COOKED.
MR. HOOPER? ARE YOU...WHO I THINK YOU ARE?
JASON, DON'T YOU REALIZE...THIS IS--
YOU MAY HAVE CORRUPTED MY SON, BUT IT'S NOT TOO LATE FOR HIM TO SEE THE LIGHT...
NO.
WAY.
...AS FOR DIANA...
...RELEASE MY DAUGHTER AT ONCE...

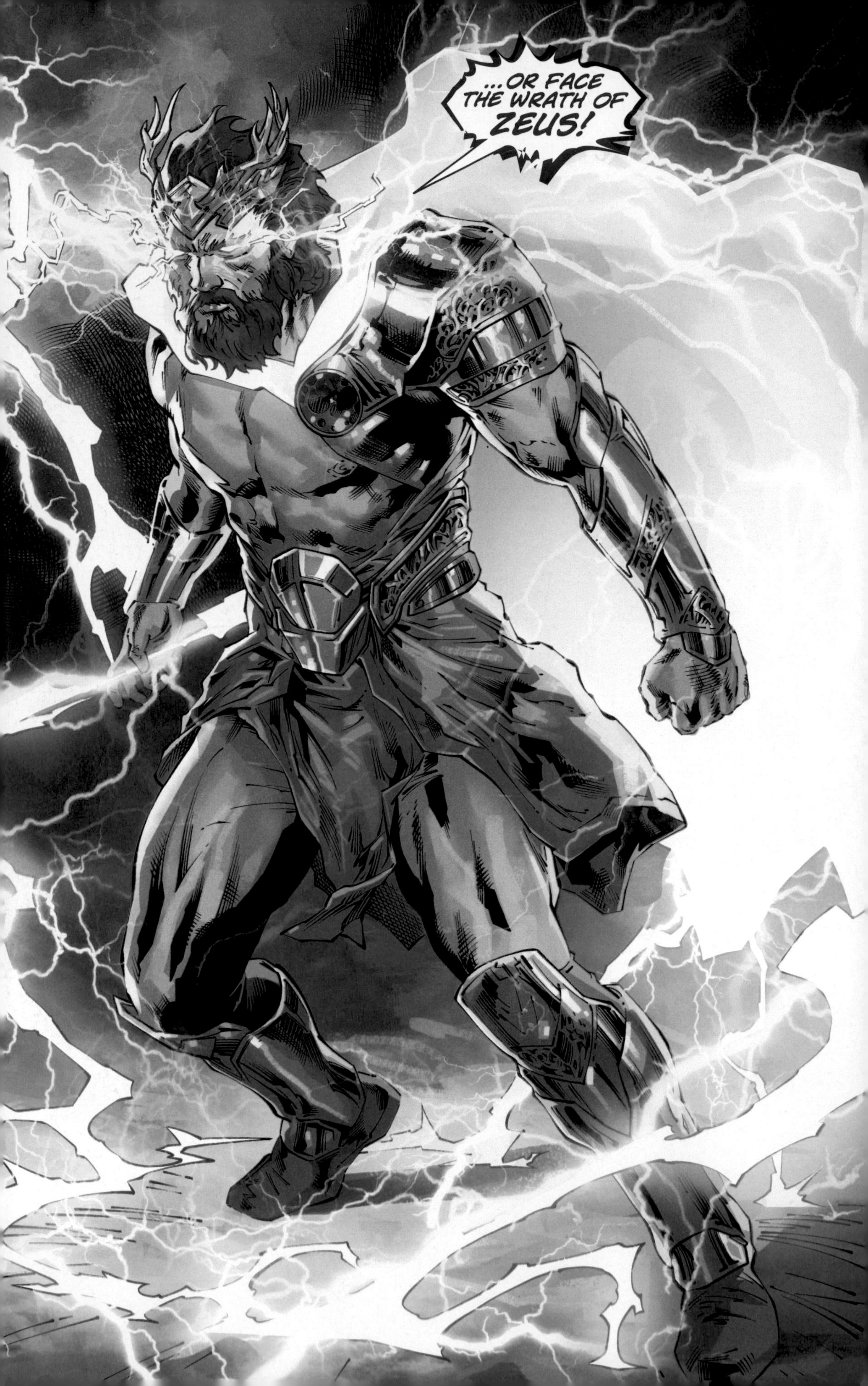
...OR FACE THE WRATH OF ZEUS!

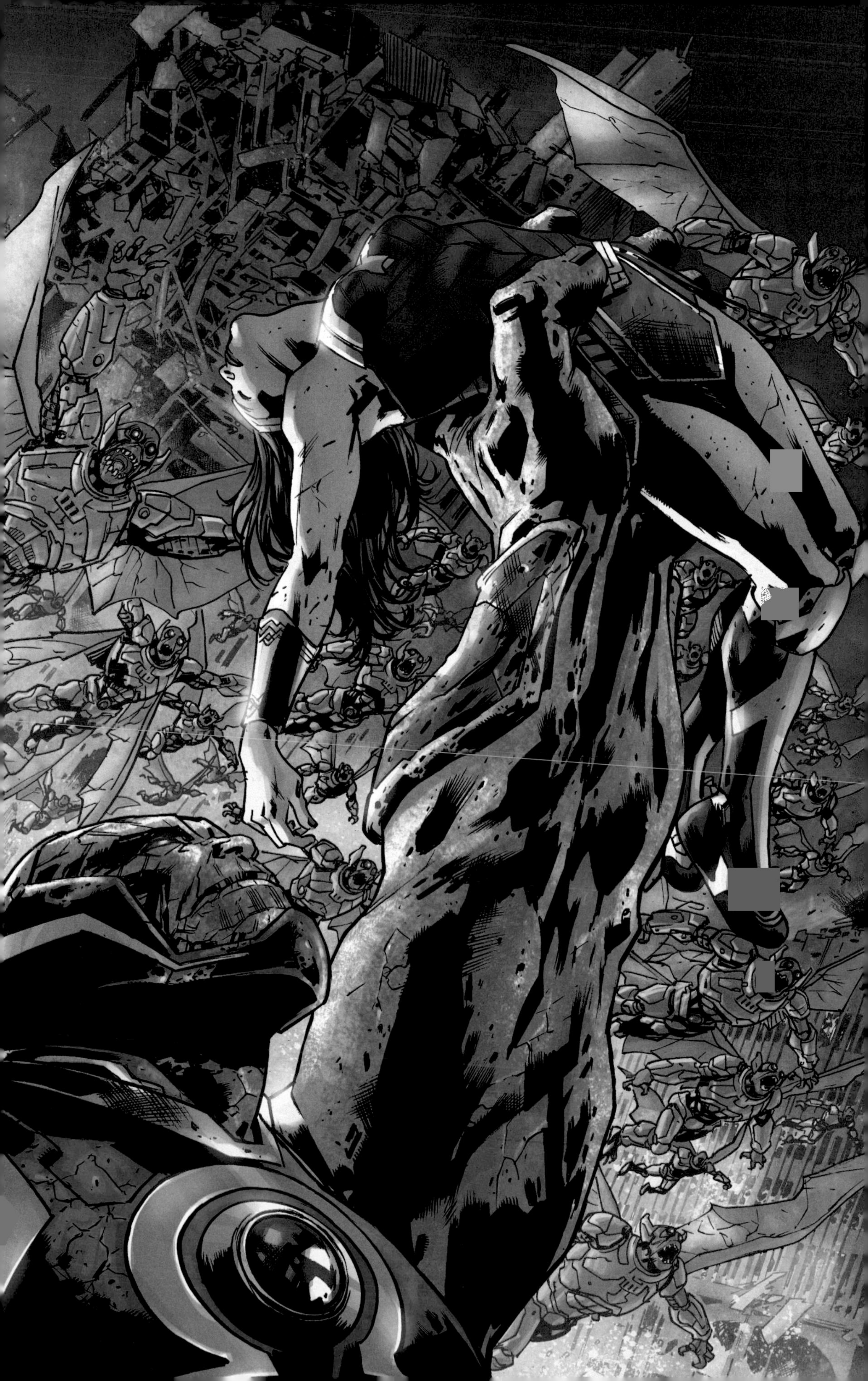

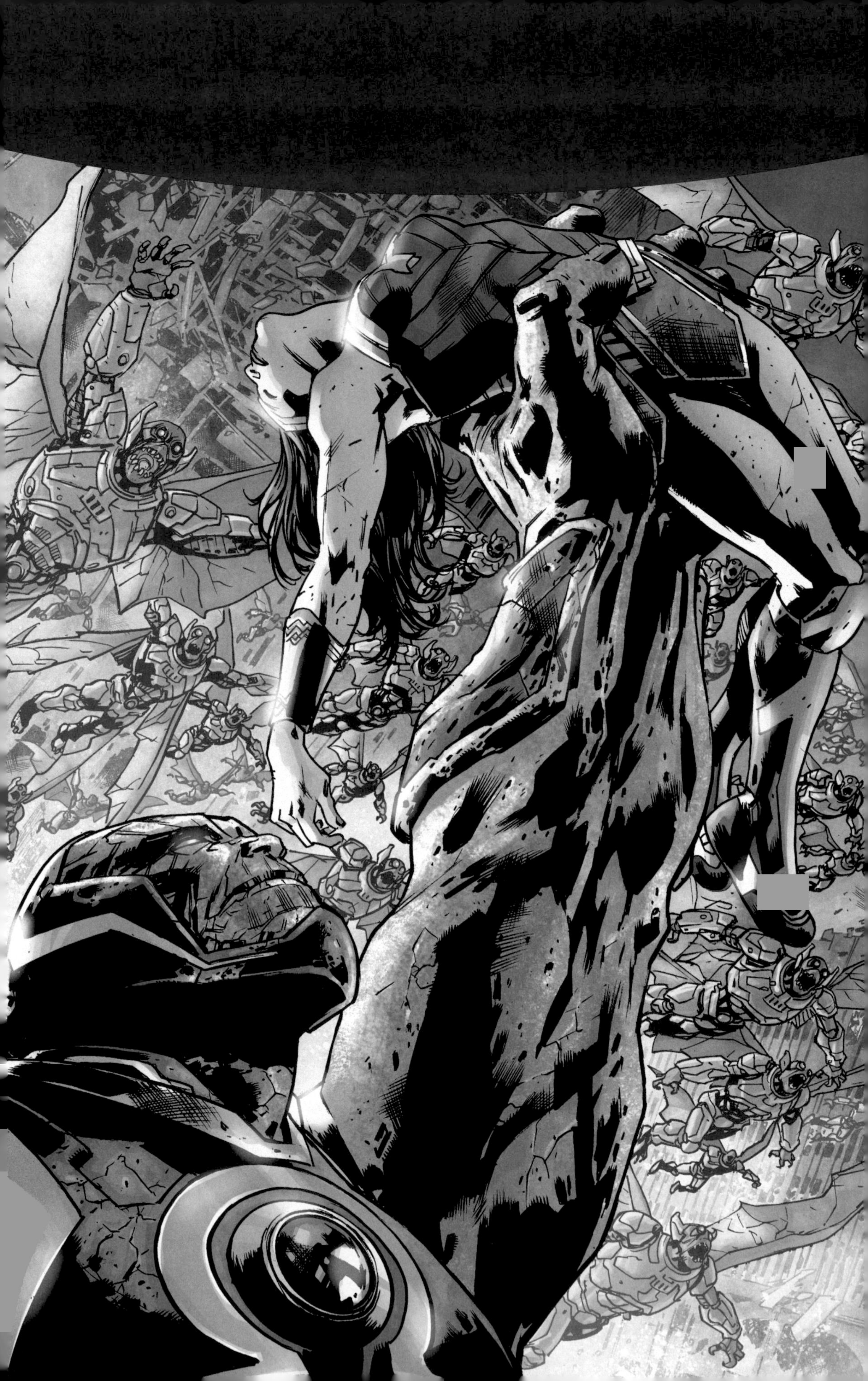

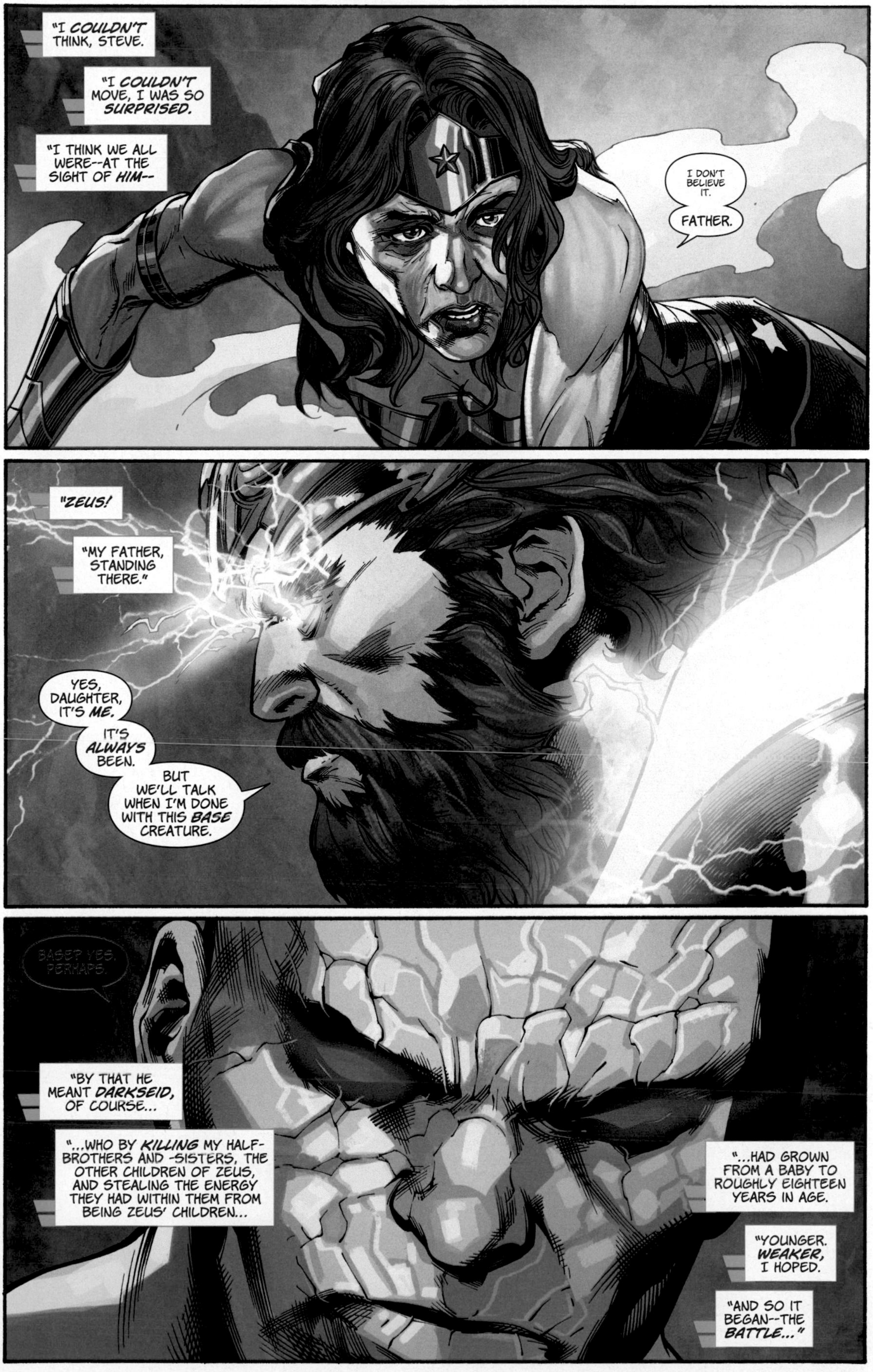
"I *COULDN'T* THINK, STEVE.
"I *COULDN'T* MOVE, I WAS SO *SURPRISED.*
"I THINK WE ALL WERE--AT THE SIGHT OF *HIM*--
I DON'T BELIEVE IT.
FATHER.
"*ZEUS!*
"MY FATHER, STANDING THERE."
YES, DAUGHTER, IT'S *ME.*
IT'S *ALWAYS* BEEN.
BUT WE'LL TALK WHEN I'M DONE WITH THIS *BASE* CREATURE.
BASE? YES. PERHAPS.
"BY THAT HE MEANT *DARKSEID,* OF COURSE...
"...WHO BY *KILLING* MY HALF-BROTHERS AND -SISTERS, THE OTHER CHILDREN OF ZEUS, AND STEALING THE ENERGY THEY HAD WITHIN THEM FROM BEING ZEUS' CHILDREN...
"...HAD GROWN FROM A BABY TO ROUGHLY EIGHTEEN YEARS IN AGE.
"YOUNGER. *WEAKER,* I HOPED.
"AND SO IT BEGAN--THE *BATTLE...*"

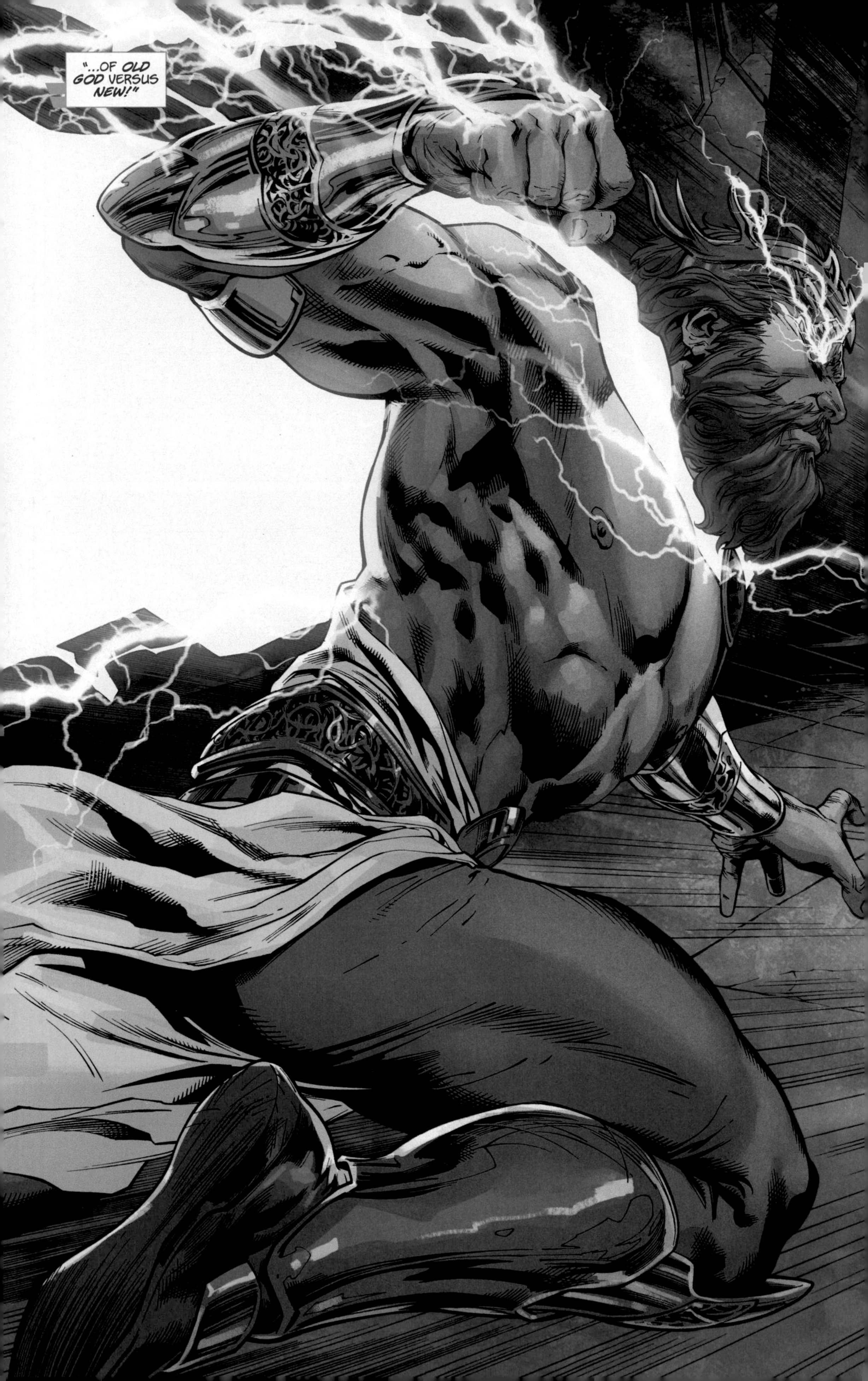
"...OF OLD GOD VERSUS NEW!"

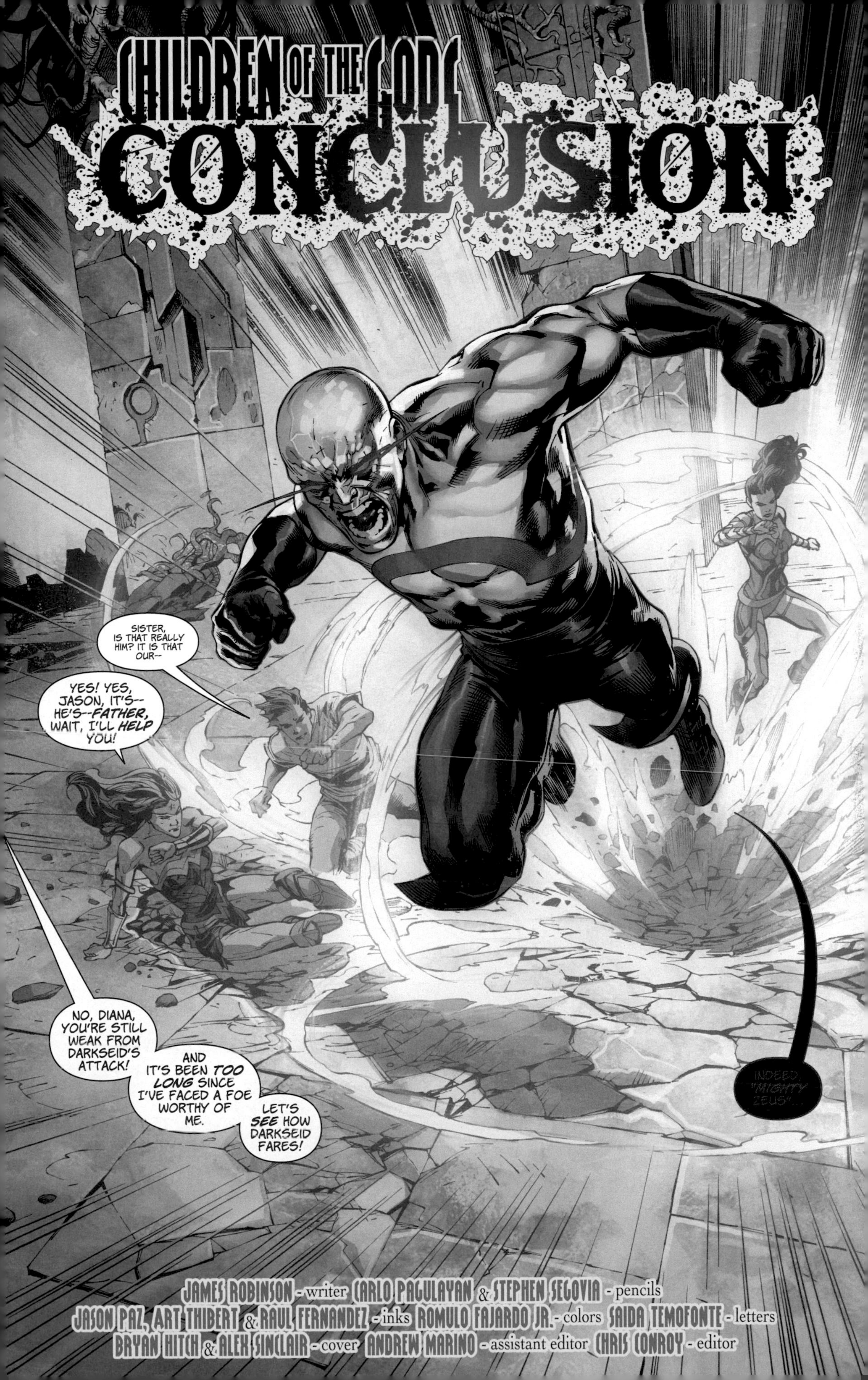

CHILDREN OF THE GODS
CONCLUSION
SISTER, IS THAT REALLY HIM? IT IS THAT OUR--
YES! YES, JASON, IT'S-- HE'S--FATHER, WAIT, I'LL HELP YOU!
NO, DIANA, YOU'RE STILL WEAK FROM DARKSEID'S ATTACK!
AND IT'S BEEN TOO LONG SINCE I'VE FACED A FOE WORTHY OF ME.
LET'S SEE HOW DARKSEID FARES!
INDEED, "MIGHTY ZEUS"...
JAMES ROBINSON - writer CARLO PAGULAYAN & STEPHEN SEGOVIA - pencils
JASON PAZ, ART THIBERT & RAUL FERNANDEZ - inks ROMULO FAJARDO JR. - colors SAIDA TEMOFONTE - letters
BRYAN HITCH & ALEX SINCLAIR - cover ANDREW MARINO - assistant editor CHRIS CONROY - editor

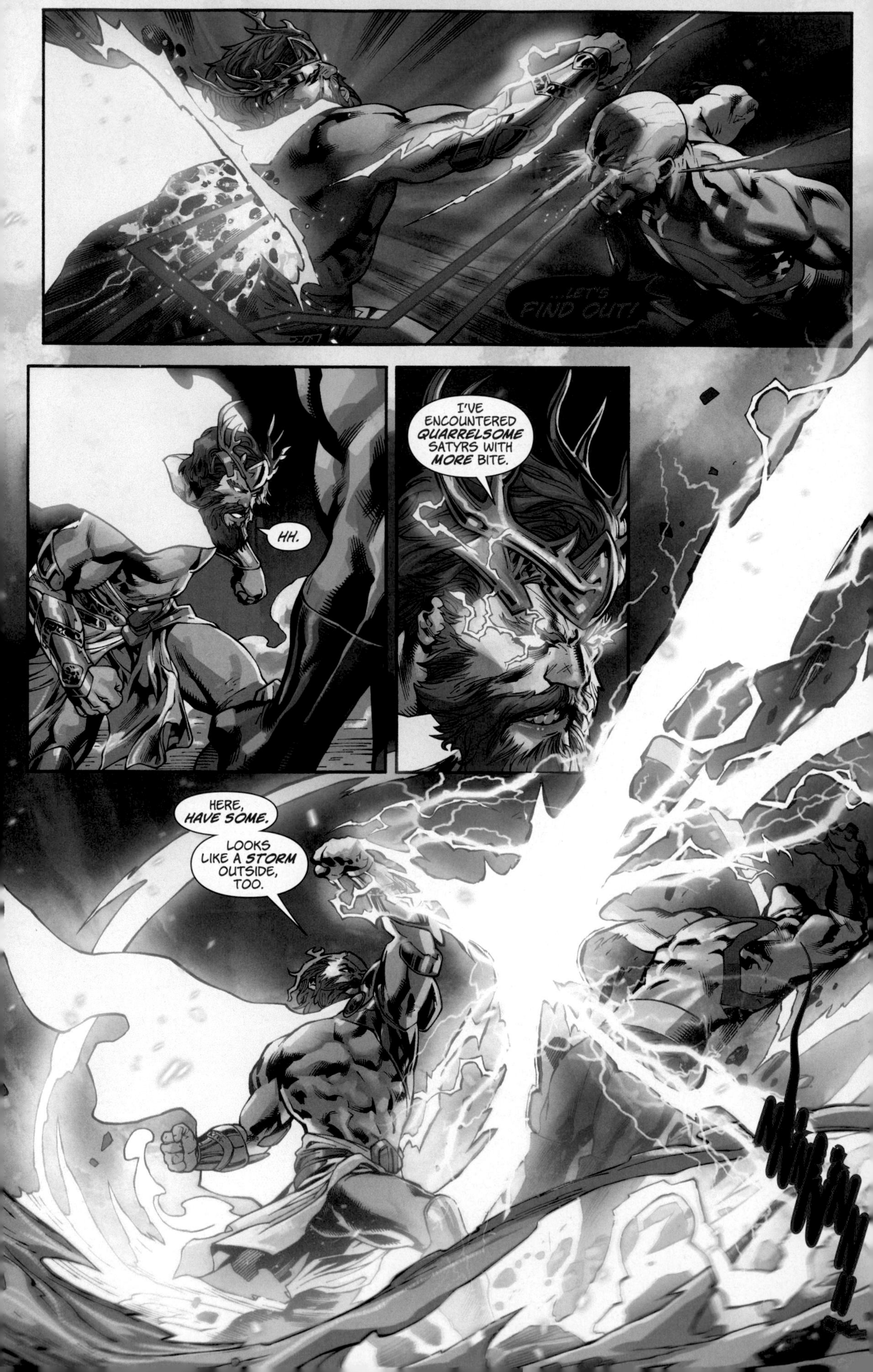
...LET'S FIND OUT!
HH.
I'VE ENCOUNTERED QUARRELSOME SATYRS WITH MORE BITE.
HERE, HAVE SOME.
LOOKS LIKE A STORM OUTSIDE, TOO.

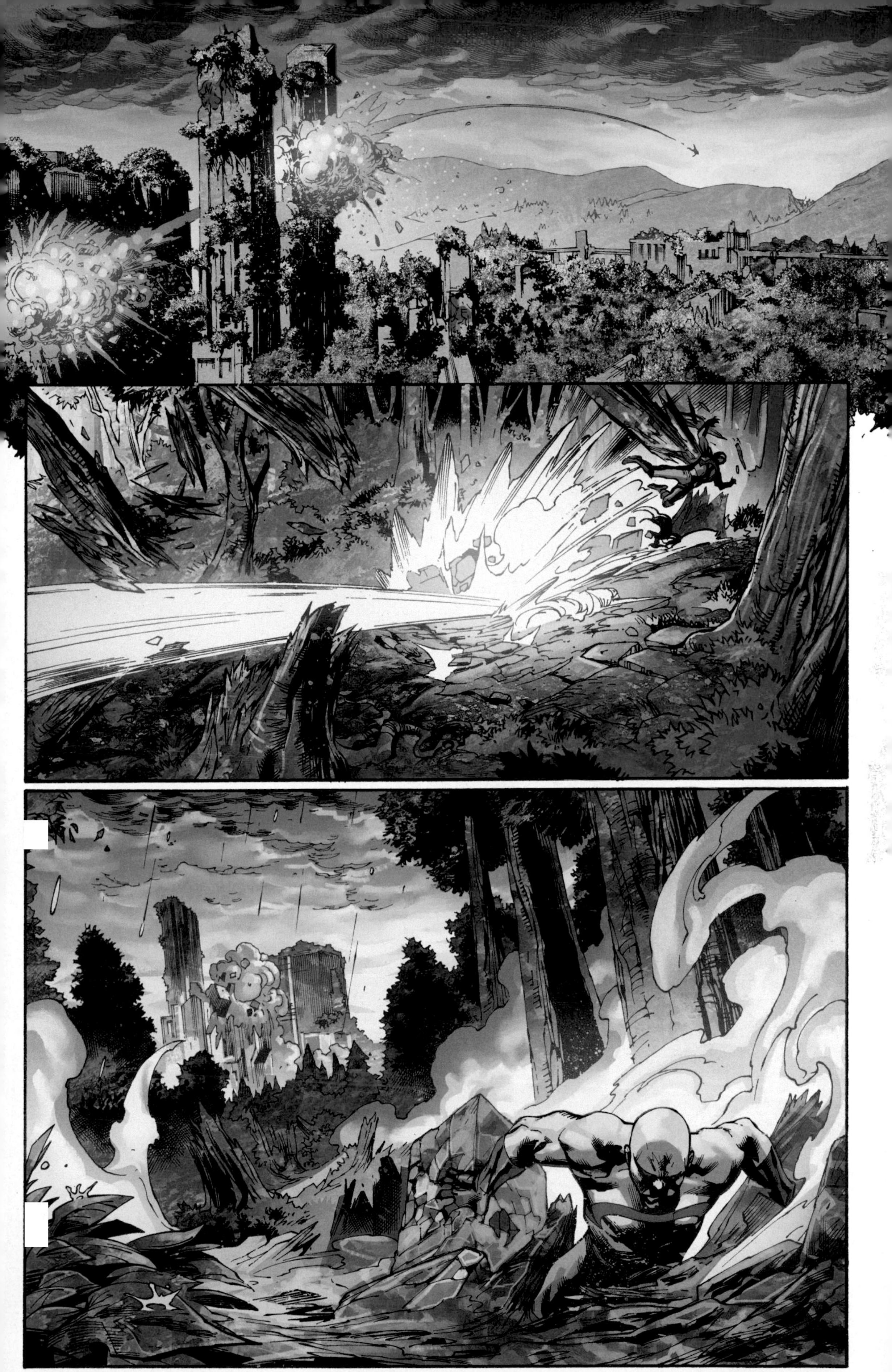

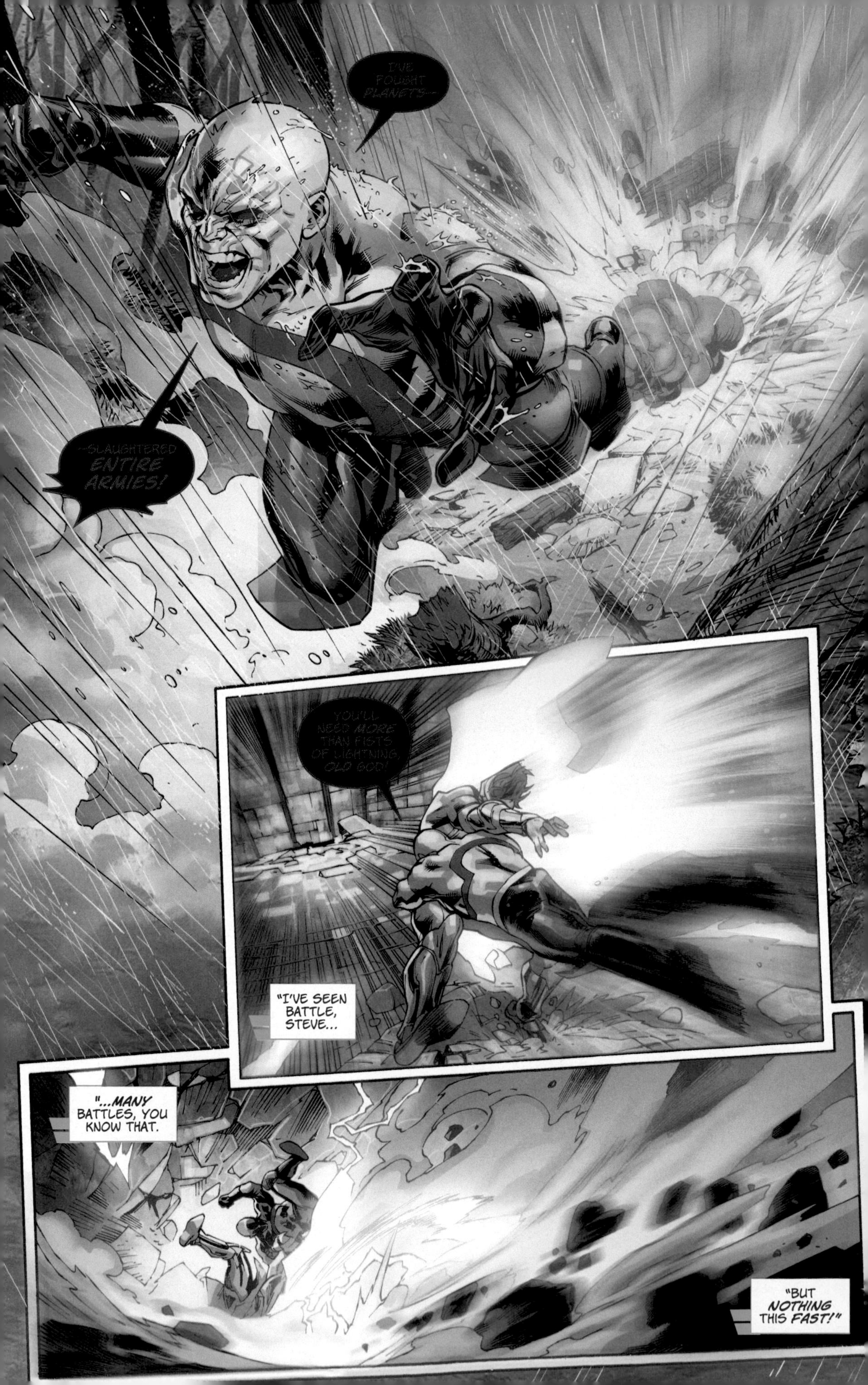
I'VE FOUGHT PLANETS--
--SLAUGHTERED ENTIRE ARMIES!
YOU'LL NEED MORE THAN FISTS OF LIGHTNING, OLD GOD!
"I'VE SEEN BATTLE, STEVE...
"...MANY BATTLES, YOU KNOW THAT.
"BUT NOTHING THIS FAST!"

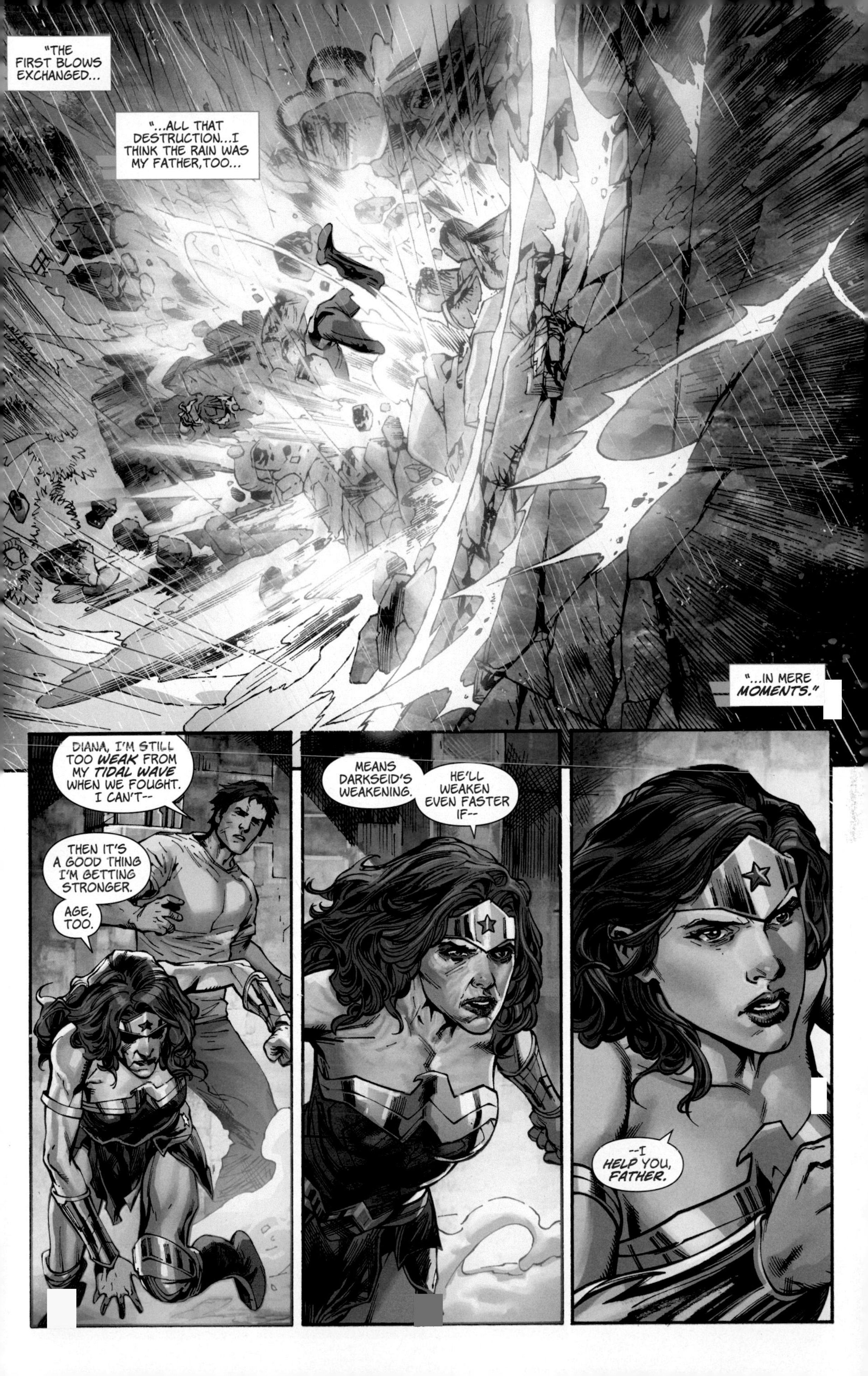
"THE FIRST BLOWS EXCHANGED...
"...ALL THAT DESTRUCTION...I THINK THE RAIN WAS MY FATHER, TOO...
"...IN MERE MOMENTS."
DIANA, I'M STILL TOO WEAK FROM MY TIDAL WAVE WHEN WE FOUGHT. I CAN'T--
THEN IT'S A GOOD THING I'M GETTING STRONGER.
AGE, TOO.
MEANS DARKSEID'S WEAKENING.
HE'LL WEAKEN EVEN FASTER IF--
--I HELP YOU, FATHER.

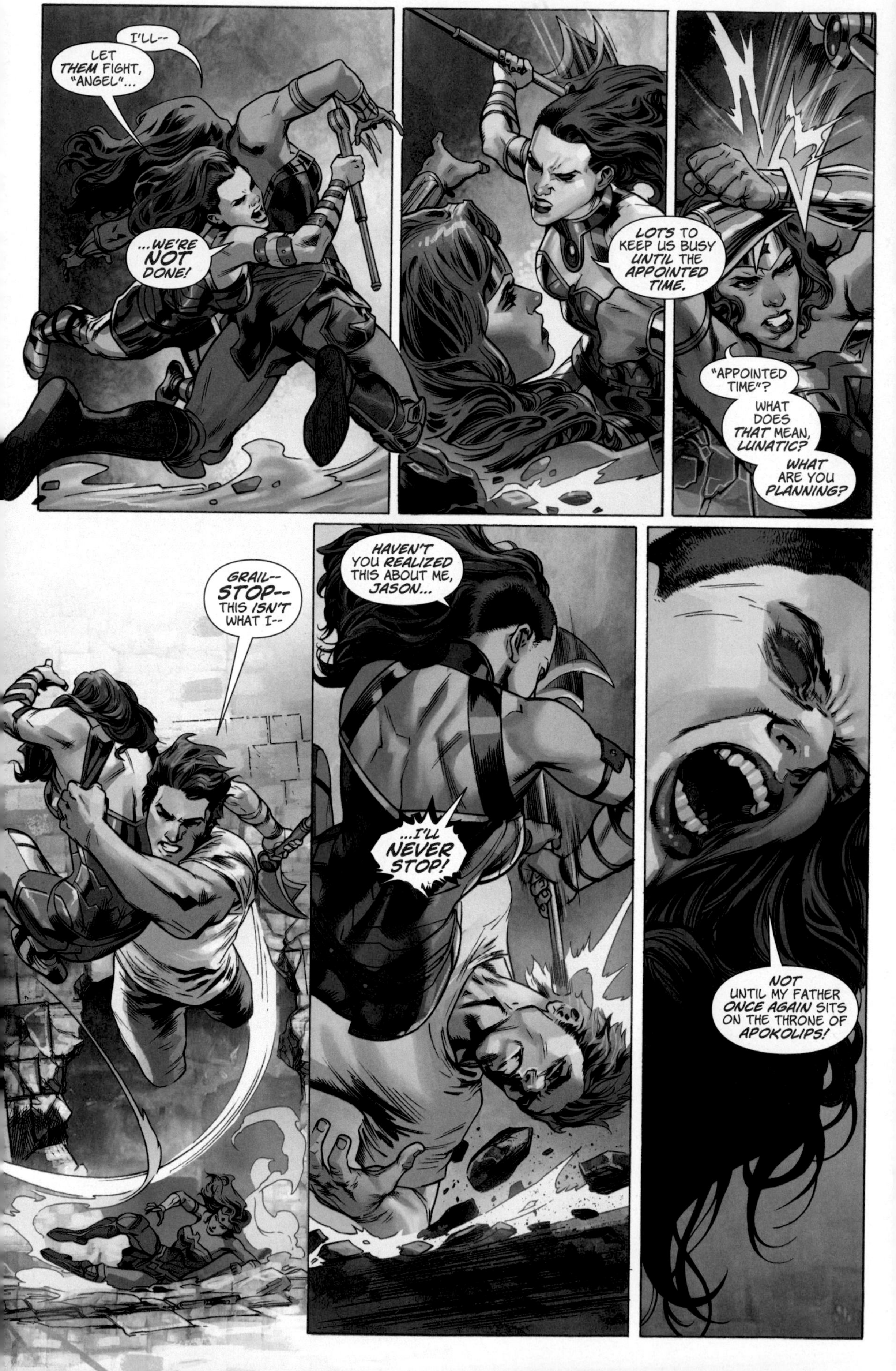
I'LL--
LET THEM FIGHT, "ANGEL"...
...WE'RE NOT DONE!
LOTS TO KEEP US BUSY UNTIL THE APPOINTED TIME.
"APPOINTED TIME"?
WHAT DOES THAT MEAN, LUNATIC?
WHAT ARE YOU PLANNING?
GRAIL--STOP--THIS ISN'T WHAT I--
HAVEN'T YOU REALIZED THIS ABOUT ME, JASON...
...I'LL NEVER STOP!
NOT UNTIL MY FATHER ONCE AGAIN SITS ON THE THRONE OF APOKOLIPS!

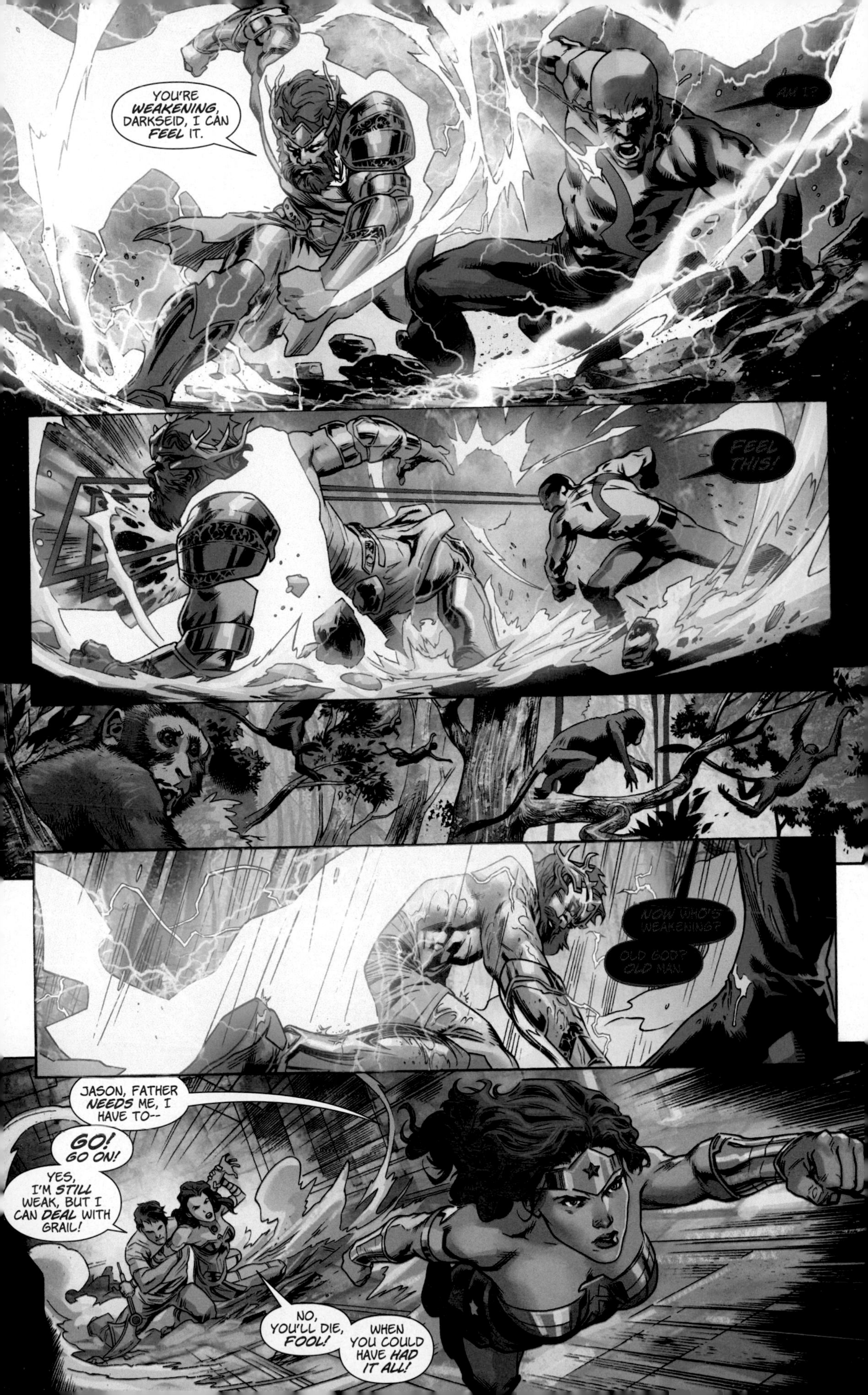
YOU'RE WEAKENING, DARKSEID, I CAN FEEL IT.
AM I?
FEEL THIS!
NOW WHO'S WEAKENING?
OLD GOD? OLD MAN.
JASON, FATHER NEEDS ME, I HAVE TO--
GO! GO ON!
YES, I'M STILL WEAK, BUT I CAN DEAL WITH GRAIL!
NO, YOU'LL DIE, FOOL!
WHEN YOU COULD HAVE HAD IT ALL!

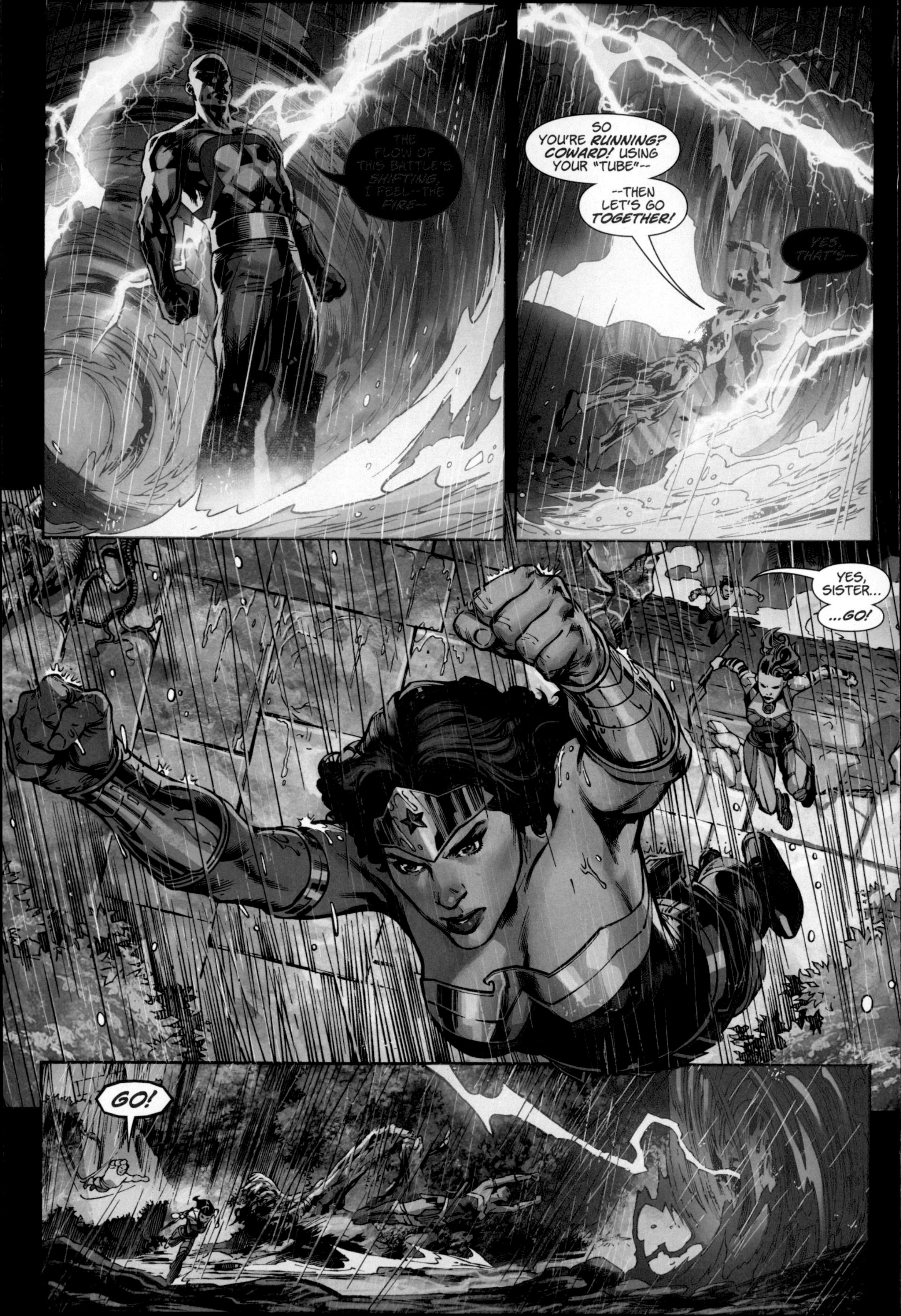
THE FLOW OF THIS BATTLE'S *SHIFTING*, I FEEL--THE *FIRE*--
SO YOU'RE ***RUNNING? COWARD!*** USING YOUR "TUBE"--
--THEN LET'S GO ***TOGETHER!***
YES, THAT'S--
YES, SISTER...
...*GO!*
GO!

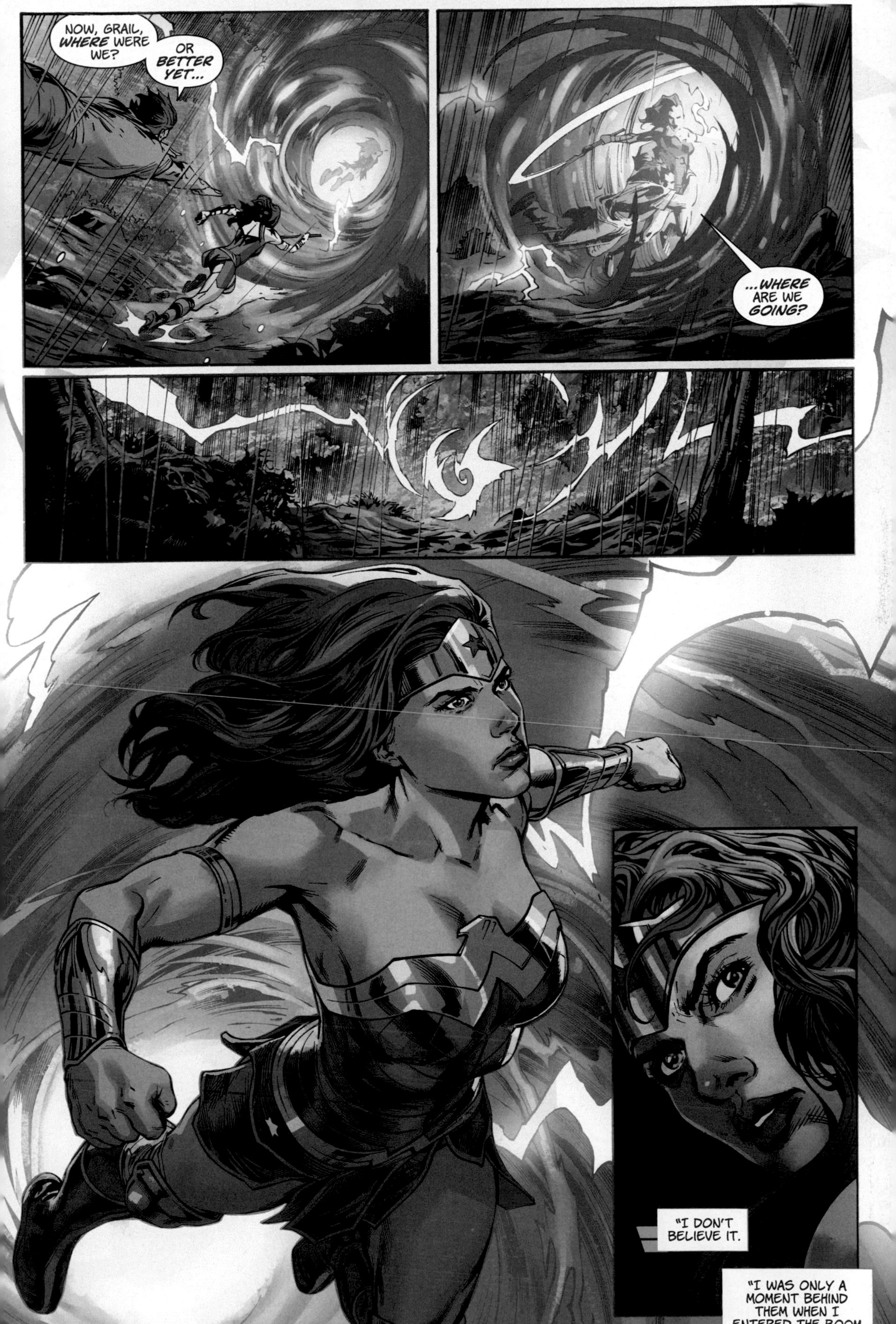
NOW, GRAIL, WHERE WERE WE?
OR BETTER YET...
...WHERE ARE WE GOING?
"I DON'T BELIEVE IT.
"I WAS ONLY A MOMENT BEHIND THEM WHEN I ENTERED THE BOOM TUBE, AND YET..."

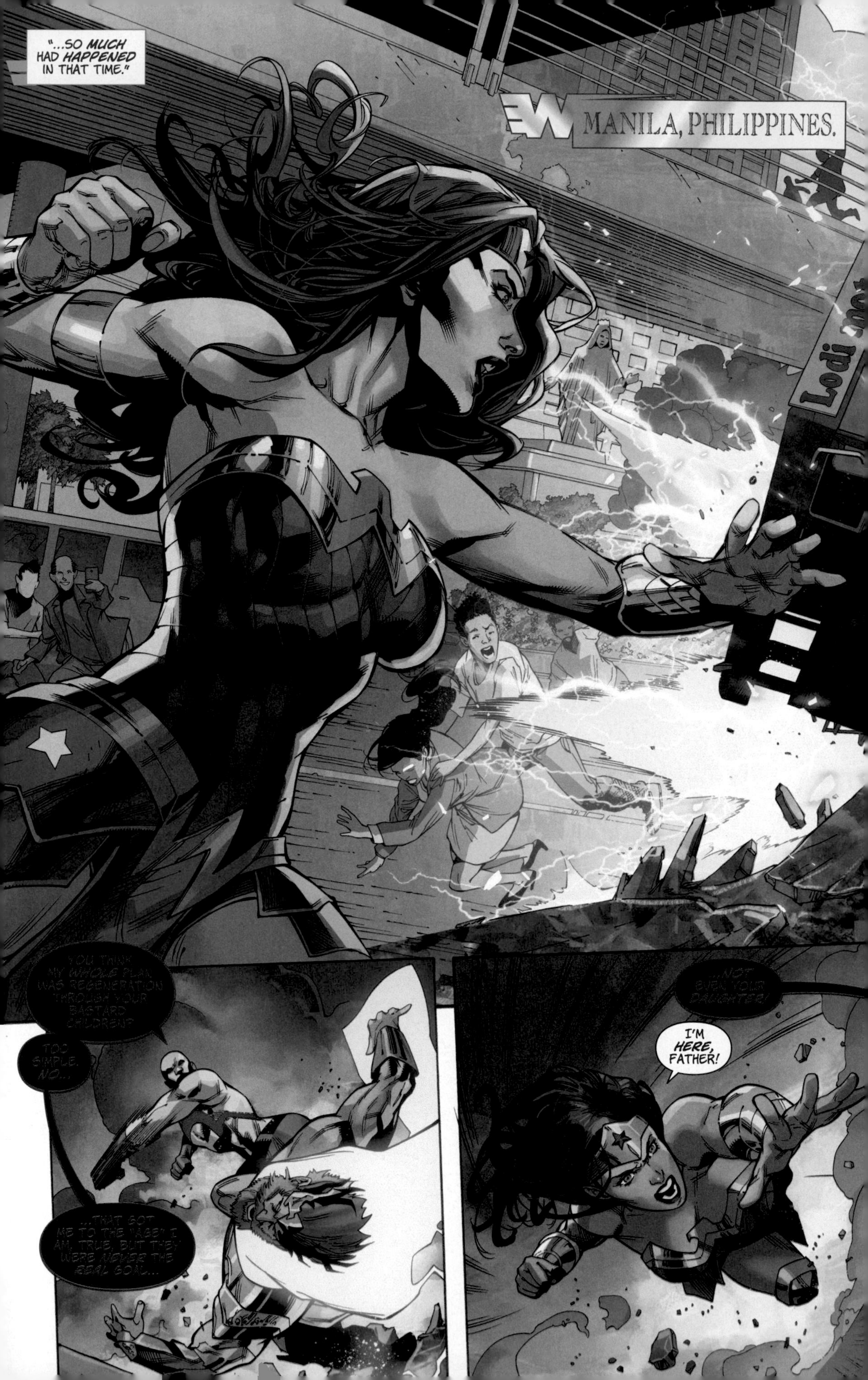
"...SO MUCH HAD HAPPENED IN THAT TIME."
MANILA, PHILIPPINES.
Lodi
YOU THINK MY WHOLE PLAN WAS REGENERATION THROUGH YOUR BASTARD CHILDREN?
TOO SIMPLE. NO...
...THAT GOT ME TO THE "AGE" I AM, TRUE, BUT THEY WERE NEVER THE REAL GOAL...
...NOT EVEN YOUR DAUGHTER!
I'M HERE, FATHER!

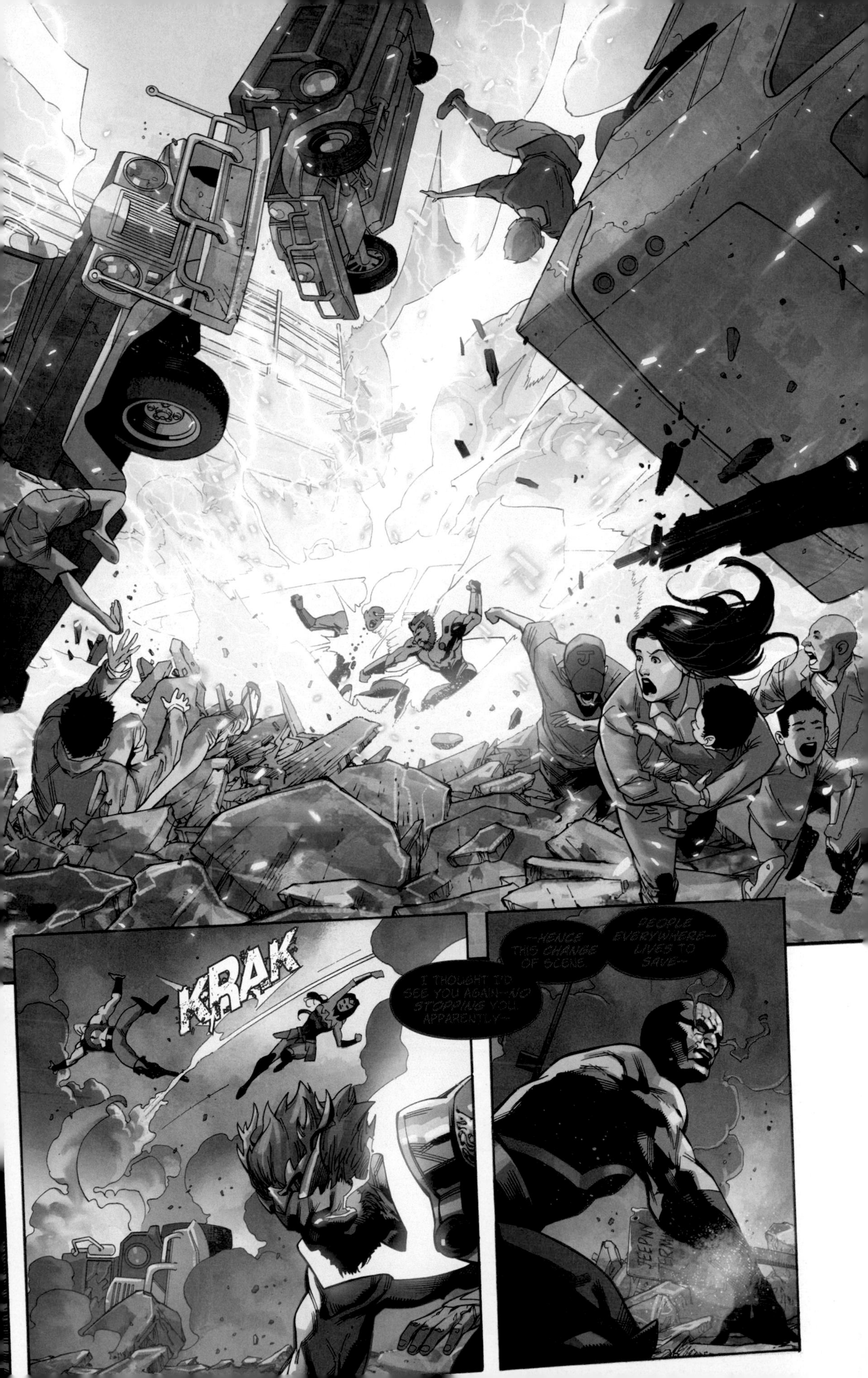
KRAK
I THOUGHT I'D SEE YOU AGAIN--NO STOPPING YOU, APPARENTLY--
--HENCE THIS CHANGE OF SCENE.
PEOPLE EVERYWHERE--LIVES TO SAVE--
JEEPNY

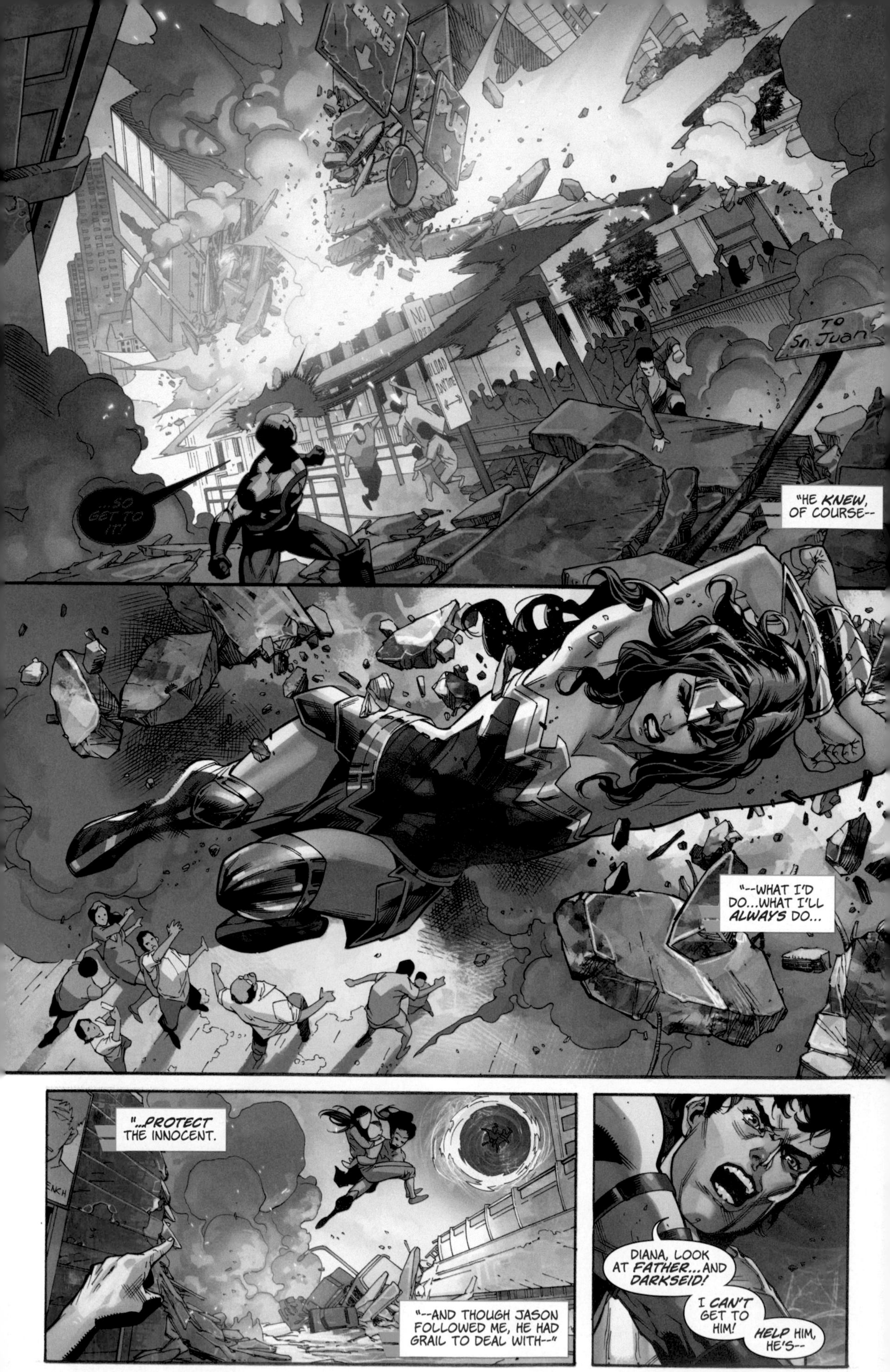

...SO GET TO IT!
"HE KNEW, OF COURSE--
TO Sn. Juan
"--WHAT I'D DO...WHAT I'LL ALWAYS DO...
"...PROTECT THE INNOCENT.
"--AND THOUGH JASON FOLLOWED ME, HE HAD GRAIL TO DEAL WITH--"
DIANA, LOOK AT FATHER...AND DARKSEID!
I CAN'T GET TO HIM!
HELP HIM, HE'S--

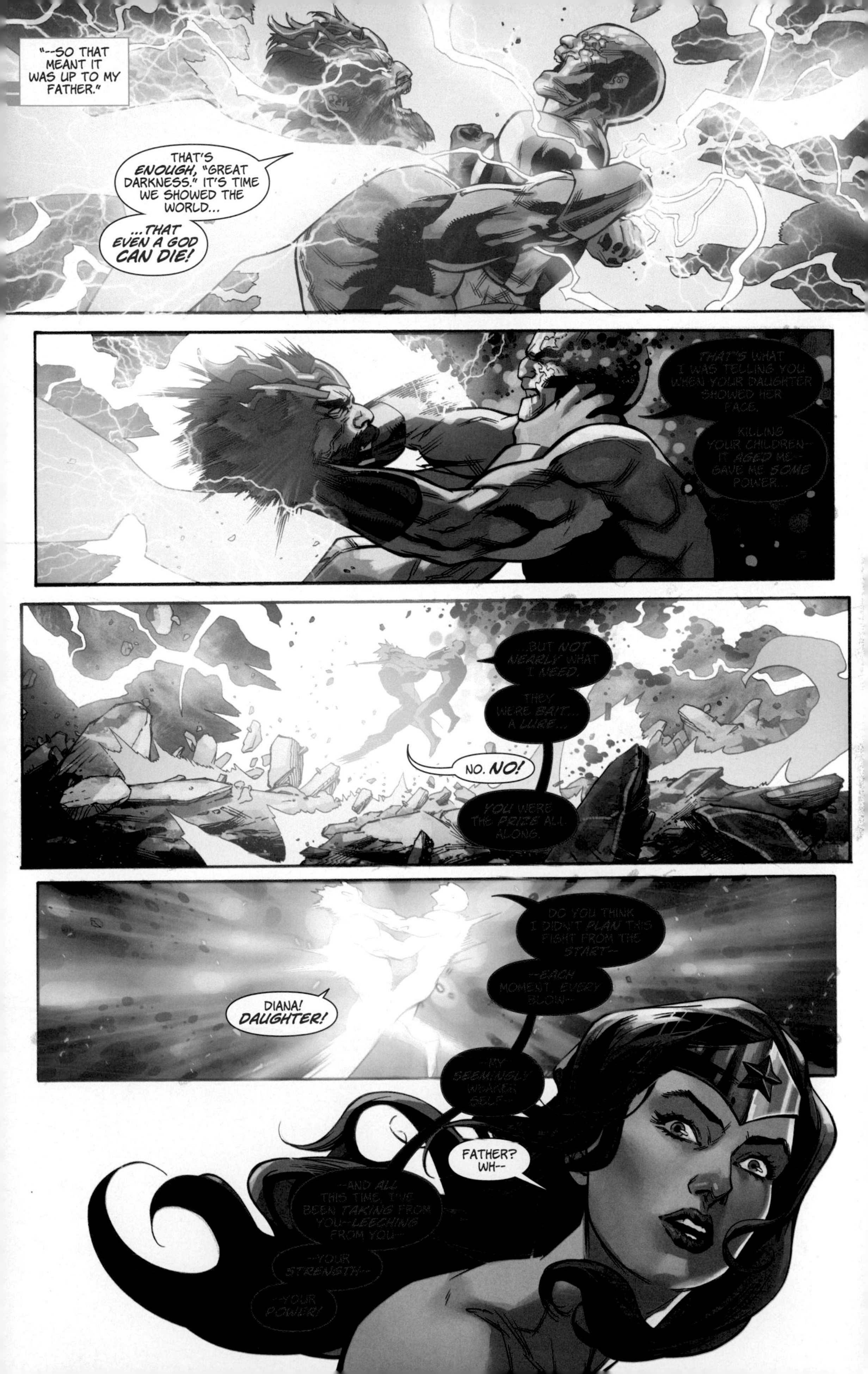
"--SO THAT MEANT IT WAS UP TO MY FATHER."
THAT'S ENOUGH, "GREAT DARKNESS." IT'S TIME WE SHOWED THE WORLD...
...THAT EVEN A GOD CAN DIE!
THAT'S WHAT I WAS TELLING YOU WHEN YOUR DAUGHTER SHOWED HER FACE.
KILLING YOUR CHILDREN--IT AGED ME--GAVE ME SOME POWER...
...BUT NOT NEARLY WHAT I NEED.
THEY WERE BAIT... A LURE...
NO. NO!
YOU WERE THE PRIZE ALL ALONG.
DO YOU THINK I DIDN'T PLAN THIS FIGHT FROM THE START--
--EACH MOMENT, EVERY BLOW--
DIANA! DAUGHTER!
--MY SEEMINGLY WEAKER SELF--
FATHER? WH--
--AND ALL THIS TIME, I'VE BEEN TAKING FROM YOU--LEECHING FROM YOU--
--YOUR STRENGTH--
--YOUR POWER!

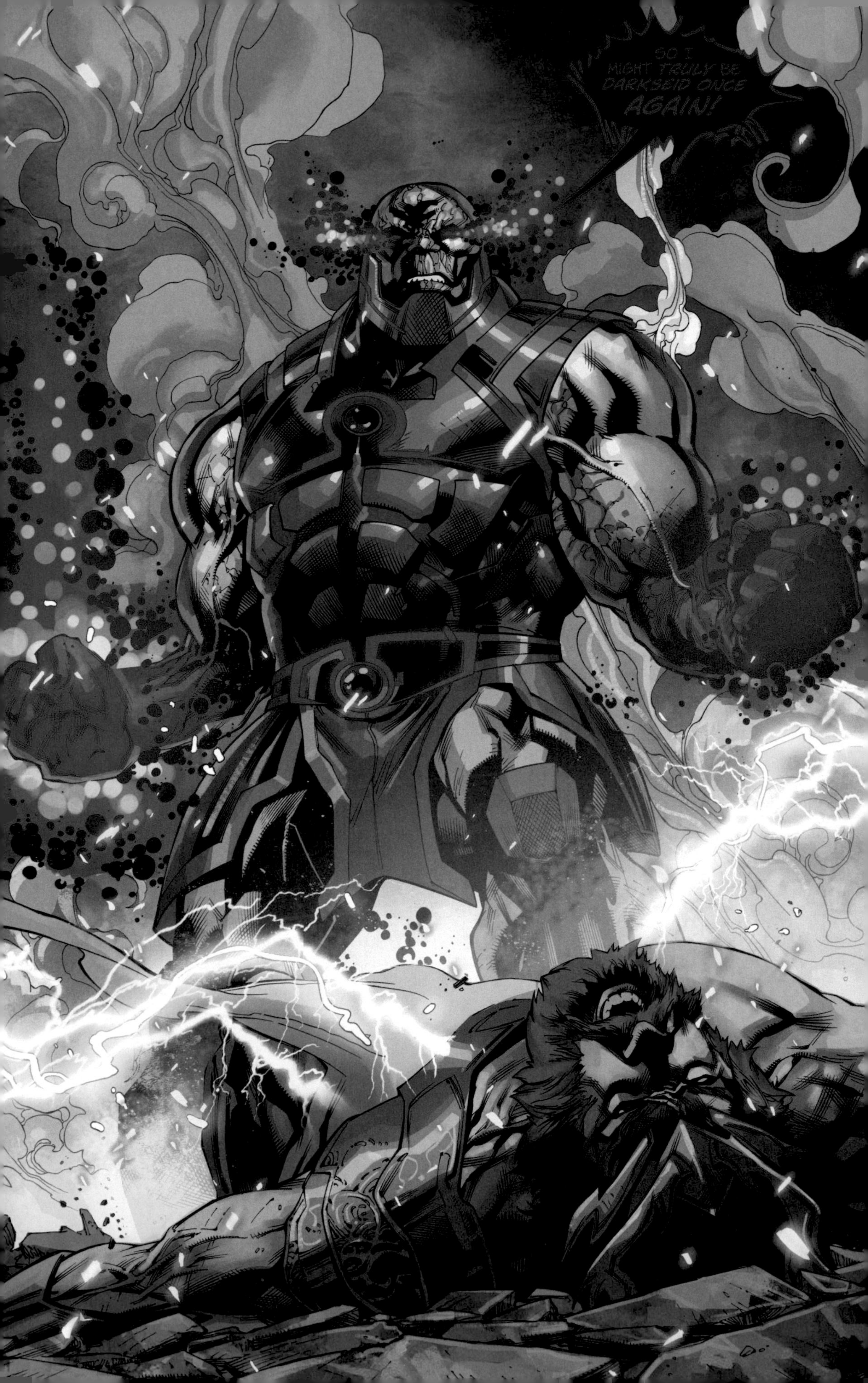
SO I MIGHT TRULY BE DARKSEID ONCE AGAIN!

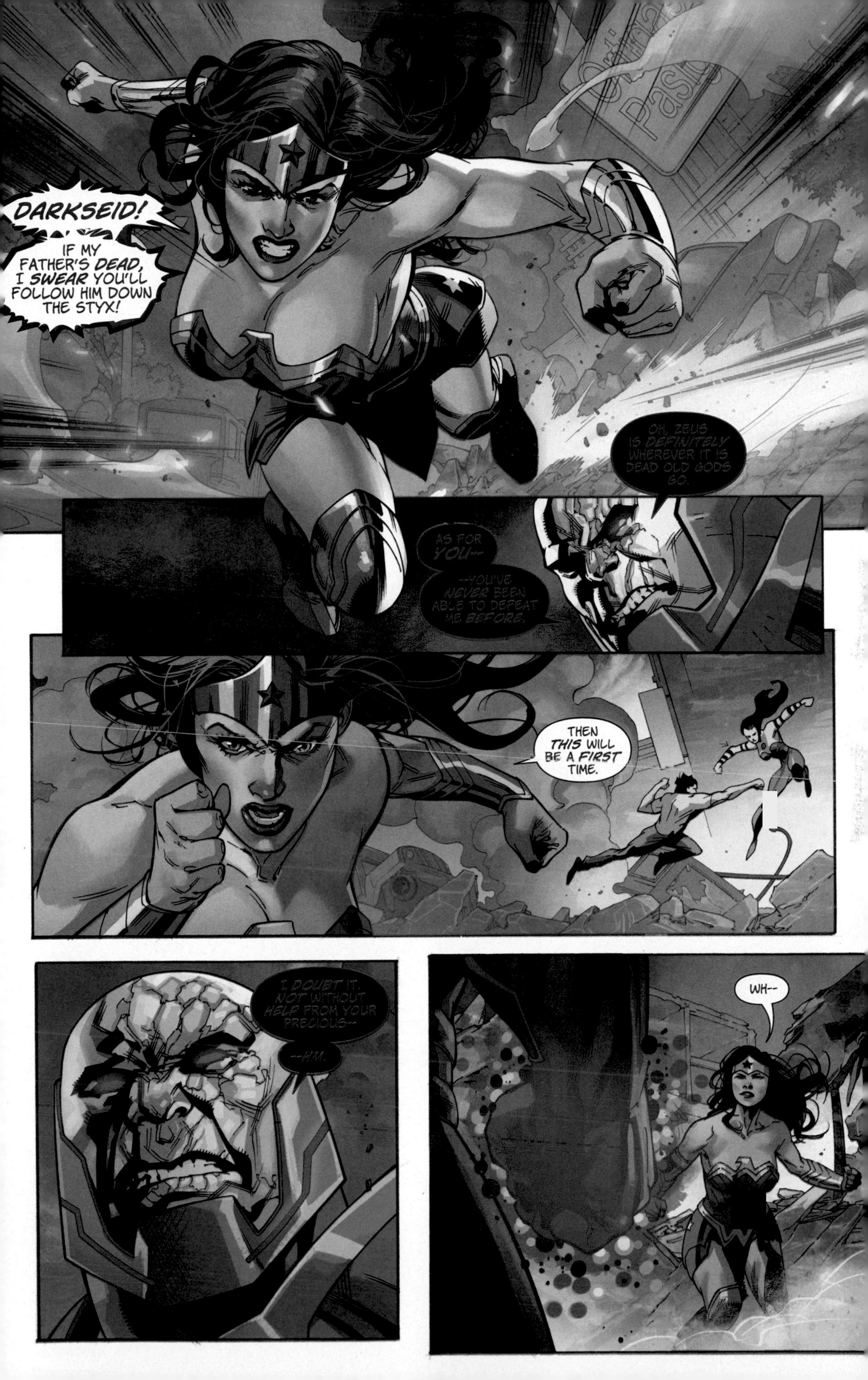
DARKSEID!
IF MY FATHER'S DEAD, I SWEAR YOU'LL FOLLOW HIM DOWN THE STYX!
OH, ZEUS IS DEFINITELY WHEREVER IT IS DEAD OLD GODS GO.
AS FOR YOU--
--YOU'VE NEVER BEEN ABLE TO DEFEAT ME BEFORE.
THEN THIS WILL BE A FIRST TIME.
I DOUBT IT. NOT WITHOUT HELP FROM YOUR PRECIOUS--
--HM.
WH--

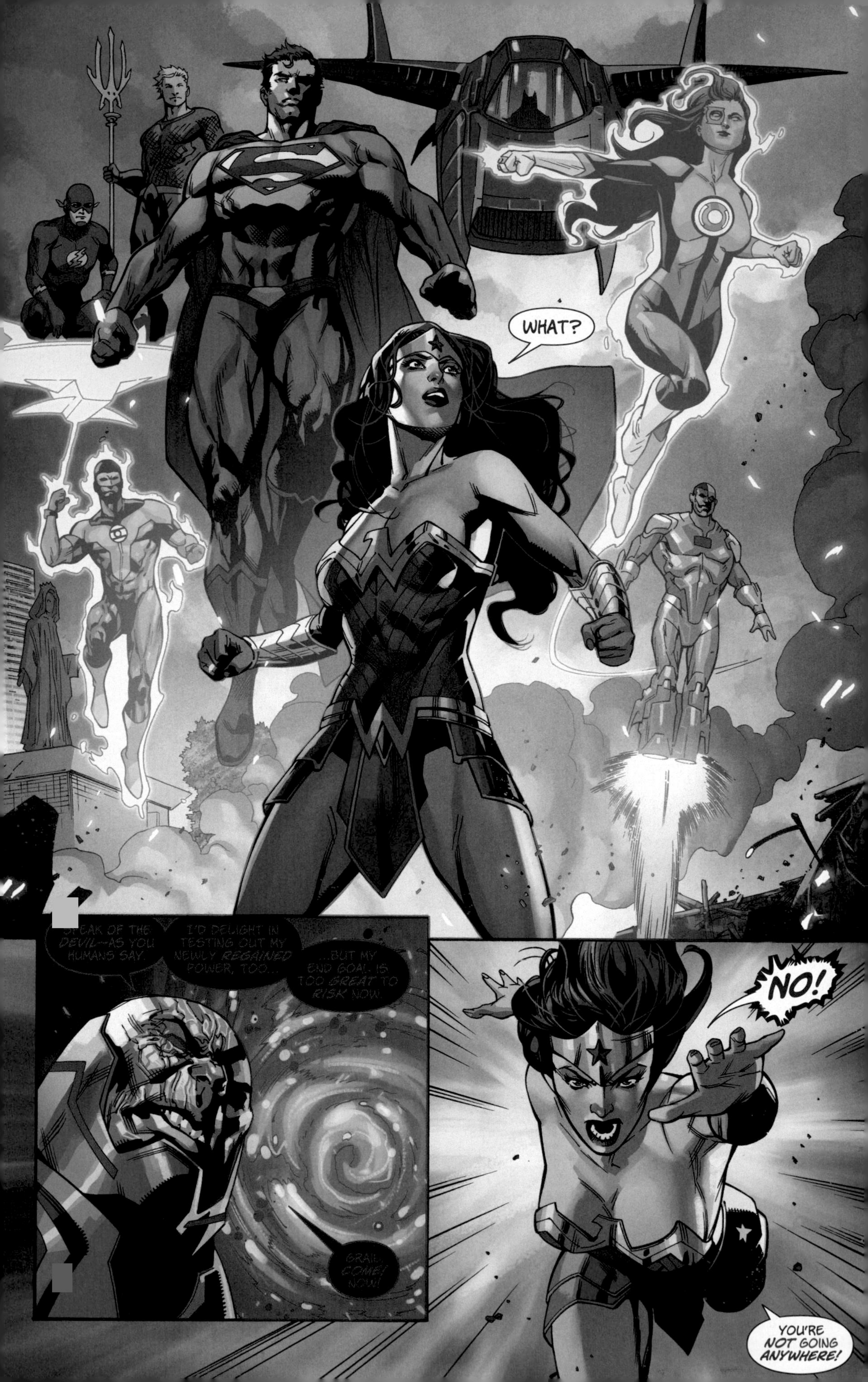
WHAT?
SPEAK OF THE *DEVIL*--AS YOU HUMANS SAY.
I'D DELIGHT IN TESTING OUT MY NEWLY *REGAINED* POWER, TOO...
...BUT MY END GOAL IS TOO *GREAT* TO *RISK* NOW.
GRAIL. *COME!* NOW!
NO!
YOU'RE *NOT* GOING *ANYWHERE!*

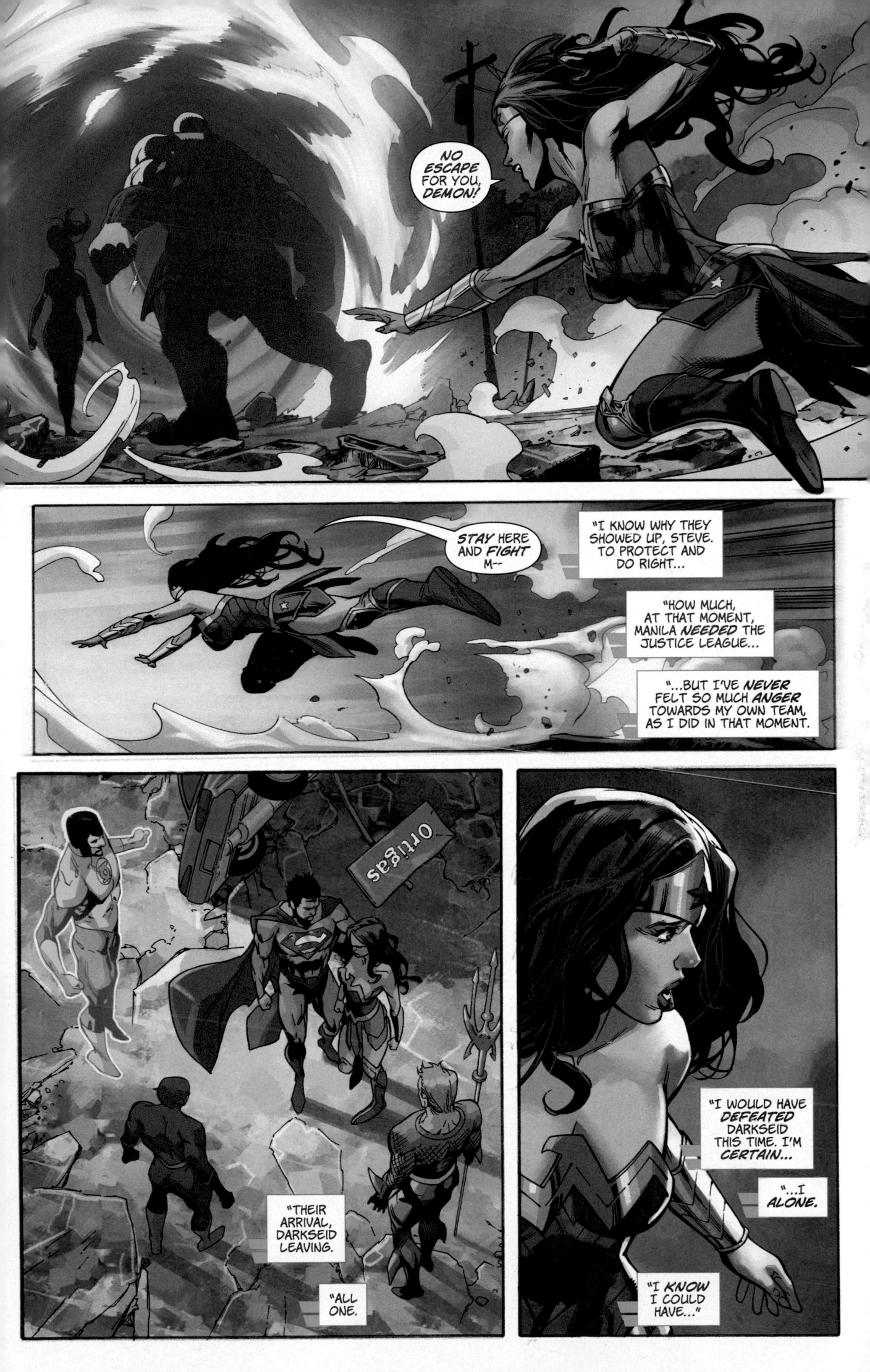
NO ESCAPE FOR YOU, DEMON!
STAY HERE AND FIGHT M--
"I KNOW WHY THEY SHOWED UP, STEVE. TO PROTECT AND DO RIGHT...
"HOW MUCH, AT THAT MOMENT, MANILA NEEDED THE JUSTICE LEAGUE...
"...BUT I'VE NEVER FELT SO MUCH ANGER TOWARDS MY OWN TEAM, AS I DID IN THAT MOMENT.
Ortigas
"THEIR ARRIVAL, DARKSEID LEAVING.
"ALL ONE.
"I WOULD HAVE DEFEATED DARKSEID THIS TIME. I'M CERTAIN...
"...I ALONE.
"I KNOW I COULD HAVE..."

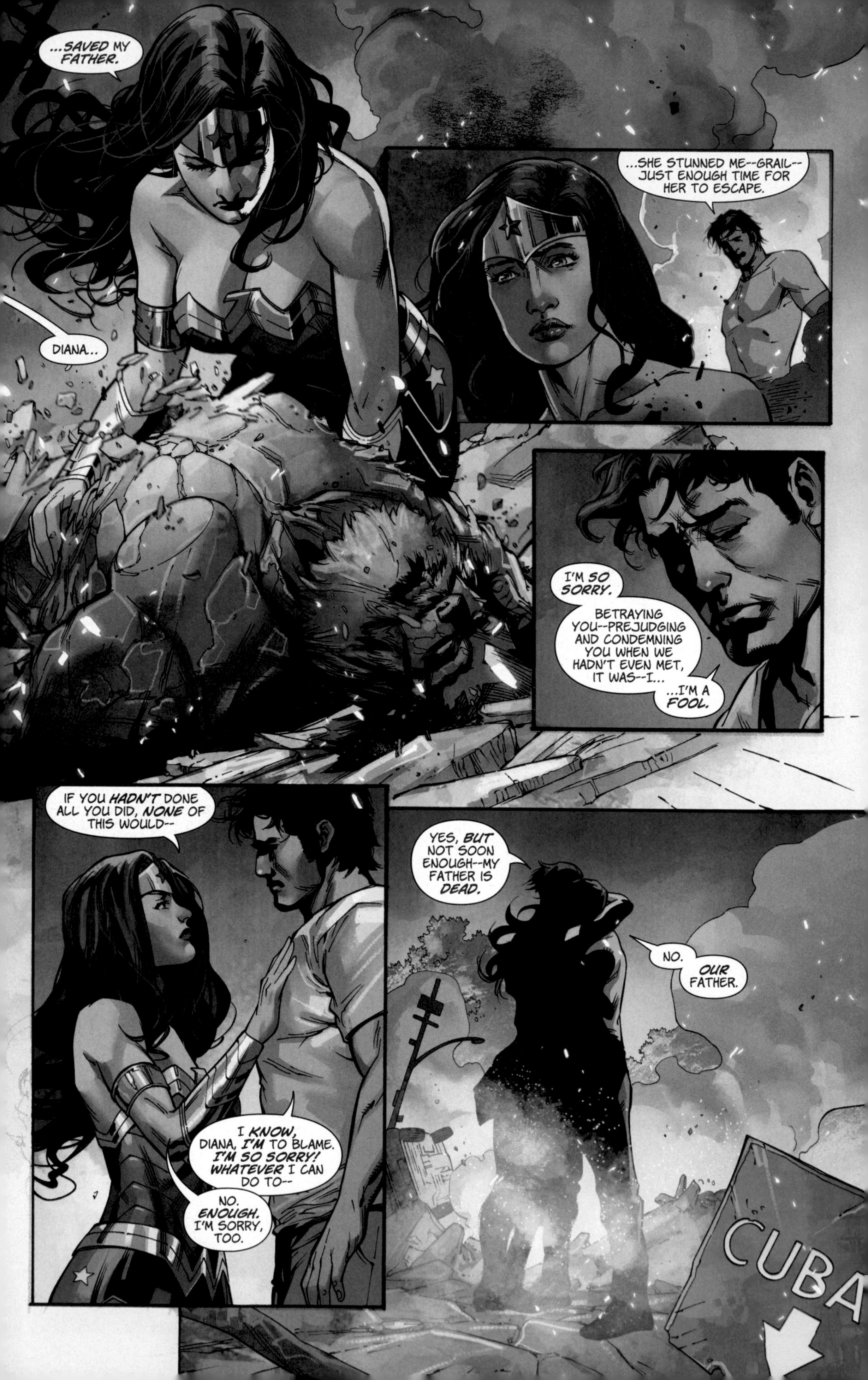
...SAVED MY FATHER.
DIANA...
...SHE STUNNED ME--GRAIL--JUST ENOUGH TIME FOR HER TO ESCAPE.
I'M SO SORRY.
BETRAYING YOU--PREJUDGING AND CONDEMNING YOU WHEN WE HADN'T EVEN MET, IT WAS--I...
...I'M A FOOL.
IF YOU HADN'T DONE ALL YOU DID, NONE OF THIS WOULD--
I KNOW, DIANA, I'M TO BLAME. I'M SO SORRY! WHATEVER I CAN DO TO--
NO. ENOUGH. I'M SORRY, TOO.
YES, BUT NOT SOON ENOUGH--MY FATHER IS DEAD.
NO. OUR FATHER.
CUBA

WONDER WOMAN

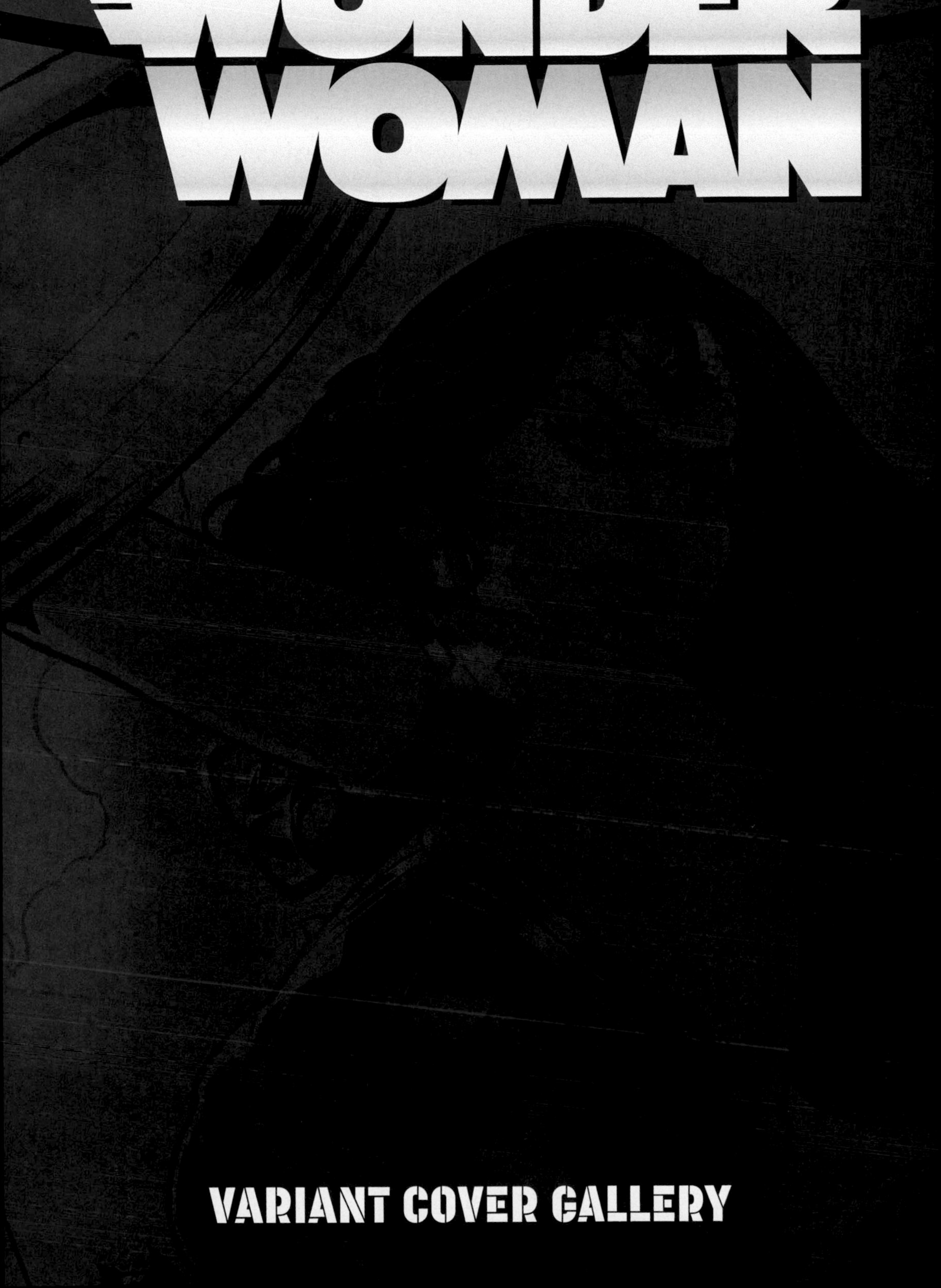

VARIANT COVER GALLERY

WONDER WOMAN #31 variant cover by JENNY FRISON

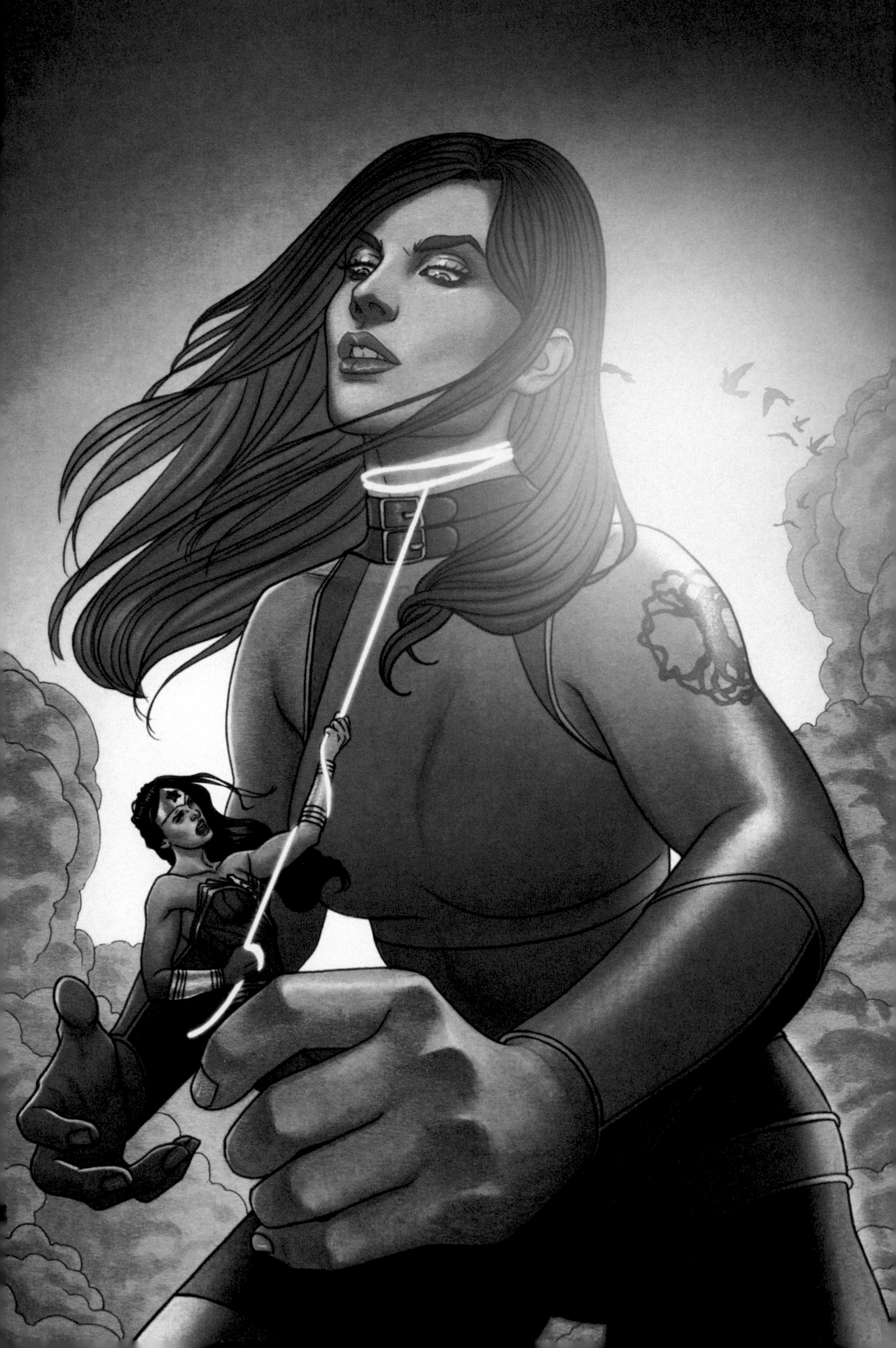

WONDER WOMAN #32 variant cover by JENNY FRISON

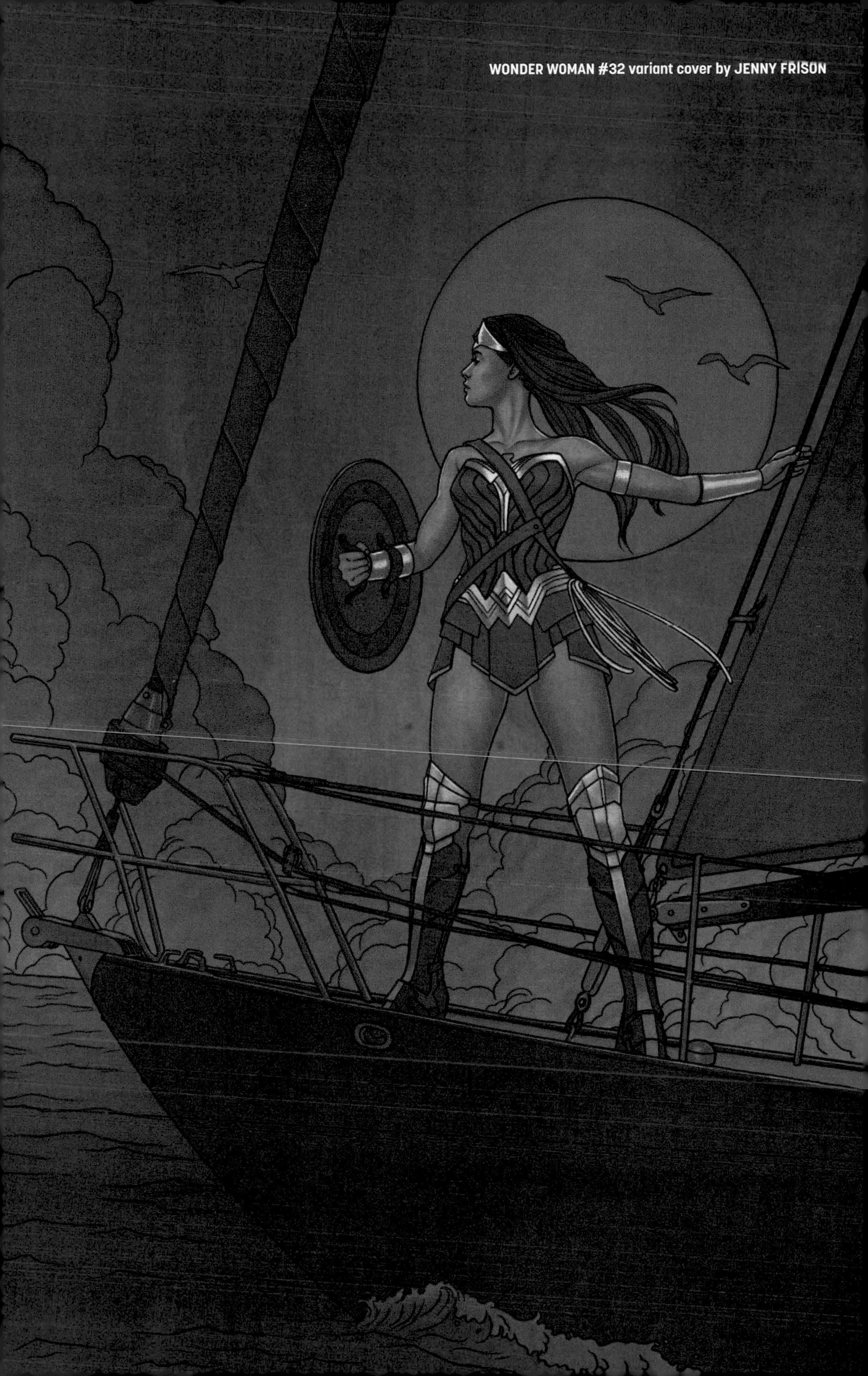

WONDER WOMAN #33 variant cover by JENNY FRISON

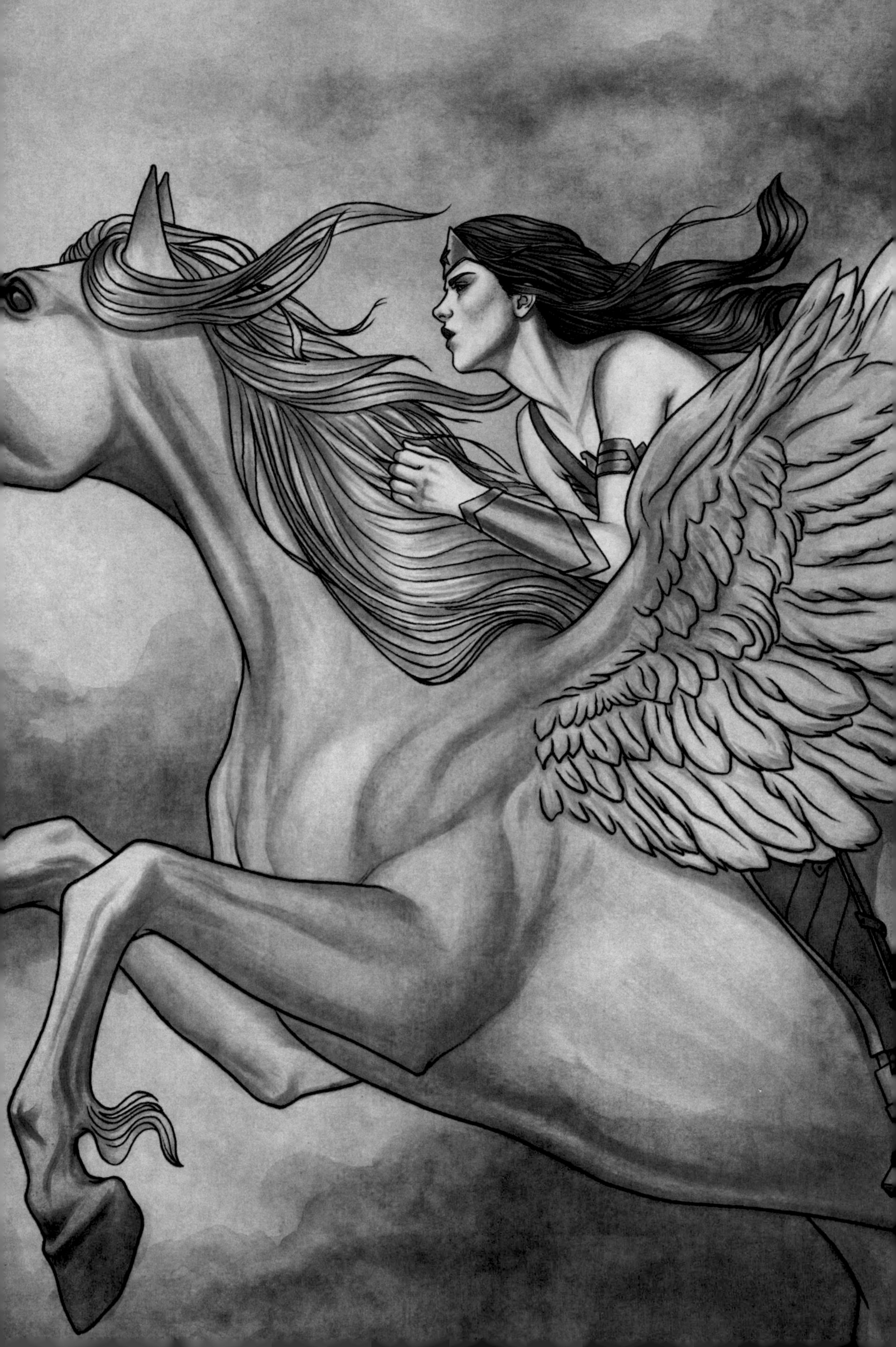

WONDER WOMAN #34 variant cover by TONY S. DANIEL and TOMEU MOREY

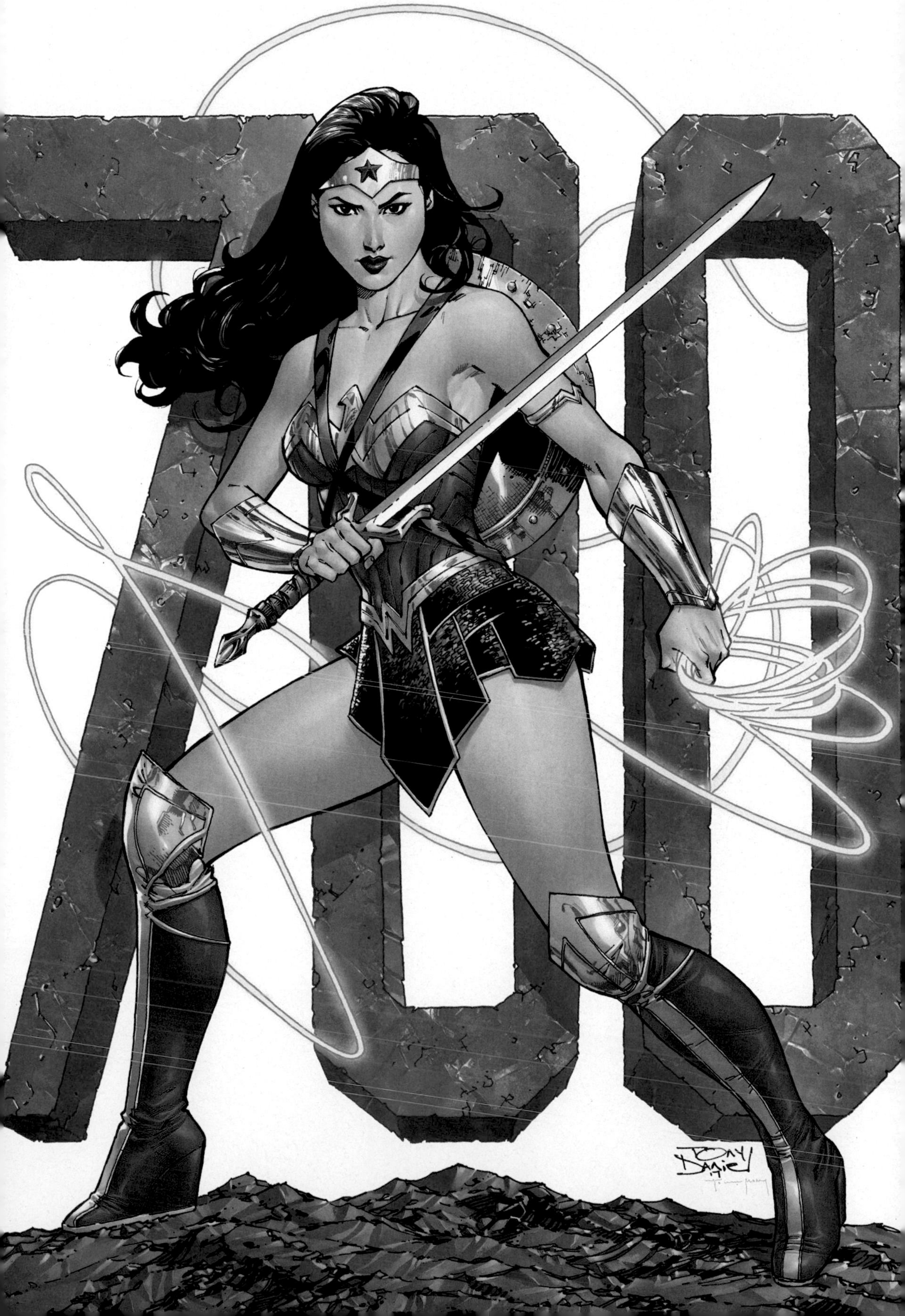

WONDER WOMAN #35 variant cover by TERRY DODSON and RACHEL DODSON

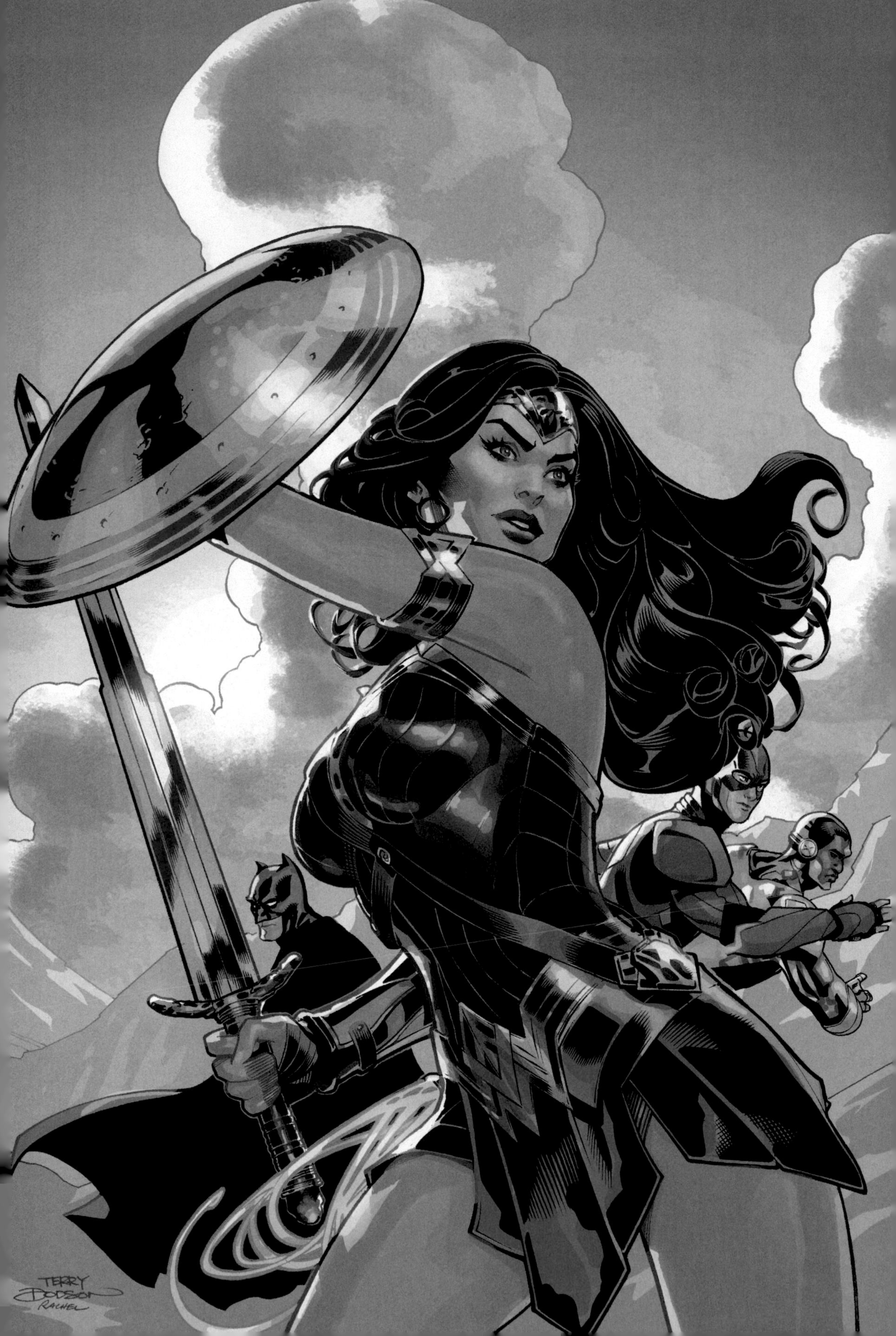
TERRY
DODSON
RACHEL

WONDER WOMAN #36 variant cover by JENNY FRISON

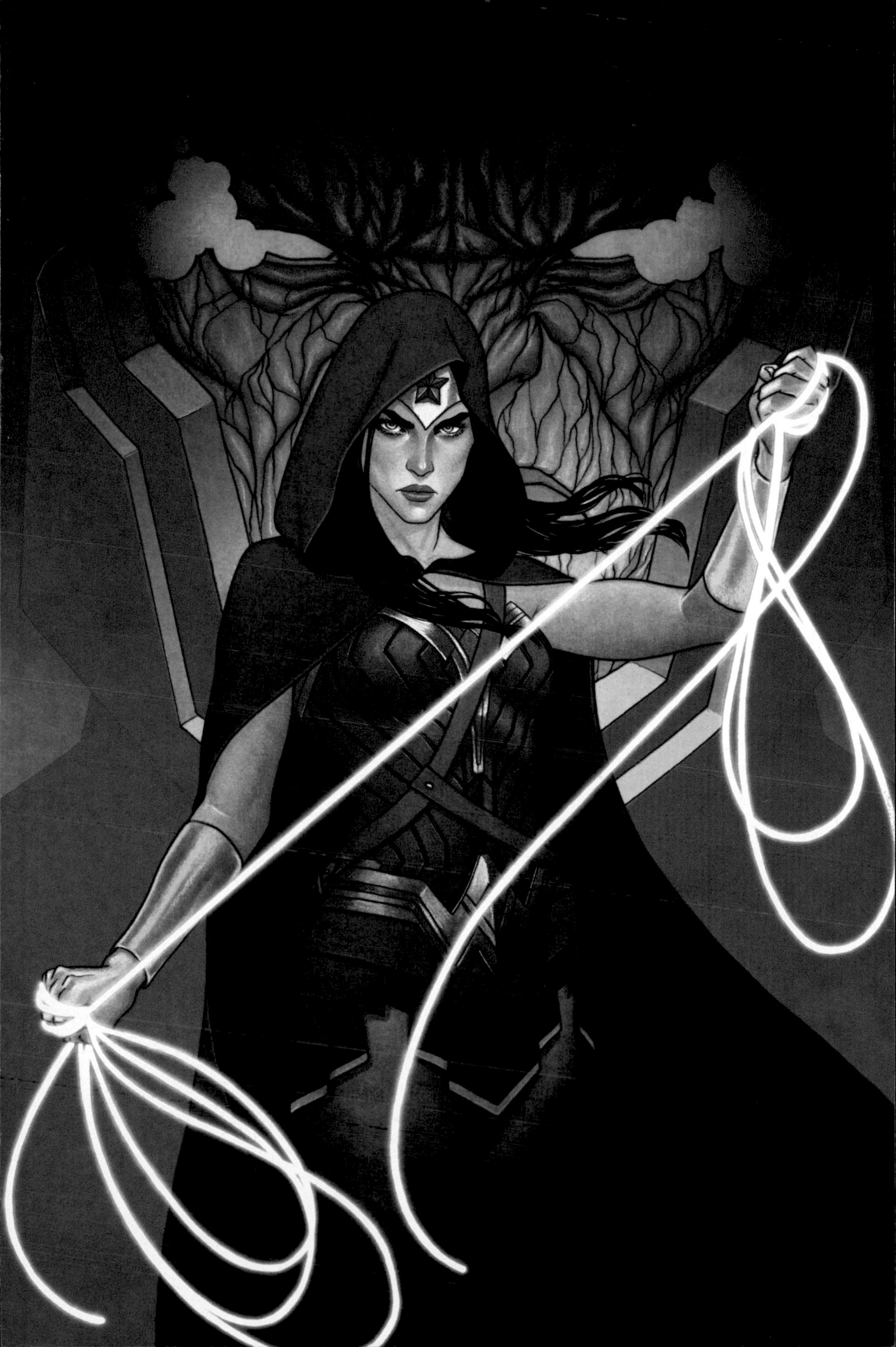

WONDER WOMAN #37 variant cover by JENNY FRISON

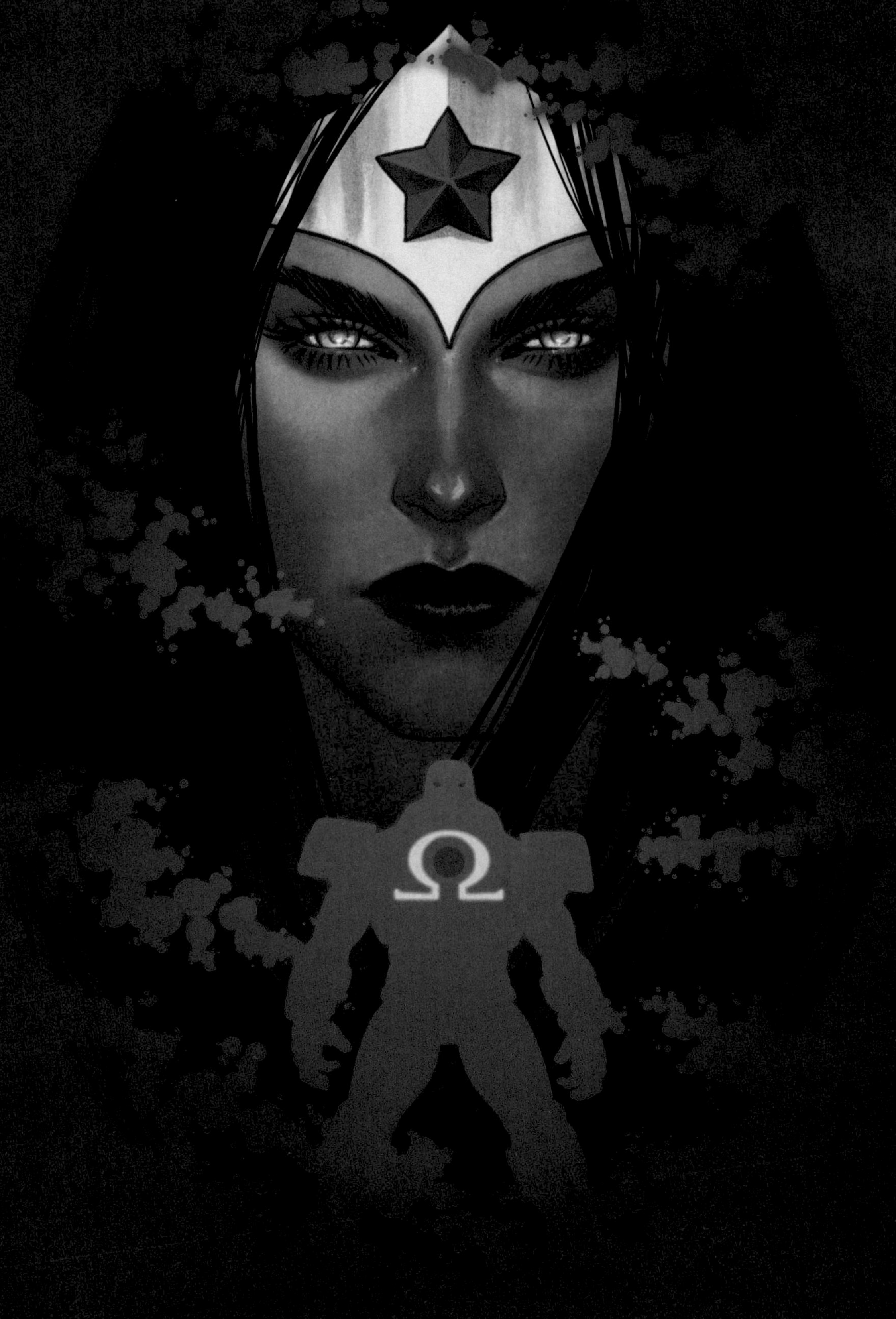

"Greg Rucka and company have created a compelling narrative for fans of the Amazing Amazon." **– NERDIST**

"(A) heartfelt and genuine take on Diana's origin." **– NEWSARAMA**

DC UNIVERSE REBIRTH

WONDER WOMAN

VOL. 1: THE LIES

GREG RUCKA
with LIAM SHARP

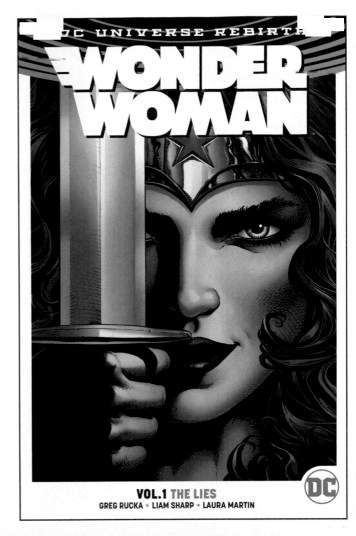

VOL.1 THE LIES
GREG RUCKA * LIAM SHARP * LAURA MARTIN

VOL.1 THE EXTINCTION MACHINES
BRYAN HITCH * TONY S. DANIEL * SANDU FLOREA * TOMEU MOREY

**JUSTICE LEAGUE VOL. 1:
THE EXTINCTION MACHINES**

VOL.1 REIGN OF THE SUPERMEN
STEVE ORLANDO * BRIAN CHING * MIKE ATIYEH

**SUPERGIRL VOL. 1:
REIGN OF THE SUPERMEN**

VOL.1 BEYOND BURNSIDE
HOPE LARSON * RAFAEL ALBUQUERQUE

**BATGIRL VOL. 1:
BEYOND BURNSIDE**

THE NEW YORK TIMES BESTSELLER
THE NEW 52!
WONDER WOMAN
"EXPECT A LOT MORE WONDER WOMAN FANS AFTER A FEW ISSUES OF THIS BOOK."
— USA TODAY
VOLUME 1 BLOOD
BRIAN AZZARELLO CLIFF CHIANG TONY AKINS

"Clear storytelling at its best. It's an intriguing concept and easy to grasp."
– THE NEW YORK TIMES

"Azzarello is rebuilding the mythology of Wonder Woman."
– CRAVE ONLINE

WONDER WOMAN
VOL. 1: BLOOD
BRIAN AZZARELLO
with CLIFF CHIANG

THE NEW YORK TIMES BEST-SELLING SERIES
THE NEW 52!
WONDER WOMAN
VOLUME 2 GUTS
BRIAN AZZARELLO CLIFF CHIANG TONY AKINS

**WONDER WOMAN
VOL. 2: GUTS**

THE NEW 52!
WONDER WOMAN
VOLUME 3 IRON
BRIAN AZZARELLO CLIFF CHIANG

**WONDER WOMAN
VOL. 3: IRON**

READ THE ENTIRE EPIC!

WONDER WOMAN VOL. 4: WAR

WONDER WOMAN VOL. 5: FLESH

WONDER WOMAN VOL. 6: BONES

WONDER WOMAN VOL. 7: WAR-TORN

WONDER WOMAN VOL. 8: A TWIST OF FATE

WONDER WOMAN VOL. 9: RESURRECTION

Get more DC graphic novels wherever comics and books are sold!

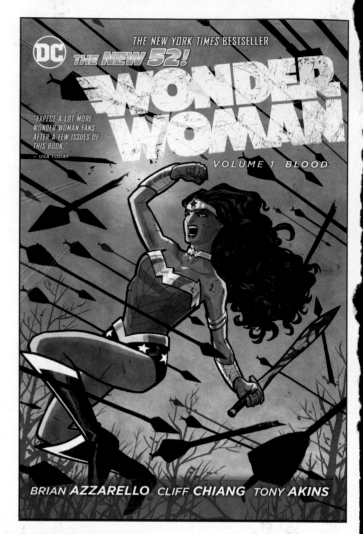

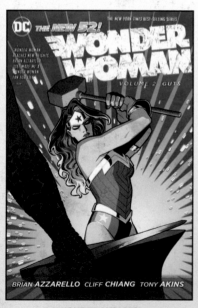